# Teaching the Italian Renaissance Romance Epic

# Teaching the Italian Renaissance Romance Epic

Edited by

**Jo Ann Cavallo**

Modern Language Association of America
New York 2018

Library of Congress Cataloging-in-Publication Data are available from the Library of Congress.

ISBN 978-1-60329-365-5 (cloth)
ISBN 978-1-60329-366-2 (paper)
ISBN 978-1-60329-367-9 (EPUB)
ISBN 978-1-60329-368-6 (Kindle)

Options for Teaching 44
ISSN 1079-2562

Cover illustration of the paperback and electronic editions: *Duello di Orlando e Rinaldo*, by Giacomo Cuticchio. 2002. © Giacomo Cuticchio. Photo courtesy of Jo Ann Cavallo.

Published by The Modern Language Association of America
85 Broad Street, suite 500, New York, New York 10004-2434
www.mla.org

# Contents

## Part IV: Comparative Themes and Topics



## Part V: Transcultural Encounters



## Part VI: Beyond the "Three Ferrarese Crowns": The Italian Romance Epic in Translation

## Part IX: The Italian Romance Epic in Modern Fiction and Video Games



## Part X: Resources

# Preface

Although today's cinematic and television epics continue to captivate audiences with stories about love and armed conflict, they often avoid representing geographic or ethnic markers in the struggle between good and evil. Indeed, some of the most popular modern celluloid epics have combined aspects of East and West in their heroic figures, whose swordplay and martial arts techniques recall both medieval European knights and Japanese samurai. Perhaps the most evident example of this cultural blending is the Star Wars series, in which the Jedi, representing the force of good, incorporate recognizably Eastern (and more precisely Buddhist) aspects. In the popular comic book and television series Teenage Mutant Ninja Turtles, the sage Master Splinter cites from Confucius, the *Tao Te Ching*, and Aesop's fables in mentoring turtles with exquisite Italian names who excel in martial arts. Among the "real American heroes" of the GI Joe franchise is the indomitable soldier Snake Eyes, who acquired his ninja skills from a Japanese clan. The East, albeit represented in these examples more by the Far East than the Near or Middle East, no longer represents a distant realm of exoticism and danger, as it did in the Orientalist writings criticized by Edward Said.

Today's college students, having grown up with the above-mentioned hits and sensitized to xenophobia, would probably view a typical Western about the United States cavalry against the Indians with some level of discomfort for the frequent distortions and demonizing of Native Americans. How, then, should instructors introduce a text like the *Orlando furioso*, which belongs to a vast body of chivalric literature backdropped by an ongoing conflict between European Christians and Asian and African Muslims referred to indifferently as Saracens and pagans?

Students who pay attention to authors' representations of non-European protagonists in the romance epic, however, may be surprised to discover historical accuracy or alternative paradigms to programmatic warfare. Indeed, the dividing line between good and evil is not equivalent to that between Christians and Saracens. Not only are there treacherous Christians and exemplary Saracens, but, for example, in Matteo Maria Boiardo's *Orlando innamorato* Ferrara's Este dynasty is founded on the love between Charlemagne's foremost warrior maiden, Bradamante, and a courteous North African knight in the enemy camp, who in turn was born of the love between his southern Italian father and African Amazon mother. Ludovico

Ariosto not only develops the Bradamante-Ruggiero story through to their marriage in *Orlando furioso*'s final canto but invents additional mixed unions, such as the ill-fated love between the Spanish Saracen Isabella and the Scottish Christian Zerbino and the happy-ever-after romance between the Cathayan princess Angelica and the Libyan infantryman Medoro.

While this volume offers tools and ideas for teaching the Italian Renaissance romance epic from a wide range of perspectives and methodologies, instructors can also reflect on issues of utmost relevance in today's increasingly interconnected and globalized—yet resistantly compartmentalized and even polarized—world.

Part 1 offers authoritative evaluations of Italian editions and English translations. Parts 2 through 9 then cover the early medieval background; the major Italian Renaissance romance epics themselves; subsequent English, French, and Spanish works; creative refashioning in art, music, and drama; and, lastly, more recent refashionings of the romance epic in cinema, literature, comic books, and role-playing video games. Essays address teaching the works in excerpts as well as in toto, according to the type of course (comparative epic, cultural studies, gender studies, global studies, history, etc.) and institutions represented (undergraduate, liberal arts, graduate). Although a few essays refer to texts not yet available in English translation, the majority of contributors discuss courses that do not require prior knowledge of Italian. Part 10 provides an overview of resources for teaching the Italian Renaissance romance epic tradition, from critical scholarship to the wealth of available audio-visual material, including online footage from Sicilian puppet theater and the epic *maggio* of the Tuscan-Emilian Apennines, the two popular folk traditions that stage adaptations of romance epic even to the present day.

Given the length of epic poems and limitations of time, no single scholar can be expected to master not only the entirety of the global epic tradition but even the Italian Renaissance romance epic variety. Our aim has been to offer critical insights, pedagogical approaches, and auxiliary materials that have proven fruitful in a number of courses across time periods and disciplines. This volume should therefore be of value to nonspecialists and undergraduate instructors as well as to established scholars seeking to venture out of their comfort zone to include new chivalric narratives and innovative approaches in their courses.

**Jo Ann Cavallo**

# Introduction

## The Italian Renaissance Romance Epic Tradition in Context

Although our English term *epic* harks back to the Greek *epos* ("word"; "song"; "speech"), cultural, national, and ethnic groups across the globe have fostered lengthy narratives with features we would think of as epic. From the Iranian *Shahnameh* to the Japanese *Tale of the Heike*, the list is seemingly endless (see Jackson). And while theorists such as György Lukács and Mikhail Bakhtin, in elucidating the complexities and particularities of the modern novel, tend to conceive the epic in rather monolithic and static terms, the truth is that no two epics are quite alike.

Even the two foremost narratives that epitomize the classical epic in Western tradition are vastly divergent in theme, structure, and substance. The *Iliad* can be summed up as the story of one man's rage, first against his leader and then against the warrior who killed his companion; the *Odyssey* features the episodic account of a man's homecoming, delayed by many fantastic digressions typical of the genre of romance. And whereas epic battles often pit good against evil, some of our most notable epics do not adopt this attitude: in the Homeric example, both Trojans and Achaians are noble and valorous warriors, leading some readers to argue that the real hero of the *Iliad* is the defeated Trojan Hector. And lest we assume that epic poets are universally engaged in glorifying military deeds,

Statius gives us an epic that unflinchingly uncovers the horrors and senselessness of war. The earliest known written epic, that of *Gilgamesh*, depicts a ruler who, after some questionable exploits with his companion Enkidu, sets out on a quest for immortality rather than caring for matters of state.

Not only are there vast divergences in narratives commonly referred to as epic, but retellings of the same epic plot can differ considerably. Epic poets not only emulate previous examples but challenge and transform their predecessors' worldview to express their own aspirations and ideology. One fascinating example is the ancient Indian epic *Ramayana* which, together with the *Mahabharata*, has been creatively rewritten in several languages and represented in various modes, from shadow puppet theater to *kuttu* performances. Despite common inclusion of certain principal episodes, interpretations can be diametrically opposed. Whereas the hero Rama is customarily viewed as the embodiment of dharma and indeed as an incarnation of the god Vishnu in traditional Hinduism, a critical refashioning of Rama's attack on Lanka posits him as a symbol of Aryan aggression over the Dravidians of southern India (Richman).

The European epic tradition most comparable to the Indian epics in narrative scale, circulation, duration, and variety of treatment are the medieval and Renaissance narratives surrounding the Frankish paladin Roland. An ambush by local Basques of Charlemagne's retreating army at the mountain pass of Roncevaux was refashioned in the *Song of Roland* and its variants into a virtual Armageddon in which Spanish Saracens (as Muslims were called at the time) massacred Roland and his rearguard companions due to his stepfather, Ganelon's, treachery. Unconditionally devoted to his religion, king, and country, Roland preferred to fight vastly outnumbered rather than call for reinforcements, thus leaving his fiancée, Aude, to die of grief back home at the news of his demise.

In the Carolingian literary tradition that passed into Italy, stories about Christians fighting Saracens competed with other narrative paradigms, in particular the internal conflicts in the Frankish court and the adventures of its paladins in the East. In the anonymous Franco-Venetian *Entrée d'Espagne* (c. 1320–1330) and its variants, notably the Italian verse redaction *La Spagna in rima*, Roland (Italianized as Orlando) leaves Charlemagne's camp in righteous anger following an offense, undertakes adventures in the Middle East (as the region is now called), and eventually conquers Jerusalem and surrounding territories, forcing the inhabitants to convert en masse, before returning to Spain in time to save Charlemagne from destruction. Pulci's *Morgante* (1483), for all its new comic episodes, iconoclastic characters, and linguistic brio, follows the narrative arc of the Carolingian tradition, beginning with Orlando's angry departure from Charlemagne's camp and culminating in the tragic battle of Roncevaux and its aftermath.

Whereas the *Spagna* narratives present Charlemagne on the offensive in a territory long subjected to Muslim rule, the twelfth-century French epic *Aspremont* and its many Italian rewritings imagine the Franks defending southern Italy from North African Saracens. It is in this prequel that the young Orlando debuts as a fighter, saving the emperor from death at the hands of the Saracen Almonte and acquiring his sword Durindana and his olifant in the process.

Carolingian epic was not, however, the only model of chivalric narrative circulating in medieval and early Renaissance Italy. Arthurian (or Breton) romances, also entering Italy from France, provided a wealth of stories about King Arthur's famed knights of the Round Table that contrasted starkly with Carolingian epic by featuring stories of individual exploits and magical adventures undertaken for love. Chrétien de Troyes' *Knight of the Cart* (c. 1177), for example, depicts Lancelot's unconditional and quasi-idolatrous romantic devotion to Arthur's wife, leading the courtly lover to cast aside both loyalty to the king and concern for his own reputation. Yet Arthurian matter not only reflected the love between Lancelot and Guinevere but also included the more austere spiritual tales involving the quest for the Holy Grail. In addition, the literary tradition of Italy embraced rewritings of ancient Greek and Roman epic poetry and history, such as Guido delle Colonne's rendition of the Trojan War in *Historia destructionis Troiae* (c. 1287) and the exploits of Alexander of Macedonia in popular legendary biographies.

Although rewritings and original compilations already complicated the seemingly straightforward opposition between Carolingian epic and Arthurian romance, Matteo Maria Boiardo organically merged the two genres in his *Orlando innamorato* (1482–83, 1495), thereby inaugurating the hybrid genre of the romance epic. In this scandalous history, kept hidden by its purported author, Turpin, so as not to embarrass the famous paladin, Orlando forsakes Charlemagne not in anger but because he has fallen in love with the princess Angelica of Cathay—despite the fact that the Italian tradition depicts him as already married to Aude, Italianized as Alda. Although the hitherto chaste Frankish paladin traverses the globe undertaking adventures for love in the guise of an Arthurian knight errant, all his efforts are for naught: as Boiardo already anticipates in the poem's opening stanzas, the previously invincible Orlando was a loser when it came to love.

If Boiardo imagines an Orlando in love, the title and opening verses of Ludovico Ariosto's continuation, *Orlando furioso* (1516, 1521, 1532), announce the hapless knight's outright insanity. Although Orlando's descent into madness is initially described as psychological, caused by the news of Angelica's sexual autonomy, we later discover that his condition was a divine punishment for having misused his God-given chivalric attributes. Indeed, Orlando's recovery of his wits, although framed in a romance adventure, catalyzes the divinely ordained destruction of the North African Saracens by the allied Christian armies of Europe and Africa.

Like Boiardo, Ariosto weaves Carolingian and Arthurian themes into an intricately interlaced plot, creatively imitating a vast range of works—from classical epic poetry and history to medieval lyric and novella traditions—in order to surprise, delight, and signify. As he continues to mix imaginary sites and the reality of a rapidly expanding globe, Ariosto not only meticulously completes the various threads of Boiardo's poem but also adds original episodes following his own creative genius and Weltanschauung.

Throughout the sixteenth century, new works continued to appear involving Charlemagne's characters in alternating Arthurian romance and Carolingian epic plots, including Torquato Tasso's *Rinaldo* (1562), which focused on the early exploits of Orlando's less prosperous but more popular cousin. Tasso wrote his better-known poem, *Gerusalemme liberata* (1581), with the Counter-Reformation in full swing and was therefore subject to a process of prepublication censorship in which he found himself compelled to defend his injection of romance adventures into his epic account of the First Crusade. Nonetheless, what most attracted artists, composers, and readers both in his lifetime and in subsequent centuries have been precisely the amorous and magical elements frowned upon by the ecclesiastical authorities.

Female authors writing in the late sixteenth and early seventeenth centuries also creatively reworked traditional paradigms to reflect their own concerns, including gender politics. Whereas Tullia d'Aragona's *Meschino overo il Guerrino* (1560) and Moderata Fonte's *Floridoro* (1581) feature secondary characters from the Carolingian tradition, Margherita Sarrocchi's *Scanderbeide* (1623) and Lucrezia Marinella's *Enrico* (1635) draw their plotlines directly from history: the life of Skanderbeg and the Christian conquest of Constantinople in the Fourth Crusade, respectively.

If we are to believe Cervantes, *El ingenioso hidalgo Don Quijote de La Mancha* (1605, 1616) was written to wipe chivalric tales off the literary map. Yet not even the priest and barber could help praising the *Orlando innam-*

*orato* and *Orlando furioso* during their ad hoc inquisition in Don Quixote's library. Ironically, though, by the time Cervantes's novel was filling the bookshelves of Spain, the epic tradition appeared to be dying out in Italy. We are hard-pressed to find new epic narratives after Tasso's revisionary poem *Gerusalemme conquistata* (1593), unless we make room for Marino's mythical *Adone* (1623), Tassoni's farcical *Secchia rapita* (1630), or the abovementioned historical narratives by Sarrocchi and Marinella. Judging from the canonized masterpieces of the following centuries, it would appear that the novel vanquished the epic. Literature in nineteenth-century Italy, despite absorbing some strands of Romanticism, culminates in verismo, an approach that attempted to represent everyday reality in a tone far removed from the grandeur of epic—even if one could argue that characters such as Giovanni Verga's *vinti* ("defeated ones") take on a grandeur all their own.

If, however, rather than limiting our attention to canonized works, we look at the undercurrents of popular culture, we find that readers and listeners still enjoyed medieval and Renaissance tales of knights and damsels thanks to both the popular press and the oral tradition. With the rise of the novel, chivalric narratives continued to be printed along with sentimental and historical prose fiction in the form of *romanzi d'appendice* ("serial novels"). Stories about Orlando and company were also daily fare in city streets up through the mid-twentieth century. In fact, storytellers in Naples were called "Rinaldi" after this much beloved character. Whereas in urban settings there is greater documentation of prose recitations and readings, in the countryside farmers and shepherds sang in ottava rima, both improvised and memorized from epic poems, especially Tasso's *Gerusalemme liberata*. Chivalric narrative also gave rise to two forms of popular theater still performed today, even if not at the same level of intensity and participation as in previous centuries: the puppet theater of Sicily and southern Italy and the epic *maggio* (folk opera) of the Tuscan-Emilian Apennines.

It is only in the second half of the twentieth century, with the production of global mass media, that the stories that drove Don Quixote to madness faded from view. Nevertheless, new stories arose, especially on the movie screen, that brought to life some of the old themes, values, and even settings of medieval and Renaissance romance epic. In *The Lord of the Rings* film sequence, for example, heroes with swords on horseback display courage, loyalty, and valor, fighting evil forces in a previous age envisioned as grander than our own. *Star Wars* combines the epic distancing of time—"a long time ago"—with an equal distancing in space—"in a galaxy far, far away"—to showcase Jedi knights who employ fancy techno-swords called lightsabers against malevolent powers in the universe. Some of today's most popular video games draw players into an alternative chivalric universe where they must set out on quests and battle monsters and evildoers. Thus, even if the knights and damsels of the Italian romance epic are no longer household names in European or American social life, the appeal of romance epic features has certainly not disappeared from the contemporary psyche.

Today's readers, then, are likely to find the Italian romance epic tradition both utterly new and surprisingly familiar. Love, betrayal, courage, temptation, deceit, ambition, power, and grief, all writ large, are woven together in a seemingly endless multitude of adventures and conflicts that continue to engage, mystify, and provoke.

## Overview of the Essays

The academic climate has changed considerably since the Einaudi edition of the *Furioso* (c. 1966) presented, with implicit endorsement, Italo Calvino's affirmation that "il *Furioso* è un libro unico nel suo genere e può—quasi direi deve—esser letto senza far riferimento a nessun altro libro precedente o seguente" ("the *Furioso* is a unique book in its genre and can—I'd almost say must—be read without reference to any other book preceding or following it"; Presentazione xxxviii). In more recent decades, on the contrary, international scholars have underscored that the romance epic genre is built on creative imitation and have therefore sought to bring into sharper focus a network of Renaissance chivalric narratives that are in dialogue with one another and with the classical and medieval literary traditions of Europe and the greater Mediterranean region.

## I. Editions and Translations

In this volume, Marco Dorigatti surveys modern Italian editions of Italy's principal chivalric poems from the fourteenth through the sixteenth centuries, discussing each work's suitability for teaching and research based on philological and practical considerations ("Italian Editions: A Bibliographical Survey of Epic and Chivalric Poems"). He also offers suggestions for transcribing and editing texts that have not been published since the Renaissance.

Joshua Reid compares English prose and verse translations of the *Orlando innamorato*, *Orlando furioso*, and *Gerusalemme liberata*, while also covering some of the three poems' translation history ("Teaching the Italian Romance Epic in Translation: Materials and Methods"). He then discusses strategies for comparative translation analysis, exploring such topics as the ottava rima stanza, the portrayal of gender, and the encounter with the foreign other.

## II. Medieval Intertexts

In this section, Leslie Zarker Morgan and Maria Bendinelli Predelli offer an essential foray into early Carolingian and Arthurian chivalric narratives. Morgan surveys the contribution of medieval Carolingian material to the Italian Renaissance romance epic, beginning with the French chanson de geste ("From Roland to Orlando: French Charlemagne Tradition and its Development in Italy"). She focuses primarily on the trajectory of the Roland/Orlando character across languages, cultures, narrative plots, and time periods. Bendinelli Predelli's essay ("Adventure, Love, and Prowess in Medieval Italian *Cantari*") takes into consideration the long tradition of medieval *cantari*, including many works of Arthurian inspiration. She distinguishes various types of *cantari* according to their characteristics, including thematic and structural features, and she discusses critical issues related to the genre, such as its connection to popular literature, folklore, and orality. Instructors will thus find that these two essays provide an important literary background, countering any students' assumption that the Renaissance poems of Boiardo and Ariosto sprang directly from ancient classics or canonical medieval authors.

## III. Boiardo, Ariosto, and Tasso in the Classroom

Italian romance epics, especially those of the "three Ferrarese crowns," as they are often called, are taught in courses that span the undergraduate and graduate curriculum, and contributors to this volume offer approaches that either compose an entire course or are integrated into courses across disciplines. Giovanna Rizzarelli suggests using sixteenth-century editions of the *Furioso* (now available online) to enter the multifaceted world of Ariosto's poem ("Teaching Ariosto's *Furioso* through Sixteenth-Century Editions"). Students delve into the topics of the poem's mixture of literary genres, the representation of love and war, and multiple layers of meaning through the early editions' paratextual apparatuses, such as glossaries, allegories, and indexes of classical similitudes. Students continue to explore the poem's reception by comparing the illustrations in these editions to other visual interpretations in frescoes, paintings, and ceramics.

Gael Montgomery discusses a series of themes and introduces students to a range of critical perspectives by following the figure of Angelica across the *Orlando furioso* ("The Transformation of Angelica"). Through close reading and analysis, she brings to bear Homer, Ovid, medieval lyric and narrative poetry, Boccaccio, and Boiardo, the creator of this alluring East Asian princess, to explore such topics as chivalry, sexuality and gender, violence, and the social position of women.

Chris Picicci shows how teaching passages from the *Orlando innamorato*, *Orlando furioso*, and *Gerusalemme liberata* can be enhanced by incorporating a variety of ancillary materials ("Figurative Arts, Music, and Film for Boiardo, Ariosto, and Tasso"). His examples include frescoes by Giovanni Battista Tiepolo for Rinaldo in Armida's garden, Claudio Monteverdi's musical compositions for the battle between Clorinda and Tancredi, and Ermanno Olmi's film *Il mestiere delle armi* for Ariosto's invective against firearms, among others.

Evelyn Birge Vitz, who has offered the undergraduate course Acting Medieval Narrative for over a decade, discusses her experience teaching the *Orlando innamorato* and *Orlando furioso* (along with *The Song of Roland* and Chrétien de Troyes's *Yvain*) through performance at New York University ("Teaching Boiardo and Ariosto through Performance"). Her performance-based approach includes students' reflections on the difference between reading the poems silently or privately and performing from them, as well as on ways the performances expressed and fulfilled—or inflected and modified—their understanding of the poems.

## IV. Comparative Themes and Topics

Essays in this section show how the Italian Renaissance romance epic can be incorporated into thematic courses with a broader reach. Walter Stephens investigates magic, monstrosity, and the marvelous in the poems of Ariosto and Tasso ("Magic, Monsters, and Marvels: Teaching Renaissance Culture through Italian Romance Epic"). His attention to supranatural manifestations brings to bear scientific as well as literary traditions and includes related topics such as proto-museums known as *Wunderkammern*, witchcraft and necromancy, oceanic and otherworldly travel, and Renaissance technologies.

Janet Levarie Smarr traces the representation of madness from Seneca's *Hercules Furens* and Ariosto's *Orlando furioso* through early modern English drama by Shakespeare, Webster, Fletcher, Ford, and others ("Ariosto's

*Orlando furioso* and Madness in Renaissance Drama"). Her comparative approach addresses universal folly versus the insanity of an isolated figure, religious and medical explanations, the convergence of physical and emotional drivers, gendered and political implications, the eliciting of varied reactions from horror and sorrow to laughter, and whether the mad bear any moral responsibility for their condition.

Susan Gaylard's essay, "Learning to Perform as a *Cavaliere*: *Orlando furioso* and Signs of Status," approaches Ariosto's poem through the context of literary and material court culture, interrogating the relation between forms of representation and political power through texts and artifacts from the mid-fourteenth to mid-sixteenth centuries. By comparing Ariosto's fictional universe to Castiglione's idealized court, Gaylard focuses on humanist education, knightly characteristics, moral relativism, the imagery of status, and public identity. In the process, students develop their own critical tools for understanding how material artifacts (such as paintings, coins, and clothing) can help uncover meaning in literary texts.

Bernd Renner argues that the *Orlando furioso*'s mixture of epic and romance is mirrored on a rhetorical level by a mixture of satire and parody ("'Truthful Jesting': Satirical Elements in Ariosto's *Orlando furioso*"). In discussing how Ariosto plays with literary conventions and extraliterary reality while transmitting satirical criticism, Renner also links satire's questioning of religious and political dogmas to the students' potential for independent critical thinking.

Bryan Brazeau focuses on earthly paradises in a comparative study of the *Orlando innamorato*, *Orlando furioso*, *Gerusalemme liberata*, and Spenser's *Faerie Queene* ("Welcome to Paradise: The Earthly Paradise Topos as Pedagogic Structuring Principle"). Brazeau's approach invites students not only to engage with these texts through a central topos but also to reflect on the ideological issues inherent in the contemporary *loci amoeni* that inform their own experience.

## V. Transcultural Encounters

A number of essays consider the Italian Renaissance romance epic from a transcultural perspective. Stephen P. McCormick proposes materials and methods that explore the connections of medieval and early modern cartography to travel texts and the romance epic ("Medieval and Early Modern Cartography and Its Intersections with Travel Texts and the Epic: From Marco Polo to Boiardo and Ariosto"). In showing how maps can help students better understand the spatial dimension of Italian epics, he also addresses 1) historically specific geographical notions such as Asia, Africa, East, West, center, and periphery; 2) the intellectual forces that shape both narrative and cartographic borders; and 3) the notion of islands and insularity as a constant source for the geographic imaginary.

Karina F. Attar's essay, "Muslims in the Novella and Romance Epic Traditions," compares the representation of Muslim protagonists in the novella and romance epic (primarily those of Boiardo, Ariosto, and Tasso). Her discussion of interfaith encounters, particularly episodes of Christian-Muslim amity and enmity, aims to better understand the philological, generic, sociocultural, and historical contexts of both genres. Issues include how the historical reality of interfaith travel, trade, adultery, marriage, and conversion inflected portrayals of Muslim protagonists and how authors expressed cultural fantasies and social anxieties about real and imagined contacts with the Muslim world.

Allison DeWitt encourages the introduction of digital tools and methods to the Italian romance epic classroom, maintaining that geocriticism and digital mapping can help students engage with the epic in a new way. In addition to discussing some of the many resources available for this approach, from the simplest to the most technologically challenging, she provides examples of projects that students can undertake independently or in a group. Her main focus is on Boiardo and Ariosto, but her suggestions provide students with opportunities to experience from a fresh perspective the vast romance epic tradition, and, indeed, the entire humanities curriculum.

## VI. Beyond the "Three Ferrarese Crowns": The Italian Romance Epic in Translation

In "Margutte's Pupils: The Ethics of Laughter in Pulci's *Morgante*," Andrea Moudarres offers strategies for teaching the *Morgante* by concentrating on the comic dimension of the half-giant Margutte, Pulci's counterpart to the giant Morgante. His essay addresses issues such as the interplay between comedy and tragedy, religious orthodoxy and parody, heroes and villains, and, more generally, ethics and aesthetics.

Stefano Gulizia's essay, "Folengo's *Baldus* and *Orlandino*," covers a range of topics that can be fruitfully addressed in teaching Teofilo Folengo's chivalric poems, including the cultural spaces of the Renaissance city and the sonic dimension of the piazza, the role of curiosity, cartography and travel writing, and Folengo's provocatively original creative imitation of Dante and Virgil. In this way instructors can help students see how Folengo relentlessly uses literary parody to enter into dialogue with such contemporary authors as Pulci, Boiardo, and Ariosto.

Of the four female authors of Italian epic now available in English translation, three are featured here in essays by the translators themselves (the fourth is Margherita Sarrocchi's *Scanderbeide*). Julia L. Hairston and John C. McLucas address issues related to teaching Tullia d'Aragona's *Il Meschino, altramente detto il Guerrino* (1560), a refashioning of Andrea da Barberino's Carolingian prose romance about a young man in search of his origins. In addition to examining gender, otherness, authorial intention, literary tradition and register, and the epic quest for identity, Hairston and McLucas also draw attention to the poet's engagement with more canonical texts from antiquity through Dante and Ariosto.

Julia M. Kisacky draws on her experience of teaching Moderata Fonte's *Floridoro* (1581), the first original Italian chivalric poem written by a woman, in conjunction with passages from Fonte's prose dialogue *The Worth of Women*. Her analysis of rulers in the poem also allows for a discussion of gender, given that some of the rulers and warriors are women. She devotes further attention to depictions of friendship, family relations, various types of love, madness, and the character of the sorceress.

In "Naming the Enemy: Linguistic Slippery Slopes in Lucrezia Marinella's *Enrico; or, Byzantium Conquered: A Heroic Poem*," Maria Galli Stampino focuses on the power of words and labels in teaching Lucrezia Marinella's heroic poem (1635). Noting that no language is ever transparent, as it always carries the weight of usage, tradition, and ideology, she demonstrates how Marinella relies on linguistic and ideological short-circuits to imagine and justify the Fourth Crusade, an expedition in which Christian troops invaded the Christian city of Constantinople rather than seek to free Jerusalem from Muslim domination.

## VII. Renaissance and Early Modern European Literary Contexts

This section moves from the Italian Renaissance romance epic into subsequent English, French, and Spanish literature, offering reflections on methodology that go beyond their specific contexts. Charles S. Ross discusses Boiardo, Ariosto, and Tasso in the context of English literary classics, such as Spenser's *Faerie Queene*, Milton's *Paradise Lost*, Sidney's *Arcadia*, and many Shakespeare plays ("The Italian Romance Epic and English Renaissance Literature"). Ross focuses in particular on the representation of female characters and on the "custom of the castle" motif to discuss how romances think about the other.

Phillip John Usher outlines an interdisciplinary and theoretically grounded approach that uses visual artifacts to show how French Renaissance epics defined themselves in dialogue with—or in opposition to—Ariosto ("A Painting of Trojans / A Map of America: Early French Reactions to Ariosto"). Usher features a painting by Toussaint Dubreuil and a New World map as points of entry into Pierre de Ronsard's *Franciade* (1572) and Marc Lescarbot's *Defeat of the Armouchiquois Indians* (1607), respectively. Such juxtapositions facilitate cross-cultural dialogue, interdisciplinary exploration, and theoretical questioning of the epic's ideological underpinnings.

Patricia E. Grieve's essay, "Moorish Lovers, Moorish Invaders, and the Call to Empire: The Inspiration of Ariosto in Early Modern Spain," proposes three pedagogical strategies to study Ariosto's relation to Spain and Spanish epics: first, compare early modern translations of *Orlando furioso*; second, consider sixteenth- and seventeenth-century Spanish romances that reflect on interactions and conflict with adherents of Islam; and third, examine creative imitations of the *Orlando furioso*, most specifically the love story of Angelica and Medoro, by Luis Barahona de Soto, Lope de Vega, and Luis de Góngora. In this way, students can better understand the geopolitical preoccupations of the time, such as fear of the Ottoman Empire and the Barbary States as well as mistrust of recent Muslim Spanish converts to Christianity.

## VIII. The Italian Romance Epic in Art, Music, and Theater

Morten Steen Hansen concentrates on pre-eighteenth-century Italian painting and sculpture inspired by Ariosto, showing how the *Furioso*'s critical status in literary debates from the mid-sixteenth century onward contextualizes artistic representations of the poem ("Ariosto in the Hands of Sixteenth- and Seventeenth-Century Artists"). Topics that highlight contrasting artistic and academic interpretations include the characteristics of epic genre, imitation, lyricism, verisimilitude, the monstrous and the grotesque, sexual desire, and societal mores.

Reminding us that stanzas from the *Orlando furioso* and *Gerusalemme liberata* were sung by people across all social strata in the early modern period, Grant Herreid finds that having graduate and undergraduate music students study and practice the singing of epic verse is an important way to understand and replicate historical Renaissance practice ("Singing Italian Renaissance Epic Verse"). In addition, he argues, this approach teaches proper scansion, illustrates humanist principles of oratorical delivery, develops the essential musical skills of ornamentation and improvisation cultivated by early modern singers, and allows students to learn and perform these important texts in an engaging and artistic way.

Characterizing the madrigal as the most forward-looking, experimental, and dramatically expressive genre of the Renaissance, Barbara Russano Hanning investigates works by late-sixteenth-century madrigal composers inspired by Tasso's *Gerusalemme liberata* ("Tasso and the Italian Madrigal"). Focusing on a few pieces based on Armida's, Tancredi's, and Erminia's monologues, Hanning shows students why Tasso's language was so attractive to musicians and how composers responded to its powerful impact. This approach leads to a greater appreciation of the sonic and expressive qualities of Tasso's poetry as well as to an understanding of Tasso's invaluable contribution to the madrigal's development.

Roberto Puggioni directs our attention to the extraordinary theatrical fortune of Tasso's *Gerusalemme liberata* from the late sixteenth to early nineteenth centuries ("Teaching Tasso's *Gerusalemme liberata* through Italian Theater and Drama"). Approaching the poem through its stage adaptations not only allows students to study a particular form of interpretation but also shows how a great epic work has participated in—and, to some extent, affected—the formal transformation of the dramatic and melodramatic genre.

## IX. The Italian Romance Epic in Modern Fiction and Video Games

The continued influence of the romance epic in twentieth- and twenty-first-century novels, comic books, and video games is explored in the volume's final two essays. Stefano Nicosia's "Rewriting Italian Romance in Twentieth-Century Italy" looks at the creative use of romance epic narratives in a range of modern genres and media, namely: 1) Italo Calvino's relation to Ariosto, from Calvino's prose version of the *Furioso* to his own fiction and essays; 2) Gianni Celati's *Orlando innamorato raccontato in prosa* (1994); 3) Gesualdo Bufalino's *Guerrin meschino* (1993), a refashioning of Andrea da Barberino's fifteenth-century work through the narrative of Sicilian puppet theater; and 4) comic book versions of Andrea da Barberino, Boiardo, and Ariosto. This approach allows students to address such issues as the relation between oral and written discourse, the intensity of fabulation, political perspectives embedded in oral culture, code-switching, and reception theory.

Andrea Privitera explores digital role-playing games (RPGs) as a tool to introduce the chivalric romance genre, in particular the *Orlando innamorato* and *Orlando furioso*, to an undergraduate classroom ("Teaching the Italian Renaissance Epic through Digital Role-Playing Games"). Privitera thereby shows how an instructor can use such games both to help students become familiar with the basic historical and narratological features of the romances and to illustrate more complex qualities of the poems, such as their intertextuality, the *entrelacement* technique, and readership involvement in the storytelling process.

In sum, this volume seeks to help instructors and students better understand the Italian Renaissance romance epic tradition in its literary, cultural, geographic, and historical context. Although the essays move chronologically from medieval models to contemporary adaptations and conceptions, numerous topics and concerns are shared across the volume. The issue of the foreign other and transcultural encounters, the explicit focus of part 5, is addressed as well by Grieve, Reid, and Usher. Women and gender studies, central to the essays on female epic poets (part 6), are broached by Attar, Hansen, Montgomery, Reid, Ross, and Stephens. In addition to the section explicitly devoted to Spanish, French, and English literature (part 7), the essays by Bendinelli Predelli, Brazeau, Morgan, and Smarr likewise consider the comparative context of European and world literature. Art, music, and theater, featured in part 8, also inform the essays by Gaylard, Picicci, Rizzarelli, and Usher. Other interpretive threads running through multiple essays include the questioning of political power and authority and the analysis of rulers (Gaylard, Kisacky, Renner, and Stampino); popular versus elite reception (Bendinelli Predelli, Morgan, Nicosia); and the use of maps and cartography (Brazeau, DeWitt, Gulizia, McCormick, Usher).

Contributors also take positions on issues related to teaching the Italian romance epic. Morgan, for example, outlines the paramount importance of medieval chivalric works in the story of Orlando to dismantle the idea that Italian Renaissance literature simply revives the ancients. Ross objects to *The Norton Anthology of World Literature*'s definition of the European Renaissance as a period of proto colonialism rather than of artistic rebirth, its meager attention to the *Furioso* compared to *Don Quixote*, and its lack of literary context in clarifying the relation between medieval

French, Renaissance Italian, and subsequent English culture. Grieve, in turning to the themes of war and conversion in interactions and conflicts with adherents of Islam, states her refusal to rehearse the continued arguments about Ariosto's influence on Cervantes.

An underlying thread of many essays is the relevance of the Italian romance epic for today's readers. Nicosia and Privitera cogently demonstrate that we continue to experience elements of the romance epic, both explicitly and covertly, in contemporary culture. Yet even beyond the question of modern adaptations and reinventions, the essays collectively demonstrate the genre's compelling and original engagement with perennial issues addressing our shared humanity and, at the same time, our alterity.

Unless otherwise stated, all Italian quotations from the *Orlando innamorato* are from Riccardo Bruscagli's 1995 Einaudi edition, and all English translations are from Charles Stanley Ross's 2004 Parlor Press edition. All Italian quotations from the *Orlando furioso* are from Cesare Segre's 2004 Mondadori edition, and all English translations are from Barbara Reynolds's 2006 Penguin edition. All Italian quotations from *Gerusalemme liberata* are from Lanfranco Caretti's 2005 Einaudi edition, and all English translations are from Max Wickert's 2009 Oxford UP edition.

## Chronology of Selected Italian and European Chivalric Narratives

English titles are provided for translated works when they differ from the original titles.

*Chanson de Roland* (*Song of Roland*) (mid-eleventh to early twelfth century)

Chrétien de Troyes, *Chevalier de la Charrette* (*Knight of the Cart*) (c. 1177–81)

*L'Aspremont* (late-twelfth-century French); *L'Aspramonte* (thirteenth- to fourteenth-century Franco-Italian; fifteenth-century Italian)

*Entrée d'Espagne* (c. 1320–30); *Li fatti di Spagna* (*The Exploits in Spain*) (late-fourteenth-century Franco-Venetian); *La Spagna* (fifteenth-century Italian)

Giovanni Boccaccio, *Teseida delle nozze di Emilia* (*The Theseid of the Nuptials of Emilia*) (c. 1340)

Andrea da Barberino, *I Reali di Francia* (*The Royal House of France*; *L'Aspramonte/Aspramont*; *Le Storie Nerbonesi*; *La Storia di Ugone d'Avernia*) and *Il Meschino di Durazzo* (early fifteenth century)

Luigi Pulci, *Morgante Maggiore* (*Morgante: The Epic Adventures of Orlando and His Giant Friend Morgante*) (1483)

Matteo Maria Boiardo, *Orlando innamorato* (*Orlando in Love*) (1482–83, 1495)

Cieco da Ferrara, *Mambriano* (1490)
Ludovico Ariosto, *Orlando furioso* (*Orlando Furioso: A Romantic Epic*) (1516, 1521, 1532) and *Cinque canti* (*Five cantos*) (composed c. 1518–19)
Teofilo Folengo, *Baldus* (1517) and *Orlandino* (1526)
Pietro Aretino, *Marfisa* (1532), *Angelica* (c. 1538), *Orlandino* (1540), *Astolfeida* (after 1547)
Gian Giorgio Trissino, *L'Italia liberata dai Goti* (1547–48)
Bernardo Tasso, *Amadigi* (1560)
Tullia d'Aragona, *Il Meschino, altramente detto il Guerrino* (*The Wretch, Otherwise Known as Guerrino*) (1560)
Moderata Fonte, *Tredici canti del Floridoro* (*Floridoro, A Chivalric Romance*) (1581)
Torquato Tasso, *Rinaldo* (*Rinaldo: A Poem in Twelve Books*) (1562), *Gerusalemme liberata* (*Jerusalem Delivered*) (1581), *Gerusalemme Conquistata* (1593)
Edmund Spenser, *The Fairie Queene* (1590)
Miguel de Cervantes Saavedra, *Don Quixote* (1605, 1615)
Margherita Sarrocchi, *Scanderbeide* (*Scanderbeide: The Heroic Deeds of George Scanderbeg, King of Epius*) (1606, 1623)
Alessandro Tassoni, *La secchia rapita* (*The Rape of the Bucket*) (1622)
Giovan Battista Marino, *Adone* (*Adonis*) (1623)
Lucrezia Marinella, *L'Enrico, ovvero Bisanzio acquistato, poema eroico* (*Enrico; or, Byzantine Conquered: A Heroic Poem*) (1635)

# Part I

# Editions and Translations

**Marco Dorigatti**

# Italian Editions: A Bibliographical Survey of Epic and Chivalric Poems

What follows is a survey of modern editions (defined as postdating 1900, excluding translations, to be treated separately) of the principal epic and chivalric narrative poems written in Italian between the fourteenth and the sixteenth centuries.[1] It aims to alert users to the editions that may be available for any given text and which should be preferred when alternative editions exist. Differences between similar editions can be subtle and hard to discern, especially for the nonspecialist, yet of great consequence, and so any recommendation will also include a reason based on philological considerations as well as on the text's intended use, whether for research or teaching purposes. All this should help the user to make an informed choice. Yet there are texts, especially numerous in this genre, that have not been published or reprinted since the Renaissance, and thus must be transcribed and edited afresh, however minimally, before they can be used in a scholarly work or in a teaching handout.

Ultimately, this essay will highlight the importance of philologically established textual accurateness and its awareness in any study on Italian narrative poems, something all too often forgotten or overlooked. But let's begin with the author who had by far more editions than any other and whose work became a bestseller already in the sixteenth century: Ludovico Ariosto.

## Ludovico Ariosto

As is well known, Ariosto published his poem three times during his lifetime. By convention, these editions are designated by the following capital letters, or sigla: A = Ferrara: per Giovanni Mazocco dal Bondeno, 1516; B = Ferrara: per Giovanni Battista da la Pigna milanese, 1521; C = Ferrara: per Francesco Rosso da Valenza, 1532. For A the only modern edition available is *Orlando furioso secondo la princeps del 1516* ("*Orlando furioso* according to the First Edition of 1516"), edited by Marco Dorigatti in 2006, whereas for B, which has never been reissued, its text can be reconstructed from the 1521 variants contained in Debenedetti-Segre's 1960 edition, *Orlando furioso secondo l'edizione del 1532 con le varianti delle edizioni del 1516 e del 1521* ("*Orlando furioso* according to the 1532 Edition with the Variants of the Editions of 1516 and 1521").[2] The latter is a unique tool in that it permits a reader to view at a glance the variants between all three versions (ABC), lending itself to a number of applications ranging from comparative studies (something that in Italian is called *variantistica d'autore*, or study of the variants made by the author) to linguistic and stylistic analyses in the classroom. As for C—that is, the poem's final version—it has had a long, virtually uninterrupted editorial tradition comprising a staggering number of editions:[3] so many, in fact, that the choice can be daunting.[4] The critical text currently considered the most authoritative and hence the most preferred (especially in scholarly works) is Cesare Segre's 1964 edition, which makes a number of corrections to the Debenedetti-Segre edition.[5] The 1964 text was later republished in the Meridiani Mondadori series beginning from 1976 and is still in print today. It also forms the basis of the following editions and their respective reprints: those edited by Lanfranco Caretti (1966), Emilio Bigi (1982),[6] and Remo Ceserani and Sergio Zatti (1997). These editions are noteworthy also for their commentaries, and Bigi's is generally regarded as the most comprehensive, particularly for his attention to classical sources, language, and style.

If the text must conform to the original typography (retaining, that is, the original spelling as well as punctuation and abbreviations), then Filippo Ermini's 1909–13 edition, *Orlando furioso di Ludovico Ariosto secondo le stampe del 1516, 1521, 1532 rivedute dall'Autore* ("*Orlando furioso* by Ludovico Ariosto according to the 1516, 1521, and 1532 Editions Revised by the Author"), might be useful, though it should be used cautiously, as it contains numerous errors, especially in the first two volumes. Still related to Ariosto's final editing of his poem is Santorre Debenedetti's much-celebrated *I frammenti autografi dell'*Orlando furioso (1937) ("The Autograph Fragments of *Orlando furioso*"), now also available in facsimile with a preface by Cesare Segre (2010), which permits the reader to observe, as it were, the author at work.[7]

For the *Cinque canti* the standard text is, once again, Segre's 1954 edition. This text was later adopted by Luigi Firpo in 1963 (*Cinque Canti di un nuovo libro di M. Ludovico Ariosto* ["Five Cantos of a New Book by Messer Ludovico Ariosto"]) but not without a few minor amendments, which were for the most part retained by Lanfranco Caretti (1977) and Ceserani-Zatti (Orlando furioso *e* Cinque canti; 1997). Hence, the latter three editions offer the most up-to-date versions of the standard text, although Segre's 1954 edition is still worth consulting.

Ariosto's other chivalric works that need mentioning are two fragments: the so-called *Obizzeide*, his earliest surviving attempt at epic poetry, and "Per la storia d'Italia" ("For the History of Italy"), a historical passage excluded from the poem's final version (see, respectively, Segre's 1954 edition of *Opere minori* ["Minor Works"; 164–71], and Casadei, "Stanze 'Per la Storia d'Italia': Testo critico e commento" ["Stanzas 'For the History of Italy': Critical Edition with Commentary"]).

Finally, when comparing any of the editions mentioned above, it is worth bearing in mind that all except Ermini and Dorigatti modernize the spelling.

## Matteo Maria Boiardo

The text of Matteo Maria Boiardo's poem, whose original title, *Inamoramento de Orlando*, is now preferred by many scholars to its old variant, *Orlando innamorato*, has not survived nearly as well as Ariosto's, because the earliest editions have all been lost, making it hard for scholars to restore. The version used throughout most of the twentieth century was based on the Trivulziano codex (a manuscript held in the Trivulziana Library of Milan) due to a belief that manuscripts predated printed works, as was assumed by successive editors (Francesco Foffano in 1906 and 1926; Angelandrea Zottoli in 1936–1937; Aldo Scaglione in 1951; Giuseppe Anceschi in 1978), culminating in Riccardo Bruscagli's 1995 edition. However, in 1999 a new, critical edition by Antonia Tissoni Benvenuti and Cristina Montagnani appeared, entitled *L'Inamoramento de Orlando*, which was based on the earliest surviving printed sources (Piero de' Piasi, 1487, for books 1 and 2, and Giorgio de' Rusconi, 1506, for book 3) and which also partly retained the original spelling.[8] This edition is now the standard work, preferred especially in scholarly contexts. But it also has a downside: the resulting text is more difficult linguistically and more demanding because of its unconventional prosody. This is due not to its editors, who have done their best, but to the disparity between the two testimonies on which their version is based, one belonging to the fifteenth century and the other to the sixteenth century. Hence this text may prove problematic in the classroom (within or outside Italy). This is the reason a new edition appeared, which tried to bridge, as it were, the two worlds, accepting some of the innovations introduced by Tissoni Benvenuti and Montagnani while preserving the legibility afforded by the Trivulziano codex: Andrea Canova's *Orlando innamorato. L'inamoramento de Orlando* (2011). Needless to say, philologically, this edition marks a step backward; it is the product of a compromise, ambivalent from the very title, but it may suit a reader who is already accustomed to the musicality of Ariosto's verse or who is approaching Boiardo for the first time.

As for the commentaries, the richest is that of Tissoni Benvenuti–Montagnani (1999), but Bruscagli (1995) and Canova (2011) are also worth consulting. Finally we should not forget Francesco Berni, whose reworking of the *Innamorato* supplanted the original text for a very long time. Today Berni's rifacimento is available only in an edition that in reality is a facsimile of Severino Ferrari and Giovanni Nencioni's 1911 edition, *Orlando innamorato di Matteo Maria Boiardo rifatto da Francesco Berni* ("*Orlando innamorato* by Matteo Maria Boiardo Reworked by Francesco Berni").

## Luigi and Luca Pulci

A milestone in the editorial history of Luigi Pulci's *Morgante* was Franca Ageno's 1955 edition. In 1962, however, Domenico De Robertis thoroughly revised its text, implementing significant improvements, so much so that it became the new standard, followed (albeit with minor departures) by all subsequent editors, namely Davide Puccini (1989), Giuliano Dego (1992), and Aulo Greco (1997). All the latter editions can be used with confidence.

The most recent edition, by Marzio Pieri and Luana Salvarani, *El famoso Morgante nella versione di Modena* (2008) ("The Famous *Morgante* according to the Modena Version"), is unconventional in that it blindly follows the earliest surviving print ("Appresso Sancto Jacopo di Ripoli"; 1481) in twenty-three cantari, even in spelling (the first modern edition to do so); yet it is not a critical edition in any way and thus remains little more than a bibliographical oddity.

This edition was complemented by a companion volume edited by Pieri and containing Luca Pulci's *Cyriffo Calvanèo*[9] (which, on his death in 1470, was continued by his younger brother[10]) and Luigi's *Morte di Orlando* ("Death of Orlando"; also known as *Rotta di Roncisvalle* ["The Roncevaux Defeat"]), a five-cantari addition that ends the so-called *Morgante maggiore*: *Il Cyriffo Calvanèo: La morte di Orlando* (2009). Planned and executed much like Pieri-Salvarani, and similarly controversial, it features nonetheless the only modern edition of *Ciriffo Calvanèo*.

## Francesco Cieco da Ferrara

Until a critical edition becomes available (currently in preparation by Jane Everson, of Royal Holloway, University of London), the only text of *Mambriano* by Francesco Cieco da Ferrara worth considering is still Giuseppe Rua's 1926 edition, *Libro d'arme e d'amore nomato Mambriano* ("Book of Arms and Love called *Mambriano*").

## Angelo Poliziano

What used to be the standard edition of Angelo Poliziano's *Stanze*—Vincenzo Pernicone's *Stanze cominciate per la giostra di Giuliano de' Medici* (1954) ("Stanzas Begun for the Joust of Giuliano de' Medici")—has now been superseded though not completely replaced. The two recommended editions are those of Stefano Carrai (1988) and Davide Puccini (1992).

## Pietro Aretino

Pietro Aretino's chivalric works, namely *Marfisa*, *Angelica*, *Orlandino*, and *Astolfeida*, are included in Danilo Romei's 1995 edition, *Poemi cavallereschi*.

## Teofilo Folengo

Teofilo Folengo's main chivalric work, *Orlandino* ("The Young Orlando"), was reedited by Mario Chiesa in 1991. For his *Baldus* see both Chiesa (1997) and Tonna et al. (*Baldo*; 2004).

## Torquato Tasso

The most reliable text of Torquato Tasso's *Gerusalemme liberata* ("Jerusalem Delivered") is in Lanfranco Caretti's *Tutte le poesie di Torquato Tasso*

("Complete Poems by Torquato Tasso"; 1957), which is based on Febo Bonnà's second impression of 20 July 1581. This was later combined with Caretti's commentary in 1961, which resulted in his 1971 edition, probably the one most widely used today. In addition to Caretti, at least two other editions of the commentary are worth consulting: Fredi Chiappelli (1982) and Franco Tomasi (2009), which offers the most up-to-date bibliography.

For Tasso's other chivalric or epic works, the recommended editions are, for *Rinaldo*, Matteo Navone (2012); for *Il Gierusalemme*, Caretti (1993) ("The *Jerusalem*: A Fragment"); and for *Gerusalemme conquistata* ("Jerusalem Regained"), Claudio Gigante (2010).

## Moderata Fonte

Moderata Fonte's chivalric poem *Tredici canti del Floridoro* ("Thirteen Cantos of *Floridoro*") was made available by Valeria Finucci (1995).

## Lucrezia Marinella

Lucrezia Marinella's 1635 "poema heroico" has been recently reedited by Maria Galli Stampino: *L'Enrico, ovvero Bisanzio acquistato, poema eroico* (2011) (*Enrico; or, Byzantium Conquered: A Heroic Poem*).[11]

## The Chivalric Tradition

The study of the chivalric tradition, for the most part anonymous, is gaining increasing attention in scholarship, but its enduring popular appeal as well as its oral qualities would make it ideally suitable also for the classroom, whenever novelty and liveliness are desired.

Beginning with Andrea da Barberino, available modern editions include Giuseppe Vandelli and Giovanni Gamberin's *I Reali di Francia* ("The Royal House of France"; 1947), which may still be used alongside Roncaglia-Beggiato (1987); Marco Boni's and Luigi Cavalli's essential editions of *L'Aspramonte* (1951; 1972); and finally, Mauro Cursietti's *Il Guerrin Meschino* (2005).

The *Aspramonte* tradition is represented by two more anonymous texts: *Cantari d'Aspramonte inediti*, edited by Andrea Fassò in 1981, and Aspramonte*: Poema del Quattrocento*, edited by Carmelina Sicari in 2003.

Another important tradition stems from *L'Entrée d'Espagne* ("The Entry into Spain"). The standard reference work remains Antoine Thomas's edition, L'Entrée d'Espagne*: Chanson de geste franco-italienne* (1913),[12] recently reissued in a modern, albeit partial, edition with parallel Italian translation by Marco Infurna (Anonimo Padovano, L'Entrée d'Espagne*: Rolando da Pamplona all'Oriente* [2011]) ("Entry into Spain: Roland from Pamplona to the Orient"). Among the various compositions directly or indirectly descending from *L'Entrée d'Espagne* are the texts forming the wider *Spagna* tradition.[13] Listed here are those that have been reedited in modern times: Michele Catalano's La Spagna*: Poema cavalleresco del secolo XIV* (1939–40) ("Spain: A Chivalric Poem from the Fourteenth Century"); Ruggiero M. Ruggieri's *Li fatti de Spagna: Testo settentrionale trecentesco già detto "Viaggio di Carlo Magno in Ispagna"* (1951) ("Exploits in Spain: Fourteenth-Century Northern Text Formerly Known as 'Charlemagne's Journey to Spain'"); Giovanna Barbara Rosiello's *La* Spagna *in rima del manoscritto comense* (2001) ("The Rhymed *Spagna* from the Como Manuscript"); Valentina Gritti and Cristina Montagnani's *Spagna ferrarese* (2009) ("The Ferrarese *Spain*"), highly recommended (despite having been criticized by both Giovanni Palumbo and Franca Strologo); Amélie Hanus's "La *Spagna Magliabechiana* e la materia cavalleresca italiana: Edizione critica e studio del ms. BNCF, II, I, 57" (2012) ("The *Spain* according to the Magliabechi manuscript and the Italian Chivalric Matter: Critical Edition and Study of BNCF, II, I, 57"); and Frej Moretti's *La* Spagna *in prosa* (2011) ("The Prose Version of the Spagna Poem").

Apart from these two traditions there are also other Carolingian poems that have been reedited: Elio Melli's *I cantari di Rinaldo da Monte Albano* (1973) ("The *cantari* of Renaud de Montauban") and *Cantari di Fierabraccia e Ulivieri* (1984) ("*Cantari* of Fierabras and Olivier"); Aurelia Forni Marmocchi's *Romanzo cavalleresco inedito* (1989) ("An Unpublished Chivalric Romance"); Sara Furlati's *I cantari del Danese* (2003) ("The *cantari* of the Dane"); and Daniela Delcorno Branca's *Buovo d'Antona: Cantari in ottava rima* (2008) ("Bevis of Hampton: *Cantari* in octaves").

Whereas the Carolingian tradition is characterized by a gradually expanding number of editions, the Arthurian tradition presents fewer titles, the most significant of which is probably Emanuele Trevi's *Tavola Ritonda* ("Round Table"; 1999).[14] But we should not forget Tristan, who more than any other hero captured the imagination of medieval Italians and resulted in a chivalric tradition well represented in modern times. For the *Tristano Corsiniano* ("Tristan as from the Codex in the Corsiniana Library"), see Roberto Tagliani's critical edition (2011) and Gloria Allaire's edition (2015); and for the *Tristano Riccardiano*, see Marie-José Heijkant (1991) and Psaki (2006). The *Tristano Panciatichiano* ("Tristan from the Panciatichi Codex") has been edited by Allaire (2002). Other works belonging to the same tradition are the *Cantari di Tristano* ("Tristan *cantari*"), edited by Giulio Bertoni in 1937, and *Il libro di messer Tristano ("Tristano Veneto")* ("The Book of Messer Tristano ['The Veneto Tristan']"), edited by Aulo Donadello in 1994.

A work that stands in between all three *matières* ("matters" or subjects) of medieval romance (classical, Arthurian, and Carolingian) is Antonio Pucci's *Cantari della Reina d'Oriente* ("*Cantari* of the Oriental Queen"), edited by Attilio Motta and William Robins (2007).

A chivalric compilation that, despite having been conceived much later (1858–1860), summed up this rich and diverse subject matter, becoming a stock-in-trade of *cantastorie* ("storytellers") and puppeteers working for the *Opera dei pupi*, is Giusto Lo Dico's *Storia dei paladini di Francia* ("Story of the Paladins of France"), edited by Felice Cammarata (1993).

## Unpublished Works

Despite the efforts of successive editors over the last century, a considerable number of epic and chivalric works, even significant ones, do not have modern editions: for example the sequels to Boiardo's *Inamoramento de Orlando* written by Nicolò degli Agostini and Raffaele da Verona,[15] the anonymous *Inamoramento de Carlo* ("Carlo in Love"), Bernardo Tasso's *Amadigi* ("Amadis of Gaul") (not published since 1837), Giovambattista Giraldi Cinzio's *Hercole* (not published since its first edition in 1557),[16] Tullia d'Aragona's *Il Meschino, altramente detto il Guerrino* ("The Wretch, otherwise known as Guerrino") (not published since 1840), and Laura Terracina's *Discorso sopra il principio di tutti i canti di Orlando furioso* ("Discourse on the Beginning of all the Cantos of *Orlando furioso*") (not reissued since 1698), to name but a few.

## Notes

1. This survey was up to date as of September 2015.

2. All works quoted are print publications unless otherwise stated.

3. The best bibliographical repertoire is still Agnelli-Ravegnani (1933).

4. On the poem's editorial tradition from the sixteenth century to the present, see Dorigatti, "Strutture filologiche: La tradizione testuale dell'*Orlando furioso*" ("Philological Structures: The Textual Tradition of *Orlando furioso*").

5. The principal of these are discussed in Dorigatti, "Dalla parola al testo: Il

cammino di Cesare Segre (1928–2014)" ("From Word to Text: The Journey of Cesare Segre"), pp. 20–22.

6. This work, formerly hard to find, is now available in a new, one-volume edition edited by Cristina Zampese (Rizzoli, 2012). Note, however, that this handy reprint contains numerous errors and should therefore not be used for textual references.

7. See Contini.

8. For example, it does retain the so-called *h* etimologica but not in all the forms of the verb *(h)avere.*

9. The accent is added purely to indicate the correct pronunciation.

10. Bernardo Giambullari eventually concluded the poem, although his addition is not included in the Pieri-Salvarani edition.

11. This edition was based on Stampino's earlier English translation, *Enrico; or, Byzantium Conquered: A Heroic Poem* (2009).

12. This edition is now also available in facsimile reprint with a preface by Marco Infurna (Olschki, 2007).

13. On this tradition see two fundamental works, both recently published: Palumbo, *La* Chanson de Roland *in Italia nel Medioevo* ("The *Chanson de Roland* in Italy during the Middle Ages"); and Strologo, La Spagna *nella letteratura cavalleresca italiana* ("The *Spagna* in the Italian Chivalric Literature").

14. On the Arthurian tradition in Italy, see Allaire and Psaki.

15. Even Raffaele da Verona's *Giunta all'*Orlando innamorato, edited by Paparelli in 1971, is only a facsimile edition reproducing the 1518 edition.

16. However, Carla Molinari is preparing a critical edition based on the manuscripts held in the Biblioteca Comunale Ariostea, in Ferrara, as well as an edition based on the printed version (Gadaldini, 1557) with Marco Dorigatti.

Joshua Reid

# Teaching the Italian Romance Epic in Translation: Materials and Methods

This essay hopes to ease the process of choosing and using an English translation of the Italian romance epics of Matteo Maria Boiardo, Ludovico Ariosto, and Torquato Tasso. The "Materials" section provides an annotated survey of English translations to equip teachers with the best editions for their courses, and the "Methods" section details strategies for comparative translation analysis, where translations become an asset, not a loss, for understanding the romance epic.

## Materials

The primary emphasis of this survey is on modern translations currently in print.[1] Mention is made of translation form (ottava rima, prose, other verse forms) and of any important paratextual materials, such as introductions and notes. Almost all modern editions include a character index, with descriptions of the characters' major actions listed by canto and stanza, an absolute necessity for navigating the romance epic's multiple strands of character and narrative. Sample stanzas from the modern editions enable comparison shopping.

In addition to the modern translations, this section addresses historical translations, as teachers may want to draw stanzas and cantos from them for comparative analysis in the classroom, a technique discussed in the "Methods" section of this essay. These classic translations are available from a variety of sources. Many have been reprinted in the twentieth century and are available in libraries, some can be found on *Google Books*, *Internet Archive*, or *Project Gutenberg*, others in cheap facsimile reprints on *Amazon.com*, and still others on databases like *Early English Books*. If seeking Renaissance English translations, *The Italian Romance Epic in English, 1590–1600* (Reid) includes multiple early translations of Boiardo, Ariosto, and Tasso in one convenient place.

## *Boiardo's* Orlando innamorato

### *Modern Translations in Print*

The only unabridged English translation of Boiardo is Charles Stanley Ross's version (2004). Ross chooses unrhymed tetrameter for his verse form, which may seem a peculiar choice, but Ross feels that the abbreviated line offers more flexibility to capture the sense of the Italian original. The introductory materials are superb, serving as essential scholarship on Boiardo, and they include a chronology of Boiardo's life, an annotated bibliography of Boiardo criticism, maps of the poem's dizzyingly circuitous geographic wanderings, and indispensable essays on Boiardo's life, the romance epic genre, and Boiardo's allegory of love. The annotations are intentionally slight, and many teachers will wish there were more. The earlier edition of Ross's translation (1989), although out of print, is in dual-language format, and the English translation is a closer line-for-line rendering.

The other English translation in print, Mark Staebler's (1989), is a dual-language version of selections that amount to about an eighth of the poem. Staebler's at times labored ottava rima stanzas provide an illuminating contrast to Ross's more accomplished unrhymed tetrameter. While it is the only modern edition lacking a character index, its introductory materials are important resources, and they include a preface by Paolo Valesio and essays on the *Innamorato*'s Italian and English reception history.

### *Historical Translations*

Historical translations of Boiardo are scarce and all incomplete. The first translation of Boiardo in English, Robert Tofte's rendering of three cantos (1598), is reprinted in full in Reid, and twelve stanzas appear in an appendix in Staebler's translation (473–76). John Addington Symonds translated over forty stanzas in ottava rima in his *Renaissance in Italy: Italian Literature*

(457–92), and John Craufurd Wordsworth included over 150 stanzas in ottava rima in *Adventures in Literature* (75–149).

### *Sampling of Stanzas (Angelica's Entrance, 1.1.21)*

They saw far down the splendid hall
four fearsome and enormous giants
enter, a lady in their midst,
escorted by a single knight.
She seemed to be the morning star,
the lily and the garden rose.
In short, to tell the truth of her,
never was so much beauty seen.

(*Orlando innamorato*,
translated by Charles S. Ross)

There came marching to the head of the room
four fierce giants, each of untoward size,
and, in their midst, in all her bloom,
a lovely lady with a knight besides.
She seemed a rose or lily, whose perfume
ascended like a star the morning skies.
Never before was seen, to tell the truth,
such a beauty in the flower of youth.

(*Selections from Boiardo's* Orlando
innamorato, translated by Mark Staebler)

## *Ariosto's* Orlando furioso

### *Modern Translations in Print*

Barbara Reynolds's translation (1975–77) is the most distinguished and most scholarly option. Its ottava rima stanzas are admirable in their accuracy and readability but may seem at times to dull Ariosto's prancing moments. The introductory materials (111 pages) are valuable: an interpretive primer to the poem, including its literary origins; a biographical sketch of Ariosto; an essay on the *Orlando furioso* and English literature, including an assessment of previous translations; as well as lists of characters, mounts, and items. The notes are the most thorough of all the Ariosto editions, including specialized resources such as genealogical tables of the Este family.

Guido Waldman provides a full prose version of the poem (1974). Released from the original's stanzas, Waldman's prose reads better as a straight story and stays true to Ariosto's narrative strengths while approximating word order (stanza shifts from the original are marked in his paragraphs with a slash). Waldman's Ariosto becomes a delightful novel, but the abandonment of poetic form entirely may seem too much of a sacrifice for accessibility. His introduction is nowhere as thorough as Reynolds's, and he includes no explanatory notes.

David R. Slavitt, an accomplished poet and translator, provides a version in ottava rima (2009), but he translates little more than half the poem. His tone is much lighter than Reynolds's, almost to the point of parody. Slavitt seems to be trying to channel Lord Byron, and, like Byron, is fully capable of using feminine rhymes for comic effect. Ariosto's serious play becomes all play here, to the point that even Ross, in his introduction to the translation, calls it "tipsy" at times (xiv). Beyond Ross's introduction, Slavitt's apparatus is minimal, with no notes and a brief translator's preface.

### *Historical Translations*

Sir John Harington's translation (1591, ottava rima) is the first of the entire poem in English. There have been a few twentieth-century reprintings of this classic, including the excellent 1972 Robert McNulty edition. Selections of the most popular episodes are available in Reid. John Stewart of Baldynneis (1585–88) wrote a fascinating abridgement of the poem in Scottish dialect and linked *ababbcbc* octaves, which was recently published in an edition by Donna Heddle (2008). Other translations include William Huggins (1755, ottava rima), John Hoole (1783, heroic couplets), William Stewart Rose (1823–31, ottava rima), Allan Gilbert (1954, prose stanzas), and Richard Hodgens (1973, prose paraphrase). Interesting fragmentary translations include one of canto 43 by Robert Tofte (1597, ottava rima), reprinted in Reid; an anonymous reappropriation of the innkeeper's tale in canto 28 (likely by George Farquhar, 1708, heroic couplets), reprinted in *Translation and Literature* (Ariosto, "Unknown English Translation"); the Olimpia episode of canto 10 by Edward Davenport (1824, ottava rima); and cantos 24 (Zerbino and Isabella) and 29 (Rodomonte and Isabella) by Henry Boyd (1785, Spenserian stanzas), which were appended to his translation of Dante's *Inferno.*

### *Sampling of Stanzas (Opening, 1.1)*

> Of ladies, cavaliers, of love and war,
> Of courtesies and of brave deeds I sing,
> In times of high endeavour when the Moor

Had crossed the sea from Africa to bring
Great harm to France, when Agramante swore
In wrath, being now the youthful Moorish king,
To avenge Troiano, who was lately slain,
Upon the Roman Emperor Charlemagne. (*Orlando furioso*,
translated by Barbara Reynolds)

I sing of knights and ladies, of love and arms, of courtly chivalry, of courageous deeds—all from the time when the Moors crossed the sea from Africa and wrought havoc in France. I shall tell of the anger, the fiery rage of young Agramant their king, whose boast it was that he would avenge himself on Charles, Emperor of Rome, for King Trojan's death. (*Orlando furioso*, translated by Guido Waldman)

Of ladies, knights, of passions and of wars,
of courtliness, and of valiant deeds I sing
that took place in that era when the Moors
crossed the sea from Africa to bring
such troubles to France. I shall tell of the great stores
of rage in the heart of Agramant, the king
who swore revenge on Charlemagne who had
murdered King Troiano (Agramant's dad). (*Orlando furioso*,
translated by David R. Slavitt)

## *Tasso's* Gerusalemme liberata

### *Modern Translations in Print*

Max Wickert (2009) is the only modern translator to replicate the original's ottava rima. Wickert succeeds with an enjoyable and accurate translation that only occasionally trips up on Tasso's tortuous syntax. The introduction is the most thorough of the modern translations and includes a chronology. Annotations are also present, as is an especially welcome appendix of each canto's influence on literature, art, and music.

Anthony M. Esolen (2000) offers a respectable alternative to Wickert. Esolen's verse form is a hybrid one, with rhyme scheme *xaxaxabb*, which allows him to follow the appearance of ottava rima while gaining more elasticity in the unrhymed *x* lines. Compared with Wickert, many stanzas feel more supple and less constrained (see lines 1–2 of the sample passages, for example). Esolen's edition has the "Allegory of the Poem" (Wickert does not) and notes. A brief bibliographical essay at the end of the volume succinctly summarizes the editions and criticism of Tasso.

Ralph Nash (1987) offers a prose option separated into stanzas, which Nash hopes will allow the reader to follow the action "smoothly and rapidly" (xxiii). His edition features notes, chronology, an introduction, and, like Esolen, he reprints the "Allegory of the Poem." In addition to the obligatory character index, he also has a glossary of biblical, geographical, and mythological names and places.

### *Historical Translations*

The earliest translation is Richard Carew's five cantos in 1594 (ottava rima), which has been reprinted in full in Reid. The most famous and important translation is Edward Fairfax's (1600, ottava rima), reprinted in the outstanding critical edition by Kathleen M. Lea and T. M. Gang (*Godfrey of Bulloigne*; 1981). Selections of the most popular episodes are available in Reid. Later translations include Philip Doyne (1761, blank verse), John Hoole (1763, heroic couplets), J. H. Hunt (1818, heroic couplets), J. H. Wiffen (1824–25, Spenserian stanza), J. R. Broadhead (1837, heroic couplets), C. L. Smith (1851, ottava rima), A. C. Robertson (1853, ottava rima), H. A. Griffith (1863, *ababccdd* octave), J. K. James (1865, *ababcdcd* octave), and Joseph Tusiani (1970, unrhymed octaves with rhymed final couplet).

### *Sampling of Stanzas (Opening 1.1)*

I sing of war, of holy war, and him,
Captain who freed the Sepulchre of Christ.
Greatly he wrought by force of mind and limb,
and greatly suffered, nobly sacrificed.
Vainly did Hell oppose him, Asia grim
vainly combined with Libya, Hell-enticed.
Heaven favoured him and guided back, to fight
under his sacred flag, each errant knight.
(*Liberation of Jerusalem*, translated by Max Wickert)

I sing the reverent armies, and that Chief
who set the great tomb of our Savior free;
much he performed with might and judgment, much
he suffered in the glorious victory;
in vain hell rose athwart his path, in vain
two continents combined in mutiny.
Heaven graced him with its favor, and restored
his straying men to the banner of the Lord.
(*Jerusalem Delivered*, translated by Anthony M. Esolen)

> I sing the reverent armies and the captain who liberated Christ's great sepulcher. Much he wrought with his wit and with his hand; much he suffered in the glorious conquest. And vainly Hell opposed herself to it, and vainly the combined peoples of Asia and of Libya took up arms. Heaven granted him favor and brought back under the holy standards his wandering companions. (*Jerusalem Delivered*, translated by Ralph Nash)

## Methods

Along with the concerns over choosing the best translation is the nagging sense of teaching a fraudulent text. This is not Ariosto; it is Ariosto in English. What is a teacher to make of such a diminished thing? Often, the text's insufficient status as translation is barely mentioned in the classroom. Teaching the Italian romance epic in translation, however, does not have to come with a sense of loss. Instead, it can become a productive catalyst of assignments and class discussion. Once the translation is made visible, it unleashes its transformative potential.

### *The Case for Comparative Translation Analysis*

The key method for making translation visible is through comparative translation analysis. The process involves giving students two or more versions of a stanza or section from different translations. It is best to include some translations from previous historical eras, as they provide some of the starkest differences and are ripest for analysis.[2]

Students will then discuss the passages as a class, analyze them in groups, or write response papers on the differences between the translations. I typically pose questions like these: What differences do you notice in the word choices of the translations? What differences do you notice in the form of the translations (ottava rima, prose, other verse forms)? How do those differences affect the interpretation of the text? Can you match the English words with the original Italian? If so, how have word placement and word choice shifted from the source text to the translation, and how have different translations approached the same Italian word? How does the translator's historical and cultural context seem to have influenced the translation?

Students relish these activities, as they already appreciate alternative versions, such as deleted scenes from their favorite movies or B-sides from music. As they discover how different cultures and translators responded to the same source text, they find that "translation is one of the most influential forms of literary criticism, for it both interprets and recreates the text it addresses" (Hammond 649). Gathering translations from different eras can show the Italian romance epic's changing reception history, particularly during the flash points of the sixteenth, eighteenth, and nineteenth centuries.

For the rest of this essay, I will briefly explore two of the matrices I have used when doing comparative translation analysis, and what they can help reveal about the Italian romance epic and its cultural reception.

## *Ottava Rima*

As the stanzaic girders of the Italian romance epic, ottava rima is worth discussion in its own right, and the English translations provide stimulating approaches to this form. Its *abababcc* scheme taxes the comparatively rhyme-poor English lexicon, particularly when rhyme words in English are usually masculine, which generates a blunting effect when replicated in the octave. Given the challenges, translators have often resorted to other forms, such as prose, blank verse, or verse couplets. In comparing these variations, students can discuss how stanza form affects the incarnation of meaning, recapitulating the debates over body and soul in verse translation. Bringing in the arguments from the translator's prefaces can accentuate the debate. For a prose translator of Ariosto like Waldman, it is folly to lay the translation on "the Procrustean bed of the 'Englished Octave'" (xvi), and Ross, who renders Boiardo in unrhymed tetrameter, "value[s] Boiardo's text more than the external form he chose for his poetry" (Introduction lxxvii). But for Staebler, the octave is a signifier that "must be duplicated, re-created, if the text is to communicate in the same form in which it was written" (58). Class discussions can focus on how external or central ottava rima is to the poem's impact or on whether or not the "Englished Octave," when present, replicates or merely diminishes the variegated power of Boiardo, Ariosto, and Tasso.

When discussing the octave, I provide a mixture of approaches. For Boiardo, I compare Ross's unrhymed tetrameter to Staebler's octave. For Ariosto, I contrast Waldman's prose translation with Harington's, Reynolds's, and Slavitt's ottava rima along with Hoole's heroic couplets. For Tasso, I use stanzas from Fairfax's and Wickert's straight ottava rima, Esolen's hybridized ottava rima, Doyne's blank verse, Hoole's couplets, Nash's prose, and Wiffen's Spenserian stanza.

Analyzing Hoole's couplets in Ariosto and Tasso, for example, helps students understand what happens when the stanzas are deconstructed:

the octave's pattern of momentum and release is not present in Hoole's metronomic couplets. Esolen's *xaxaxabb* stanza compared to Wickert's ottava rima shows how both translators dealt with Tasso's difficult syntax. Reynolds and Slavitt cope differently with English's rhyme resources, which in turn drastically affects the translations' tone: Slavitt embraces feminine rhyme as few have since Byron, producing humorous moments, while Reynolds is more conservative and staid. Waldman's and Nash's translations claim to contain the spirit of Ariosto and Tasso and use prose to retain the narrative sense. Their attempts at dynamic equivalence can be tested against the formal equivalence of Reynolds's and Wickert's octaves. Pairing some of the earliest translators (Harington and Fairfax) with translators from the eighteenth and nineteenth centuries shows how different eras have sought to "English" the octave according to conventional poetic practice, such as Doyne's Miltonic blank verse, Hoole's neoclassical heroic couplets, or Wiffen's fascinating Spenserians stanzas, which force him to add a ninth line.

## *The Other: Foreignness and Gender*

The Italian romance epic provocatively explores gender and the foreign other, and the genre provides dynamic conversation topics for students who see these texts working through current social and geopolitical concerns. Students are particularly fascinated with the texts' treatment of gender and foreignness as fluid and porous, with cross-dressing characters (Ricciardetto), women knights (Bradamante, Marfisa, Clorinda), women posing as male knights (Erminia), and characters moving through foreign and religious divides (Ruggiero and Armida). Each tale's narrative stage becomes a contact zone for encounters with gender and the foreign other, whether it's Charlemagne's tournament in Boiardo, Agramante and Charlemagne's war in Ariosto, or Goffredo's crusade in Tasso.

When the contemporary translations are paired with historical ones, students can see how cultural pressures shaped the way translators processed these Italian texts for their target audiences. For example, when Ariosto describes Agramante's forces, he uses many different descriptors for nationality and religion. This variety helps to reinforce pagan multiplicity versus Christian uniformity. In the corresponding passages in Harington's 1591 translation, he turns everyone into "Turk." Not once does Ariosto use "turco" to describe Agramante's warriors. Harington's version reorients the central conflict in Ariosto from Christian solidarity versus pagan multiplicity to Christian solidarity versus the unified Turkish horde. When converting Ariosto's diverse pagan masses into the Turk, Harington restructures the narrative geopolitically to fit his understanding of the conflict between Turks and Christians in the 1580s, a decade of particularly keen hostility and fear toward the Ottoman Empire. A discussion of this seemingly innocuous word change often leads to consideration of other contemporary ways we use language to monolithically generalize entire regions and peoples.

The representation of women is also an interesting source of conflict with the translators. As Selene Scarsi has noted about the Renaissance translations of the Italian romance epic, "it is exclusively the female characters who seem able to attract the imagination of the English readership and, more importantly, 'translatorship.'" (84).[3] Harington, for instance, systematically diminishes female knights like Bradamante, perhaps threatened by their power. One of my favorite scenes to look at with students is Armida's entrance into Goffredo's camp in *Gerusalemme liberata* 4.27–32. Tasso's masterful tap dance of revelation and concealment tests the translator's talents, with some peculiar results. Fairfax, for example, diverges wildly from his source texts in the entire episode, running his description through a Petrarchan blazon familiar to his Elizabethan audience.

## Romance Epic as Translation

It is fascinating that a translator like Fairfax seems to wander, to go errant, in his translation at the same moment that Armida draws the eyes and hearts of Goffredo's knights. In the process of re-creating their texts, these translators re-experience them, and they are drawn into the same dynamic forces of romance and epic that animate this genre. Translation isn't really distancing us from the romance epics of Boiardo, Ariosto, and Tasso after all; rather, these translations release the genre's defining features. Making translation visible in my classroom helps my students see transformation as a central process of the Italian romance epic: it is fixated on continual reshaping across borders of genre, character, religion, nationality, and gender. The Italian romance epic, we begin to see, *is* translation.

## Notes

1. Other useful surveys of English translations include Reynolds, "Epic and Romance: Pulci and Boiardo" and "Epic and Romance: Tasso"; Cox, "Epic and Romance: Ariosto"; and Braden, "Non-dramatic Verse."

2. See the "Materials" section for a list of historical translations to draw from. My edition, *The Italian Romance in English, 1590–1600*, was written to facilitate comparative translation analysis, as Renaissance translators of the same source text—such as Robert Tofte and Sir John Harington for Ariosto, and Richard Carew and Edward Fairfax for Tasso—are paired in a dual-translation format.

3. Scarsi's chapters "Ariosto's Female Knights," "Ariosto's Other Female Characters," and "Tasso's Female Characters" provide many excellent passages to focus on in this area.

# Part II

# Medieval Intertexts

Leslie Zarker Morgan

# From Roland to Orlando: French Charlemagne Tradition and Its Development in Italy

Ludovico Ariosto's Orlando is but one of many preceding, contemporary, and later Rolands, part of a shared European tradition. Roland and his peers arrived in Italy through French tradition in various ways—artistic, oral, and written—and developed in different directions: in poetry and in prose, in long and short forms, and in different languages. These together form the Carolingian (after *Carolus*, Latin for Charles) background of the *Orlando furioso*. Studying other Rolands in the context of Ariosto's poem allows readers to understand the contribution of Carolingian material to the *Furioso* and thus appreciate Ariosto's innovations. The challenges of such study include language (few early Carolingian texts are translated into English or modern Italian), length (by definition, epics are long), and historical context (spanning more than five centuries over a large, heterogeneous geographical area). To assist instructors in preparing and presenting the material through which aspects of Roland's character appear, this essay suggests selections in translation from primary texts preceding Ariosto in addition to passages from secondary works treating literary and cultural context.

## Origin of Roland

Many critics analyze the *Song of Roland*'s development either as the afterlife of Old French chansons de geste or as the protohistory of Ariosto. Roland leads the way among the strands of French epic tradition that feed into the *Furioso.* Three useful secondary sources for that tradition are Jane Everson's "Epic Tradition," which summarizes each of the works and their development; Aline Laradje's *Légende de Roland*, which comments on Roland episodes chronologically up through the *Furioso*; and François Suard's *Roland*, which continues Roland through modern times.

Primary texts demonstrate the development of characters, motifs, and narrative technique from the Old French *Chanson de Roland* through Ariosto's masterpiece. Roland's story begins in 778, with a battle between Charlemagne and local groups on the return of Frankish armies through the Pyrenees. Official Carolingian history, the Royal Annals of 801, does not mention the battle. The Royal Annals of 829 state that Basques attacked Charlemagne's rearguard, slaying many. Some versions of Einhard's *Life of Charlemagne*, written between 829 and 836, mention "Roland, duke of the March of Brittany" (Kibler, "Rencesvals" 53–54; Thorpe 181–83; Suard 14). Other references mention Roland as well but are not helpful in identifying him.[1] Thus, a shadowy figure, Hruotlandus, not traceable to any historical individual, begins the tradition.

The best-known version of the *Chanson de Roland* is the Oxford Bodleian Library Manuscript Digby 23 (referred to as "O") dating to approximately 1100. Since it contains the first literary appearance of Roland, it is frequently translated into modern languages (e.g., Burgess; Bensi; Short).[2] A class should read the entire poem, but three scenes in particular illustrate Roland's reputation: Roland's agreeing to lead the rear guard of Charlemagne's army (laisses 58–65); his refusal to call for help by blowing his horn, the olifant, despite overwhelming enemy numbers (laisses 78–87); and his finally blowing the horn (laisses 128–138), thereby killing himself. Roland's exchanges with Olivier in these last two passages have come to be interpreted as evidence of overwhelming pride and lack of restraint, *démesure* (for a contrary view, see Jones, "Roland versus Oliver"), an important element in the development of his fictional life. He vows that all the pagans will die, resulting in the poet's much-discussed comment, "Roland is brave and Oliver is wise" (Burgess, laisse 87, line 1093). However, the initial laisses where the Saracen army decides to trick the Franks, and Ganelon's comments about Roland (laisses 1–6, 20–52) that precede them, remind readers that we initially view Roland through Ganelon's eyes. Bands of companions in twelfth-century France, "a mob of young men let loose in search of glory, profit and female prey, by the great noble houses in order to relieve the pressure on their expanding power" (Duby 122), remind us of issues in French society of the time. Rulers' councils that begin and end the epic (both Marsile's and Charlemagne's) can be examined for the poem's presentation of the ruler, the responses of different groups of nobles, the reception of messengers, and the interplay between messenger and recipient. These offer fruitful discussions for classes and form elements of Ariosto's plot.

A different but contemporary literary context for Roland derives from the Latin *Historia Karoli et Rothlandi*, known as the Pseudo-Turpin *Chronicle* (Poole; Meredith-Jones). The *Chronicle* is book 4 of the *Codex Calixtinus* or *Liber Sancti Jacobi*, dated to approximately 1150. There Roland appears in three parts: first, in battle during Charlemagne's initial literary expedition to Spain (ch. 11); second, where he fights a Saracen giant, Ferragus (ch. 17); third, at Roncevaux (ch. 21). In this text Roland appears as a fearless fighter, jousting successfully after many others have been captured. His courtesy is unparalleled: he allows Ferragus to nap unharmed during their combat. Elements of humor appear in that encounter, such as Ferragus punching Roland's horse to death on the first day and Roland countering Ferragus's sword with a long twisted pole on the second (Poole 43).[3] Roland attempts to convert Ferragus in a famous theological debate by comparing the Trinity to a zither, an almond, a wheel, and a human body, illustrating concepts in medieval scholarly rhetoric. Ferragus reveals that he is vulnerable only at the navel, and Roland is thus finally able to kill him. At the battle of Roncevaux, there is no discussion of the rearguard or mention of Ganelon's relation to Roland. Roland initially survives with a few others and kills many Saracens. Other important episodes include a miracle: Roland prays and fasts, making the walls of Grenoble fall so that he can depart to help Charlemagne. As Suard suggests, Roland appears there as a Christlike martyr for the faith (32). There is no love interest at all, unlike in the *Song of Roland*, where his betrothed appears briefly only to die on hearing of his death. The *Chronicle*'s popularity grew particularly after Charlemagne's canonization in 1165, and European vernacular translations began to appear during the mid-thirteenth century. The Pseudo-Turpin *Chronicle* presents an inkling of peculiarities to come: comic elements like fighting with unusual weapons, fisticuffs against a giant, and, in particular, the combat with Ferragus, which takes on a life of its own.

## Spread of Roland Tales

How chansons de geste like the *Song of Roland*, in assonanced, varying-length stanzas called *laisses*, grew and spread is the topic of numerous controversies and is important for understanding the development of Roland stories in Italy. The two main theories are the traditionalist and the individualist. Nineteenth-century traditionalist scholars like Gaston Paris believed that epics arose from the people, that popular singers elaborated on historical events in oral tales that were later written down. Joseph Bédier, on the contrary, suggested that the poems "were composed by individual poets of genius who drew their inspiration from local legends preserved in churches and monasteries along pilgrimage routes" (qtd. in Jones, *Introduction* 4; cf. Bennett 58). The traditionalists enjoyed renewed popularity in the twentieth century in the advent of studies about oral formulaic theory by Albert B. Lord and Milman Parry, who discovered oral epic in Yugoslavia: traditionalists seized upon the orally performed Yugoslav poems as proof of their theory.

During the twentieth century, scholars hotly contested the topic, yet, in the Italian context, both oral and written poetry are essential, for both helped spread Carolingian material to Italy. Legal documents testify to street singers presenting tales of Roland and other heroes: laws attempt to clear street singers out of public thoroughfares in Bologna in 1289 (Palumbo 51–52), and the name Roland occurs frequently among signatures to documents in the Italian peninsula (Rajna, "Contributi"; Palumbo 29–33). Statues of Roland and his future brother-in-law, Olivier, appear in civic sites (Lejeune and Stiennon; Palumbo 35–45). On the other hand, inventories of manuscripts, the first of which dates to 1407, list works in "lingua francigena" ("French language"), attesting to these stories' written presence—and written requests for copies further demonstrate their popularity (for an English summary, see Duggan, *Chanson* 2: III/25–III/29).

In the Italian peninsula, Old French texts were initially reproduced through copying. Three of ten copies of *Roland* are in mixed French and Italian. Not only does the form of the poem differ in those manuscripts but so do the narrative and Roland himself. Laisses are partially rhymed instead of wholly assonanced. The two Italianate groups of the *Song of Roland* are known as $V^4$ (Biblioteca Nazionale Marciana, Venice, MS Fr. Z. 4; dated to the end of the thirteenth century) and C-$V^7$ (Bibliothèque Municipale, Châteauroux, MS 1 and Biblioteca Nazionale Marciana, Venice, MS Fr. Z. 7;

dated to the first half of the fourteenth century). All have been edited; there is also a translation into English of C-V[7] (Duggan and Rejhon). The Venice versions are considerably longer than the Oxford MS: C-V[7] is 8,397 lines compared with the Oxford manuscript's 4,002. Three important segments for Roland's character offer expanded battle scenes that further illustrate his prowess and provide slightly different details regarding his family and friends that cast a new light on his character (e.g., laisses 204–05). First, his religious observance is emphasized; when he is nominated for the rearguard, he recalls being in church that morning (C-V[7] laisse 93). Second, his relationship to Aude, his betrothed and Olivier's sister, is stronger; he calls on her at his death. After Roland's death, that relationship is further expanded by Aude's dying between Roland and Oliver in their tomb (laisses 369–81; Duggan, "L'épisode d'Aude"). Third, in addition to the poet initially presenting Roland through Ganelon's eyes as arrogant and prideful, in C-V[7] the extended conclusion proves Ganelon a liar. Ganelon flees the court, saying he is testing his horse (laisses 399–407), and confesses to having Roland killed (laisse 434); Ganelon's demonization leaves a closing image of Roland markedly different from that in the Oxford manuscript. Roland's relationship to Aude/Alda and other women is a motif followed in later texts, like his battling giants and theological debates with them.

Like adventure stories today, chansons de geste were so popular that sequels and prequels expanded them. Traditionally, these involved three phases: the childhood of the hero (*enfances*), knightly deeds of manhood (*chevalerie*), and old age (*moniage*). Numerous Franco-Italian fourteenth-century manuscripts include tales of Roland's adult heroism. The most famous of these, the *Entrée d'Espagne* (Biblioteca Nazionale Marciana, Venice, MS Fr. Z. 21), has not been translated into English, but Nancy Bradley-Cromey translates segments of it and provides a complete résumé in her appendix (269–76); Marco Infurna has translated parts of it into Italian. Roland's capturing Nobles alone, having left Charlemagne besieging Pamplona (lines 9,410–10,944), and his returning to Charlemagne, guided by a hermit in the wilderness, to prepare for death at Roncevaux (lines 14,648–15,805) illustrate the development of his character. Roland's travels in the Orient—where he enchants numerous pagan damsels but remains ever-faithful to Aude—add to his reputation of sanctity. However, humorous moments appear again during his battle with Ferragu (lines 1,632–4,204), and he again debates the immaculate conception (3,832–3,880). Bradley-Cromey argues for the moral nature of the work, maintaining that Roland has to learn to accept his role (see Sturm-Maddox). Not everyone agrees with this interpretation, similar to debates among critics of the Italian epic in their reading of ethical teachings (see Murrin, *Allegorical Epic*; Franceschetti, "Rassegna"). The religious element, overshadowed by crusade experiences demonstrated in place names and trips to the East, looms large over plot twists. In the *Entrée d'Espagne*, Roland's relationship to Saracens is problematic for a religious epic: he works for the Sultan of Persia and teaches courtly ways to the Sultan's son, who then accompanies Roland back to Spain.

The period before Roncevaux is reworked numerous times in the tradition of the "Spagna group" (Everson, "Roland" 99–101), which narrates Oriental travels and battles alongside pagan warriors. Trevor Dean's essay about the rise of the *signori* and E. R. Chamberlain's chapter about warrior princes (152–84) speak to political and cultural background as reasons for the popularity of Carolingian tales in northern Italy. The novelty of Roland's defying Charlemagne after a rebuke for disobedience in the *Entrée* opens new possibilities for the epic; Roland's travels through the Mediterranean world demonstrate his valor and allegiance to Christian ideals. Instructors and students can note motifs such as the beautiful Saracen princess and humility of a disguised Christian knight that reappear in future poems.

## Further Developments in Italy

Residents of the Italian peninsula adopted Roland as their own. One of the major traits of chansons de geste was lineage: *geste* means not only "deeds" (from the Latin *gesta*) but also "family." Charlemagne's family is his *geste*, to which Roland belongs. Part of the mystery in Roland's success was his origin: who was his father? How did he come to such bravura? *Enfances* tales sought to answer this question. Pio Rajna named a manuscript containing a series of poems linking the noble lines of France and dating to the first half of the fourteenth century *Geste Francor*; the manuscript is missing its initial folios and lacks a title, as Rajna explains in the brief preface to his photographic reproduction of the text (Rajna, *Geste Francor*). It offers an exciting tale of Roland as an illegitimate child of Charlemagne's half sister. The daughter of an imposter, she was destined to marry an important political figure but instead falls in love with a courtier. She becomes pregnant and the couple flees, raising their son in a forest in Italy

(*Geste Francor* 637–55, 708–27).[4] The story is available online in both English and Italian translations (Morgan, "Berta and Milone" and "Orlandino"; Fernando). Roland appears as a bully, in a gang with other town youth, and threatens even Charlemagne. His descent from Ganelon's clan, the evil line, through his mother's side, partially explains his fits of anger and attractively rebellious fighting. In these poems, Roland is called Orlandino, reflecting his absorption into the Italian tradition. Orlandino's use of *furbizia* ("cleverness") and his capture by courtiers also foretell future Italian epic trends.

This is not, however, the only episode of Roland's youth that appears in Franco-Italian texts; there are also versions of *Aspremont*, an Old French chanson de geste in which Roland and his youthful friends appear. The Italian versions are currently being edited, and there is no reliable English translation of either the Old French or the Italian. The Old French (c. 1190) tells of Roland and his friends eluding supervision and battling the Saracen invaders. Roland subsequently averts Charlemagne's demise by clubbing to death a Saracen opponent, Eaumont. Consequently Charlemagne, despite initial hesitation, allows Roland to fight by knighting him; Roland thereby acquires his horse, his horn (olifant), and his sword, Durendal. Roland is eager to fight and to take risks even as a youth. This poem's popularity seems in part related to its location in the Italian peninsula; Keith Busby notes the connection between stories that continue in Italy and those that take place elsewhere in southern Europe (2: 629). These same stories of origins, youth, and battles reappear throughout the Charlemagne tradition in Italian.

The Franco-Italian poems, dated to the early fourteenth century, coincide with Dante's *Commedia* (c. 1314–20). Dante, unlike his successors, distinguishes between characters from the chanson de geste and those from romance.[5] Boccaccio, shortly after Dante, mentions Orlando in the same company as the romance heroes Tristano and Lancelotto in his *Corbaccio* (c. 1365), without distinction (Boccaccio, *Corbaccio* [Padoan] 264; Boccaccio, *Corbaccio* [Cassell] 49–50). The joining of the romance and epic traditions was thus already then underway.

## Italian New Creations: *Cantari*

Saving Christendom and converting pagans to the Christian faith are major goals in chansons de geste, sometimes re-elaborated in shorter poems focusing exclusively on such events. Among those are Orlando's battle against Ferragu, leading to the latter's conversion, and the birth of Roland, senator of Rome (*Entrée d'Espagne*; *Geste Francor*) and defender of the Christian faith. In the fourteenth century, the language of the poems changed from mixed French and Italian to regional varieties of Italian, while the form shifted from laisses to ottava rima, which became the form of choice for Carolingian narrative as well as for Arthurian and classical subjects.[6] These poems are *cantari*, which vary in length from twenty-two *ottave* (*Cantare del padiglione*) to multiple books of *ottave*: *Orlando*, the basis of Luigi Pulci's late-fourteenth-century *Morgante*, is comprised of sixty books of thirty-four to forty-eight *ottave* each (Allaire, "Cantare" 370–71). It is telling that of the two most recent English-language essays about *cantari*, one appears in a book about oral tradition (Morabito) and the other in a volume about textual culture (Bendinelli Predelli, "Textualization").

Unfortunately, few Italian *cantari* have been translated into English and none in the Carolingian tradition. The subjects are many: one *cantare* (c. 1380–1420), a boast poem, lists subjects about which the speaker can recite stories (Rajna, "Cantare dei cantari"); it includes not only Carolingian but also biblical, classical, and Arthurian topics. Among these are versions of Roland's birth similar to the Franco-Italian version (Barini 45–78). Comparing the presentation of Roland there—he cleverly tricks the French court in order to get food but is subsequently tricked himself—with that in Franco-Italian and in Andrea da Barberino's later version (discussed below) requires careful attention to detail and is a useful exercise in close reading for students of Italian.

Another *cantare*, "Fioretto de' paladini," portrays an escapade away from court, with Orlando not only a wise and valorous fighter but also a calmer of Rinaldo (who is there pictured as his brother). It includes magic and religion as well as travels through Spain, Portugal, Africa, and "India minore." Furthermore, Orlando is married to Alda (Barini 79–131). This "Vanto dei paladini" consists of twelve self-introductions, first by Charlemagne, then one by each knight. Roland follows Charlemagne:

> Io sono il conte Orlando paladino,
> fontana della casa Chiaramonte:
> e Ferraù, quel franco saracino,
> con le mie mani uccisi e lo re Almonte.
> Le mie prodezze per ogni cammino
> e le mie gentilezze ancor son conte.

> Son nipote di Carlo imperïero
> e sono il fior d'ogni altro cavaliero. (Barini 35)

> I am the count Roland, paladin,
> fountain of the Clermont family:
> and Ferraù, that brave Saracen,
> as well as King Almonte, I killed with my hands.
> My bold deeds and courtly actions
> are still recounted along every route.
> I am nephew of Charles the emperor
> and I am the flower of all knights. (my trans.)

This linking of heroes—combining Orlando with Arthurian and classical protagonists—points to Orlando's future adventures, as the *cantari* indicate the rhyme form that will illustrate his chivalric feats.

## Italian Prose

Prose tales narrating Roland's story appeared at the same time as the *cantari*. Perhaps the most famous writer of these is Andrea da Barberino (c. 1370–c. 1431), whose *Reali di Francia* retells the tales of the *Geste Francor* in the context of world history, from Constantine through his descendants to Charlemagne and Roland, ending with an extended list of the family genealogy and announcing a sequel, *Aspramonte*. Again, there are no texts translated into English. Andrea's Roland shares qualities with the earlier texts: as a child he bullies local children yet stands up to a bigger bully. He becomes the most beloved of all the children, receiving more alms than anyone (*Reali* [Roncaglia] 672). He steals from Charlemagne's court at Sutri to feed his mother; that night, Charlemagne dreams of a lion cub saving the French in battle. For those studying in Italian, chapters 58 to 70 (669–90) provide scenes that can be compared with "Orlandino" and *cantari*. Andrea's *Aspramonte* therefore continues the Old French *Aspremont* and provides a version of Roland's early feats, before the Spanish expedition and Roncevaux ([Boni], bk. 3, chs. 38–60). Orlando's attributes—horse, horn, and sword—can thus be followed through their acquisition, loss, and return.

Some humanists disdained these chivalric stories in nonclassical form; Lovato de' Lovati (1241–1309), called the "father of humanism," wrote perhaps the most famous negative review, speaking of the "little people" listening to a singer who mooed the stories of Charlemagne in barbarically deformed French (Foligno 49). Poggio Fiorentino (1380–1459) writes in his Latin *Facetiae* (*Witty stories*; 1450) of a man distraught on hearing of the death of Roland, the last hope of all Christianity (Hurwood 81). These writers, contemporary to *cantari* and to the prose romances, reveal their familiarity with the texts and their characters—including Roland—as they disparage them. The popularity of *cantari* among all classes is demonstrated by their appearance in personal inventories and their use as textbooks (Grendler 274–77).

## Renaissance Epic: Suggested Examples of Roland/Orlando's Development

Roland, then Orlando, continues to charm through the sixteenth century in the Italian peninsula in Renaissance poems that are better known than Franco-Italian chansons de geste and *cantari*. What follows are short suggestions that feature characteristics from earlier texts. Pulci brings Orlando to a court milieu, but a court—that of the Medici in Florence—very different from those of twelfth-century France and its dependencies. Pulci's Orlando continues his previous characteristics of loyalty and prowess as he wanders through the Mediterranean, working for various potentates and encountering Christian peers as well as pagan threats. *Morgante* cantos 1, 18, 19, and 26 to 28 demonstrate the novelty of Pulci's work in its links to tradition. Gano (Ganelon) offends Orlando in canto 1, leading Orlando to depart from court. In his travels, Orlando battles giants and ultimately converts Morgante. In cantos 18 and 19, Morgante, for the moment separated from Orlando, encounters Margutte, a half-giant, and their culinary and scurrilous escapades parallel Orlando and Rinaldo with the complicity of Dantean echoes. The final three cantos retell the battle of Roncevaux: in 26.11–15 Pulci rewrites Oliver's request that Orlando blow his olifant. Orlando's elegant sermon before the final battle evokes New and Old Testament figures together with classical heroes (26.24–41), reminiscent of the fully developed theologian who appears in the *Entrée d'Espagne* with Ferragu.

Roland's ceremonial interment in the Aix tomb, inscribed "Uno Iddio, uno Orlando ed una Roma" ("One God and one Orlando and one Rome"; 27.220), commemorates the lost past of large-scale national battles. Orlando's development as a superhero leads to super-enemies as well, such as Gano, whose machinations intertwine with Orlando's throughout the entire poem, concluding with the death of Gano's son Baldwin at

Roncevaux (27.47). In the text, Gano's punishment is prolonged: he is slapped around in court and then paraded through town on a cart while food is thrown at him, and the pieces of his quartered corpse are thrown to wild animals. As in the *Roland*, the story begins and ends with the antagonist rather than the hero. Florence's link with France and the idealization of past chivalric codes characterize Pulci. The suggested passages, including Charlemagne's legendary refoundation of Florence after its destruction by barbarian tribes (28.100; see Maissen), develop earlier readings.

Ferrara's Ercole I d'Este requested a copy of Pulci's *Morgante* in 1478 (Carrara 147), demonstrating an ongoing interest in Ferrarese ruling circles for Carolingian materials. The title and the opening canto of Matteo Maria Boiardo's *Orlando innamorato* announce, however, a novelty for Orlando: "L'alta fatica e le mirabil prove / Che fece il franco Orlando per amore" ("stupendous feats, amazing labors / Love caused Orlando to perform"; 1.1.1). We can follow this new theme by examining Orlando's encounter with Ferragu (1.3.68–81), his battle against Agricane (1.18.29–1.19.17), his rescue of fellow knights from Morgana's realm (2.7.36–2.9.44), and ultimately his own liberation from the Laughing Stream by a group including pagan knights guided by Fiordelisa (3.7.1–55).

The poem's introduction and the four selections above illustrate love as a motivator to action, a motif absent from our earlier poems; female magic, also new to the genre; and finally, the strongly moralizing tone found in portions of the poem. These appear in a complex series of interwoven plots that can confuse the reader (for interlace, see Lot; Weaver, "Lettura dell'intreccio"). Although Orlando is married to Alda (1.1.22), he acknowledges, "Io che stimava tutto il mondo nulla, / Senza arme vinto son da una fanciulla" ("I, whom the whole world could not tempt, / am conquered by an unarmed woman!"; 1.1.30). Orlando's duel with king Agricane of Tartary resembles that against Ferragu in earlier poems (1.16.2–26, 1.18.29–55, 1.19.1–17). However, instead of arguing religion, they discuss love (1.18.45). The episode's novelty derives first from their interest in love, instead of religion or pride, as source of war, and second, from learning being one of Orlando's positive traits (his intelligence is not praised earlier).

Book 2 takes place during Agramante's invasion of France, which he undertakes to attain glory and avenge earlier losses. There, Orlando's rescue of knights imprisoned in Morgana's lake features Orlando's wits, which assist his valor in this quest. A chase scene through rough terrain (appealing to students), instead of hand-to-hand combat, brings Orlando to free all but one prisoner, whom Morgana loves. The final contrasting passage, in book 3, relates Orlando's liberation from the Laughing Stream. With friendship and mutual aid, Saracens assist in releasing Orlando, demonstrating further the changing narrative relationship between Christian and pagan.

Boiardo's Orlando is no longer the great Christian crusading hero; he is a vassal to love rather than to Christ. Like others, he forgets his duties in order to follow his beloved: it becomes difficult to distinguish Orlando's adventures from those of other knights, male and female, Christian and pagan. In the *Entrée d'Espagne* he was already bald (lines 13650–61); Boiardo makes him bushy-browed and squinty (2.3.63). He also appears incapable of or uninterested in amorous encounters (cf. Leodilla [1.24.14]; Angelica [1.25.39]), making his adventures with women throughout the tradition worth discussing. Religious and national allegiance are lost; Orlando prays for Charlemagne's army to be defeated so he might win Angelica (2.30.61), though we wonder what winning her would mean.

Three selections in Ariosto's continuation of Orlando's tale in particular follow earlier readings: Atlante's castle (12.1–38), Orlando and Mandricardo's duel (23.71–99), and Orlando's madness (23.99–24.115; 29.39–74; 30.4; 39.36–61). The first episode tells of Orlando hearing a damsel in distress, seemingly Angelica (12.5–6), whom he pursues to the illusion of a castle. The second incident does not follow earlier battle patterns for serious duels. Orlando does not want to fight, but Mandricardo's accusation of treachery finally riles him sufficiently to do so. Mutual insults, not philosophical discourse, precede the battle. Mandricardo and Orlando fight with staffs "come duo villan per sdegno fieri / nel partir acque o termini de prati" ("Like yokels quarrelling about a field, / Or where an irrigation-ditch to fix"; 23.83). Continuing with their hands, Mandricardo knocks Orlando (still in his saddle) to the ground; Orlando pulls the bridle off Mandricardo's horse, which flees, ending the battle, in a parody of earlier combats.

Loyalty to duty and single-minded dedication to individual quests cause Orlando to lose himself and his possessions (see Zatti, *Il* Furioso 69–89), and eventually, to lose his wits. When his metaphysical hell ends, he returns to duty for Charlemagne and the Christian cause on Lampedusa, where he, Brandimarte, and Oliver confront the three pagan champions (41.68–42.19). The battle is unlike that of chansons de geste: no long prayers precede combat. The battle is commented on like a modern sports event: Sobrino "gli crede il capo tôrre . . . / . . . sí ch'espedito all'altra vita vada" ("thought to cut off [Oliver's] head . . . / . . . in order to send [Oliver] rapidly to the next world"; 41.88.2; 41.89.2; my trans.). This should be read with versions of Roncevaux.

With these selections, readers appreciate the transformation of Roland into Orlando. Boiardo expands the cast of characters, including positive and negative, male and female, Christian and pagan figures, who draw the spotlight from Orlando. Ariosto refocuses that spotlight on Orlando, but paradoxically also back to the original text: Orlando's positive values—valor and single-mindedness in a cause—are taken to the extreme for an inappropriate cause and become negative. Instead of physical death through personal sacrifice, an Aristotelian violence against self, society, and God expiate Orlando's deviation from loyalty to lord and cause. Orlando returns to rescue Christianity, unlike the physically gigantic and fanatically driven Rodomonte, Orlando's pagan double, who is sent cursing "alle squalide ripe d'Acheronte" ("to Acheron's sad shores"; 46.140), where he will not likely amuse others, unlike Margutte.

Following Roland's development to Orlando through five centuries acts as a thread through the labyrinth of languages, literary forms, and cultural milieux. Narrative structure influences our interpretation: the order in which the tale is told—who or what gives us our first impression, as well as who leaves us with our final images—frames our interpretation of him. The deployment of epic motifs like the council, the courtly woman, and single combat demonstrates literary style and social context. Suard asks how to appreciate Roland in modern times, since the *Song of Roland* contains no psychological sense of the hero, and responds by saying, "La rigidité et la relative pauvreté du type est . . . corrigée par la lecture que les personnages épiques proposent les uns des autres" ("The rigidity and relative poverty of the type [epic character] is . . . corrected by the reading that the epic characters propose of each other"; 325; my trans.). We read Roland/Orlando through his actions, his antagonists, and his entourage, including the narrator-poet. The selections suggested here begin to navigate the intricate interwoven paths of romance epic character and adventures: readers trace the changing hero, Roland, through narration over time.

## Appendix

## Syllabus of Readings to Follow the Development of Roland/Orlando

* *Available in English translation in addition to the original (in Italian or another language).*

† *Available only in Italian.*

* *Song of Roland* (O [Oxford, Bodleian Library MS Digby 23; trans. Burgess])

Roland's acceptance of the rear guard, laisses 58–65; his refusal to blow the olifant, 78–87; his finally blowing the horn, 128–38 (and possibly Ganelon's prejudice against Roland, 1–6, 20–52; and Ganelon's trial, 272–89)

**Song of Roland* (C-$V^7$ [Châteauroux, Bibliothèque Municipale MS 1 and Venice, Biblioteca Nazionale Marciana, MS Fr. Z. 7; trans. Duggan and Rejhon])
Aude's death (laisses 369–81); Ganelon's trial (399–407, 434)

**Chronicle* of Pseudo-Turpin (see Poole)
First expedition to Spain (ch. 11)
Fight with Ferragus (ch. 17)
Roncevaux (ch. 21)

*Entrée d'Espagne*
Roland's taking of Pamplona alone (lines 9410–10944); †returning to Spain (lines 14648–15805)

**Geste Francor*
Berta and Milone and Orlandino

*Dante Alighieri
*Hell* (canto 31)

†*Cantari*
"La storia di Milone e Berta e del nascimento d'Orlando" (Barini 45–78)
"Fioretto dei paladini" (Barini 79–131)
"Vanto dei paladini" (Barini 35–41)

†Andrea da Barberino
*Reali di Francia*, story of Roland's parents and his youth (bk. 6, chs. 58–90)
*Aspramonte*, Orlandino saving Charlemagne and gaining his weapons, horse, and horn (bk. 3, chs. 38–60)

*Luigi Pulci, *Morgante*
Orlando leaving the Christians, offended by Gano (canto 1)
Morgante and Margutte (cantos 18–19)
Roncevaux (cantos 26–28)

*Matteo Maria Boiardo, *Orlando innamorato*
Presentation of Orlando and the novelty of the work (1.1)
Orlando encounters Ferragu (1.3.68–81)
Orlando fights Agricane (1.18.29–2.19.17)
Orlando saves fellow knights from Morgana (2.7.36–2.9.44)
Orlando rescued by pagan knights (3.7.1–55)

*Ludovico Ariosto, *Orlando furioso*
Atlante's Castle (12.1–38)
Orlando and Mandricardo's duel (23.71–99)
Orlando's madness (23.99–24.114, 29.39–74, 30.4, 39.36–61)

## Notes

1. For example, the signature "Roland" is found on a document with the written date 778 (it actually dates from the beginning of the tenth century), and the *Nota Emilianense* (dating to the eleventh century) mentions "Rodlane" along with eleven others (Bennett 60–61; Suard 15).

2. For the differences in laisse numbers between editions and an explanation, see Kibler, "Editions" 12–13.

3. Humorous since it was contrary to the code of battle for chivalrous knights; not, of course, humorous for the horse.

4. In the *Geste Francor*, Orlandino is born at Imola (lines 9,363–70), and a month later the family continues to Sutri (lines 9,435–44). Later versions (*Reali di Francia* and its derivatives) designate Sutri as the location of Orlandino's birth.

5. Hell echoes with Roland's horn between the eighth and ninth circles (*Inf.* 31. 16–18), and Roland himself inhabits heaven with Charlemagne and other warriors for Christ (*Par.* 18.43–48), while romance characters abide in Dante's hell: Tristan, representative of Arthurian tales, is in the circle of the lustful (*Inf.* 5.67).

6. Though the origin of the form is debated, its popularity is attributed to Boccaccio (Everson, *Italian Romance Epic* 113–26; Balduino, "Misteriose origini").

**Maria Bendinelli Predelli**

# Adventure, Love, and Prowess in Medieval Italian *Cantari*

## The Facts

### *Characteristics of the Genre*

Popular culture, that is to say, the products of an artistic-artisanal process widely known throughout the social strata, can be found today in cinema, television, pop music, and the novel. In the Middle Ages, the function of this type of cultural pursuit, which simultaneously satisfies the goals of entertainment, art, and instruction, was fulfilled in large part by the *cantari*. The characteristics defining this genre are as follows:

The means of communication, occurring for the most part orally: the name itself, the infinitive of the verb *cantare* (to sing) used as a noun, tells us that these compositions were sung in public. They were often accompanied by a vielle, played by the *canterino* ("minstrel") himself or by a musician accompanying him.

The public: the *cantari* were intended not for a chosen public but a generic and diversified one, comprising therefore all the social strata of a medieval Italian court or town.

The meter: the *cantari* were written mostly in *ottave*, eight-line stanzas or octaves (a strophe of eight hendecasyllables and an *abababcc* rhyme scheme), sometimes in six-line stanzas or sestinas (with an *ababacc* rhyme scheme). Much has been written about this meter's origin, but there is still no convincing or commonly accepted theory. The first known literary works written in this meter are the *Filostrato* and the *Teseida*, youthful poems by Giovanni Boccaccio, produced between 1335 and 1341, and the first documented *cantare* appears no later than 1345. Unfortunately, it is not possible to know the exact melody in which the *ottave* were sung, but we can derive an approximation from those recorded in the Renaissance or modern times.

The subject matter of the romances: the genre will in any case be narrative poetry. As the next section illustrates, the themes could be rather diverse, but generally speaking they provoked wonder and admiration in the audience because of either the presence of fantastic elements, such as fairies and spells, or the extraordinary nature of the exploits described.

## *Themes and Precursors*

The topics discussed in the *cantari* were many and varied. Most of them can be arranged into the following types: Carolingian romances; classically themed narratives; chivalric romances.

The narratives of *cantari* derived from a long line of earlier traditions. From the late eleventh century, the European narrative lore had found artistically relevant and socially prestigious works in France (in French) in the chansons de geste, which sang the epic feats of French warriors against Muslims, and the chivalric romances, often featuring King Arthur's knights encountering marvelous adventures for the sake of their ladyloves. Such poems spread throughout the Carolingian Empire and even beyond: they were sung or translated in Germany, Scandinavia, Iceland, England, and Italy. In Northern Italy, a literature relating to the Carolingian court was born, written in a hybrid language mixing French and local dialects, known as Franco-Italian literature. Also belonging to this body of literature are works written in Italy by Italians but in French. There were in addition prose translations of French romances into the Tuscan vernacular. This entire legendary heritage relating to people considered historical, and to stories whose popularity and appeal had already been substantiated, extends into the *cantari*.

Broadly speaking, this narrative tradition splits into three large branches, clearly identified in Jean Bodel's *Chanson des Saisnes*: "Ne sont que trois matières à nul home entendant / de France, de Bretagne et de Rome la grant" ("There are but three matters that no man should be without, / That of France, of Britain, and of great Rome"; lines 6–7; my trans.). It should therefore not surprise us to find a *Storia di Re Alessandro* ("History of King Alexander"), a *Guerra di Troia* ("The Trojan War"), and an *Apollonio di Tiro* among the Italian *cantari*. The most beloved and widespread were, however, the stories relating to Carolingian heroes: the French Roland and Renaud were Italianized into Orlando and Rinaldo and became the protagonists of important Italian *cantari* (*La Rotta di Roncisvalle*, *Spagna*, *Cantari di Aspramonte*, *Orlando*, *Rinaldo da Montalbano*). They generally provided material for extremely long poems, which could not be completed in one *cantare* session. A poem like *Spagna*, for example, is subdivided into forty cantos—but in the vocabulary of the time, each *cantare* session covers one canto: thus every canto is called a *cantare*, and the titles of the poems are often labelled as the *Cantari* of [. . .] (*Lancillotto*, *Rinaldo*, *Aspramonte*, etc.).

Shorter poems, which could be completed in a couple of *cantari*, offered a different type of adventure, inspired by a narrative tradition of contes, for which we do not have precise precursors, since they were transmitted orally. In French literature, the lais (for example, the lais of Marie de France) drew on this tradition, as did short poems in *couplets d'octosyllabes*, some of which were artistically developed and well-appreciated in aristocratic French circles (for example, the poems of Chrétien de Troyes). This literature often (although not always) derived characters and motifs from a preexisting narrative tradition among the Breton peoples of the British Isles (the Celtic narrative). The stories of King Arthur, originally representing only one branch of this literary trend, became so famous that this entire type of narrative took the name of Arthurian literature. In Italy, the oldest and most renowned *cantari* belong to the short genre, notably *Fiorio e Biancifiore* (the oldest *cantare* of which written evidence has reached us, 1343–45), *Il Bel Gherardino*, *Bruto di Bretagna*, *Carduino*, *Ultime imprese e morte di Tristano* ("Tristan's Last Exploits and Death"), *Il duello di Tristano e Lancillotto al petrone di Merlino* ("The Fight between Tristan and Lancelot at the Rock of Merlin"), *Febus e Breus*, *Ponzela Gaia*, and *Gibello*. In the *cantari* of this type we recognize certain motifs from that distant Celtic origin—for example, the love between a knight and a fairy—and others dating back to an ancient narrative style such as the quest sequence. Normally (with the exception of the *cantari* of Tristan and the story of Febus), they are love stories with a happy ending.

Other short *cantari* fit into a novella-type tradition and became increasingly profuse from the moment the *Decameron* launched and definitively legitimized the new novella genre: *La Dama del Vergiù*, *Madonna Elena*, *Ginevra degli Almieri*, *Ottinello e Giulia* (see *Cantari novellistici dal Tre al Cinquecento*) and, later on, *cantari* explicitly derived from the novellas of the *Decameron* in the fifteenth and sixteenth centuries (*Cantari di Griselda*; *Cantari tratti dal* Decameron). The subgenre includes works that may reach considerable length, such as the series that tells the *Storia dei Sette Savi* ("The Seven Sages' Story") in twenty-three *cantari* (see *Storia di Stefano figliuolo d'un imperatore di Roma*) and a later poem titled the *Storia di Campriano contadino* ("The Story of Campriano the Peasant").

Another important fourteenth-century experiment is represented by the Florentine Antonio Pucci's seven *Cantari della Guerra di Pisa* ("Cantos of the Pisan War") as well as the short *Cantare degli Otto Santi* ("The Eight Saints' Cantare"), also attributed to Pucci. These are the only *cantari* of historical subject matter of the fourteenth century (this genre would return in full force in the fifteenth and even more so in the sixteenth century).

Perhaps halfway between the classical *cantare* (sung in public) and the poem meant for either silent reading or recitation before a small audience (such as Boccaccio's poems in *ottave*), are several fourteenth-century religious *cantari* dedicated to Catherine of Siena's followers: *La leggenda di Santo Giosafà* ("Saint Josafat's Legend"), by Neri Pagliaresi; *La fanciullezza di Gesù* ("Jesus's Childhood"), by friar Felice Tancredi from Massa; and *La Passione* ("The Passion") and *La Risurrezione* ("The Resurrection"), by Niccolò Cicerchia (*Cantari religiosi senesi del Trecento*). The length of the *Fanciullezza di Gesù* and the *Passione*, as well as the unusual division of the *Risurrezione*, remind us more of literary creations and do not fit completely into the *cantari* tradition. Later on, however, even the religious *cantare* became a full-fledged participant in the classical *cantare* genre adopting all of its characteristics.

### *Geographical Distribution*

Since the majority of *cantari* came down to us in the Tuscan dialect, it has been hypothesized that the birthplace of this literature would indeed be Tuscany, particularly Florence and Pisa, whose commercial traffic easily brought them into contact with the romance literature of France. French prose romances were translated or elaborated in Tuscan prose, and it is from these works that many *cantari* derived. This filiation has been ascertained, for example, in the cases of the *Guerra di Troia*, the *Febus e Breus*, the *Apollonio di Tiro*, and the stories of Tristan, all of which are considered to be Tuscan. It is true, however, that Franco-Italian literature of trans-Apennine Italy first received and revitalized French romance literature and subsequently served as inspiration for Tuscan romance writers such as, for example, Andrea da Barberino (c. 1370–1432). Scholars have thus observed that the first documented *cantare*, *Fiorio e Biancifiore*, preserves traces of a Northern pronunciation and that certain *cantari* were written in a trans-Apennine language: *Ponzela Gaia*, for example, is written in decidedly hybrid Tuscan and Venetian. There are two versions of *Madonna Elena*, one from Tuscany and one from the Po Valley, and the latter could well be older than the former. The hypothesis is therefore that some *cantari* may be of Northern origin. The *cantare* genre would have very quickly reached southern Italy as well, or at least the court of Naples. In his introduction to the prose romance *Filòcolo*, Boccaccio states that he was reworking a most beautiful story "non . . . con debita ricordanza . . . essaltata da' versi d'alcun poeta, ma lasciata solamente ne' fabulosi parlari degli ignoranti" ("which merits to be rendered in the most exalted form—poetry—but that was instead handed down to us only in the fabled words of the unlettered"; 772; my trans.). In fact, a version of *Fiorio e Biancifiore* found in a southern Italian manuscript has readings that seem to belong to an early stage of the text. Versions of Carolingian poems written in northern and central dialects have also been found: thus, even if the largest number of *cantari* were written in the Tuscan dialect, the genre had an immediate success and rapidly circulated throughout Italy.

## Canterini *and Authors*

We have little concrete information regarding the *canterino* who sang these stories. A descendant of the minstrel, the *canterino* often possessed not only the artistry of narrating through song but also the abilities of a musician and juggler. Generally speaking, the *canterino* performed outside, on a city square, probably on Sundays, when most people did not work and could pass the time listening to him. A small stage made him conspicuous and allowed him to project his voice: for this reason the *canterino* would also be called *cantimpanca* ("street-singer" or "stage-singer"). The *cantare* would often occur weekly in the same place. In Florence, for example, the *canterini* performed in the small square of San Martino, close to the Cathedral.

The *canterino* could himself be the author of the songs, but often he received the texts from others, more expert in creating poetry, whom perhaps he paid. He would need an excellent memory to remember entire poems (see, for example, the subjects proposed by the *canterino* in the *Cantare dei cantari* [Rajna, "Cantare dei cantari"]), but he would also need an aptitude for storytelling and a capacity for modifying the text to fill in memory gaps or to be more in tune with his audience.

In communicating with the public, the *canterino* did not behave like someone who tells a story he has invented (or at least composed); rather, he considered himself the custodian of a narrative heritage that he was now passing on. If anything, he cared about expressing his loyalty to the accepted tradition, and in relation to the story, the *canterino* was the first to feel the emotions of wonder and admiration that he communicated to others.

Very few authors of *cantari* are known: most *cantari* are anonymous. Some texts hand down the name of a *canterino* but nothing else. Two notable exceptions are Antonio Pucci (c. 1310–88) and Piero da Siena (1343–c. 1419). The first was a well-known author of *cantari*, although he cannot be considered a real *canterino*, given that he had a respectable position in the civic administration. He knew Boccaccio, and we have many more of his poetic compositions in different genres, as well as a *zibaldone*, a notebook in which he summarized his many readings. His *cantari* include *Apollonio di Tiro* in six *cantari*, *La Reina d'Oriente* in four, *Gismirante* in two, and *Madonna Leonessa* and *Bruto di Bretagna*, both in a single *cantare*. That Antonio Pucci's stature may be superior to a career *canterino*'s is demonstrated by the speed with which he recognized the new genre's value (*Bruto di Bretagna* is the first known Arthurian *cantare* composed in Italy) and by his efforts to create inventive and original *cantari* rather than simply repeat previously written stories (*Madonna Leonessa*). In addition to the above, he wrote the seven *cantari* of the *Guerra di Pisa*, the first Italian experimentation with a historical *cantare* (see Pucci, *The Four Cantari* and *Gismirante*; *Madonna Leonessa*).

Piero "*cantarino*" da Siena is the author of *La Bella Camilla* (in eight *cantari*), the *Lamento in morte di Gian Galeazzo Visconti* ("The Plaint for Galeazzo Visconti's Death"), and other works of entertainment. Many newly revealed archival documents outline a professional profile similar to Pucci's. In fact, Piero was an employee (*familiaris et custos librorum* ["domestic and bookkeeper"]) in the Office of Statutory Auditors (Regulators) and a *canterino* in the dining hall of the Priors of the Comune di Siena (Municipality of Siena).

### *The* Cantari *in Literary History*

Artistically speaking, *cantare* literature reaches only modest heights, even if the charm of the stories and myths had a long-term effect on the popular imagination. The relevance of this artistic output, however, resides not only in the fact that it represents the popular culture of our ancestors between the Middle Ages and the Renaissance but also in the fact that the *cantari* were the cultural and artistic background from which works of higher artistic standard drew inspiration, works such as the great epic poems of the Italian Renaissance (*Morgante*, *Orlando innamorato*, *Orlando furioso*). The relation between *Morgante* and a long, anonymous *cantare* with an incomplete ending (called *Orlando* by Huebscher, its first and only publisher) is intriguing. In fact, except for the adventures of Margutte, the plot of *Orlando* is practically identical to *Morgante*, and Pio Rajna maintained that Pulci indeed composed his *Morgante* by rewriting *Orlando*. On the other hand, the contemporary scholar Paolo Orvieto hypothesizes that the relation is most likely reversed, and the issue is still sub judice. But even Matteo Maria Boiardo and Ludovico Ariosto, as well as Torquato Tasso, were undeniably acquainted with the *cantari* and drew inspiration and motifs from them. From the *cantare* tradition is derived the use of prologues and epilogues; the textual invention of a direct relation between narrator and audience; and the use of certain stylistic traits such as hyperbole, dramatization, and, naturally, characters, motifs, and situations. The literary corpus of the *cantari* thus becomes important in European literary history because it acts as the indispensable *trait d'union* between the French chansons de geste and *roman courtois* and the artistic flowering of the Italian Renaissance's epic-chivalric poems.

## What to Read

The study of this body of literature is made difficult by its richness and diversity. One may meet this challenge by grouping works around some essential themes (for example, the encounter with the fairy, the venture to the Orient, amazing adventures, the novella-like genre). One could thus read one or more works representative of each group; for example, *Bel Gherardino* for the encounter with the fairy; *Rinaldo da Montalbano* for the venture to the Orient; *Gismirante*, *Bruto di Bretagna*, and *Carduino* for amazing adventures; *Madonna Elena* and *Madonna Leonessa* for the novella-like *cantare*. Students should be shown that a *cantare* often develops a specific version of a narrative theme already present in various forms in Europe. Students could read, for example, the *Lai de Lanval* for the fairy encounter theme or compare *Decameron* 2.9 with *Madonna Elena* and the wager cycle.

## Critical Issues

After students are acquainted with some of the texts, they can tackle critical issues that arise from studying *cantari*.

### *The Question of Popular Literature*

It may be interesting to discuss the value of so-called popular, or widely circulating, literature in relation to literature representing high or elite art. A few pages of Pier Paolo Pasolini's extensive introduction to a collection of popular poetry are enlightening (31–41), even if they simplify the issue. Pasolini identifies three categories of literary production: the literature of high art, usually the prerogative of the aristocratic classes; a middle literature represented by a contamination or vulgarization of high art with folkloric elements, as it circulates through the lower social classes; and the folklore heritage itself. The *cantari*, which circulate but also modify stories derived from more literary compositions, seem to confirm his formula. A comparison between the *Lai de Lanval* and the *cantare* of *Bel Gherardino*, or between *Decameron* 2.9 and the *cantare* of *Madonna Elena* might be useful for discussion: why is the *Lanval* or the *Decameron*'s novella considered more artistically valid? What modifications does the *cantare* introduce when it replicates the content of its models? What do the *cantari* and certain contemporary pop culture creations (songs, film, plays) have in common?

### *The Relation with Folklore*

Many of these *cantari* are considered similar to fairy tales, and often their plots correspond to motifs identified in Hans-Jörg Uther's *Types of International Folktales* and the Aarne-Thompson *Motif-Index of Folk Literature* (see Thompson; also available online at sites.ualberta.ca/~urban/Projects/English/Motif_Index.htm). One could have students find in the Aarne-Thompson index the type of corresponding fairy tales or the motifs in the studied *cantari*. The relation with folklore may also be explored structurally, by trying to ascertain, for example, whether the Italian *cantare* contains a basic format similar to that identified for the fairy tale by Wladimir Propp.

### *The Relation between Written and Oral*

The *cantare*, especially in the fourteenth century, was to be recited before an undifferentiated audience, often in episodes, and as such it involves stylistic traits that carried forward into the written romances of Boiardo and Ariosto. The oral communication explains the constant presence of prologues (usually some sort of religious invocation) extending for one or more *ottave*, in order to give spectators time to gather, and of epilogues, in which the *canterino* sometimes expresses the need for a drink, invites the audience to return for the sequel, and reveals some captivating elements of the *cantare* to follow. If the story is divided into several *cantari*, often the middle *cantari* will end at a crucial point (the hero in danger, for instance), just as serial television narratives do. Another typical aspect of the *cantari* is dramatization: while the prose-romance spends time analyzing a character's frame of mind, the *cantare* will express the character's feelings and thoughts mostly through dialogue or a monologue. The outcome of an action or situation will be presented in dramatic form to astound the audience. Students may discover signs of the oral performance within the texts they read and also appreciate how difficult the texts' continuous *mouvance* is for scholars who wish to provide a critical edition of the *cantari*.

### *Enduring Archetypes*

Students may recognize the myths introduced by the *cantari* and the connections between literary creations and the societies that express them. The so-called myth of the hero and the princess, the exaltation of a warrior, and the love of adventure are also the basis of so much modern literature and cinema (popular novels, western films, science fiction films, television dramas, etc.), and they seem to be enduring myths (see Uther). But do they truly remain unchanged? In what way do these myths reappear and how are they modified in works of contemporary popular culture? In what way do these modifications correspond to transformations across time periods and cultures?

## Editions and Critical Readings

A comprehensive bibliography, also useful for research purposes, is available in Bendinelli Predelli, "Italian Cantari." I indicate here a few publications that may be appropriate for students' and teachers' perusal.

Texts and criticism in English are unfortunately rather scarce. Two short *cantari* by Pucci (*Gismirante* and *Madonna Leonessa*) have been translated into English and prefaced with a useful introduction by Bendinelli Predelli, who has also contributed the chapter "Arthurian material in Italian *cantari*" to the collective volume *The Arthur of the Italians*. Marie-José Heijkant and Raffaele Morabito deal with signs of orality in the written texts of *cantari*.

Literary criticism is naturally more abundant in Italian, often prefacing the editions of texts. A 1968 anthology, *Poemi cavallereschi del Trecento*, prepared by Giuseppe Guido Ferrero, offers sections of the most important Carolingian poems. The two-volume anthology *Cantari novellistici* provides the text of most short *cantari*, while Daniela Delcorno Branca compiled the anthology *Cantari fiabeschi arturiani*. An Italian version of the French *roman Mort Artu* is found in the *Cantari di Lancillotto*, recently published under the title of *La struzione della tavola ritonda* (edited by Bendinelli Predelli). General overviews that include the *cantari* tradition can be found in Emilio Pasquini and in Marco Villoresi, *La letteratura cavalleresca*. Various aspects concerning the *cantari* literature are discussed in volumes edited by Michelangelo Picone and Bendinelli Predelli, Picone and Rubini, and Bendinelli Predelli (*Cantari e dintorni*), as well as in essays by Branca, Armando Balduino ("Letteratura canterina"), Margherita Lecco, and Jacques Monfrin (in French). Tito Saffioti provides a collection of historical documents concerning the figure of the *canterini*. Maria Cristina Cabani's *Le forme del cantare epico-cavalleresco* is still the reference work as far as the question of orality and writing is concerned. An old but still interesting study by Gaetano Mariani identifies stylistic traits that Pulci's *Morgante* inherited from *cantari*.

# Part III

# Boiardo, Ariosto, and Tasso in the Classroom

**Giovanna Rizzarelli**

# Teaching Ariosto's *Furioso* through Sixteenth-Century Editions

In recent decades, early editions have increasingly been considered a crucial component for better understanding the reception of Italian literature classics. The publishing history of a text presents the fortune of literary works in a unique way and lets us analyze these works through innovative perspectives. The *Orlando furioso* is an ideal platform for this teaching approach because from a very early date—even before the publication of the poem's final form in 1532—its reception was deeply intertwined with editorial issues and publishing strategies. This essay suggests that the use of sixteenth-century editions of the *Furioso* in the classroom enables a new and highly effective approach to the multifaceted world of Ludovico Ariosto's poem and discloses an efficacious method of teaching its topics and themes. The course that I envisage here is aimed at graduate students who, in addition to having an interest in the Italian Renaissance, can read the original Italian or follow the text with the help of an English translation.

I will focus on five Venetian editions, which were printed by Niccolò Zoppino (1536), Gabriele Giolito (1542), Giovanni Andrea Valvassori (1553), Vincenzo Valgrisi (1556), and Francesco de' Franceschi (1584). These editions share two features that are especially fruitful as teaching tools: they provide editorial support in understanding the text (through glossaries, *allegorie*, indexes of classical similes, etc.), and they are richly illustrated. Three teaching approaches to the *Furioso* benefit from the analysis of these features. First, they allow us to explore the mixture of literary genres in Ariosto's poem (e.g., epic, romance, short tale, lyric). The sixteenth-century editions mark out these different forms by using iconic and textual apparatuses. Second, the editions' illustrative sets and the paratextual apparatuses allow us to investigate the poem through a thematic perspective. The representations of "arms" and "love" in sixteenth-century engravings and their characterization in the moralistic summaries given in the *allegorie* provide important clues for a thematically centered analysis. Finally, the comparison of Ariosto's octaves with the illustrations of sixteenth-century editions and other visual interpretations of the poem (frescoes, paintings, maiolicas) provides an interdisciplinary approach.[1]

## Teaching the *Furioso* through Genre

The first part of the course centers on the advantages of a generic approach to teaching the history of literature. Ever-changing, alive, and imbued with historicity, literary genres may be examined by observing the principle junctions and turning points that have characterized their development over time. In presenting the history of literature through genre, we can focus on a canon that is not only Italian but, crucially, European and that allows us to relate modes of writing to modes of reading. Genre is the first element to condition the audience's horizon of expectation, thereby influencing both the moment of the text's composition and its reception (see Jauss; Iser).

Thus we may see how the *Furioso* lends itself to be read through the lens of literary genres. First, it displays a specific case study of how important the codification of literary forms became in the sixteenth century: there was a well-known *querelle* concerning the *Furioso*'s adherence to the rules of different literary genres. Second, Ariosto's poem is a highly representative case of how literary genres usually incorporate other literary forms. The *Furioso*'s mingling of such forms is intrinsic not only to the narrative poem but also to the dialogue, and, in the modern age, to the novel. Finally, Ariosto's poem is emblematic of how a work's generic definition lies in a territory halfway between the author's intentions and the readers' expectations. In order to tackle these various issues it is indispensable to bear in mind both Ariosto's intentions and how his contemporaries interpreted them.

A first part of the course should therefore focus on the sixteenth-century debate on genre and on the polemic regarding the *Furioso*, which eventually led to its canonization.[2] Despite what may seem a textbook oversimplification, the debate surrounding literary genres became from the middle of the century onward an unprecedented phenomenon, as is attested by the book market's large corpus of treatises aimed at precisely defining the characteristics of each genre. The production of these texts was mainly motivated by a progressive classicism driven by the desire not to emulate antiquity but to modernize the classical genres.[3] Aristotle's *Poetics* entered actively into this process and, far from hindering modernity, was instrumental in justifying the birth of new vernacular forms. Nevertheless, simultaneous with a modernist current, which understood the definition of genres in a progressive manner, a more rigid vision of the Aristotelian precepts, underpinned by a die-hard conservatism, also gained ground. The *Furioso* was early on accused of disobeying the rules of the *Poetics* for the following reasons: the poem did not tell the story of one single hero; Ariosto excessively interfered, thereby contravening the *Poetics*'s recommendation to mask the narrative voice (section 24); the poem lacked verisimilitude, as it narrated facts that were fantastic and scarcely credible; and the poem's title was unsuitable, because Orlando's madness was not the narrative's only theme.

At the same time, however, numerous voices defended Ariosto's poem, such as Lodovico Dolce, in his *Apologia di Ludovico Dolcio contra ai detrattori dell'autore* (*Defense by Ludovico Dolce against the Author's Detractors*; 1535) and Simone Fornari, in the *Apologia brieve sopra l'Orlando Furioso* (*Brief Defense of the Orlando Furioso*) included in his *Spositione di m. Simon Fornari da Rheggio sopra l'Orlando furioso di m. Ludovico Ariosto* (*Exposition of Mr. Simone Fornari from Reggio on Mr. Ludovico Ariosto's Orlando Furioso*; 1549–50).[4] Fornari's defense of the *Furioso* is didactically effective because it establishes the *Furioso*'s full subscription to the Aristotelian precepts. The Venetian publishers deployed roughly the same arguments as Fornari to legitimize the poem they were printing, thereby contributing to the canonization of the *Furioso*.

One of the most precious sixteenth-century editions of the *Furioso*, printed by Gabriele Giolito de' Ferrari in 1542, exemplifies this legitimization through the printed book. Both the printer and his sophisticated collaborator, Dolce, wished to underscore the poem's close dependency on Virgil's *Aeneid*. To achieve this end, Dolce wrote the first commentary on Ariosto's imitations, where he pointed out the ancient models on which the similes in the *Furioso* were based and in particular marked out the episodes derived from Virgil (for example, Ruggiero and Alcina as Aeneas and Dido; Rodomonte's rampage in Paris like that of Turnus in the Trojan camp; Cloridano and Medoro as Euryalus and Nisus).

The edition published in 1556 by Vincenzo Valgrisi, with the collaboration of Girolamo Ruscelli, also shows how deeply the canonization of the *Furioso* was intertwined with the Venetian publishing houses. Though Ruscelli openly argued with Dolce, he nevertheless followed in his footsteps and signaled to readers the greatest possible number of similarities between the *Furioso* and the *Aeneid*.

It is, however, useful to alert students not merely to the theoretical debate around the *Furioso* and the manner in which the editors intervened directly on the text but also, and indeed more important, to Ariosto's own intentions. In *Il* Furioso *tra epos e romanzo*, Sergio Zatti describes the *Furioso* as a site of hesitation between two codes: one inherited from the medieval and popular tradition (the chivalric romance), another distinctive of a new emerging genre (the modern epic poem). Ariosto, therefore, orchestrated this migration from the chivalric pole to the epic pole, and indeed two opposing tendencies seem to cohabit in his work.

An open question, which may be put to the class, is how clear this tendency was to Ariosto himself or indeed to his contemporaries (see Sangirardi, "Quanti sono"). The information on the early readers of the *Furioso*, both common and expert readers, suggests that many saw it simply as one of the countless sequels of Matteo Maria Boiardo's poem; Ariosto himself is likely to have shared the same horizon of expectation. Emulating the *Inamoramento de Orlando*, he conceives his poem as a mixture of genres and attempts to radicalize what Boiardo had already experimented. The *Furioso* displays multiple allusive processes referring to texts and codes external to the traditional chivalric narrative, but such hybridizations always remain visible. The diverse narrative forms, already present in the *Inamoramento*, achieve in the *Furioso* both a quantitative and a qualitative improvement on its model; looking at the novella or the other short narrative forms that both poems willingly incorporate make this evident.

What are the peculiarities of the novelle contained in the *Inamoramento* and the *Furioso*?[5] An anomalous trait immediately jumps to the eye in both poems' short narratives: these are not prose but verse. Moreover, in both poems' novelle the narration is always entrusted to one character (second-degree narrative), and the stories have a linear and closed development, according to a typical characteristic of the genre. It is not, however, simple to identify exactly what parts in the two poems truly belong to the novella genre; this difficulty also depends on the variety of terms with which these narrative insertions are mentioned. Boiardo and Ariosto do not use distinctive terms to indicate the novelle in their poems—terms that would clearly signal their presence within the complex narrative tissue. Boiardo calls them "novelle" on various occasions—for example, when introducing the story of Prasildo, Iroldo, and Tisbina (1.12). Ariosto, on the other hand, never uses the term "novella" to indicate a part of his poem. He more often calls the *Furioso*'s short narratives "istoria" ("story") or "esempio" ("example"). Remarkably, in the sixteenth-century editions of the *Inamoramento*, the *Tavole degli argomenti* (tables of contents) systematically associate the term *novella* with the various brief narratives. The same happens in the *Furioso* printed by Giolito in 1542. The printed book, therefore, actively partakes in the text's reception, influencing its reading in relation to the definition of genres, even simply by furnishing clear tags through which they may be classified.

## Teaching the *Furioso* through Themes

Like very few other texts in our literary tradition, the *Furioso* is an arena for an extraordinary variety of themes, a fact that has determined the persistence and vitality of its fortune throughout the centuries. The poem's ability to isolate, within the unfolding plot, a series of particularly memorable episodes has favored the fortune of certain motifs connected to political, cultural, social, and religious issues central to the early modern world. The poem, therefore, seen also through the lens of its sixteenth-century editions, lends itself to being taught in terms of the universal themes with which it engages. The methodological advantages of a thematic approach, which is the premise to the second part of the course, must be listed: 1) it can mediate, through the various centuries, the reconstruction of the relation between past and present; 2) it mostly implies a multidisciplinary dimension; 3) it creates bonds between literary texts and the lived experience of their readers. However, one must not consider the theme as independent from the literary form through which it is expressed. The close connection between structure and sense emerges clearly in the *Furioso*, where there exists a perfect correspondence between the narration *en entrelacement* and the central theme of the quest (Zatti, *Il* Furioso 18). The most important thematic nuclei through which the poem may be read are love, arms, and madness, to which the reader's attention is drawn right from the *proemio* of the first canto (1.1.1–2 through 1.2.1–4). These motifs point at access routes to the work, which are easily suitable to a thematic reading.

The sixteenth-century printed book thus either emphasizes or obliterates some of the poem's most significant themes. As Daniel Javitch (*Saggi sull'Ariosto*) and Klaus W. Hempfer (*Diskrepante Lektüren*) have shown, the early publishers of the *Furioso* and their editorial collaborators used the text's packaging to provide important keys to interpret the poem's great themes. The paratextual apparatuses, especially the *allegorie* that in the early editions opened the cantos and presented the reader with a moral interpretation, are the site where recurring themes of Ariosto's poem are read through a clearly identifiable ethical antithesis between right and wrong (Ellero; Lo Rito). By comparing the *allegorie* in the sixteenth-century editions it is possible, for example, to establish that the theme of love takes on a markedly negative connotation and may be redeemed only through eschewing this original sensual bias, while the theme of arms is charged with positive values (that often distort, or at least ignore, the subtle irony through which Ariosto treats many episodes of duels or battles). One clear example of this interpretation of the theme of love is offered by the way the Giolito edition (1542) presents one of the *Furioso*'s best-known erotic episodes—namely, Ruggiero's journey to the island of Alcina in canto 7:

> per Ruggiero, dato in potere di Alcina e poi liberato per virtù dell'annello, postogli in dito da Melissa, dimostrasi similmente che a trarci dalla servitù amorosa e dal vizio, nei quali traboccati siamo, fa di bisogno dell'aiuto della sola ragione, ritornata in noi per somma e speciale grazia e non per consiglio o avedimento che sia in noi. (*Orlando furioso* [Giolito], fol. 29r)

> For Ruggiero, fallen under Alcina's spell and set free by the power of the ring that Melissa placed on his finger, similarly demonstrates that the help of solely reason, which derives not from our own understanding, but from the highest and special grace, is needed to release us from the servitude of love and vice into which we have fallen.

The *allegoria* offers a significantly biased reading of the episode and the theme of lascivious love, which is associated with abasement and deviation from a morally higher condition, to which Ruggiero must return after repenting. Arms, being thematically opposite to love, naturally furnish an equally strong interpretative key. For the same reason it is useful to examine the *allegorie* that comment on one of the most famous duels in the *Furioso*, that between Ruggiero and Rodomonte, which closes the poem.

Here, for instance, are the remarks on the duel in the Valvassori and Valgrisi editions:

> Nel duello di Ruggiero e di Rodomonte appare che molto più vale nel combattere l'arte e la destrezza, che il furore e la forza estrema. Sotto la morte violenta di Rodomonte crudele e dispregiatore di Dio, contiensi che rarissime volte, o non mai, si vede che un dispietato ed empio faccia buon fine. (*Orlando furioso* [Valvassori], fol. 259r)
>
> The duel between Ruggiero and Rodomonte shows that art and dexterity are in fighting much more valuable than fierceness and great force. The violent death of the cruel and godless Rodomonte exemplifies that the vicious and impious end well most rarely, or never. (my trans.)
>
> Nella morte poi di Rodomonte, et nell'ultima vittoria di Ruggiero, con che si finisce il libro, restano molto meglio edificati et più sereni gli animi de' lettori et de gli ascoltanti che in quella di Turno presso Vergilio, poiché Rodomonte era venuto con tanto torto et con tanta temerità a disfidar Ruggiero; là ove il misero Turno non avea di nulla offeso già mai Enea. . . . (*Orlando furioso* [Valgrisi] 520)
>
> Rodomonte's death and Ruggiero's final victory, which concludes the book, educates and relieves the readers and the listeners even more than Turnus's death in Virgil, because Rodomonte defied Ruggiero so unjustly and recklessly, whereas the unfortunate Turno never wronged Aeneas. . . . (my trans.)

The moral reading given in the *allegorie*, on the one hand, emphasizes virtue, which is always victorious and expresses its valor through weapons; on the other hand, it underscores the connection between this duel and its model in Virgil, only to conclude by upholding Ariosto's superiority because his hero's reasons for killing his arrogant antagonist are just. Thus sixteenth-century readers could not only learn a very specific interpretation of the episode but also recognize its textual source along with the originality of Ariosto's rewriting.

## Teaching the *Furioso* through Images

The final part of the course uses an interdisciplinary approach to literature, centering not on the relationship between the reader and the work but on the interaction with other disciplines. In what follows, particular relevance is given to the relations between literary works and other arts, both performative and visual.

The *Furioso* is particularly well suited to an investigation of connections between literature and visual culture.[6] Ariosto's poem is one of very few literary texts to have been immediately and extensively translated into images, as episodes from all its cantos were illustrated. Even before the definitive forty-six-canto version was assembled, the Zoppino edition, printed in Venice in 1530, complements each canto with a woodcut representing one of its episodes. The following Zoppino edition (1536) does the same for the final version of the poem. Each canto's image functions as an aide-mémoire and guides the reader's attention toward one episode, highlighting certain specific narrative nuclei to the detriment of others (see galassiaariosto.sns.it/opere/orlando-furioso/zoppino-1536/1-Canto-I). The iconographic apparatus thus offers a powerful testimony of what type of reading the poem elicited from some very special users, such as artists and engravers.

Only six years after the second Zoppino edition, Giolito's richly illustrated *Furioso* (1542) set an editorial standard that would be observed throughout the century and beyond: the engravings, while still of a relatively small size, are placed at the beginning of each canto and accompanied by the above-mentioned *allegorie* (see galassiaariosto.sns.it/opere/orlando-furioso/giolito-1542/47). Through this visual transposition and moralistic interpretation, sixteenth-century readers were handed a text already mediated by other readings, which aimed—either directly or indirectly—to condition its reception. The Giolito edition paved the way for highly complex illustrative solutions, which became progressively richer and more sophisticated across the sixteenth century. Unlike the 1536 Zoppino edition, the Giolito illustrations represented two or three carefully selected episodes from each canto, which offered a clearly defined interpretation of both the text and the type of reading put forward. The illustrator here wishes not merely to create brief cycles that focus on the adventures of a single hero but to systematically exclude those episodes in which the romance (i.e., more romantic and erotic) seems much more relevant. The arms, in other words, are significantly more central than the love, and indeed the female characters feature decidedly less prominently than the knights.[7] The images contributed to affirming the *Furioso* as a modern classic, and they show students how publishing houses shaped the definition of vernacular genres.

The edition printed by Valvassori in 1553 also presents extremely high artistic standards. Its illustrations follow many technical innovations introduced by Giolito: the images are placed at the beginning of each canto and have a multinarrative structure. Valvassori, however, goes one step further and enriches the images with an increasing number of details (see galassiaariosto.sns.it/opere/orlando-furioso/valvassori-1553/101-Canto-IX). These make the dialogue between the iconic and verbal language ever more intense. The images now attempt to mirror the poem's complex narrative time, as the illustrator tries to suggest a succession of events in line with the chronology of the canto. Only a few years later, the Vincenzo Valgrisi edition (1556) represents a further radical innovation in the visual apparatuses: the engravings now take up a whole page and illustrate the highest possible number of episodes from the relevant canto (see galassiaariosto.sns.it/opere/orlando-furioso/valgrisi-1556/148-Canto-X). The sixteenth century closes with another elegant edition, Francesco de' Franceschi's 1584 *Furioso*, embellished with chalcographic engravings by the Paduan artist Girolamo Porro (see galassiaariosto.sns.it/opere/orlando-furioso/de-franceschi-1584/289-Canto-VI). Here the serpentine movement of the Valgrisi illustrations, which seemed to compete with the *entrelacement* of the narrative, are replaced by orderly representations, organized along different perspective planes, where each episode occupies its own distinct narrative unity. By significantly simplifying the earlier visual and narrative chaos, de Franceschi's illustrations seem to endow the poem with a greater respect for the Aristotelian precepts.[8]

The iconographic corpora of these five editions are accessible online as a digital archive, *L'* Orlando furioso *e la sua traduzione in immagini* (www.orlandofurioso.org). The archive is entirely devoted to the examination of text-image relations in the *Furioso*. A further, more complex archive, *Galassia Ariosto*, dedicated to the *Furioso*'s influence on the editorial format of other chivalric poems, is now available online (www.galassiaariosto.sns.it).[9] Both archives provide the search tools to discover which octaves of the *Furioso* inspired the various illustrations and offer further information in individual entries on the verbal paratexts; additionally, *L'* Orlando furioso *e la sua traduzione in immagini* contains a virtual gallery gathering numerous works of art inspired by the poem. Such archives, therefore, have a significant didactic potential, as they give us a synchronic picture of sixteenth-century visual interpretations and may be used by teachers in more ambitious courses.

The archives' tools allow us to combine the three teaching approaches I have described, as the illustrated editions and other figurative works can be analyzed as visual interpretations of both the different relevant genres and the poem's most significant themes. Users of the archives can not only easily compare the interpretations of love and arms offered to sixteenth-century readers of the *Furioso* but also ponder the strategies adopted to represent the poem's combined genres. For instance, the class can examine the *Furioso*'s second-degree narratives by considering the corresponding images. Starting from the apparatuses of the Giolito edition, where, as we have seen, the digressive narratives are placed under a single heading (novella), the instructor may analyze their visual transposition: Which novellas found their way into the illustrations? How were they represented? And were these illustrations also transposed into the iconographic material of the other Venetian editions? The digital archives are equally helpful in discussing why some thematic nuclei were more successful than others: How much room, for example, did duels and battles occupy in the textual and figurative apparatuses? How often did the illustrators choose instead to represent the amorous adventures of Ariosto's characters? Again, the visual transpositions reexamine various interpretations of the poem.

The sixteenth-century editions of the *Furioso*, along with the digital archives, therefore prove to be an innovative, versatile, and extremely valuable didactic tool in several respects. Those editions, combining words and images, represent highly sophisticated interpretative instruments, which can be usefully deployed to better understand and teach the *Furioso*'s complex universe from a variety of viewpoints.

## Notes

The research leading to the results noted in this essay received funding from the European Research Council under the European Community's Seventh Framework Programme (2007–2013) / ERC Grant agreement n. 295620: ERC Advanced Grant 2011, Looking at Words Through Images: Some Case Studies for a Visual History of Italian Literature.

1. Useful strategies for teaching literature are also to be found in Luperini.

2. On the debate surrounding the *Furioso*, which later led to its canonization, see primarily Javitch, *Proclaiming a Classic*.

3. For the debate on the genres in the sixteenth century, especially in relation to the chivalric poem, see Weinberg; Baldassarri; Zatti, *L'ombra del Tasso*; Javitch, "Nascita"; and Sberlati.

4. Both works are available in *Google Books*.

5. On the novelle of the *Furioso*, see Franceschetti, "La novella"; Bigazzi; Cavallo, *Romance Epics* 99–125; Sangirardi, "Les nouvelles du *Roland furieux*"; and Salwa.

6. On the fortune of the *Furioso* in the figurative arts, see Bolzoni et al.; Caracciolo and Rossi; and Bolzoni, *L'*Orlando furioso *nello specchio delle immagini*. These volumes also mention the relevant earlier bibliography.

7. On Giolito's woodcuts, see Cerrai.

8. On the relation between the illustrations and Ariosto's narrative strategies, see Rizzarelli, "Tempo" and "Vedere"; Pezzini, "Il disegno"; and Izzo.

9. For further details on the archives, see two pages of the Centro di Elaborazione Informatica di Testi e Immagini nella Tradizione Letteraria Web site: www.ctl.sns.it/progetto_furioso.html, www.ctl.sns.it/progetto_ERC_galassia_ariosto.html; see also Pezzini, "The Digital Collections"; Urbaniak.

**Gael Montgomery**

# The Transformation of Angelica

A useful way to present a poem as intricate, pluralistic, and contradictory as *Orlando furioso* is to focus primarily on one character's journey through the poem. This lightens the teacher's task considerably and makes the *Furioso* less daunting for the student. Moreover, there is no risk of oversimplifying the material, since each principal character's strand is complex and intersects with many other strands. Angelica is an ideal choice for this approach, and a natural point of departure is the competition to sexually possess her that opens Ariosto's poem. Angelica's travels between cantos 1 and 30 offer students an overview of many characters and plot lines and also show certain key themes of the poem: love and its different meanings and manifestations, chivalry and male competition, gender roles and sexual aggression. Angelica's episodes contain rich poetic language and incorporate multiple literary citations, providing students with an introduction to close reading and acquainting them with important sources for the *Furioso*, including its direct predecessor, Matteo Maria Boiardo's *Orlando innamorato*.

The character of Angelica, Boiardo's original creation, is an essential link between *Orlando furioso* and *Orlando innamorato*. As the object of Orlando's passion in the *Innamorato*, and the putative cause of his folly in the *Furioso*,

Angelica can be regarded as the raison d'être for both poems. Although Boiardo is rarely considered integral to courses on Ludovico Ariosto, one cannot fully appreciate the *Furioso* without some familiarity with the *Innamorato*. A brief study of Boiardo's great poem gives students an idea of how thoroughly Ariosto's continuation appropriates and transforms the material, using Angelica as the motive force. It also amplifies our understanding of fifteenth- and sixteenth-century Ferrara and the Este court—the cultural environment in which Ariosto wrote—and allows us to contextualize Ariosto's accomplishment. Moreover, a comparison of Boiardo's and Ariosto's treatments of Angelica can be used to incorporate narrative theory into the course.

## Structure of the Course

I describe here a semester-long seminar with two meetings per week, designed to be taught in Italian and with primary texts in Italian. The course can easily be taught in English and thus cross-listed; the pacing still allows some analysis of the original texts, aided by English translations, so that students can better appreciate the poetics of *Orlando furioso* and the linguistic and stylistic differences between Boiardan and Ariostan ottava rima. (I recommend the Charles Stanley Ross version of the *Innamorato* and the Barbara Reynolds version of the *Furioso*, which preserve the octave and nicely convey the qualities of the original poems.)

In the first week we briefly discuss the history and development of Roland/Orlando, from the *Chanson de Roland* up to the time of Boiardo (see Morgan in this volume), and acquaint ourselves with Ferrara and the Estensi. This is an apt time to note that knowledge of classical texts and literary models was fundamental to Renaissance humanism and literature and that far less emphasis was placed on originality, as we conceive of it today, than students might expect. Thus, reading a romance epic necessitates understanding the many literary conventions and citations it incorporates and, often, reinterprets. It is in this context that we discover originality: the innovations of Boiardo during the second and third weeks of the course, followed by the brilliant inventiveness of Ariosto.

## Boiardo

We devote week 2 to *Orlando innamorato*'s canto 1 and portions of other cantos from the first book (2.1–29, 3.31–78, 5.13.6–31, 8.1–26, 8.52–64, 9.1–25, 9.38.3–41.4), along with selected source readings. Vital elements in these verses (such as the ring of invisibility, Angelica's flight and sexual pursuit, contradictory love enchantments, a harrowing escape from an accursed monster) will have reverberations, parallels, or counterpoints in the *Furioso*.

Week 3 includes later cantos of book 1 (25.36–61, 27.37–62, all of canto 29) and parts of book 2 (3.60–66.4, 15.42–64, 20.44–60, 21.1–21). These readings largely deal with the sexual characterizations and behavior of Angelica and Orlando, which Ariosto will alter drastically in the *Furioso*. Our study of Boiardo concludes as Angelica is captured by Charlemagne's forces and given in custody to Duke Namo of Bavaria. It is here that Ariosto will begin his story.

Each canto of Boiardo's poem offers a variety of source readings to choose from. Those for the first canto might include Virgil's tenth eclogue, with its famous verse "omnia vincit Amor; et nos cedamus Amori" ("Love conquers all things; let us surrender to Love"; verse 69)[1] alluded to several times in Boiardo's incipit (verses 1–3). This, in fact, becomes the guiding ethos for the *Innamorato*, although with comic rather than tragic results. Orlando's speech of self-reproof upon falling in love with Angelica is filled with Petrarchan language (1.1.30–31), and his statement "io vedo il meglio ed al peggior m'appiglio" ("I see what's best and hold on to what's worst"; 1.1.31) directly cites the final line of Petrarch's canzone 264, which itself references Ovid's *Metamorphoses* 7.20–21, wherein Medea attempts to resist her love for Jason. Yet Boiardo's tone is humorous, and in following this literary chain we can trace how the device alters as it is used in different contexts. An obvious choice for canto 3 is *Metamorphoses* 1.504–24, cited by Boiardo in 1.3.43–45 as Angelica plays Apollo to Ranaldo's Daphne. Ariosto, like Boiardo, will frequently cite Petrarch and Ovid but to quite different effect, allowing us to analyze the disparate ways he and Boiardo use these sources to structure character and determine meaning.

As students begin to read Boiardo, there are fundamental questions they should consider: How does the narrator present himself? How detectable is his presence in the poem, and what is his relationship with his audience? What novelty is he promising to his readers? What about the pacing of his narrative—is it relaxed or rapid? Is the tone serious, comical, or a mix of the two? With what type of language does the narrator construct Angelica as well as the knights who become enamored of her? Do these characters produce direct speech? Whose voices do we hear, whose points of view? These questions will prepare students for both the similarities and the radical changes they will encounter in Ariosto's text and will be posed repeatedly while they read the *Furioso*. As students proceed with the *Innamorato*, we can raise more complex issues: How are female and male sexuality, and sexual desire, presented in Boiardo's poem? How is Angelica's situation in the poem—sexual and otherwise—affected by her status as Saracen and other? How much autonomy does Angelica have, given her circumstances and also given the fact that she is under the influence of magic? Again, these issues will be essential to our reading of Ariosto's poem.

## Ariosto

As with Boiardo, we also study sources related to Ariosto and now add critical works as well. A principal source for much of Ariosto's first canto is, of course, *Orlando innamorato*. Although the *Furioso* commences where the *Innamorato* has left Angelica, it is also a rewriting of the *Innamorato*. The *Furioso*'s incipit is modeled in part on the *Innamorato*'s, but it shows evident divergences between the poems' narrators, regarding both their narrative styles and the ways they condition readers' perceptions. A chief difference is the volatility and instability of the *Furioso*'s narration: the biased interventions and commentaries of Ariosto's narrator, especially regarding women, love, and madness, seem designed to manipulate the reader yet are often contradicted by the events he recounts. As in Boiardo's poem, Angelica flees while Charlemagne's knights contest possession of her. However, whereas Angelica enters the *Innamorato* a free and well-connected woman, the *Furioso* transforms her into an isolated and defenseless prisoner. At the same time, Angelica is also presented as the powerful cause of Orlando's madness.

Ambivalence and contrariness regarding femininity and female sexuality pervade every section featuring Angelica (cantos 1, 2.1–18, 8, 10.92–115, 11.1–12, 12.23–65, 19.17–42, 29.58–66). The poem's contrasting perspectives are enhanced by literary references, which themselves often contain much ambiguity. For example, in Sacripante's lament comparing a woman's virginity to an untouched rose that loses its value when plucked (1.42–43), Ariosto recycles a simile used countless times by previous poets, among them Poliziano, Lorenzo the Magnificent, and Nicolò degli Agostini (Rajna, *Fonti* 84n187, 86n192). The comparison's familiarity may lead the reader to accept it at face value; yet if we look at the initial inspiration, Catullus 62.39–47, we find an epithalamium: a nuptial hymn sung in alternating parts, first by young men who advocate that the bride give herself over to the groom and then by girls who oppose them, protesting that the bride loses her value once she is married and no longer virgin. Catullus's poem empathizes with the girls' fears of leaving the protection of the family and losing their social milieu, and their worth, along with losing their virginity. This is Angelica's situation precisely, but without benefit of marriage.

The simile recurs in verse 1.58.1–2, in which Sacripante plans to pluck Angelica's rose; in the subsequent lines (1.58.3–8), as Sacripante claims that despite a woman's resistance, nothing is more pleasing to her than being forced, we find references to Ovid's *Ars Amatoria* (1.663–78), *Pamphilus* (A. Elliott 109–14), and Chrétien de Troyes's *Perceval* (3858–77). This embarrassment of sources provides excellent material for in-class presentations: as students become more familiar with Ariosto, and more adept at close reading, they can elucidate the relation between source readings and the text, identifying where, and to what effect, Ariosto uses particular citations.

Although Angelica virtually disappears midway through the poem, her influence persists. Her importance is manifested in Orlando's madness and violent behavior; her experiences are reflected in those of other female figures in the poem. Therefore, we also read cantos featuring characters who are closely connected with Angelica—Orlando, Ruggiero, Medoro—or who serve as counterparts or foils—Alcina, Isabella—thus further illuminating the ways her character is represented (cantos 6 and 7 for Ruggiero and Alcina; 12.66–94, 13.1–44, 20.132–44, 23.52–69, 28.95–102, 29.1–38 for Isabella; 18.163–92, 19.1–16 for Medoro; 23.100–36, 24.1–93, 29.39–74, 30.1–17 for Orlando). These passages, too, are marked by ambiguity and by contrast between the narrator's interventions and the events of the narrative. The honorable hero Orlando becomes unthinkably violent out of sexual frustration. Ruggiero, fictive ancestor of the Estensi, is both unfaithful lover and failed rapist. Medoro, the only man Angelica finds sexually attractive (and, not coincidentally, whom she does not find sexually menacing), is of low birth and status. Incongruities exist between characters as well: Isabella is celebrated for protecting her virginity while Angelica is depicted as cold and disdainful for not relinquishing hers.

Not surprisingly, Angelica has given rise to an abundance of commentary and to disparate, even discordant, points of view. I prefer to elicit student reactions to selected cantos and related sources before discussing pertinent scholarly works, generally focusing the first of the weekly meetings on primary texts and the second on supplemental readings and scholarship. The discussion of critical works is then guaranteed to engage the students' own critical faculties and to generate lively and even passionate debate. How do scholars support their interpretations of various passages? Do students agree with a particular reading? What textual evidence do they propose to corroborate or refute it?

For instance, Ariosto's description of Angelica's flight from Rinaldo in verse 1.34 compares her to a frightened fawn, citing Horace, ode 1.23. In D. S. Carne-Ross's reading, Angelica's experience is beside the point, and Ariosto's use of the citation is entirely aesthetic (206). For Deanna Shemek, on the other hand, Angelica's fearful perspective dominates the imagery and determines the tone of the passage (*Ladies Errant* 56). Marcello Turchi ascribes Angelica's repeated flight from her male pursuers to "transcendental coquetry" (133), Valeria Finucci to Angelica's fear of being raped (*Lady* 110). Angelica's function is often disputed: Eduardo Saccone and Eugenio Donato are not concerned with Angelica as the object of the knights' desire but rather with the longing she and other objects stimulate in the *Furioso*. Indeed, Donato sees Angelica as interchangeable with any other thing that provokes rivalry among the knights (33, 40). Mario Santoro, however, regards Angelica as a specifically female object who is valued for her beauty and the pleasure her pursuers obtain from her (58–59). Ita Mac Carthy examines Angelica not only as object but as desiring subject, pointing out that the encounter of Angelica and Medoro in canto 19 is one of the few instances of requited love and satisfied desire in the poem (62–63). Jo Ann Cavallo adds a political interpretation: Angelica's union with Medoro, which makes him ruler of Cathay, may reflect the Este family's acquisition of power through dynastic and intercultural marriage (*World Beyond Europe* 34–35).

As students encounter conflicting interpretations of Ariosto's poetry, we can introduce the notions of open and closed texts and of narrative determinacy. Does the text direct us toward a particular reading or does it lend itself to multiple and even simultaneous interpretations? As we discover that interpretations often correspond to the generation or gender of the critic, we can also ask whether there is such a thing as social determinacy and whether readers themselves can be relatively open or closed. An interesting exercise is to have students interpret single passages multiple times: first, based on the narrator's direct comments, then on his descriptions of a male character's experience, and finally on a female character's experience. The diverse perspectives that emerge may surprise teachers as well as students and ensure that none of us remains a complacent reader.

## Note

1. All translations are mine.

**Chris Picicci**

# Figurative Arts, Music, and Film for Boiardo, Ariosto, and Tasso

There are myriad ways to present the Italian romance epic. Taking into consideration that most undergraduates are unfamiliar with the Ferrarese *tre corone* and the genre at large, I use a selective approach. I have taught Italian epic poetry in its original language and in English translation in courses on both Italian Renaissance literature and epic poetry; typically, my students enroll in a cross-listed Italian and English course. In the past, I have designed supplementary lessons for *italianisti*, requiring students to read selections of the poems out loud and discuss them in Italian. In addition to choosing specific passages in accordance with my course's thematic content, I also emphasize topics like plot structure (its multiplicity, intercalated stories, abundance of characters, and narrative unpredictability), poetics (the ottava rima, the use of hendecasyllable with specific accentuation and rhyme scheme, along with the meaning of rhetorical figures), as well as other basic linguistic particularities. I encourage students of Italian to always read the original text before looking at the English translation.[1] Including ancillary materials like art, music, and film enhances comprehension in both monolingual and bi- or multilingual students, allowing them to better understand and appreciate selected passages.

For my courses in Italian Renaissance literature, I include a unit on the Renaissance chivalric tradition, highlighting topics such as origins, oral and musical attributes, the role of the hero(es), the inclusion of myth and (pseudo-) history, and the presence of an authorial voice. In my Love and Deceit in Epic Poetry course, I include selections from ancient, medieval, and Italian epic poems. Students often appreciate the parallels they find in an assortment of texts from different periods and literary traditions.

## Figurative Arts

Passages from Matteo Maria Boiardo's *Orlando innamorato*, Ludovico Ariosto's *Orlando furioso*, and Torquato Tasso's *Gerusalemme liberata* can be contextualized by selecting pictorial works that complement specific passages; such images often depict continuous narrations, representing lines from more than one octave. All three poems inspired visual interpretations of poetic passages—included either as illustrations in the poem's various editions or completed as independent frescoes, sketches, paintings, and other art forms (e.g., sculpture, majolica, terracotta); indeed, the relation between the written and artistic mediums spans five centuries. Instructors can make appropriate selections for their course or ask students to find pictorial representations on their own; students should be encouraged to examine the symbiotic relation between the original poetic texts and the rich visual images they inspired.[2]

When discussing the role of love and war in the *Innamorato*, I ask students to comment on the opening canto's presentation of Orlando (1.1.2), along with the often-anthologized proemial statement in which the author draws attention to his fusion of epic and romance: "Però diversamente il mio verziero / De amore e de battaglia ho già piantato" ("My garden has variety. / I've planted it with love and war"; 3.5.2). I pair this with the narrator's apostrophe to Venus (2.12.1–3)[3] while simultaneously presenting the fresco entitled *Allegory of April: Triumph of Venus* by Francesco del Cossa (1436–1478) in the Hall of the Months of Ferrara's Palazzo Schifanoia.[4] Students draw parallels between the passages and the fresco, discussing the role of love and war and their allegorization as the mythological figures Venus and Mars. In the fresco, the seated goddess of love appears victorious over the god of war, who is chained and kneeling in front of her. Furthermore, Mars is not facing the viewer, his shield and helmet seem more ornamental than useful, and his scimitar remains in its sheath. Students sometimes compare this fresco to Botticelli's well-known

*Primavera* (1482), given the similar mythological aspects, the centrality and prominence of Venus, and the presence of the Three Graces, who act as her companions in both works.[5]

Contemporary paintings and illustrations of the poems are also excellent prompts for discussion. I include the artist Emanuele Luzzati's fanciful pieces inspired by the *Orlando innamorato.* Many of his images are sketched in extraordinary detail with geometric patterns. His use of collage and tribal patterns speaks to the twenty-first-century spectator, and is therefore often appealing to students. *Dell'amore, dell'avventura:* L'Orlando innamorato ("Of Love, of Adventure: *Orlando in Love*") combines verses from the *Innamorato* together with Luzzati's vivid and whimsical sketches.

Although the diffusion and popularity of the *Furioso* overshadow the *Innamorato*, I stress that Ariosto's poem is a continuation or sequel of Boiardo's masterpiece. The variety of subject matter, interlaced plot, and characters in Boiardo's poem are models for Ariosto and are masterfully resumed and adapted by him (see Brand, "Ariosto's Continuation"; Marinelli; and Cavallo, "Denying Closure"). Asking students to analyze the artistic depiction of Angelica—and of other female characters in the *Furioso*—frequently leads to discussions of the poem's purported philogyny or misogyny. Additionally, attention to Ariosto's female characters may further complicate opinions on the poem's treatment of women, underscoring their dominance and the narrator's ambivalent attitude toward them.

Angelica is a central character in the *Innamorato* and *Furioso*, and Ariosto highlights her virginity as well as her beauty. Described through idealized Petrarchan tropes, she is often depicted as fleeing from her many suitors. This aspect is rendered especially vivid in the terracotta work *Angelica che fugge* ("Angelica Fleeing") by the contemporary sculptor Giuseppe Bergomi, first displayed with other pieces of art in an exhibition at the Palazzo Magnani in Reggio Emilia in commemoration of Ariosto's 540th birthday. In this 2014 bust sculpture, the naked Cathayan princess looks behind her right shoulder with a terrified expression, her arms extended forward and her thick straight hair flowing backward in flight, thus forming an equal opposition that balances the composition.[6]

The episode of Angelica's enamorment of Medoro has inspired numerous artistic representations through the centuries. In *Angelica si innamora di Medoro* ("Angelica Falls in Love with Medoro"), by Simone Peterzano (1535–1599), for example, students can detect the physical characteristics that coincide with Ariosto's verses and the aesthetics of archetypal beauty.[7] Angelica's intense gaze and tender caress of the naked wounded soldier, along with her exposed breast, intensify the sensuality of the scene, focusing attention on the two figures rather than the surrounding landscape—the horses, the deceased Dardinello and Cloridano, and the shepherd tending to the latter. Following the Ariostan source text, Peterzano depicts Medoro less like an African soldier and more like an idealized Greek or Roman sculpture with curly golden hair and fair skin (see Cavallo, *World* 32–35). A question I often pose to students is, How is Angelica's compassion, conveyed in the poetic lines (19.20), communicated in the painting?[8]

Another episode with a rich pictorial tradition is Ruggiero's rescue of Angelica from the Orca and the rescue's aftermath. One of the best-known images is *Ruggiero Rescuing Angelica* by Jean-Auguste-Dominique Ingres (1780–1867), a neoclassical interpretation depicting Ruggiero as he rides his hippogriff, his lance positioned in the mouth of the sea monster, with a naked Angelica bound by chains to the rock (10.91–104).[9] Students often note the inauspicious setting, the emotive qualities evoked by the dominant dark colors, and the painting's upward motion despite the downward blow of the lance. They point out the agitated waves created by the monster, the upward flow of Ruggiero's cape, and the awkward position of Angelica's head. Both the poem and Ingres's painting emphasize Angelica's illuminated white skin and golden hair (10.100), despite the terror of her situation. Students also observe her facial features, bejeweled hair, and contrapposto pose. Students may also discuss how the sea monster measures up to Ariosto's description of it as "una gran massa che s'aggiri e torca; / né forma ha d'animal, se non la testa, / c'ha gli occhi e i denti fuor, come di porca" ("A writhing, twisting mass. . . . / No other feature can Ruggiero note / By which to recognize it as a beast, / Save head and eyes and tusks and gaping throat"; 10.101). Additional artistic interpretations of this episode include the sixteenth-century woodcuts published in Venice by Gabriel Giolito, Titian's detailed drawing of the passage from the 1550s, Eugène Delacroix's *Ruggiero libera Angelica* ("Ruggiero Frees Angelica"), with its dramatic landscape and emphasis on Ruggiero slaying the monster, and Gustave Doré's nineteenth-century illustration with its monochromatic intensity of line and dream-like interpretation.[10]

In order to emphasize the importance of additional female characters in the *Furioso*, I include paintings of female subjects by Dosso Dossi, the Renaissance painter and court artist to the Este family. His depiction of *Circe and her Lovers in a Landscape* incites discussion on the nefarious sorceress Alcina and her similarities to the witch-goddess in Homer's *Odyssey* along with the depiction of trapped lovers on her island (cantos

6–8).[11] Another Dossi canvas entitled *Melissa* (previously called and still sometimes referred to as *Circe*) is effective in discussing magic and its role in the poem. Students comment on the idyllic setting, the canine with the human-like eyes imperfectly positioned behind an empty cuirass, and the elegance and detail of Melissa's dress.

There are many visual representations of Orlando's descent into madness (23.100–36), one of the most outlandish and entertaining moments of the poem. Instructors should consider, for example, the Venetian Giolito woodcut of 1542 with its simple lines and depiction of a naked and enraged Orlando uprooting a tree or Giovanni Boulanger's *Orlando impazzito per amore* ("Orlando Gone Mad for Love"; 1650–52) in the Palazzo Ducale in Sassuolo (see Everson, "Every Picture").[12] The seventeenth-century artist captures the paladin in a bucolic setting, shedding his armor and clothing while Cupid (without a quiver or arrows) holds Orlando's sword. This image is an excellent segue into a philosophical discussion on humanism and its notion of mankind's capacity to descend to base depths or, as Giovanni Pico della Mirandola would argue, become godlike. Despite Orlando's superhuman physical strength, he reveals his mental fragility with his uncontrollable emotional state and irrational behavior.

Lastly, Grazia Nidasio's illustrations for Italo Calvino's retelling of the *Furioso* offer straightforward colored sketches and visual support to the original and glossed selections of Ariosto's text for the contemporary reader. The blotches of color and minimalist structures reduce the epic's complex poetics to a more tangible aesthetic experience, especially for younger readers. This work contrasts with the mostly Renaissance and baroque examples and gives students a sense of the poetry's continuity and endurance.

Several episodes of Tasso's *Liberata* have also been visually interpreted in the fine arts. When assigning the poem, I select a variety of corresponding artworks that depict the famous combat between Tancredi and Clorinda in canto 12, Armida and Rinaldo in her garden in canto 16, and Erminia finding Tancredi wounded in canto 19.[13] I prefer artworks that dramatize the verses, portraying the sense of pathos and frenetic movement present in Tasso's octaves. Well-known examples by French painters include Nicolas Poussin, whose theory of painting was influenced by Tasso's poetry (see Unglaub); Claude Lorrain, whose *Liberata*-inspired paintings suggest idealized landscapes; and Jean-Honoré Fragonard, who produced Rococo paintings and sketches of passages inspired by the *Liberata* and the *Furioso*.

Also interesting for discussion is the use of chiaroscuro in works like Guercino's *Erminia Finding the Wounded Tancredi*, now in the Doria Pamphilj

Gallery, Rome, Italy (c. 1618).[14] The figures' emotion, underscored by the outstretched arms of Erminia, the uncontrollable bleeding of Tancredi, and Vafrino's gentle assistance, contributes to the dramatic intensity of the scene (19.104–05). The vivid blue, black, white, and yellow of the copious textiles appear to blend with the dark, ominous clouds, rendering an eerie sky. The striking contrast of light and dark defies any verisimilitude of natural light, intensifying the emotional impact, while Tancredi's nude body in the foreground highlights the scene's sensuality.[15]

## Music

Musical renditions of specific episodes, such as operatic performance or orchestral composition, allow students to experience the inherent musicality of epic poetry, recalling the original aurality of epos.[16] Although operatic renditions do not always maintain the sources' literary integrity, they are nonetheless useful in helping students realize the passion and intensity of the original poetry. Students appreciate the melodic dramatization of the libretto along with the music's rhythmic flexibility, which convey the poetry's affect.

To introduce students to operatic rifacimenti of the Italian epic tradition, I play a variety of musical works, including selections from Antonio Vivaldi's *Orlando finto pazzo* ("Orlando, the Fake Madman"; 1714) and his *Orlando furioso* (1727), both of which debuted at the Teatro Sant'Angelo in Venice. For the former, which is based on Boiardo's *Innamorato*, I prefer the aria "Se in ogni guardo" sung by Argillano (act 1, scene 5) and "Anderò, volerò, griderò" ("I will go, I will fly, I will shout") sung by Origille (3.11). A compact disc of the work is available from the Istituto di Musica Antica Academia Montis Regalis, Mondovi, Italy (2004). Before presenting scenes from Vivaldi's *Orlando furioso*, I discuss some of the operatic alterations of the original text (e.g., the action takes place on Alcina's enchanted island; Orlando, Angelica, and Medoro meet under the sorceress's watchful eyes; Orlando hugs the statue of the wizard Merlin, thinking it is Angelica). I play Orlando singing the praises of being a Christian soldier (1.1) and Angelica singing her love to Orlando, making Medoro jealous ("Tu sei de gl'occhi miei" ["You are for my eyes"]; 1.5). I also play the scenes depicting Angelica and Medoro in postnuptial bliss, followed by Orlando's madness (2.9–10) and Alcina's farewell aria, "Anderò, chiamerò dal profondo" ("I will go, I will call you from below").[17]

George Frideric Handel's three *opere serie* derived from Ariosto's poem emphasize the impact of the Renaissance epic on musical and dramatic mediums. Handel's *Orlando* (1733) is based on the love triangle between Orlando, Angelica, and Medoro. In highlighting textual differences, students recognize the transformation from verse narrative to the abbreviated dramatic lyric and appreciate opera as a performing art. The most obvious difference is the added character, Zoroaster, whose magical deeds and constant presence is markedly distinct from Ariosto's poem. Students note Astolfo's absence and discuss Orlando's regained sanity and its difference from Astolfo's journey to the moon.

Handel's *Alcina* (1735) very loosely follows the Alcina episode of the *Furioso*. Ruggiero witnesses the island's true landscape, as opposed to its idyllic illusion, and confirms this in act 2, scene 12 with his aria "Verdi prati" ("Green meadows"). Bradamante's previous request "fuggiam l'infame loco" ("let's escape the vile place") incites Ruggiero to flee Alcina's island, intensifying the situation's pathos. Students often comment on Alcina and the authenticity of her love for Ruggiero in the opera. They enjoy the destruction of the urn, the source of Alcina's magic, in the final scene. Ultimately, this act brings about her demise and the restoration of her former lovers to their original selves.

Handel's *Ariodante* (1735) is an adaptation of the love story between Ariodante and Ginevra. It enriches discussions on the role of women in the *Furioso* and the moral standards to which they are held for their sexual behavior. Issues of fidelity, betrayal, motivation, loyalty and sexual propriety are all potential topics of discussion. Handel's notes often extend beyond the range of the staff, allowing him to highlight tonal variation in this opera. Students may discuss the effect of this feature, for example, in "Dopo notte" ("After night") (act 3, scene 8).[18]

Claudio Monteverdi's *Combattimento di Tancredi* ("Tancred's Fight") reproduces the actual octaves from canto 12 of the *Liberata*, providing instructions to the performers, and ultimately developing one of the most dramatic baroque musical performances based on epic poetry. Clemens Risi describes the work as a "musical contact zone of sorts" (153).[19] The *Combattimento*'s musical techniques highlight the acoustical dimensions and palpable immediacy of the dramatic encounter, particularly the duel and baptism of Clorinda. Monteverdi's *concitato* ("agitated") genre is intended to convey the emotions and sounds of war (153). Monteverdi interprets the pathos of this episode, highlighting the tension of combat and the compassion of the final baptismal scene. Various techniques (forte, pianissimo, syncopations, semitones, dissonance, etc.) contribute to the mounting tension as Clorinda's death nears (see Moses; La Via).

## Film

Cinematic interpretations of epic poetry are another tool for student engagement. Film is particularly useful for emphasizing the poetry's most dramatic episodes. This contemporary medium appeals to twenty-first-century students and gives them the opportunity to visualize the texts on screen. I often show clips after conducting close readings of corresponding passages. Students compare and contrast the filmic representation for accuracy, prompting discussions on content, character, and interpretation. Cinematic productions can also be discussed in conjunction with the technical and theoretical components inherent to film studies; certainly, film as an image-based medium requires a different set of protocols, strategies, and analysis from the printed text.

Luca Ronconi's *Orlando furioso*, a film adaptation of his theatrical production, presents a wide variety of episodes from the poem, including several already mentioned in this essay.[20] The scenes I select for students of Italian (given the lack of subtitles) include Angelica and Ruggiero, the sorceress Alcina and her enchanted island, the presentation and use of the harquebus, the figure of Olimpia (Mariangela Melato), Orlando's madness, and Astolfo on the moon. Students find that Ronconi's faux set designs are, at times, too artificial for our modern tastes: the horses slide on fixed trolleys, the theatrics are slow moving, and all scenes take place indoors. Nonetheless, the occasional narrative interjections and close representation of literary characters sustain the viewer's attention. This theatrical-cinematic project maintains Ariosto's living narrative with a kind of poetic dialogue, larger-than-life characters, and multiplicity of narrative action in a remarkable attempt at ultramodern experimental filmmaking.

Another film appropriate for students of Italian is Ermanno Olmi's *Il mestiere delle armi* (2001). The title comes from the *Furioso*'s phrase "per te il mestier de l'arme è senza onore" ("No honour now attaches to the art / [o]f soldiering"; *Orlando furioso* 11.26) and revolves around the figure of the condottiere, Giovanni delle Bande Nere. It emphasizes the introduction of artillery (the falconet) into combat and focuses on the relation between the ethics of warfare and technology, highlighting how firearms, with their destructive power, forever changed the art of war. Various clips can be paired with the poem's foretold resurrection of artillery from the sea and its lamented revolutionary effect on contemporary combat. Students discuss Ariosto's invective against firearms (11.21–28) or what he calls a "scelerata e brutta / invenzïon" ("hideous invention"; 11.26) and his belief that its use initiates the ruination of traditional soldiering. The poet's nostalgic stance may also be compared to Machiavelli's writings on maintaining traditional military tactics and strategies in *The Art of War* (see books 2, 3, and 4).

Tasso's poem influenced the production of Enrico Guazzoni's dated *Gerusalemme liberata* (1910–18), which was eventually reissued with sound in 1935, and Carlo Ludovico Bragaglia's 1957 *La Gerusalemme liberata* (*The Mighty Crusaders*). Instructors may instead consider the more recent film *Kingdom of Heaven* (2005), produced by Ridley Scott and written by William Monahan, which presents a fictional account of the Crusades, imparting the magnitude of the bloodshed between Christians and Muslims, and thus offering material that invites a discussion of current events. The stunning cinematography, gruesome battle sequences, and set design dramatically recreate an example of the many medieval fights for Jerusalem.

Teaching the Italian Renaissance epic can be a challenging yet intellectually stimulating experience for both instructor and students. Calvino's famous idea that a classic never stops telling us what it has to say can be applied to the entire Italian epic tradition. With every reading, there exist countless interpretations, new ideas for potential course offerings, and possible avenues of research. The fluidity and lyricism of the poetic form, the evocation of numerous literary traditions, and the complexities of multiple plot structures are significantly underscored by introducing the figurative arts, music, and film inspired by the poetry. In my classes, I help students appreciate the rich dialogue between epic literature and various art forms, emphasizing the inherent qualities of the poetry's open-ended hermeneutics and its potential for interdisciplinarity. Furthermore, visualization and oral experience of the poems enhance student understanding of specific passages, allowing them to further internalize the literature, and, in turn, generate more substantive classroom discussion.

## Notes

1. I prefer Ross's facing-page translation of the *Innamorato* and Reynolds's verse translation of the *Furioso* to promote the musicality and rhythmic qualities of the original poem. When presenting Tasso's *Liberata*, I have used both Nash's prose and Wickert's verse translation. All the translations mentioned above provide

informative introductions and extensive notes and commentary for anglophone readers.

2. See Prampolini, *"Storie di Orlando"*; Fumagalli et al.; Rivoletti; and Bolzoni, *L'* Orlando furioso, a magisterial volume with essays highlighting the *Furioso*'s relationship with the figurative arts.

3. Boiardo repeatedly emphasizes the tension between love and war and the power of love in the *Innamorato.* Some additional short passages instructors may want to consider include 1.28.1–2, 2.8.1, and 3.7.1–2.

4. For the painting, see commons.wikimedia.org/wiki/File:Francesco_del_Cossa_-_Allegory_of_April_-_Triumph_of_Venus_%28detail%29_-_WGA05405.jpg.

5. For further analysis of this fresco see Via 41–44. More generally, Joseph Manca presents an informative essay on Boiardo's poem in relation to Ferrara's visual arts. The author emphasizes the late Gothic style in both Boiardo's writing and Ferrarese fifteenth-century art, both of which contain "a thirst for novelty, romantic escapism, and transportation to an impossible realm (i.e., the marvelous) in which wonderfully improbable things can happen" (262).

6. For the sculpture, see www.7per24.it/wp-content/uploads/2014/10/Giuseppe-Bergomi-Angelica-che-fugge.jpg.

7. For the painting, see it.wikipedia.org/wiki/Simone_Peterzano#/media/File:Peterzano_-_Angelica_and_Medoro.jpg.

8. Additional pictorial representations of Angelica and Medoro that warrant inclusion in class discussion include Matteo Rosselli's *Angelica cura Medoro ferito*, Lorenzo Lippi's *Angelica e Medoro*, and Giovanni Battista Tiepolo's *Angelica e Medoro.*

9. The original 1819 canvas is in the painting collection of the Louvre Museum: en.wikipedia.org/wiki/Roger_Freeing_Angelica_(Ingres)#/media/File:Jean_Auguste_Dominique_Ingres_-_Roger_Delivering_Angelica.jpg.

10. For more information on the Giolito woodcuts, see Everson, "Every Picture" 117–32. See L. Freedman 287–300 for more on Titian. Freedman underscores Angelica's unbound naked body recumbent in a beautiful landscape setting; she identifies Angelica as allegorically personifying *Voluptas* and as the embodiment of a Venus-like temptress. In addition to Doré, Titian, Delacroix, and Giolito, I also recommend including pieces by the seventeenth-century artists Bilivert, Bravo, and Tacca. See Hansen's essay in this volume for a historical perspective of these baroque masters.

11. For the art, see www.nga.gov/content/ngaweb/Collection/art-object-page.12147.html.

12. For Boulanger's painting, see www.studiarapido.it/orlando-furioso-di-ludovico-ariosto/.

13. For important Italian and French seventeenth- and eighteenth-century pictorial representations of the *Liberata*, see Lee, "Poetry." See also Wickert's English translation of the *Liberata* for an informative appendix on the poem's influence on other literary works, art, and music ("Appendix").

14. For Guercino's painting, see www.doriapamphilj.it/roma/en/i-capolavori-doria-pamphilj/giovan-francesco-barbieri-detto-il-guercino/.

15. In canto 19, Tasso highlights the play between day and night in this passage: "e di tenebre il dì già gli s'appanna" ("darkness comes flooding in, the lights recede"; 19.28) and "agiato il porti anzi più fosca sera" ("find shelter for him before nightfall"; 19.115).

16. Although opera (*dramma per musica*) evolved after the epic poems discussed in this essay, its combination of music, drama, visual arts, and dance creates an explosive art form to enliven the original poetry and diffuse the written word as performance.

17. Pieri Luigi Pizzi's 1989 production with the San Francisco Opera starring Marilyn Horne as Orlando and Kathleen Kuhlmann as Alcina has exceptional staging, elaborate costumes and memorable performances. Additionally, *La Compagnia del Madrigale*'s 2011 compact disc offers a repertoire of soothing madrigals inspired by the *Furioso* and sixteenth-century *canzoni*, evoking episodes from the poem's cantos. A booklet with an informative essay by Cecilia Luzzi, entitled "*Orlando furioso* in the Music of the Sixteenth Century," accompanies the recordings.

18. For more on Handel's operas derived from the *Furioso*, see Jorgens; Feinstein.

19. Such a definition calls to mind Mary Louise Pratt's *Imperial Eyes: Travel Writing and Transculturation*, where she discusses "contact zones" as loci of encounters with the other.

20. See Bernardi for the transformation of Ronconi's original theatrical production into a five-episode television series for Radiotelevisione Italiana.

**Evelyn Birge Vitz**

# Teaching Boiardo and Ariosto through Performance

## The Course

I taught Matteo Maria Boiardo's *Orlando innamorato* and Ludovico Ariosto's *Orlando furioso* at New York University in spring 2015, in a course titled Acting Medieval Literature, in which the students perform from all the texts that we read; I have taught this course yearly for almost fifteen years. The texts studied vary from year to year—but we always focus on narrative works that were originally intended for live performance of some kind, not just for silent, private reading. In the spring 2015 course, we read *The Song of Roland* and Chrétien de Troyes's *Yvain; or, The Knight with the Lion*, and then, moving beyond the medieval period for once, we turned to Boiardo and Ariosto—to these two great Renaissance works with such strong grounding in medieval French epic and romance. (Later in the semester we also performed a number of short medieval texts.)

The class is capped at twenty. For the most part, the students in this course come from the Tisch School of the Arts at NYU, many of them from its several drama studios; other students typically come from dramatic literature and medieval and Renaissance studies. The young actors—and the other students as well—bring many and varied skills to the course, but they also learn some new ones since our focus is not on theater or purely on the Middle Ages but rather on performance of narrative and on the arts of storytelling—in particular, the art of the one-man band.

## The Structure of the Course

We spend a week or more talking about each text in general terms. Thus, we discuss historical background, genre, form, plot, characters, and other key features of the work. But even at this preliminary stage, we are already looking toward performance. Thus, for example, we ask: What is the quality of the narrator's or author's voice? How widely does it vary—what is its range? How might one embody each of the various characters in the story? What sorts of gestures and behaviors characterize them? How do they sound—what are their voices like? Would one want props or costumes to do justice to the scenes in which these characters figure?

In the class following this preliminary discussion, each student performs, from memory, roughly twenty to thirty lines from the text; the choice of passage is theirs.[1] After three or four students have performed, we pause to give feedback—always some praise for what was achieved but perhaps also questions concerning performance choices, suggestions for improvement, or thoughts about how the scene might have been performed differently. (If a performance was underprepared, I might ask the student to redo it in the next class.) The performances are video recorded in the classroom by students.

## Working with Boiardo and Ariosto

From Boiardo's *Orlando innamorato*, we took large sections from book 1 in Charles Stanley Ross's translation (the students bought it on *Amazon*) and some sections from books 2 and 3. For Ariosto's *Orlando furioso*, the students read passages taken from the Barbara Reynolds translation, including the opening passages; Alcina's Isle; the siege of Paris; Orlando goes mad; Orlando's madness; hell, paradise, and Orlando's wits; and the very end of the work, to provide closure. This year, during the discussion and performance phase, students also read aloud since both works—especially, we felt, Ariosto—invite that performance mode. We discussed the art of effective reading aloud, including careful preparation and practice, using the book to give authority to the reader, variation in voices (both the storyteller and the characters), and the dramatic deployment of changes in pace and of pauses. The students also wrote in class about the differences between reading Boiardo privately, performing him, and watching him performed; the same for Ariosto.

The students loved both Boiardo and Ariosto. They enjoyed the distinctive voice of each great writer and storyteller as well as the many and varied characters and the twists and turns of the plots; they delighted in the magic and in the mythology. For example, my student David, speaking of Ariosto's epic, said, "It is not only accessible and pertinent, it is also riveting." As he read he was struck by the "overflowing creativity, grandeur and scope of the epic."

But while the students liked reading these epics, they enjoyed performing from them even more: it gave them pleasure, and they also felt that this allowed them to go more deeply into the text and to bring it to life. Student responses included the following:

Coral said, "I enjoyed reading it but performing it was FUN!"

Gwen said, "I feel that it is hard to keep track of all the characters and their interactions while simply reading—I tend to latch on to one story line or another and track it through the text while many of the other characters become a bit muddled. In the performance, every single character comes to life. [All have] their own personalities, behaviors, gestures that imprint their existence within the epic more firmly in my mind."

One student noted, "When I'm reading I'm trying to understand what's happening and where the plot is going in a general sense. It's easy to skim and gloss over the details that make the text so fun. While isolating a small passage for performance it's easier to delve into every nuance and decide how your unique interpretation would play out."

Jared said, "As I approached the text to perform, I had to dig deeper and ask myself a few questions: How do the characters feel toward one another? What do they want? These questions, along with many others, are answered in depth to bring life to the scene. The performance allows us to slow down the scene, maybe creating an entire world from one line and exploring it in depth."

Katrina, who had also been trying to keep track of the "grand scheme of things" in the plot, noted that it was "only through performance, mine and others, that I realized that it was easier and more fun to just hear the stories as they were being told."

The students certainly enjoyed performing from these works, but they all agreed that they liked watching others' performances even more—and there were many fine performances, ranging from the fun and entertaining to the chilling and hair-raising. The students also thought they learned a great deal from the differing interpretations of the text, even of the same scene—and indeed it happened several times that, quite by accident, two students performed the same passage. Connor said, regarding the variety of performances and interpretations, "People were able to find in the very same text moments of horror, pure slapstick, parody, and intense drama. I witnessed things that not for a moment crossed my mind while reading the text." Again, speaking to the variety of interpretations that emerged in performance, Victoria said, with amazement and appreciation, "My Angelica was completely different from Sandra's—and Stephen's was super chill and really cool." They found this variety exciting and eye-opening. (It can take lots of scholarly reading to bring this important concept home to students—performances did it painlessly.)

While they especially appreciated the performance dimensions of the course, the students felt that performing also helped them to read better and more carefully. Jillian noted that the reading of the works can seem "distant" and the "performing feels relevant and current"—but she added that "you need to have one in order to have the other. I can see our performances getting so much better and in part I think it's because we are all becoming more accustomed to reading this kind of text and becoming better at seeing deeper into them. The intellectual experience of reading Boiardo closely lends itself to more well-thought out and better developed characters and scenes."

The students were sensitive both to the strong elements of continuity between the two works—and several expressed their gratitude that Ariosto had chosen to continue and complete Boiardo's work. But they were also very sensitive—perhaps particularly so as performers—to the substantial differences between these epics.

## Results

The students came up with some wonderful performances. For some examples from the class, I invite you to search under Boiardo and Ariosto on the Web site *Performing Medieval Narrative Today* (mednar.org).[2] But let me briefly evoke a handful of performances. From Boiardo, Brooks performed the scene where Orlando sees Angelica for the first time—he played both characters, shifting back and forth, and generating a great deal of appreciative laughter (*Orlando innamorato* 1.1.28–31). Gwen performed the old woman in Castle Cruel who tells how, in revenge against her faithless husband, she killed and chopped up her children (1.8.37–40). Circling the room, Gwen created a compelling and hair-raising performance. Stephen performed the fight between Mandricardo and the giant (3.1.57–63); he sat in a rolling classroom chair, in which, as Mandricardo, he rolled effortlessly around and from which he barely bothered to rise—he was so smooth and such a master with the sword—as he dispatched the giant. He also was the storyteller Ariosto—and he played the ladies as well. A marvelous performance! From Ariosto, Katrina performed part of the scene where Astolfo, who has been transformed into a myrtle bush by the sorceress Alcina when she tired of his love, reveals that he is now the bush to which Ruggiero tied his hippogriff (*Orlando furioso* 6.50–52). With simple but clever costume and props, Katrina was truly that talking myrtle. David first read aloud and later performed from memory another scene from Ariosto, dramatic though told in rapid narrative summary, where Orlando, now completely "furioso," kills shepherds (24.4–7). We saw the madman tear off a shepherd's head "as a man might easily / Pluck blossom or an apple from a tree" (24.5). One student chose to perform a scene from Ariosto as an episode from the TV drama *Game of Thrones*, another as a stand-up comedian, both of them drawing on recorded music and computer special effects.

The students especially enjoyed performing from Boiardo, in whose epic they relished the voices and gestures of so many unforgettable characters as well as the entertaining and enjoyable ways in which Boiardo's voice intervenes with asides, picks up and drops the stories' threads, and opens and ends cantos. In the *Orlando furioso*, they were particularly struck by Ariosto's highly distinctive voice, but fewer scenes, they felt, invited dramatic impersonation since many consist largely of monologues, lengthy description, or rapid narrative summary—the last being especially difficult to act out. But the students enjoyed performing some of the highly memorable scenes. They thought that Ariosto lent himself either to weird and outlandish performances (and we had a few of those) or, on the other hand, to reading aloud with effective gestures and interesting use of voice, and we experimented much with this, to good effect.

## Reflections

These romance epics turned out to be a real delight to read and perform, and I would love to do them again soon. There were, however, complications. They were of two kinds: the first resulted from the length of the texts. Works such as these were intended for audiences with a great deal of leisure. This is a kind of leisure that we—and most college students—just do not have in the course of a semester. Moreover, this was not a class whose primary focus was on Italian Renaissance epic—it had broader and somewhat different goals. Therefore we could not give these grand works the time they so richly deserve. As I pointed out to the students, one would like to be able to read these books during a lengthy but pleasant convalescence, with plenty of time on one's hands.

The second and related issue was the texts' availability. The Ross translation of Boiardo—excellent but expensive—was said to be out of print just as the semester began; some students were able to buy it used online but others not in time (or at all). Therefore they were passing the book back and forth, and a few had to read parts of it in prose translation online. For Ariosto, the marvelous two-volume translation by Reynolds was of course prohibitive for our needs—and we were also a bit more pressed for time at that part of the semester—so I put sections into a course pack, to give them a number of great passages and at least some sense of the whole.

While these complications were somewhat frustrating for them and for me, working with these epics was more than worth it. The students really admired Boiardo and Ariosto—and performing from them greatly enhanced their enjoyment as well as, in my view, their deep appreciation of the works. I'll do it again as soon as I can.

## Notes

1. Visit mednar.org to see some of the performances this course has generated; there is also advice on how to use the site, under "Teaching Tips."

2. On the Web site there are also marvelous performances from Boiardo by Paolo Panaro and from Ariosto by Enrico Messina.

# Part IV

# Comparative Themes and Topics

**Walter Stephens**

# Magic, Monsters, and Marvels: Teaching Renaissance Culture through Italian Romance Epic

A broad interdisciplinary focus on primary texts can stimulate undergraduates and early career graduate students to understand and appreciate the romance epic as an encyclopedia of Italian Renaissance culture. I offer my 400-level seminar Magic, Marvels, and Monstrosity in the Renaissance in English, without prerequisites. The core of the course is built around discussions of Ludovico Ariosto's *Orlando furioso* and Torquato Tasso's *Gerusalemme liberata*. I use my own anthology of related texts, rather than a commercial textbook, to prepare students to enjoy these otherwise daunting narratives. I use relatively few secondary sources to supplement class discussions.

## Objective

Students will learn why the Renaissance has been called "the age of the marvelous." Rediscovery of ancient civilizations, coinciding with an expanded view of the spatial world, inspired Italians to strip the Greeks and Romans of their medieval Christian vestments and imagine them in more authentic guise, while exploration beyond the Pillars of Hercules led to the discovery of previously unknown places, peoples, customs, flora, and fauna (Bynum; Daston and Park; Kenseth).

Italian romance epic reflected the kaleidoscopic richness of these new worlds, becoming a cumulative encyclopedia, part travelogue, part ethnography, part natural history, that underlies modern views of antiquity, the Middle Ages, and the Renaissance. Romance epic enshrined a fantastic world of dreams beneath the mundane realities of court, boutique, and counting house. An expanded repertoire of literary, historical, and philosophical reference and a deeper understanding of philology enabled exploration of how the imagination inspires fiction, fantasy, and even forgery. The two Valla cousins, Lorenzo and Giorgio, provide a useful example of disciplinary kinship. Lorenzo, more durably famous, demolished the forged *Donation of Constantine* (1440) in a masterpiece of philological criticism and oratorical argumentation that brilliantly contested the temporal powers of the papacy. Giorgio, though primarily interested in natural history, translated Aristotle's *Poetics* into Latin in 1498, a decade before its first edition in Greek, and half a century before Francesco Robortello's pioneering commentary (1548) made Aristotle the center of Renaissance poetic theory. In these seemingly unrelated texts, the magical, the monstrous, and the marvelous permeate considerations of verisimilitude or probability in unexpected ways.

## Organization

Under the staffing constraints of our small Italian program, I include Italian majors and novice graduate students in the primary (English) section of the course. Italian majors and graduates form a supplementary discussion section in Italian and perform all written work in Italian.

This course presents the *Furioso* and *Liberata* more broadly than would a graduate seminar. Given the length and complexity of the *Furioso*, I have students read all of cantos 1 through 7 but thereafter reserve discussion only for episodes that typify the course themes, particularly adventure and eros. Unless they have marvelous elements, massed battle scenes and episodes of the Bradamante-Ruggiero subplot are excluded, but a detailed plot handout allows students to envision the poem as a whole. No such guide is necessary for the briefer and more linear *Liberata*, which the students read in full. Tasso's Counter-Reformation theory of the "Christian marvelous" in his *Discourses* (Tasso, *Discourses on the Heroic Poem*; Rhu) allows for an effective contrast between early and late Renaissance attitudes.

## Syllabus

In the English section, the first fourteen meetings situate the course themes in Renaissance intellectual history. Day one comprises a long slide show (posted online afterward) introducing course themes through Renaissance art and artifacts. A required visit to the permanent *Wunderkammer* in the Walters Art Museum of Baltimore supplements slides with realia. In a short (500-word) reaction paper, students imagine themselves as a sixteenth-century observer of the natural, artisanal, and artistic wonders displayed. These preliminary experiences furnish a vivid archive of remembered images students can relate to their readings.

Days 2–14 cover a variety of texts from Latin humanism to vernacular novelle and comedy:

Days 2–3: Marvel: Antiquity Lost and Found entails a book-historical analysis of antiquarian enthusiasm from Petrarch, Boccaccio, and quattrocento humanists to Machiavelli.

Days 4–6: Marvel: The "Dark Ages" and the "Renaissance" contrasts Petrarch's and Lorenzo Valla's philological critiques with the fantastic philology imagined in Francesco Colonna's *Hypnerotomachia Poliphili* and Annius of Viterbo's "antediluvian" forgeries (Stephens, *Giants* 98–138).

Days 7–10: Humanists and Magic explores Giovanni Pico's *Oration on the Dignity of Man*, Giambattista Gelli's *Circe* (dialogues 1 and 10), and Gianfrancesco Pico's *The Witch* (abridged).

Days 11–14: Magic, Marvels, Rationalism centers on marvelous and pseudomagical trickery in the *Decameron*, Antonio Manetti's *Grasso legnaiuolo* (*Fatso the Carpenter*); optional: Bernardo Dovizi da Bibbiena's *Calandra* and Machiavelli's *Mandragola*.

Days 15 through 18 examine *Orlando furioso*; days 19 through 22 the *Gerusalemme liberata*. Days 23 through 26 include comparative discussions, presentations, and discussions of individual projects. Despite tight scheduling, the syllabus works if approached thematically.

Besides the *Furioso* and *Liberata*, both undergraduates and graduate students enjoy Luigi Pulci's *Morgante*, Matteo Maria Boiardo's *Orlando innamorato*, and Teofilo Folengo's *Baldus*. I would not substitute any of these in toto for Ariosto and Tasso, but extracts can replace some of the non-epic works for comparison with the *Furioso* and the *Liberata* (particularly in the majors-graduates section). Moderata Fonte's *Floridoro* allows a gendered comparison of romance ethos.

## Thematic Rationales

### *Magic*

J. R. R. Tolkien and *Harry Potter* distort students' understanding of the intellectual history of magic. While Italian epics treat all varieties of magic as plot devices and usually display some whimsy or satire, magic was persecuted as a menace to Renaissance society. Renaissance magic was quadripartite: necromancy, witchcraft, natural magic, and hermetism.

Most of the magicians in epic are necromancers (*maghi*). Malagigi dominates *Morgante*; Atlante has a major role in Ariosto and Boiardo. Merlinus Coccaius is a character in Folengo's *Baldus* but is also ostensibly its highly unreliable author. Tasso stages two principal necromancers, the apostate Christian Ismeno (*Gerusalemme liberata* 2.2 [canto 2, stanza 2]) and the pagan or Muslim king Idraote (4.20). Female necromancers are *maghe*: in *Orlando furioso*, Melissa, the guardian *maga* of Bradamante, plays a major role; Manto makes an appearance (canto 43) as Melissa's competitor and the tutelary *maga* of Mantua. The sisters Alcina and Morgana are malevolent fairies (*fate*) and *maghe* in both Boiardo and Ariosto. Armida is Tasso's consummate representation of human charm, both sexual and magical. Mainly an herbalist endowed with magical songs (19.112–13), Tasso's Erminia presents a deceptively languid foil to overtly powerful and dangerous Ariostan and Tassian enchantresses.

In pagan antiquity, necromancy involved magically compelling the dead to prophesy the future: aside from Odysseus (*Odyssey* 11) and Simon Magus (Acts 8, etc.), the most famous ancient necromancers were women: the woman of En-dor who foretold Saul's defeat (1 Sam. 28) and Erichtho, who foretold Pompey's (Lucan, *Pharsalia* 6.413). Early church fathers, including Tertullian and Augustine, debunked necromancy by declaring that dead bodies were animated or impersonated by demons. By reverse engineering, a medieval clerical underground of inquisitive exorcists transformed necromancy into demonic nigromancy, or black magic, in which magicians deliberately conjured demons to reveal forbidden knowledge. (Kieckhefer's *Magic in the Middle Ages* is an excellent short introduction.)

Given their clerical origins, Renaissance necromancers were literate and bookish (O. Davies), and their well-read culture appears throughout the epics. Reading her grimoire aloud, Melissa commands demons to impersonate Bradamante's descendants (*Orlando furioso* 3); aloft on the Hippogriff, Atlante jousts "by the book" (4.17); Alcina reads aloud on whaleback to charm fishes and Astolfo (*Orlando innamorato* 2.13.59 [book 2, canto 13, stanza 19]; *Orlando furioso* 6); Armida uses her book to transubstantiate knights-errant into fishes (*Gerusalemme liberata* 10.65–66). To defeat the necromancer Orrilo, Ariosto's Astolfo consults his counter-grimoire; its index handily identifies the means to destroy Atlante's illusory palace (*Orlando furioso* 15.79, 22.16). A similar book enables Carlo and Ubaldo to liberate Rinaldo from Armida's enchanted island (*Gerusalemme liberata* 16.8). No necromancer, Boiardo's Orlando kills the Sphinx after forgetting to consult his guidebook (*Orlando innamorato* 1.5.66–76).

Necromancy and witchcraft were not identical, and female necromancers were not *streghe* ("witches"). Historically, accused witches were rarely literate: though necromancers commanded demons, *streghe* were their dupes and sexual slaves (Stephens, *Demon Lovers*). *Streghe* are rare in Renaissance epic: in canto 13 of *Gerusalemme liberata*, *streghe* and their incubus lovers reputedly celebrate their sabbath in the forest; *streghe* dominate the final books of Folengo's *Baldus* (Capodivacca). Like *streghe*, male witches were supposed to copulate with demons—female succubi rather than male incubi—but male *stregoni* are even rarer than *streghe* in romance epic. Tasso's Ismeno, like Marlowe's Faustus, has witch-like traits but is indisputably a necromancer (*Gerusalemme liberata* 2.1, 13.5–11). The rarity of male witches in romance reflects a rigid societal stereotype; historically, around eighty percent of witchcraft persecutions targeted women. As a supposed fact of Christian society from the early 1400s until nearly 1800 (Levack), witchcraft was too real a preoccupation for the fantasies of romance. Necromancers could be imagined as long ago, far away, erudite, and noble, but witches were stereotypically contemporary, near, and sordidly plebeian. Catholics and Protestants imagined witches as a massive Satanic conspiracy, the enemy subverting Christendom. Thus 30,000 to 60,000 accused witches were executed during three hundred years.

Nondemonic magic rarely figures in Renaissance epic. Ariosto's Logistilla (*Orlando furioso* 6.43) and Tasso's Christian Magus of Ascalona (*Gerusalemme liberata* 14–15) are the only examples presented in enough detail to contrast with necromancers. Like the ideal magus of Giovanni Pico's *Oration*, these figures expand the implications of natural and hermetic magic into an idealistic vision of human intellect and imagination.

Gelli's *Circe* shows a lighter version of Pico's allegorical anthropology, since only one of Ulysses's metamorphosed companions abandons his bestial contentedness for human rationality.

### Nonhuman Wonders

Several characters in Boiardo and Ariosto are humanoid but have wondrous characteristics. Foremost are the *fate*, fairies endowed with seemingly innate magical powers (Green). *Fate* can be fairy-godmothers (Ariosto's Melissa) or approximations of personalized fates (the protectresses of Grifone and Aquilante in *Orlando innamorato* and *Orlando furioso*). Ariosto's magus Orrilo (*Orlando furioso* 15.66) is the son of a *fata* and a *folletto* (imp); his life depends on a single fatal hair. But evil fairies exist: Boiardo's Falerina (*Orlando innamorato* 1.17.8), his and Ariosto's Alcina and Morgana (*Orlando innamorato* 1.25.5; *Orlando furioso* 6.38). These fairies provoke a Carolingian apocalypse in Ariosto's *Five Cantos*, excluded from the *Furioso*.

### Monsters

Monsters in epic rarely conform to the technical definition of natural philosophy, which classified monsters by anomalies of conception, birth, and physical form. The etymology of *monstrum* was explained as demonstration (*monstro/monstrare*) or warning (*moneo/monere*): as with comets and other extraordinary phenomena, monsters were a warning of impending disaster. Epic monsters are fearsome but wondrous, often monstrous without being deformed. Technically, whole species could not be monsters, since they reproduced predictably. But Pliny the Elder described monstrous human races in exotic locales; these endured in medieval anthropology and were illustrated in the *Nuremberg Chronicle* of 1493 (Friedman). Vernacular romance and chanson de geste frequently presented non-Western peoples as monstrous; this prejudice lingers in *Morgante*, in Ariosto's Amazons (*Orlando furioso* 19.57), and in his portrait of Ethiopians in the story of Argia and Anselmo (43.135).

Giants are the most frequently encountered aberrant human specimens in romance epic. They are essential to epic wonder but were also defined technically in natural-scientific discourse and were seriously discussed as races of extinct anthropoids until twentieth-century endocrinology declared them impossible. The real—that is, biblical and classical—giants were unremittingly, even congenitally evil (Ovid, *Metamorphoses* 1; Gen. 6.4, etc.). They occur in Augustine's *City of God* (15.23), in *Inferno* 31, and many other ancient, medieval, and Renaissance texts. Tales of giants' tombs and bones, as in Boccaccio's *Genealogy of the Pagan Gods* (4.68), were inherited from antiquity (Mayor). Reports of gigantic peoples, such as Patagonians, from early modern explorers ensured that the Renaissance epic's fanciful giants reflected a consensus about reality (Stephens, *Giants*).

Homer's cannibal Polyphemus belonged to a society of Cyclopes (*Odyssey*, book 9), but his descendants are usually solitary. Ariosto inherited the anonymous Orco (*Orlando furioso* 17.29) directly from *Innamorato* (3.3.27); Ariosto transforms Homer's blinded Polyphemus into a congenitally sightless, phallomorphic, cannibal herdsman who segregates his human flocks by sex. Ariosto's other giant cannibal, Caligorante (*Orlando furioso* 15.43), resembles Zambardo, the net-bearing giant of *Orlando innamorato* (1.5–6). The giants of medieval French romance are less uniformly evil (Cohen; Huot).

The archetypal giants of Italian romance epic are Pulci's Morgante and Margutte. According to Don Quixote (part 1, ch. 1), Morgante was the only well-behaved giant. He had been evil but converted to Christianity after a divinely inspired dream, like that other giant, Saint Christopher (Stephens, *Giants* 43–50). Presumably, Folengo calls Fracassus, Baldus's giant companion, a descendant of Morgante owing to the affability and loyalty of both colossi to their friends (4.53–59). Margutte was only a half-giant; his stature of 7 cubits (*braccia*) alludes to the evil giants of Genesis 6.4, whose height Bible commentators traditionally gave as 15 cubits. Margutte's "confession of faith" when he meets Morgante (*Morgante* 18.113) shows a perversity parodying that of biblical giants. But Margutte dies by exploding from laughter; Malagigi symbolically resurrects him as Marguttino, a demonic automaton who dupes and cremates the towering pagan giants Falalbacchio and Cattabriga (*Morgante* 24.92–97).

Like Margutte, other large warriors have evil, giant-like traits. Because giants are always enemies of God in Jewish and Christian tradition, Dante includes Nimrod, the "mighty hunter before the Lord," among them (Gen. 10.8–9; *Inferno* 31.46–81). Rodomonte, the most formidable pagan warrior of the two *Orlando* poems, is a descendant of Nimrod and inherits Nimrod's hauberk of dragon hide (*Orlando furioso* 14.118), alluding to Revelation 13. Tasso's Adrasto is enormous (*smisurato*), bestrides an elephant instead of a horse, and wears a hauberk of serpent skin (*Gerusalemme liberata* 17.28), but neither he nor Rodomonte is actually called a giant.

Some nonhumanoid epic beings are mythic monsters. The harpies who torment Senapo (Prester John) in *Orlando furioso* 33 descend from pre-Homeric Greece through Virgil and inherit their demonic aspect from *Inferno* 13. Given their size, whales are depicted as monsters in Pulci, Boiardo, and Folengo. Ariosto's Orca (*Orlando furioso* 10–11) resembles her modern namesake, the "killer whale." Representations of marine creatures in ancient, medieval, and Renaissance sources will help students visualize the sea as a frightening kingdom of monstrosity. Both text and illustrations of Ambroise Paré's *On Monsters and Marvels* provide striking examples of species that, while not technically monsters, were exotic and rare enough to earn the reputation of monstrosity. Ariosto's Hippogriff, born from a mare and a griffin, may look like a monster but is "real and true, a prodigy of Nature," thus neither monster nor "magic creature" (*Orlando furioso* 4.18–19). Ironically, there could be a grain of reality to griffins. Adrienne Mayor conjectures that Herodotus's gold-guarding griffins reflect ancient Scythian lore about fossils of Protoceratops skulls (15–53).

## Angels

Angels and demons (fallen angels) were particularly significant in the Renaissance, owing to the discourse of witchcraft and spirit possession. The theory of demonic witchcraft, consolidated around 1420 to 1460, was particularly concerned with corporeal interaction between humans and demons. Although theologians defined demons as separate (incorporeal) spirits, Aquinas (d. 1274) and others affirmed that demons could confect temporary bodies from air and vapors. These could be given any shape, whether natural (e.g., horse or person) or monstrously composite (as in illustrations of St. Anthony's temptation). In canto 4 of the *Liberata*, the demons that Plutone (Satan in epic guise) summons to his conclave arrive in the shape of sphinxes, centaurs, gorgons, hydras, chimerae, Polyphemuses, and Geryons, while in cantos 13 and 18, Ismeno summons demons who impersonate human souls and animate the trees of Sharon Wood as if they were dryads or Dantean suicides.

Incubi and succubi were functions, not species, of demons and could supposedly sire children of the Devil such as Merlin and Ezzelino da Romano (d. 1258) by stealing semen and injecting it into women. This theory of human/demon intercourse was doubly useful. On a practical level, it was a topos of witches' confessions, which provided supposed epistemological evidence that demons and other separate spirits, including the immortal human soul, were real. Explicit in some witchcraft literature by 1450, the defense of demonic reality grew until the mid-eighteenth century, when Sadducistic and Epicurean materialism became widespread attitudes rather than slanderous accusations and witchcraft became an object of ridicule or mere curiosity (Stephens, *Demon Lovers*). Gianfrancesco Pico, whom Ariosto mentions in *Orlando furioso* 46.17, used his dialogue *Strix* to argue that demons were not imaginary (Stephens, "Skepticism"). When Astolfo strikes the harpies, their bodies, like the demonic lover of Gianfrancesco's Witch, have the consistency of bags packed with stubble (*Orlando furioso* 33.122). Possession of humans by spirits is rare in epics, though Tasso's Solimano welcomes his own invasion by the fury-demon Alecto (*Gerusalemme liberata* 9.11–12), Malagigi makes demons possess horses in *Morgante*, and a necromantic hermit in *Orlando furioso* 2.11 can conjure up an illusory demonic "varlet."

### *Travel and Technology*

Travel is a source of wonder, thanks not only to the Hippogriff and to preternatural horses like Rabicano but owing to human ingenuity and inventions. As Piero Boitani explains, Renaissance epic rewrites the sin of Dante's Ulysses, making him the prototype of Columbus's oceanic exploration (50–57, 73–77). The inquisitor of Pico's *Strix* contends that Spanish and Portuguese navigation is more wondrous and incredible than the bodily intercourse of demons and witches. Earth's Western hemisphere is not the only "other world," however. Voyages to a Celtic-seeming otherworld are especially notable in *Orlando innamorato*; Ariosto's Astolfo travels to the realms of Alcina and Prester John but also visits the moon and a hell that recalls both *Inferno* 5 and its parody in *Decameron* 5.8. Necromancers travel in wondrous vehicles: the chariots of Ismeno and Armida (*Gerusalemme liberata* 10 and 16) are magical. Tasso's Dantesque Fortuna or Occasio ("fatal donzella," *Gerusalemme liberata* 15.3) governs a providential boat. Fantastic travel, both earthly and infernal, animates the final five books of Folengo's *Baldus* (Capodivacca).

Other human technologies are similarly wondrous. Swords, preeminently Orlando's Durindana, and Hector's armor, which Ruggiero appropriates when he kills Mandricardo, have preternatural qualities. Rinaldo's wondrous new shield in *Gerusalemme liberata* 17 recalls the one Hephaestus made for Achilles. These characteristics reflect not only the superhuman expertise of smiths such as Hephaestus and the legendary Wayland of Germanic myth but also the fantastical creations of fifteenth- and sixteenth-century armorers (Springer). The unchivalrous harquebus of Ariosto's Cimosco (*Orlando furioso* 9.28) threatens to end the utility of armor and negatively echoes the importance of cannon to Ariosto's Este patrons (14.2–9). Major museum collections of arms and armor and illustrated catalogs are valuable visual correctives to distorted representations in modern popular culture. Romances celebrate the wonder of figural art: frescoes and bas-reliefs adorn the tombs of Merlin (3.10), Atlante (36.58), and Sveno (*Gerusalemme liberata* 8.38–40); Melissa's demons bring the prophetic canopy Cassandra wove for Hector, to adorn Ruggiero and Bradamante's wedding bed (*Orlando furioso* 46.77); Armida's garden and labyrinth display the superhuman artistry of her demonic servants (*Gerusalemme liberata* 15–16).

Writing as a technology is pervasively present in Renaissance epic. The grimoires of various necromancers celebrate the power of the written word over the limitations of reality. Mysterious writings abound: when Tasso's Tancredi penetrates the enchanted wood, he finds an inscription in Egyptian hieroglyphics (*Gerusalemme liberata* 13.38). The contiguity of history and forgery is a venerable joke: comic poets cite "Turpino" tongue-in-cheek as their source, spoofing the forged twelfth-century Latin Roland chronicle. Pulci provides an extravagantly ridiculous source for the death of Margutte (*Morgante* 19.152–54), passing the original through an improbable eight successive translations as "through Nimrod's very tower it passed" (19.154). In a prefatory letter, Folengo applies the commonplace of the rediscovered manuscript to the entire *Baldus*, providing the work an absurd odyssey of adventures and duelling author-editor-forger-plagiarist figures. Suspicious writings abound on the moon: St. John denounces writers as liars and history as sycophantic forgery but admits that his writings also glorified his patron (Christ) and earned a reward (*Orlando furioso* 35.25–29).

Modern readers can easily overlook the lingering awe Renaissance authors expressed for the art of writing. Following classical precedent, Ariosto and Tasso habitually compare writing and weaving as wondrous technologies (*Orlando furioso* 2.30, 34.90; *Gerusalemme liberata* 1.2, 19.61). Polydore Vergil's encyclopedia *De inventoribus rerum* declares that "only the use of letters makes memory endure, and protects things worthy of memory from all damage of forgetfulness"; thus he treats the history of writing "before anything else" (*On Discovery* 77). The writings of Petrarch, Boccaccio, Poggio, Machiavelli, and other humanists are permeated with this reverence, which endured well into the nineteenth century (Stephens, "Writing").

Given modern students' diminishing contact with printed books, anyone teaching magic and marvel in the Renaissance epic should have the class visit a rare book collection, no matter how small. Along with the experience of a *Wunderkammer* (even online), engagement with centuries-old books as material objects provides powerful motivation for undergraduates. Museums may be similarly unfamiliar to them, and a trip might be arranged. Various other activities can be integrated, given adequate time. In fall 2015, my course hosted a lecture and demonstration by a professional swordsmith and armor maker.

## Written Assignments

I interview students and tailor term paper topics to their individual interests, requiring a prospectus, draft, and final version. In 2015, I received expository essays on witchcraft, necromancy, imitation of Plautine comedy, representations of Muslim women in the *Decameron*, and doubt and disbelief in the *Decameron*. I also offered a creative writing option: one undergraduate turned the episode of Ginevra, Ariodante, Dalinda, and Polinesso (*Orlando furioso* 5–6) into a stage play; another converted Isabella's last hours (29) into a short story. The year 2016 brought literary histories of the hippogriff, tricksters, and classical and Renaissance antecedents of the superhero as well as studies of Armida, Clorinda, women warriors, and Ariosto's society of "homicidal women" (20). A graduate student is developing his 2016 essay on heresy and carnivalesque in a sixteenth-century manuscript from Lucca into his dissertation prospectus. In earlier iterations of the course, an Italian major from a nonwestern culture developed his term paper on philosophy in Gelli's *Circe* into a senior thesis; a graduate student scripted, cast, and filmed an English-language production of Calandrino and the heliotrope (*Decameron* 8.3); and another translated *Mandragola*'s intermezzi into English verse.

Janet Levarie Smarr

# Ariosto's *Orlando furioso* and Madness in Renaissance Drama

Madness fascinates everyone and draws students to explore earlier texts than they might otherwise read. It has many facets: religious, moral, medical, and social. Twenty-five years ago, inspired by the realization that many of the greatest Renaissance works deal with madness, I taught a comparative literature seminar on madness in Renaissance culture, addressing works that ranged from Erasmus and Ludovico Ariosto in the early 1500s to Shakespeare and Cervantes roughly a century later. Changing universities and shifting into a theater department, I have modified the course's focus mainly to English drama in the early seventeenth century. The English plays, arranged by topic and usually, but not consistently, by chronology, are Shakespeare, *King Lear*, 1605 (real and fake madness); John Webster, *Duchess of Malfi*, 1612–13 (sin and the sick society); Shakespeare and John Fletcher, *Two Noble Kinsmen*, 1613–14 (women's madness); John Ford, *The Lover's Melancholy*, 1628–29 (theatrical medicine and the doctor); Philip Massinger, *A Very Woman*, licensed 1634 (medicine and the doctor, plus gender differences); Thomas Middleton and William Rowley, *The Changeling*, 1621 (the asylum).[1]

Despite the focus on drama, Ariosto's *Orlando furioso* remains an early reading.[2] I do not claim that Ariosto's poem directly influenced English drama, although Harrington's English translation was available by 1591,[3] and some Englishmen could read Italian; rather, I let the poem establish issues and features that can be recognized in the plays.[4]

I introduce early on the theory of humors: chapter 1 of Lawrence Babb's *The Elizabethan Malady* presents the humors, while chapter two discusses causes, effects, and cures of melancholy; primary sources include selections from André Du Laurens (Andreas Laurentius), Timothy Bright, and Robert Burton's *Anatomy of Melancholy*, which I use as a reference work for the class. Confusingly, Burton, Bright, and Du Laurens, use "melancholy" to refer to many types of madness as well as to the types specifically associated with the humors of melancholy or black bile. All suggest a mutual influence of the mental and physical: mental or emotional states are shaped by the imbalance of humors and by other physical influences such as weather, light levels, exercise, and sleep; emotional stress can, in turn, unbalance the humors. The association between types of madness and different humors becomes useful in our analysis of characters, while the interconnection of the physical and mental establishes a foundation for discussions of causes and cures. On the one hand, it implies that appropriate diet, exercise, and environment can rectify instabilities. On the other, it indicates the need for helping the sufferer deal with real causes of distress.[5]

In discussing physical and emotional causes of madness, I bring in Cicero's *Tusculan Disputations* 3.5–6, which considers whether one is morally responsible for maintaining a healthy balance or whether even the wise man can become mentally as well as physically ill. A person's moral responsibility for their mental imbalance informs many of our plays and lingers today in the stigma attached to mental illness. Students need to become aware, furthermore, of the difference between mind and soul. Du Laurens's second chapter asserts that the soul remains incorruptible even when the mind is beset by delusions and causeless fears. Bright, first a physician and later a clergyman, discusses the differences between physiological mental illness and the effects of sin, between a mind perturbed and a soul already suffering damnation (ch. 33).

Connected to the question of moral responsibility is a recurring image, going back to Plato, of the individual as analogous to a state well or poorly governed. Middleton and Rowley's *The Changeling* puns:

> *Jasperino*. Tush, I know what physic is best for the state of mine own body.
> *Diaphanta*. 'Tis scarce a well-govern'd state, I believe. (1.1.138–39)

Babb cites passages from Thomas Wright's *The Passions of the Minde* (1601) that compare the passions to unruly servants and the imagination to "a deceitfull Counsellor" (17–18; see also Kitzes, who develops this topic). Reason is supposed to govern this little state of man but can succumb to misinformation or outright rebellion. Yet the image cuts two ways, suggesting that political revolt is madness.

The humoral differences supposed between men and women produce different types of mental and emotional disorder: men, being hotter, are more prone to choleric behavior; women, cooler, more subject to "mopishness."[6] Gender differences in the representation and treatment of madness are a recurring topic of discussion regarding the drama *Hamlet. Two Noble Kinsmen* and *A Very Woman* contain both male and female insanity, distinct in its gendered manifestation and treatment—but that topic leads us away from the *Orlando*.

As Ariosto's title draws obviously from Seneca's *Hercules furens*, we begin with Seneca's drama.[7] Although each hero's madness has a divine cause, both raise the question of whether emotional excess led to the violent delusional fit or where madness actually begins. The stepfather is horrified when Hercules comes to the altar with bloody hands, but Hercules finds this human blood a fitting offering; is this already madness? Is Hercules's strange prayer, spoken as if he were Jupiter controlling the cosmos, insane hubris: "Ipse concipiam preces / Iove meque dignas. Stet suo caelum loco / tellusque et aequor" ("I shall pronounce prayers, ones worthy of Jove and of myself. May heaven stand in its place, and earth and sea"; 926–29)? Once his hallucinations begin, Hercules doubts Jupiter's promise and threatens to seize heaven by force; his stepfather exclaims, "Infandos procul / averte sensus; pectoris sani parum, / magni tamen, compesce dementem impetum" ("Banish those monstrous notions! Restrain the crazy impulses of your mind, which is great to be sure, but scarcely sane"; 973–75). Is insanity inflicted on a good man by the goddess, or does it well up from within? Juno claims to be using Hercules' own qualities to destroy him (68–70, 89–90). His self-confidence and ambition make him vulnerable.

After his return to sanity, overwhelmed by the horrid massacre of his family, Hercules must be persuaded to live with himself for his final labor. The move from Thebes to Athens for purification presents the topoi of dysfunctional versus well-governed states and of violent passions versus rational control; this pair of cities reappears in *The Two Noble Kinsmen* with similar significance.

When we ask what caused Orlando's madness, Ariosto's poem gives us two answers. The first (canto 23) is that Orlando is overwhelmed by the discovery of Angelica's love for Medoro. After increasingly desperate attempts to ignore this knowledge, Orlando, likened to a bottle neck that prevents its contents from pouring forth (23.112–13), is unable to release the turmoil within him and explodes into violent insanity (23.129). Emotional trauma is aggravated by his failure to eat or sleep for three days (23.132). Here madness is explained as a combination of emotional and physiological stresses. The second answer is given to Astolfo by St. John (34.62–66): God inflicted Orlando's madness as punishment for his betrayal of Charlemagne's cause, which the knight abandoned to pursue a pagan woman. Thus we ask, as with Hercules, whether madness arises from within or without and at what point it begins: is the love that motivates Orlando's departure from the French camp when he is needed already a kind of madness? Are the causes of insanity natural or supernatural? Is Orlando morally responsible for his insanity?

Similar questions arise for *King Lear*, which we read directly after the *Orlando*, and for *The Two Noble Kinsmen*. When is Lear mad: already in the first scene, where Kent calls him "mad" (1.1.147–48) or only when his verse turns into incoherent prose? In *Two Noble Kinsmen* when the wooer finds the jailer's daughter, like Lear, decked with weeds and, like Ophelia, in danger of drowning, she is clearly insane. Yet earlier in the day, her father, noticing with annoyance that she was answering foolishly, had not labeled this behavior "mad" (4.1.37–41). When she releases Palamon, an important political prisoner, from her father's jail, is she already in some sense mad? In a more rational moment, she feels guilty that she has probably caused her father to be hanged (3.2.22–24). For both her and Lear, as for Orlando, emotional turmoil aggravated by a lack of sleep and food causes increasing incoherence and delusion. All three cases involve grief at an unrequited love, erotic or parental, but that love also provokes a loss of good judgment. Ariosto links love with madness in his opening comment to canto 24, and Orlando at the restoration of his wits is freed from his love for Angelica (39.61).[8]

Orlando's attempts to fend off the truth provokes another question: can delusion be a good thing when it protects us from emotional trauma, or is the honest truth always better, regardless of consequences? Rinaldo refuses the host's invitation to drink from a cup that would reveal whether his wife is faithful and is praised for this avoidance (43.6–10); seeking to know about a woman's infidelity is as crazy as seeking to fend off that knowledge. Hercules too was protected temporarily by delusion; Seneca's chorus comments before he awakes:

> pelle insanos fluctus animi,
> redent pietas virtusque viro.
> vel si potius
> mens vesano concita motu,
> error caecus qua coepit eat:
> solus te iam praestare potest
> furor insontem
>
> Drive the waves of madness from your spirit,
> may the hero's goodness and heroism return.
> Or rather
> may your mind still race with insanity;
> may blind error continue as it began:
> the only thing now that can offer you
> innocence is madness. (1092–97)

So too Meleander, in *The Lover's Melancholy*, observes:

> Whilst I am frantic,
> Whilst throngs of rude divisions huddle on,
> And do disrank my brains from peace and sleep,
> So long I am insensible of cares. (Ford 4.2.94–97)

But truth eventually prevails.

Orlando's mad actions include the scattering of his armor and clothing (23.132–33) and the indiscriminate eating of raw as well as cooked food (24.12–13). His reason lost, he becomes more animal than human. Ariosto's comment in 24.2 compares the mad lover to someone lost in a forest.[9] The forest into which maddened Orlando runs (23.125, 129) parallels Lear's heath; both have left civilization to roam in wilderness. King Lear repeats the scattering of clothes and reversion to the "bare, forked animal" as he tries to remove his clothing (3.4.111–12), inspired by the nakedness of Poor Tom. In *The Duchess of Malfi*, Ferdinand's lycanthropy is the ultimate animalization.

Orlando's neglect of his horses' needs parallels his neglect of his own (30.8 and 11–14). Control of horses is a recurring motif in Ariosto's poem, which can be readily connected to Plato's image of the charioteer reason and his horses of desire and anger (*Republic*, bk. 4). The image of Orlando carrying or dragging the horse reflects an upside-down psyche

(29.69).[10] When Ruggiero's friends, rescuing him from suicidal depression, put him back on his horse (46.46–47), students see the action as a restoration of rational control. When in John Webster's *Duchess of Malfi* Antonio is twice praised for his horsemanship (1.2.8–9, 60–65), are we to recognize an evocation of this topos?

Just as Orlando's emotional explosion results from the bottle neck that prevented safer venting, so too Lear invites explosion by bottling up his grief:

> touch me with noble anger,
> And let not women's weapons, water-drops,
> Stain my man's cheeks! . . .
> . . . You think I'll weep;
> No, I'll not weep:
> I have full cause of weeping, but this heart
> Shall break into a hundred thousand flaws
> Or ere I'll weep. O fool! I shall go mad. (2.4.278–81, 285–89)

Lear's gendering of emotions, while aligned with the science that saw men as hotter and women as moister, denies him the outlet of grief that might have balanced him. Thus the scattering of clothing or armor has a double valence: an effect of emotional explosion as well as a return to animal nakedness. Ruggiero's scattering of armor in his haste to rape Angelica (10.115–11.1) becomes a comic variation on this trope, illustrating the frenzy of lust. Unsurprisingly, the image of controlling a horse appears here too.

Orlando's counterpart is Rodomonte. Both physically invulnerable but emotionally overthrown, they abandon human society for a parallel cause: their love object has asserted herself as a subject with her own desires and chosen someone else.[11] Furious, Rodomonte leaves the camp, seeking "le selve e le rive più sole" ("the remotest wood or shore") where, like a wounded bull, "muggir non cessa . . . né però scema l'amorosa rabbia" ("he bellows ceaselessly . . . without assuaging his love-pangs"; 27.111).[12] He too becomes an animal seeking the solitary wilderness. His wounded pride turns into ranting misogyny, as will King Lear's.

We first meet Rodomonte in the *Furioso* not as a lover but as a furious fighter at the siege of Paris. Whereas Orlando is normally the consummate Christian gentleman, Rodomonte is demonic. He curses God (14.117) and wears the armor of his ancestor Nembrot, who built the tower of Babel, and whom he resembles as "superbo e furibondo" ("proud and rabid";

14.118–19). In his final appearance, he attacks Ruggiero for becoming Christian, opposing Ruggiero's "senno e valor" ("prudence and valour"; 46.133) with "a maggior rabbia, a più furor si mosse" ("increasingly maddened rage and fury"; 46.121; my trans.). In the epic's last stanza, he dies "bestemmiando" ("cursing"); thus his entrance and exit from the poem are marked by cursing, a sign of damnation.

Canto 14 describes Rodomonte's reckless savagery: not only does he terrify the Christian army by leaping over the city walls and killing the soldiers inside, he also causes mass death among his own troops, who are caught in the moat and burn to death: "la misera gente che peria / nel fondo per cagion de la sua guida" ("the poor wretches perishing in the fosse through the fault of their leader"; 14.134). Ironically, love-maddened Rodomonte is later compared to the invaded city; like the Parisians helpless against Rodomonte, he cannot rid himself of his distress: "Di ripararsi il misero non vede, / da poi che gli nimici ha ne la terra" ("The poor wretch could see no defense since the enemy was within the citadel"; 28.87–88).

The vivid presentation of war's collective insanity extends the idea of madness beyond the individual. Ariosto opens canto 15 contrasting leaders who protect their followers with those whose recklessness causes their destruction. So too *The Duchess of Malfi* opens by praising the healthy government of France and then introduces the sick government, secular and ecclesiastical, of Calabria. Burton notes that societies, like persons, can be diseased (1.79). The heads of state who spread corruption embody Burton's "immoderate in lust, hypocrites, . . . of no religion, but in show . . . ringleaders oftentimes of all mischief" (1.81–82). Webster demonstrates how rulers affect the health of the entire realm. Although Ferdinand murders his sister to purge the corrupted blood of his lineage, it is ultimately the killing of both duke and cardinal that cleanses and restores the society.

Orlando in his insanity massacres neither family nor followers but peasants. Modern readers have the uncomfortable but probably correct feeling that this combat was seen as a comic parody of epic battles. The class discusses what might make this scene, or violent madness generally, comic rather than horrifying. Is Orlando's madness comic?[13] His increasingly desperate defense against the blatant truth is funny. Is his treatment of horses—sorry as we may feel for them—humorous? His proposal to trade a dead horse for a live one evokes laughter. Is his swinging one peasant to knock down others funny? Would Ariosto's courtly audience have viewed it that way? We must lack concern for horses and peasants to find their slaughter comic. Other characters feel fear or pity for Orlando, but they have to deal with him; readers view him from a safety that enables laughter. The scene in Ford's *The Lover's Melancholy* where the raving Meleander frightens his household with a poleax humorously imitates Hercules and Orlando (4.2); students analyze what makes it comic.

*Two Noble Kinsmen* offers another example of comic insanity. Students argue whether the two knights merit being called insane, but their rapid shifts from affection to hostility provoke laughter. "Men are mad things," says Emilia in that scene, not yet aware of her observers (2.2.126). The play reverses norms, for we respond more seriously to the deepening melancholy of the lower-class jailer's daughter than to the comically irrational behavior of the nobles. Yet the country folk consider themselves made—that is, their success assured—by her joining their morris dance (3.5.69–73); her madness will increase their entertainment value and profit. Is the noble kinsmen's violent rivalry as amusing as mad dancing? Is the irrational frenzy of love comic in itself?

Besides characters whose fury threatens violence, Ariosto presents a figure of extreme melancholy in the suicidal Ruggiero. Convinced that he has lost forever—and by his own doing—the chance of marrying Bradamante, Ruggiero, like other madmen, wanders off into the countryside and aggravates his mental state by neither eating nor sleeping for the usual three days (46.21–28). But this is not an explosive fury with scattered arms. Rather, Ruggiero lies on the ground, fully armed, weeping continually and waiting to die.

The pair of mad types, one suffering from choleric frenzy, the other from suicidal melancholy, recurs in several plays. When the new enlarged Bedlam was built in 1667, a set of statues at its gate represented the raging and the melancholy madmen, but that motif had long and frequently been visible on stage. King Lear's raging threats are coupled with Gloucester's melancholy and attempted suicide. Lear and Gloucester are parallel figures: fathers who harm their innocent child and are deceived in trusting the other children, but the pairing of choler and melancholy contrasts their reactions. The Duchess of Malfi's two brothers are another such pair. Ferdinand, acknowledging his "choller" (2.5.19), rages so extremely that his brother exclaims: "You fly beyond your reason. . . . Come, put yourself / In tune. . . . Are you stark mad?" (2.5.62, 80–81, 87). Meanwhile the cardinal is described as "a mellancholly Church-man" (1.2.76–77). Bosola labels Ferdinand's guilt-ridden lycanthropy "a fearful judgment" by God (5.2.92–93), and the cardinal's melancholy similarly reveals a guilty conscience: entering with a book, the typical image of the melancholic, he ponders a question about hellfire (5.5.1–4). Unlike Lear and Gloucester, this pair's madness is marked as damnation.

Ford's doctor in *The Lover's Melancholy* has two patients: the first, a melancholy prince, enters with a book. The doctor accuses him of wallowing in his illness: "A book! Is this the early exercise / I did prescribe? Instead of following health, / Which all men covet, you pursue your disease" (2.1.48–50). Meleander, on the other hand, enters in a rage with a poleax. These diverse reactions have the same cause: the loss of Eroclea, the prince's fiancée and Meleander's daughter. Like Ruggiero, both are cured by her return. Meanwhile, the doctor employs elaborate means first to diagnose the prince, then to bring the old man to his senses. The pair thus highlights the doctor's professional virtuosity, a new aim for this persistent trope. The highly theatrical nature of his treatments implies that the glorification of the doctor is also a glorification of theater, suggesting its curative function—and an audience in need of its aid.

Meleander and Lear need a double treatment: physical and emotional. The doctor takes care of the physical problems—for example, with soporifics—but only the return of the daughter, safe and loving, can treat the emotional cause of derangement. So too Ruggiero must be given food, drink, and rest, but the cause of his depression is removed by Leon's offer to restore Bradamante. *The Duchess of Malfi*'s doctor fails because the cause of madness, sin and divine judgment, remains unaddressed. In Philip Massinger's *A Very Woman*, the doctor single-handedly treats and cures both physical and psychological trauma, caring for Martino as a physician and donning a friar's costume to rescue him from spiritual despair. Thus Caroline plays gave the doctor a new starring role. Nonetheless, representations and understandings of madness, including the contrast of frenzy and depression, the interaction of emotional and physical causes, and the combination of moral, religious, and scientific explanations, continued to share *Orlando furioso*'s models.

## Notes

1. I have varied this ten-week syllabus from time to time. Occasionally I include Dekker, *The Honest Whore, Part 1*, the first English play to put an asylum on stage; the play also features a patience so extreme that it is considered by other characters a form of madness.

2. We cannot read the entire work. My selections follow a few main characters and lines of plot and raise issues relevant to the drama: In week 1, we read cantos 1.1–4.50, 10.90–12.65, 13.45–14.9, 14.68–15.15, 18.156–19.42, 22–24; in

week 2, 27.1–30.16, 33.96–35.30, 38.37 to the end of 39, 42.97–43.49, 44.35 to the end of the poem.

3. Already in 1592, Robert Greene produced his play *The Historie of* Orlando furioso, albeit with considerable changes to the story (Chapman). See also Marangoni on theatrical elements in the *Orlando*, Cairneross on the poem's use by Shakespeare, and Nicholson for its use by commedia dell'arte performers.

4. Useful essays on madness in the *Orlando* include Weaver, "Reading"; Valesio; Donato; Anconetani; Di Tommaso; Calabritto; Segre.

5. This double aspect continues in psychology and psychiatry, one exploring emotional issues, the other offering medicinal aids. I want students to understand the scientific views of the early modern era but also how those views, outlandish as they may now seem, could be accepted for nearly two millennia by intelligent and experienced people.

6. This word, which shows up in *Two Noble Kinsmen* for the jailer's daughter (3.2.25), was frequently used by clients of a seventeenth-century doctor to describe the behavior of female patients. MacDonald analyzes the doctor's notebooks in chapter 4 of his *Mystical Bedlam*, "Popular Stereotypes of Insanity."

7. On Ariosto's sources see Romizi; Rajna, *Fonti*. Kromm discusses visual images of madness.

8. Donato notes, "It is important to underscore the fact that Orlando's madness differs from desire only in degree and not in nature or in essence" (55). Burton has much to say about love melancholy, and students find his discussion intriguing.

9. Valesio points to the analogous example of Tristan in the woods (203–04).

10. Cozzarelli contrasts Orlando's and Astolfo's relations with their steeds.

11. Doralice thus parallels Angelica; for her choice and Rodomonte's response, see 27.105–11.

12. I use the translation by Guido Waldman because that of Barbara Reynolds either fails to translate these phrases or translates them in a roundabout and less clear way; Waldman's translation is more accurate, clear, and succinct.

13. Bakhtin comments on "the special role that the motif of madness played in the figure of the 'comic Odysseus'" and on the popularity of the comic Hercules: "Hercules, the monstrous glutton, the playboy, the drunk and scrapper, but especially Hercules the madman—such were the motifs that lent a comic aspect to his image." But Bakhtin's idea that "[t]he comic Hercules is one of the most profound folk images for a cheerful and simple heroism" does not seem applicable to Ariosto's complex, aristocratic and ironic poem ("From the Prehistory" 54, 55).

**Susan Gaylard**

# Learning to Perform as a *Cavaliere*: *Orlando furioso* and Signs of Status

This essay focuses on teaching *Orlando furioso* in the literary and material cultural contexts of sixteenth-century courts; it draws from undergraduate seminars taught in Italian on symbols of authority in late medieval and Renaissance Italy. The primary goal of the seminar is to encourage students to interrogate relations between political power and forms of representation. By studying a range of texts and artifacts from around 1340 to the mid-sixteenth century, and by taking responsibility for their own visual analyses, students see continuities in the imagery of status and learn how Italians used material objects to fashion their public identity. In reading Ludovico Ariosto's *Orlando furioso* and Baldassare Castiglione's *Cortegiano* (*Book of the Courtier*), we examine the shifting meaning of the word *cavaliere*—from arms-bearing knight in the twelfth century to courtier in the Renaissance—in the context of humanist ideas of education. In order to show the centrality of performance in Ariosto's and Castiglione's projects of educating knights, the class focuses on objects that enhance aristocratic display.

Much of the course helps students develop their own critical tools for understanding how material artifacts (like paintings, coins, clothing, and so on) can elucidate literary texts. Each week's reading is tied to a research project on an art object or aspect of material culture. After choosing a topic (e.g., armor), students learn to find general information through library resources (from reliable sources rather than *Wikipedia*), high-quality images (from databases like *ARTstor*), and recent scholarship (from a range of databases, depending on the object of study). Over the course of the term, students choose and write a critique of a scholarly article; in a class presentation they synthesize both general information and their new expertise on recent scholarship; and they discuss the relevance of the topic to the week's literary readings. The research presentations build on each other and are closely integrated into midterm and final exams.

## Objects, the Noble *Cavaliere*, and the New Elite

We use Boccaccio's fourteenth-century story of the aristocratic Federigo degli Alberighi to introduce the interrelated ideas of the noble *cavaliere* and the ideal nobleman's education (*Decameron* 5.9). This tale focuses on the depletion of Federigo's own wealth and status for the sake of his true love. While Federigo's sacrifice seems to highlight his true nobility and worth, it also problematizes noble consumption as heedless dissipation. The symbolism of objects such as Federigo's falcon gains force when supported by visuals depicting the hunt: in Ambrogio Lorenzetti's *Allegory of Good Government*, completed around 1340, just a few years before Boccaccio's *Decameron*, richly clad aristocrats on horseback with their falcons contrast starkly with the peasants to whose status Federigo was reduced. As the first research topic of the term, the Lorenzetti frescoes need not be assigned to a student; instructors can model the ideal project for the class.

Boccaccio's tale leads us to consider the new mercantile elite emerging at the end of the Middle Ages, epitomized in book 3 of Leon Battista Alberti's *Libri della Famiglia* (*On the Family*; 1434), which focuses on how to accumulate and preserve wealth. The significance of increasing displays of wealth is easier to understand when seen alongside what Luke Syson and Dora Thornton have called "objects of virtue": expensive signs of status that circulated in Renaissance Italy. There are many potential research presentations to assign here—for example, on coin-collecting, portrait medals, birth trays, and marriage chests. Such presentations open various avenues of exploration: the link between coin collecting, portrait medals, and the so-called rise of the individual; birth trays as a symbol of status; the often elaborate imagery on marriage chests and its purpose. Such emergent status objects are rather different from the self-consciously chivalric symbols sought by Ariosto's knights (swords, horses, helmets, armor—e.g., *Orlando furioso*

1.10–63), and, as the course continues, interrogating these differences enhances appreciation for the parodic force of Ariosto's project. At the same time, it is helpful for students to understand both the pedagogical value often invested in signs of wealth as well as *Orlando furioso*'s frequent mocking of those signs.

## Objects and Humanistic Education

Alberti's advice on husbandry derives from the display of status, which represents one approach toward humanistic education projects. Fifteenth-century writers advocated learning from one's reading, following examples from history to become in turn an exemplar for future generations.[1] Donatello's *Gattamelata* statue in Padua (c. 1445–53) and Andrea del Verrocchio's *Bartolomeo Colleoni* in Venice (1483–88) show idealized virile heroes on horseback, clarify the idea of imitating the ancients, and document the emerging trend of commissioning a statue to oneself. While in themselves exceptional, these sculptures help students recognize the frequent conflation of the idealized autonomous and heroic medieval *cavaliere* with classically derived humanistic models and ideas. In order to help students understand the value of educating by visual example, one could ask how viewers were supposed to react to these statues. Why, moreover, were the statues considered controversial when they were commissioned?

The negative reactions to these statues help to clarify the *Furioso*'s ridiculing of the heroic *cavaliere* and his knightly education. The pursuit of Angelica becomes absurd as sworn enemies team up on a single horse (1.23), and the initial object of desire—the woman—is successively substituted when knights seek further objects: a helmet, a sword, a horse, the woman. Ariosto's knights actually define themselves through the lack of accoutrements that should mark their status, often allowing their desire for objects to threaten any claim to knightly identity (as in 1.60–72). This parody of signaling identity through artifacts ties in well with student projects on the luxurious status objects that first gained currency in the fifteenth century.

## New Political and Material Realities: From Knight to Courtier

Ariosto is often taught alongside his historical context: the culture of the northern Italian courts as well as the political crises and devastating wars that turned the Italian peninsula into a battleground for foreign conflicts, starting with the French invasion of Naples in 1494 (at the invitation of Lodovico

Sforza, Duke of Milan) and culminating with the sack of Rome by Charles V's imperial troops in 1527. The intellectual elite who served as poets, secretaries, and ambassadors were dispersed from one court to another and continually forced to change allegiances. My students, however, often ask, What is a court? Andrea Mantegna's *Camera Picta* (*Camera degli Sposi*) in Mantua offers an excellent background for understanding Ariosto's struggle with patronage and the *Furioso*'s many snide comments about patrons (perhaps most famously in the episode of Astolfo on the moon, 35.3–30). The frescoes show both an idealized visual depiction of the duke, his family, and courtiers and the kinds of enigmatic symbolic imagery that became increasingly typical in the sixteenth century. The frescoes thus usefully correlate with the simultaneous visual legibility and illegibility that is problematized by Ruggiero's education trajectory. Students might reflect on the differences between Mantegna's courtiers—depicted in static and decorative fashion, wearing modish clothes that seem to constitute a kind of livery—and Ariosto's knights, who race around autonomously, dressed in individualized armor.

Considering the striking differences between Ariosto's knights and the idealized court of the *Camera Picta*, it is also helpful to investigate the evolution of firearms and their impact on war in this remarkably volatile period: the swords, shields, and other weaponry frequently lost and sought in the *Furioso* elucidate how quickly and dramatically the art of war was changing.[2] Armor in particular often fascinates students, as it changed in style and function from utilitarian twelfth-century styles to sixteenth-century ornament. Indeed, by the time of Ariosto's writing, armor was largely decorative, since it did not provide reliable protection from the new firearms. Students' research projects immediately beg the question, Why are Ariosto's knights perpetually dressed in, or seeking to be dressed in, armor? Viewing varieties of armor from around 1200 to 1550 helps students understand both the kind of identity confusion possible in Martano's theft of Grifone's armor (37.11–35) and the many moments in which Bradamante is assumed to be a man (because she is clad in armor—e.g., 1.60), as well as the nostalgic mockery inherent in a sixteenth-century text in which all the knights are presumed to be clad in armor most of the time.

## Identity, Appearances, and Deception

The *Furioso*'s continual emphasis on the representation of identity and status through material objects throws into relief Ruggiero's failed education as a worthy knight (2.30–55, 4.1–50, 6.17–81, 7, 8.1–21, 10.35–58, 10.112–15), which is framed through the impossibility of reading appearances.[3] Ruggiero's initial redemption depends on both belief in false appearances (Bradamante's deception of Brunello; Melissa's disguise as Atlante) and the revelation of truth beneath deceptive exteriors (Bradamante's ability to see through Atlante's visual trickery; Alcina's unveiling as a hag). The multiplying contradictions suggest that, in a visually deceptive world, it is impossible to embrace the humanist ideal of following history's examples—the idea of being inspired by monuments to become a monument oneself. Indeed, Ruggiero ultimately nullifies his education and loses his newly acquired knightly accoutrements (11.1–21), ending up where he began: one of many knights trapped in an enchanted palace, chasing visions of his own desires (12.17–22).

In addition to the status objects sought by knights in the text, the materiality of the poem's early editions offers further insights into the representation and questioning of political power. A student research project could focus on the successive editions of the *Furioso*, with special attention to the author's famous *impresa* (device). This depicts a fire beneath a hive, the bees fleeing, with the motto *Pro bono malum* ("evil in return for good"). Typically understood as attacking the ingratitude and stinginess of Ariosto's patrons, this *impresa* shows how personal emblems became a fashionable means of veiled self-expression in a politically fraught environment. In class, students might develop and then explain their own personal *impresa*, clarifying also how the *impresa*'s individual specificity differs from the traditional chivalric emblems worn by Ariosto's characters (as in 10.77–89, 36.3), and how such traditional signs of identity function or fail in the text.

## Performing Power through Clothing

The discussion of personal emblems offers an excellent lead-in to Castiglione's *Cortegiano*, which was composed in the same years as the *Furioso*, and offers a complementary response to the fraught politics of the early sixteenth century. One evening entertainment mentioned early in the text is the invention of personal emblems (1.5), although the conversation detailed in the dialogue engages in a different kind of identity-formation project: to imagine an ideal courtier. Since the *Cortegiano* and the *Furioso* are very different, it can be useful to ask questions relating specifically to the differences between Ariosto's knights and Castiglione's courtiers. The latter are imagined by Lodovico da Canossa in *Cortegiano* 1.16–21 primarily as autonomous knights on horseback, despite the fact that the courtiers in the text (both the interlocutors and the ideal courtier they discuss) are engaged in fairly sedentary service to despotic and often unstable political powers. It can be helpful to contrast the *Furioso*'s quests for armor and weapons with the political and tactical discussion of clothing in *Cortegiano* 1.25–27. Research projects on men's clothing of the early to mid-sixteenth centuries can illuminate the longing for an imagined chivalric past. Students are generally fascinated by the codpiece, which is more easily understood as an assertion of bellicose masculinity in the context of armor's decline as a functional tool of war.[4]

Two sets of visuals can help contextualize differences between the imagined knights of the *Furioso* and the pragmatic advice of Castiglione's text: thirteenth- and fourteenth-century manuscript illustrations of chivalric romances depicting knights in battle (for example, the Princeton University Library Garrett MS 125) and Bronzino's enigmatic *Portrait of Ugolino Martelli*, at first glance a straightforward painting of a man. In contrast with early manuscript knights, whose external appearance (their actions and their armor) typically makes their identity clear, Bronzino's painting combines elements in a way that raises a series of questions—rather like a personal emblem and in many ways echoing the advice of Castiglione's text to both display and hide oneself (as in 1.26, 1.38).

## Gender Anxiety

The *Cortegiano*'s anxiety concerning clothing and the threat of effeminacy (as in 1.19, 2.27) helps contextualize the *Furioso*'s detailing of material objects and instances of gender muddling (for example, the Ricciardetto-Bradamante episode in canto 25).[5] The threat of gender confusion in both texts, and the much-discussed role of the court lady in Castiglione's book 3, gain some clarity when studied alongside women's dress and ideal comportment, perhaps epitomized in such paintings as Domenico Ghirlandaio's *Portrait of Giovanna Tornabuoni* (c. 1489) and Piero della Francesca's *Battista Sforza* (c. 1465; a useful counterpart is the other half of the diptych, *Federico da Montefeltro*). Considering these portraits' highly stylized and idealizing nature, one might ask what the images suggest about the women. Conversely, how do the gender confusion episodes in the *Furioso* threaten this ideal? Lorenzo Lotto's problematic *Lucretia* (c. 1530–32) provides a useful visual contrast to the above paintings, as the subject's active stance and disheveled clothing defy visual and social convention but are more relatable to readers of Ariosto.

## Status Objects and the Performance of Chivalry

The idealization of the courts and the political importance of visual display are perhaps most easily explained through the ducal palace in Urbino, designed for Federico da Montefeltro in the later fifteenth century and the imagined physical setting for Castiglione's *Cortegiano*. The palace famously blurs into the city, inviting admiration not only for its beauty and idyllic hilltop site but also for its collections of rare status objects (*Cortegiano* 1.2). Students might investigate why Castiglione chose this particular setting for his dialogue. How do the palace structure and its contents reflect (or not) the ideas set out in the *Cortegiano*? To what degree might the Urbino palace resemble the *Furioso*'s enchanted castles (e.g., the richly decorated palace in which characters are imprisoned in 12.7–22)?

Ruggiero's failed education project and the significance of material display for Renaissance identity gain further clarity when read alongside the trajectory of Castiglione's dialogue, which initially proposes that the courtier is primarily a *cavaliere*, an outstanding horseman characterized by virtue (1.17, 21). Later, however, Federico Fregoso clarifies that the calculated and elegant display of virtue is what matters: the courtier's behavior is conditioned by considerations of his own gain or loss (1.6–10, 21–24; see Cox, *Renaissance Dialogue* 57). Federico's view prevails, despite opposition from Gasparo Pallavicino, who links concern for appearances with deception, women, and effeminacy (2.27–28, 33–35, 40).[6] Federico's insistence on external signs correlates with the *Furioso*'s knights seeking material objects of virtue rather than waging war (as in canto 27, where chivalric contests over objects distract from the real military crisis). Yet while the *Cortegiano*'s emphasis on appearances offers the potential for a positive outcome (as the courtier will lead the prince to govern wisely in 4.4–47), the *Furioso*'s frequent episodes of deception and mistaken identity clarify that appearances, though paramount, cannot be trusted. Taken alongside the author-narrator's condemnation of Italy's current leaders in precipitating the Italian wars (34.1–3), concern for chivalric furniture in the *Furioso* assumes a deep irony.

By the end of the course, students have thus interrogated many Renaissance cultural tropes about chivalry and humanistic education, in addition to acquiring research tools and new expertise in at least one aspect of early modern visual and material culture. Students are often surprised by their own enthusiasm about the research projects and remark on the challenge of becoming experts and of teaching their colleagues about political representation in literary texts.

## Notes

1. For the idea of exemplarity and its failures, see Hampton; Rigolot.

2. One or two brief scenes from Ermanno Olmi's film *Il mestiere delle armi* (2001) vividly show the uselessness of armor against the new warfare.

3. See the analysis of Ruggiero's education in Ascoli, *Ariosto's Bitter Harmony* 121–257.

4. For the display of men's bodies through clothing and armor, see McCall; Springer. For the codpiece, see Lüttenberg.

5. For Bradamante and the problem of gender, see especially Shemek, *Ladies Errant*; for the question of gender more generally, see Stoppino.

6. For gender in the *Cortegiano*, see Freccero; see also Milligan; Gaylard.

**Bernd Renner**

# "Truthful Jesting": Satirical Elements in Ariosto's *Orlando furioso*

A main characteristic of the early modern period is the rise of and radical change in satirical writing. The rediscovery of the Greco-Latin heritage enriched medieval satirical texts (farce, sotie, *prosimetrum*, *fatrasie*) by linking them to Roman satura, which became the official gold standard of Renaissance satire, but also to other forms of verse satire (Catullus, Martial), to Menippean satire (Lucian), and to the etymologically unrelated satyr-play, whose crudeness and dramatic form integrated popular medieval theatrical variants into the satirical mixture. The blending of these various traditions is the trademark of early modern satire and transformed the form from a well-defined genre (*satura*) into a technique or attitude prone to infiltrating all literary genres (Renner).

Epistemologically, we distinguish between two main orientations of satirical discourse: the dominating strand of ad hominem satire, usually blunt and straightforward criticism of a historical event, abuse, or perpetrator(s), on the one hand, and a more universal or abstract variant (*divina satyra* ["divine satire"]) that transcends a particular time period or historical persona. While the former is quickly outdated to the point of incomprehensibility—the pamphlet war between Protestants and Catholics constitutes one major illustration—the latter more readily retains its future pedagogical value, as it addresses moral, ethical, or social issues that affect societies throughout time. Satire's objective, healing societal ills, is thus transformed into a perpetual battle, an ongoing undertaking, and the lessons of this approach have no expiration date.

Ludovico Ariosto's masterpiece *Orlando furioso* is not known for its traditional satirical qualities, especially when compared to the author's seven satires published near the end of his life (1534), which illustrate contemporary society within the paradigms of Horatian gentleness and Juvenalian indignation, the two main models for satirical writing at the time. And while satire is certainly not the main concern of Ariosto's epic—hence the neglect of this angle in most scholarship—there are definite satirical elements that warrant a closer scholarly as well as pedagogical consideration. This approach helps fulfill several objectives that facilitate access for our students to a long and often quite convoluted text. Some of the main issues my seminar addresses are satire's functions within the status of fiction, the rhetoric of praise and blame, and the assessment of folly. Students usually undertake guided close readings of select cantos from the poem's first half to introduce them to the satire's mechanics; they subsequently work on the second half of the epic for their written assignment, most often grappling with the notion of folly, instrumental in early modern satire but too extensive to be dealt with properly here. They will have read at least one of the two major texts that redefine folly, Sebastian Brant's *Ship of Fools* (1494) and Erasmus's *Praise of Folly* (1511), which present an opposition between Brant's straightforward, moralizing approach and Erasmus's more perplexing linguistic virtuosity and narrative irony, a mock encomium that "hasn't been performed altogether foolishly" (Erasmus 5).

This essay presents sample readings of cantos 7 and 14 to 18, which combine different satiric strategies, ranging from the conventional criticism of social structures as well as religious and political authorities (concrete satire) to, more important, Ariosto's dichotomies of appearance/reality and reality/ideal rooted in the power of language, the satire's main target because of its potential of abuse (abstract satire). The latter approach is more difficult to gauge, often diluted by polemic or parody, but it appears all the more persuasive as it attempts to attack the causes of the problem instead of particular symptoms or effects, which is the realm of concrete satire. This opposition seems also the main distinction between Ariosto's *Satires*, begun in 1517, and the *Orlando furioso*. Given the scholarly neglect of the mock epic's satirical angle, it seems significant that, in the first *Satire*, the author addresses Ruggiero, a hero of the *Orlando* and mythical founder of the House of Este, in order to complain about unfair treatment when he refuses to accompany Ippolito d'Este to Hungary: "Ruggier, se a la progenie tua mi fai / sì poco grato, e nulla mi prevaglio / che li alti gesti e tuo valor cantai, / che debbo far io qui?" ("Ruggiero, if you make me so little welcome among your progeny, and I achieve no distinction by singing of your noble deeds and valor, what should I do at your court?"; 1.139–42).

Praise and blame in *Orlando furioso* have a clear satirical purpose in highlighting moral and social ills, as this unmasking of useful flattery indicates; tellingly, the poem closes with these two characters, as renewed praise of Hippolytus is followed by the final epic combat between Ruggiero and Rodomont. The duel effectively ends the pagan menace thanks to the House of Este's bravery and provides a model of exemplary behavior for dealing with the Turkish threat. The power of Ariosto's language therefore does not merely entertain or provide moral edification; it also engages with reality in a way that is not restricted to the author's personal fate but extends to the society at large. Appearance and thus a lack of sincerity, a main result of the abuse of language, is attacked time and time again, frequently behind a veil of irony, as in satire 1, where the aforementioned appeal to Ruggiero functions both as a veiled criticism of Ariosto's protector Hippolytus of Este's threats to withdraw his poet's ecclesiastical benefits if he refused to accompany him (fall 1517) and as an implicit acknowledgement of the material and pragmatic motivation behind the praise that Ariosto has lavished on the House of Este in the *Orlando furioso.* It is in such passages that satire has an undeniable albeit subtle impact on the text's intentionality.

## Canto 7: *Quod Vidimus Testamur*

Canto 7 opens with an appeal to the reader from the eyewitness narrator:

> Chi va lontan da la sua patria, vede
> cose, da quel che già credea, lontane;
> che narrandole poi, non se gli crede,
> e stimato bugiardo ne rimane:
> che 'l sciocco vulgo non gli vuol dar fede,
>
> . . . . . . . . . . . . . . . . . . . . . . . . . . . . . . . .
>
> A voi so ben che non parrà menzogna,
> che 'l lume del discorso avete chiaro.

> He who has left his native country sees
> —As further off he goes—things far removed
> From what he thought to find; and when he is
> Recounting them at home may be reproved
> For telling lies, since ignoramuses,
> Unless with touch and sight they've plainly proved
> A thing, will not believe it;
> . . . . . . . . . . . . . . . . . . . . . . . . . . . . . . . . . . . .
> To you alone, my lord, do I pay heed,
> Who follow clearly all the threads I wind. (1–2)

The narrator will insist on several issues found in this comment throughout the text. First and foremost, the notion of truth is problematized in a tale full of magic, monsters, and improbable combats. The subtle irony of the assertion is underscored on numerous occasions, as the narrator is not shy to doubt accounts from other sources (8.58) or to indulge in comic hyperbole directed at historiography (15.4). Similar to Matteo Maria Boiardo, author of *Orlando innamorato*, Ariosto frequently shores up his authority through references to Turpin, Archbishop of Rheims and the presumed author of *Life of Charlemagne*, but the same ambivalence to factual truth prevails in many of the source references (e.g., 33.85 and 34.86). Authority, whether a legendary historiographer's or even the author's, is set up to be undermined by the diligent readers who should be incited to arrive at their own judgment. The dismantling of authorial authority is reflected in the often ambiguous use of Turpin (e.g., 26.23) and the insistence on the interchangeability of sources (24.44–45).

Such healthy skepticism, distinguishing between factual and allegorical truths, between authoritative sources and the readers' judgment, is a main concern of early modern satire and constitutes a strong indicator of the Greek cynic Lucian of Samosata's influence on the form, which was widespread at the time; even Thomas More and Erasmus translated him. The beginning of the aptly named *True Story* announces the aforementioned passages from Ariosto, when Lucian not only confesses that he tells "all kinds of lies in a plausible and specious way" but goes on to insist on the difference between himself and "the poets, historians, and philosophers of old, who have written much that smacks of miracles and fables": "But my lying is far more honest than theirs, for though I tell the truth in nothing else, I shall at least be truthful in saying that I am a liar" (249–53). Sixteenth-century authors used this premise not only to critique authority but also to challenge their readers to search for hidden criticism of contemporary social, political, and religious ills, for which the seriocomical approach of satire, *spoudogelaion*, provided the ideal breeding ground. François Rabelais, author of *Pantagruel* (1532), a mock epic filled with grotesque creatures and fantastic adventures similar to Ariosto's and clearly inspired by the Italian model, parodies and satirizes the Lucianic premise in his prologue (1532): "May you suffer from bloody-stools; . . . and may you fall into the sulphurous fire of the Pit like Sodom and Gomorrah should you not firmly believe everything that I shall relate to you in this present *Chronicle*" (13–14). Such passages fulfill several purposes: the protective veil of satire hides serious concerns behind comical, vulgar, or obscene language, a necessity given the precarious position of authors who undermined religious and secular authorities (Renner). Factual veracity appears to be sacrificed for moral sincerity, which is precisely what distinguishes concrete from abstract satire. This moral dimension willfully provokes the readers in order to ensure that their moral integrity and intellectual independence does not buckle in the face of overwhelming (authorial) assertions; hence the liberty to call Turpin a liar.

Magic and monstrosity, of particular interest in Ariosto, had an ambivalent, even ambiguous status at the time and often used grotesque or fantastical exaggerations to convey higher truths, as many studies have shown (Céard; Huet; Daston). We are in the realm of truthful lying that has been linked, at least since Aristotle's *Poetics*, to the mimetic function of literature and to which my conclusion will briefly refer back. The concept places satire in general and Ariosto in particular in a rich literary tradition that is of particular pedagogic interest, as it enables students to better understand the big picture and add to the present-day significance of early modern texts.

The distinction between benevolent and malevolent magic is closely related to these observations and also finds one of its many illustrations in canto 7. Whereas the kind enchantress Melissa attempts to rescue Ruggiero and "trarlo . . . alla vera virtù, mal grado d'esso" ("pull him . . . against his will, to virtue's victory; 7.42), love-sick Alcina's evil spell had quite the opposite effect (7.55). We recognize the magical roots of satire, which, like a spell or an incantation, can change reality by virtue of the mere power of the verb, the almighty logos (R. Elliott), oscillating between constructive criticism and destructive abuse. The violent satirical pamphlets during the religious strife in Europe for much of the century—Ariosto comments on the early stages of this conflict—exemplify the destructive potential of language that the author criticizes. One ought not underestimate the power of these pamphlets' incendiary language, bad verbal magic if you will, whose problematic status runs throughout the history of human conflicts. Beyond the question of legitimacy, one could consider the effectiveness of such radical versions of the satirical cure—often more damaging than healing—compared to, for example, Logistilla's book, which provides infallible antidotes for malevolent spells (22.16).

## Cantos 14 to 18: Propaganda, Deceiving Appearances, and Satirical Cure

These chapters not only illustrate the impact of abstract satire on the text but also underscore the epic's subtle epistemological coherence. Canto 14 showcases a transparent allegorical satire directed at the conventional target of the clergy, which had abandoned traditional values in favor of the seven deadly sins that now govern monastic life. The ideal is presented as a mere state of appearance, whereas the ugly reality is exposed as soon as the archangel Michael arrives at the monastery (14.80). This type of reality check can then trigger a counter-reaction, aimed at reaching a satirical cure that will attempt to reestablish the ideal state of religious life. The archangel quickly identifies the allegorical figure of Discord as the main culprit, who had left her natural habitat, Hades, to dominate "questo nuovo inferno" ("this new-made hell"; 14.82). The loss of true Christian values and the internal schism of Christendom are the ills that the transformative power of the satirical verb is meant to remedy, and, triggered by Astolfo and his companions' sojourn in Jerusalem, Ariosto lauds the actions of Charlemagne and his knights against the Moors as an example for contemporary Western leaders in their struggle against the Turks:

> Purgati de lor colpe a un monasterio
> che dava di sé odor di buoni esempii,
> de la passion di Cristo ogni misterio
> contemplando n'andâr per tutti i tempii
> ch'or con eterno obbrobrio e vituperio
> agli cristiani usurpano i Mori empii.
> L'Europa è in arme, e di far guerra agogna
> in ogni parte, fuor ch'ove bisogna.
>
> Some days in penance in a monastery
> They duly spend; then pass to contemplate
> Christ's Passion and its every mystery

> In all the churches, which the Turks of late,
> To our eternal shame and contumely,
> With their usurping presence desecrate,
> While Europe blazes, everywhere at war,
> Except where Christian arms are most needed. (15.99)

Passages like these resonate with students, who seize their modern geopolitical relevance and see how the abuse of such powerful language shows the danger of invective and polemics that constantly weigh on satirical discourse. Later, Ariosto will contextualize such calls to arms for his contemporary readers when he depicts a future Christian union of Europe's leaders (Francis I, Maximilian, Charles V, and Henry VIII) under the leadership of Pope Leo X (26.35–36). The poet's verb is essential for this call, as it outlines a proper code of conduct for rival leaders in the face of imminent danger, all the more significant given Francis I's temptation to ally with the Turks against the emperor.

Internal religious strife, loss of Christian values, and political conflicts (Francis I vs. Charles V) dominate the grim reality, far from the ideal that the satire is aiming to restore. The narrator increasingly links the fictional medieval past to the flawed present—for example, by conflating Moors and Turks while putting the blame explicitly on godless Europe, whose leaders' behavior is far removed from that of Charlemagne's exemplary knights:

> Or Dio consente che noi siàn puniti
> da populi di noi forse peggiori,
> per li multiplicati et infiniti
> nostri nefandi, obbrobrïosi errori.
> . . . . . . . . . . . . . . . . . . . . . . . . . . . . . . . .
> Doveano allora aver gli eccessi loro
> di Dio turbata la serena fronte,
> che scórse ogni lor luogo il Turco e 'l Moro
> con stupri, uccisïon, rapine et onte.
>
> Now God consents that we should punished be,
> By other races who perhaps are worse,
> For all our manifold iniquity.
> . . . . . . . . . . . . . . . . . . . . . . . . . . . . . . . . . . . . .
> The Christians must have caused by their excesses
> A clouding of the Father's countenance.
> On every side the Saracen oppresses
> With murder, rape and all incontinence. (17.5–6)

One can only imagine the seriousness of the Christians' vices in the face of the crimes committed by the pagan foes. Only the members of the House of Este are spared in this satirical purge; they are even juxtaposed with the warlike Pope Julius II, the symbol for the ills of Christendom, as early as canto 3, which allows the author to compare his own project to Virgil's praise of Augustus. The parochial thinking of the different European factions—Spain, France, Switzerland, Germany, and Italy are named explicitly—continues to dominate Ariosto's ferocious criticism of a deplorable reality:

> Se Cristianissimi esser voi volete,
> e voi altri Catolici nomati,
> perché di Cristo gli uomini uccidete?
> perché de' beni lor son dispogliati?
> Perché Ierusalem non rïavete,
> che tolto è stato a voi da' rinegati?
> Perché Constantinopoli e del mondo
> la miglior parte occupa il Turco immondo?
>
> If "the most Christian" rulers you would be,
> And "Catholic" desire to be reputed,
> Why do you slay Christ's men? Their property
> Why have you sacked, and their belongings looted?
> Why do you leave in dire captivity
> Jerusalem, by infidels polluted?
> Why do you let the unclean Turk command
> Constantinople and the Holy Land? (17.75)

Confronted with a crisis of existential proportions, the author gives in to his exasperation and drops the veil of the legendary epic. Yet again, he pushes the satire dangerously close to pure polemic. The cure almost morphs into a call for utter destruction instead of aiming at healing the patient; Juvenalian indignation gains the upper hand over Horatian gentleness in this wake-up call directed at Western Europe.

The narrator's frequent predictions of a future based on Charlemagne's present, which is actually in the past at the time of the epic's composition, legitimize the author's appeal to end religious strife and achieve European unity. This ultimate objective of the satire confirms the poet's power through a subtle ruse, mixing fake predictions and moral exhortations, a ploy that places Ariosto firmly among the happy few who elude fate's power by being able to foretell the future. This capacity transforms the poet into a true magician of the logos, even surpassing Homer and Virgil in a complex illustration of *translatio studii et imperii*, the Renaissance obsession to surpass the classical models in all domains of intellectual and political life.

Epic and satire share a common referential system (Debailly), and its major factors are to be found in abundance in *Orlando furioso*: both forms require at least two levels of interpretation based on epidictic rhetoric, allegory, and the interplay of the explicit and the implicit, of appearance and reality, all of which is rendered even more complex through irony.

As satire is the form of literary expression most closely linked to reality, the pedagogical advantages of studying it are numerous. In the early modern period, an era of rapid gains in knowledge that mirrors our own, the form usually questions received truths supported by religious and political authorities bent on preserving their absolute powers. Satire thus teaches indispensable skills that college faculty endeavor to instill in their students, first and foremost critical thinking independent from the often arbitrary mainstream positions. This is one of the most important didactic purposes of a humanities seminar: teach students to come to their own conclusions by questioning received truths. Ariosto deals with such questions in his multifaceted account of courtly love and his satirical treatment of the disastrous role of religion in love and war. A short list of examples would include the aforementioned condemnation of Christian excesses (canto 17), the moral lesson addressed to Rodomont, who criticizes the female sex (29.1–3), or the subtle mockery of rigid patterns of courtly love (29.8). Even Orlando's folly could be a realistic dismantling of courtly love patterns that elevate the unreachable lady in the chaste knight's noble quest.

By attacking the abstract cause of the vices it deplores—the often abused power of language that, paradoxically, can be countered only by the magical qualities of satirical discourse, the verb mirroring the inherent ambiguity of all human action—the text's satire preserves a timeless quality that values the problem-solving skills of independent critical thinking in the face of untrustworthy sources and dubious authority. Moreover, by focusing on the plausible (*argumentum*) and therefore bridging the gap between the ideal and reality, between *fabula* and *historia*, satire is firmly anchored in the realm of committed fiction, applying criteria that are at the forefront of classical theory (Aristotle's *Poetics*; *Ad Herennium*). Truthful lying or truthful jesting (*serio ludere*) underscore satire's intermediary position between literary, aesthetic, and pragmatic tendencies and demonstrate a firm grasp on issues of real, everyday life (the problematic status of authority; personal responsibility; independent thinking). Satire demonstrates the relevance of such old texts in students' lives and the practical benefits of closely studying them (which often trumps literary concerns), and while this is certainly not the main focus of Ariosto's epic, it adds a valuable angle and enhances its timeless qualities.

**Bryan Brazeau**

# Welcome to Paradise: The Earthly Paradise Topos as Pedagogic Structuring Principle

This essay stems from a survey course of medieval and early modern Italian literature organized around the theme of the earthly paradise that I designed and taught in fall 2011 at New York University. The focus on paradisial spaces helped students structure their reflections in the course and provided them with various analytical points of entry into rich yet difficult texts. Consideration of the dynamics that emerge when thinking about earthly paradises, furthermore, allowed students to draw connections in their weekly reflection papers between contemporary *loci amoeni*—such as music festivals or vacation resorts—and the selections we discussed in the classroom. Such a course relies on a claim made by A. Bartlett Giamatti, in his excellent, albeit dated, study *The Earthly Paradise and the Renaissance Epic*, that the earthly paradise topos functions as a central organ of these poems. As such, episodes featuring this topos represent in miniature many of the ambiguities and tensions that undergird these poems as a whole (6). Another central claim in Giamatti's study and in this course is that the paradises of early modern chivalric epic are distinguished from their medieval counterparts by their illusory, enchanted nature. While Dante was concerned with the location of the historical Eden, the *loci amoeni* depicted by later poets only appeared to be what Eden once was (119).

The present essay discusses how this theme might structure a mid- to upper-level undergraduate seminar on the early modern romance epic tradition in either an Italian or a comparative literature department. To outline the pedagogy of such a course and the resources used, this essay is divided into six sections: a general introduction, four sections each focused on a particular work, and a final section on possibilities for evaluation, useful digital resources, and ideas for optional workshops that can help students who are approaching the texts in Italian. The texts under discussion are Matteo Maria Boiardo's *Orlando innamorato*, Ludovico Ariosto's *Orlando furioso*, Torquato Tasso's *Gersualemme liberata*, and Edmund Spenser's *The Faerie Queene*. In each section of the course, I provide prompts for one-page reflection assignments to foster critical thought before class sessions, along with one or two relevant secondary sources. Throughout the semester, students take turns summarizing and commenting on these articles in five- to seven-minute presentations, which foster further class discussion. If weather and space permit, some of the class sessions should be scheduled in a quiet park or nearby garden.

## Course Introduction

Students are assigned Giamatti's introduction and first chapter, which cover much preliminary ground, discussing the three main discursive traditions that inform thinking about earthly paradises in the early modern world: classical myths about the golden age, traditions of Latin and vernacular love poetry set in gardens, and medieval discussions about the Christian earthly paradise (3–86). Key points in this analysis are the influence of Claudian's *Epithalamium* as fixing "the convention of the natural bower . . . dedicated to Venus and her pastimes" (50), the description of the space as spatially or temporally remote (or both) and therefore protected or fortified (83), and inaccessible desires conveyed through stylistic negation—describing what is not present in the paradisial space (84). Students may also read Dante's *Purgatorio* 27–33, which engages with these themes. The earthly paradise in Dante serves as a site of spiritual and personal growth, as emblematized in the pilgrim's meeting with Beatrice and the farewell to Virgil (*Purg.* 30.40–57), along with the pilgrim's transformative immersion in Eden's two rivers (*Purg.* 31.91–96; 33.127–45). Before moving on to enchanted earthly paradises in chivalric epic, we discuss Petrarch's "Chiare, fresche, et dolci acque" ("Clear, fresh, and sweet waters"; *Petrarch's Lyric Poems* 244–47, poem 126) to demonstrate the transformation of Dante's

Edenic space into a deceptive paradise of false images that do not offer the possibility of dynamic spiritual growth. Class discussion is based around Nancy Vickers's intertextual analysis, which provides a useful framework in which to consider the shift from Dantean to Petrarchan paradises. In their reflection papers, I ask students to think of contemporary earthly paradises that fit these two models and to describe their dynamics.

## Boiardo

As Boiardo's *Orlando innamorato* is the first chivalric epic featured in the course, it can be useful to begin the unit introducing basic themes of the genre, such as the combination of Carolingian and Arthurian traditions and the narrative techniques of *entrelacement*. For the first class, students are asked to read from book 1 the entire first canto and the first twenty-nine stanzas of the second. In this class, I also give a general plot summary, underlining the dynamics of dispersal and congregation as well as the geographic polarities of Paris in the West and Cathay in the East. I highlight as well how a character's absence on occasion catalyzes the poem's action as much as their presence. To illustrate this last point, it can be helpful to assign the remainder of 1.2, which describes the Christians' poor performance in a tournament due to the absences of Orlando and Ranaldo.

Once students have a general overview of the text, I assign from book 2 all of canto 4 and the first twenty-four stanzas of canto 5, which describe Falerina's allegorical garden, Orlando's escape, and the destruction of the space.[1] I underline Boiardo's anticipation of the garden throughout the text and ask students for their general thoughts on the symbolic aspects of the episode.[2] I prompt the class to focus in particular on Orlando's guidebook, the various guardians, Orlando's method of overcoming each one, the rain of golden apples, and the magical tree at the center of the garden. Through discussion, students discover how the destruction of Falerina's garden implies personal growth and the overcoming of Orlando's own sensual desires. We then compare the garden's overarching motifs to those in Dante's *Purgatorio*; while thematics of inner transformation are nonetheless also present in Boiardo, the genius of the space is inverted. Orlando's personal growth is signaled by the destruction of the paradisial space; as we saw with Petrarch, the garden is no longer a place of transformation but one that threatens a dangerous stasis.

For in-class presentations, students might discuss Jo Ann Cavallo's chapter on the garden of Orgagna, as it situates the episode in the broader narrative and allegorical arc of Boiardo's text (*Boiardo's* Orlando innamorato 90–95). Michael Murrin's chapter on Falerina's garden (*Allegorical Epic* 53–86) could also be presented, as it offers a systematic account of the episode's complex allegory and introduces the concept of allegory itself, which will be important in later discussions on Tasso and Spenser.

## Ariosto

*Orlando furioso* is a rich text for discussion of paradisial spaces. Alcina's garden is the most sustained of these and fits squarely into the enchanted garden trope found in other chivalric epics. Students are assigned cantos 6, 7, and 8.1–21. Discussion begins with Astolfo's cautionary tale, which opens the episode with the topos of the enchanted garden as a prison where lascivious knights are lured into a trap by their own desires (6.27–53). The final stanza, where Astolfo doubts that Ruggiero will obtain "giovamento" ("a lesson") from his story (6.53), along with Ruggiero's own self-deception (7.16–17), provide occasion to introduce the Horatian idea of poetry as "dulce et utile" ("sweet and useful"). Here, I ask students to write reflections on how the earthly paradise topos extends beyond sexual dalliance or debauchery—in the word's etymological sense—and also serves as a site to explore cultural anxieties about the social role of visual, musical, and literary arts.

The disenchantment of the garden in Ariosto's text differs from that in Boiardo's. In the *Innamorato*, Orlando destroys Falerina's dangerous garden by battling its various guardians and, later, with Falerina's cooperation. Ariosto, however, depicts the disenchantment of Alcina's paradisial space thanks to Melissa's intervention and Angelica's magical ring (7.70–74). This tension between magical enchantment and ironic disenchantment can introduce students to broader themes in the *Furioso*, including its playful interruptions and conscious subversions of its own plot. *Furioso* 10.35–11.12 may be assigned for a second discussion—here, students reflect on the overarching allegorical aspects of Alcina's garden and Ruggiero's training to ride the hippogryph under Logistilla's tutelage. We also consider why Ariosto confounds readers' expectations when Ruggiero attempts to rape Angelica at the beginning of canto 11. Articles for in-class presentations include William J. Kennedy's "Ariosto's Ironic Allegory," which further develops the students' understanding of allegory in the earthly paradise, and Daniel Javitch's "Cantus Interruptus in the *Orlando furioso*," which provides an excellent overview of Ariosto's use of *entrelacement.* Time permitting, one may also discuss the *locus amoenus* where Angelica and Medoro fall in love (19.16–42), along with Orlando's exclusion from this paradisial space and subsequent destructive madness (23.100–136). This episode can also be used to introduce a discussion of security and paradisial spaces, building on the theme of the paradise as prison, seen in both Falerina's and Alcina's gardens. With regard to this theme, Michel Foucault's short but insightful article "Of Other Spaces: Utopias and Heterotopias" may be assigned for an in-class presentation or for the weekly reflection paper, exploring to what extent the paradises discussed in the course compensate for or expose the shortcomings of the real space of the epic battlefield.

## Tasso

Armida's garden represents a clear reworking of Alcina's. We begin discussion of the *Gerusalemme liberata* with passages that provide essential context: the initial stanzas of the poem (1.1–28), Erminia's description of the Christian knights to Aladino, and Tancredi's encounter with Clorinda on the battlefield (3.1–28). Earlier discussions of Alcina's garden will have prepared students to discuss the social role and pedagogical value that Tasso assigns to his poem, particularly the Lucretian metaphor of the honeyed cup of medicine in 1.3. Such metapoetic reflections provide a useful opportunity to discuss the broad strokes of Tasso's poetic theory, while also preparing students for the tensions between nature and imitative art in the episode of Armida's garden. If the course develops allegory as a dominant theme, one might have the students read and reflect on Tasso's *Allegoria della Gerusalemme liberata*, considering the extent to which Tasso's allegorical overlay corresponds with the poem.

Moving now to Armida's garden, I assign cantos 15 and 16 to begin the discussion with Carlo and Ubaldo's magical journey and the analogous use of European images of paradise to depict the conquest of the New World. In this regard, I assign passages from Christopher Columbus's *Four Voyages* for in-class presentations and bring in images of premodern maps locating the earthly paradise (Columbus 30–36; Scafi 98–140). When reading canto 16, students learn to pay close attention to the description of Armida's garden, which builds on both earlier discussions concerning the protection of the paradisial space and the cultural anxieties about human art exceeding nature's craftsmanship. The classical references in the ekphrastic description of the gate can prompt a useful mini-assignment for students to research at home and discuss in their reflection papers or present in small groups (16.2–7). We compare the ideological aspects of Armida's garden with the enchanted paradisial spaces seen in Boiardo and Ariosto. Here, it can be particularly helpful to discuss the parrot's song in 16.15–16 and the description of Rinaldo and Armida in stanzas 18–26, both of which demonstrate the tensions between narcissism and the crusading knights' greater social mission. Tasso's treatment of individualism is also a good occasion to point out the differences between the values of a late-sixteenth-century reading public during the Catholic Reformation and the values students may hold. Such discussions may help them approach the text with a historical consciousness, avoiding anachronistic interpretations. One should, however, also emphasize the diversity of Tasso's public, noting the differences between his religiously minded censors in the Roman Curia and courtly readers who expected to be delighted by chivalric romances similar to Ariosto's. In this regard, students might compare the parrot's song from *Gerusalemme liberata* 16 to the chorus's celebration of a hedonistic golden age in act 1 of Tasso's *Aminta*, the pastoral play performed in the paradisial Belvedere gardens only eight years before the publication of the *Liberata*.

We close our discussion of Tasso with a consideration of Rinaldo's moral conversion, Armida's lament, her disenchantment of the garden, and their reunion at the end of the poem in the garden-like "chiusa opaca chiostra" ("dark and sheltered spot") outside the walls of Jerusalem (20.122). This provides an excellent opportunity to discuss Armida's agency in her garden's creation and destruction, which may be compared to the disenchantment of Falerina's and Alcina's gardens. For in-class presentations, I assign Marilyn Migiel's "Secrets of a Sorceress" and Jane Tylus's "Reasoning Away Colonialism." The former piece provides an excellent overview of Armida in the poem, asking that readers consider her not simply as a sorceress but rather as a strong woman whose threatening power stems from her careful self-presentation along with the rhetorical and linguistic control she exerts over her origin story. Tylus links Tasso's poem with themes of New World colonialism, while providing a clear and elegant framework for the ideological tensions that undergird the *Liberata*.

At this point, I invite students to consider how the earthly paradises we have seen are heavily gendered spaces, reflecting male anxieties about female sexuality. In this regard, I dedicate one class to earthly paradises in female-authored chivalric epics, such as Moderata Fonte's *Floridoro* (5.1–40),

Margherita Sarrocchi's *Scanderbeide* (13.1–45), and Lucrezia Marinella's *Enrico* (5.57–100), focusing on how these works rewrite the figure of the enchantress in a positive light.[3]

## Spenser

Should this course be taught with a comparative approach, one may compare cantos 15 and 16 of Tasso's *Liberata* with book 2, canto 12 of Edmund Spenser's *Faerie Queene*. Students are assigned the section on the Bower of Bliss (2.12.42–87). Moments of imitation, expansion, and, at times, direct translation from Tasso's poem provide useful prompts for the students' reflection papers. One such example is *Faerie Queene* 2.12.58–59 / *Gerusalemme liberata* 16.9–10, where Spenser extends the tension between nature and art, showing not only how art convincingly imitates nature in the Bower but also how nature itself seeks to imitate art. Another is found in *Faerie Queene* 2.12.60–68 / *Gerusalemme liberata* 15.58–66, where Spenser abbreviates Tasso's description of the playful maidens and adds a classical simile comparing the scene to the birth of Venus (2.12.65.3–4).[4] Students might also compare the image of Armida and Rinaldo in *Gerusalemme liberata* 16.19 to the image of Acrasia and Verdant at *Faerie Queene* 2.12.73.6–7. Students may wish to further explore Giamatti's description of the scene as "vampirish" in their reflection papers (279), asking whether the early modern literary topos of the earthly paradise as a projection of sexual anxieties might not find a contemporary equivalent in vampire fiction.[5] For in-class presentations, one might assign Robert Durling's "The Bower of Bliss and Armida's Palace," which discusses Spenser's transformation of Armida's palace and could provide prompts for further discussion.

While at first glance Acrasia's Bower of Bliss elicits themes similar to Armida's island and seems to function as a similar enchanted garden episode, there are also several key differences that may be discussed in class. While Rinaldo's rescue from Armida's garden is crucial for the plot of the *Gerusalemme liberata*, Verdant's rescue from Acrasia's bower has little impact on the plot of the *Faerie Queene*, other than to demonstrate Guyon's mastery of temperance. Perhaps the greatest difference between Spenser's depiction of the earthly paradise and that of other authors studied in the course concerns the destruction of the space in *Faerie Queene* 2.12.81–87. Students will recall Falerina's complicity in the destruction of her enchanted garden, Melissa's breaking of Alcina's spells, and Armida's agency in causing her realm to vanish. Guyon and the Palmer's trapping of Acrasia, along with the "rigour pitilesse" with which Guyon destroys, burns, and razes Acrasia's bower, emerge as surprising in their violence when seen in the light of other earthly paradises discussed in the course.

## Digital Resources and Final Evaluations

When discussing Ariosto, *L'*Orlando furioso *e la sua tradizione in immagini* (Bolzoni) provides a wealth of resources for lectures and student presentations. These include illustrations from early Cinquecento editions of the *Furioso*, artworks inspired by the text, and the ability to compare various illustrations (see Rizzarelli in this volume). For example, one may discuss representations of Alcina in paintings inspired by the poem (selecting the following menus: Opere d'arte > Personaggi > Alcina). Students might be asked to reflect on Alcina's various presentations as a seductive maga, a courtly lady, or a deceptive crone and how such visual interpretations could shape one's reading of this *Furioso* episode. Another possibility would be to navigate to Edizioni > Luoghi > Giardino di Alcina and compare illustrations of Alcina's paradise across the Zoppino (1536), Giolito (1542), Valvassori (1553), and Valgrisi (1556) editions of the poem. When teaching Ariosto and Tasso, the digital versions of these texts from the Italian verse project can be quite useful for students; the texts are presented alongside parallel translations, plot summaries, and a list of characters (Robey).

For student evaluation, the weekly reflection papers help improve the quality of the discussion in class and factor into the participation grade. Students' short presentations summarizing secondary sources broadened our critical perspective, while also preparing the students for their final project. A midterm exam may be assigned, asking students to discuss themes embodied in a particular passage or to compare and contrast aspects of two different earthly paradises. If the course also introduces rhetorical figures, it can be helpful to have the students identify these in a passage, along with rewriting several stanzas into Italian prose to demonstrate comprehension. Following the midterm, students are asked to prepare a research essay, with short presentations on their outline one to two weeks before the final paper is due. When I taught this course in 2011, topics ranged widely and students were encouraged to explore texts the class may not have fully addressed, including female-authored chivalric epics, poems from the pastoral tradition, or the relation of the earthly paradise topos to utopian literature. If the general caliber of the final papers is high, as it was when I taught this course, it can be fruitful to organize a mini-conference in the following semester for students to present their work.

## Notes

1. Falerina's garden, as opposed to Dragontina's in 1.5–6 or Angelica's pleasure palace in 1.8, is, I believe, more helpful for the students, as it allows them to see how Boiardo crafts anticipation of future events throughout the work, engages in a sustained allegory, and most clearly foreshadows the thematics of the paradisial space as a dangerous prison for unsuspecting and easily seduced knights. Each of these elements of the poem can form the basis for engaging in-class discussions.

2. In 1.17, Iroldo describes how he became a prisoner in Falerina's garden and nearly a meal for her dragon. He is saved by Prasildo, who takes his place as prisoner; no sooner has Iroldo finished telling the tale than prisoners on their way to Falerina's garden pass by, whom Ranaldo promptly liberates. Fiordelisa is among the prisoners and describes the complexities and dangers of Falerina's garden (1.17.1–46). Later on, in 1.28, when Orlando is about to deliver a fatal blow against Ranaldo, Angelica asks him to destroy Falerina's garden in the kingdom of Orgagna in order to save the knight she loves (1.28.28–32).

3. For an excellent overview of these three works and their unique enchantress figures, see Cox, *The Prodigious Muse* 164–212. I would also like to thank Virginia Cox for suggesting these passages as I put together this course's syllabus.

4. For a broader overview of Tasso's reception in early modern England and for how Spenser adapts Tasso for an English audience, one might also bring in passages from Edward Fairfax's English translation of the *Gerusalemme liberata*, which was heavily mediated by Spenser's *Faerie Queene*. The text of Fairfax's translation is available alongside Tasso's Italian original in Robey. Braden provides a fascinating overview of both Spenser's and Fairfax's classicizing additions to Tasso's text, which served to shape and rework the *Gerusalemme* for an early modern English audience ("Edward Fairfax"). This article might also be assigned for an in-class presentation.

5. An accessible short survey of vampire fiction and sexual anxiety from *Dracula* to *Twilight* can be found in Acocella.

# Part V

# Transcultural Encounters

**Stephen P. McCormick**

# Medieval and Early Modern Cartography and Its Intersections with Travel Texts and the Epic: From Marco Polo to Boiardo and Ariosto

The amplified geographic perimeter of Italian epic, perhaps most artfully expressed in *Orlando innamorato* and *Orlando furioso*, opens up interdisciplinary approaches to teaching the Italian Renaissance romance epic. A major impetus for the romance epic's new focus on Africa and the Far East stemmed from merchant readers trading exotic goods in distant lands. Michael Murrin discusses this phenomenon in his book *Trade and Romance*, arguing that merchant travels beyond the Mediterranean basin amplified the early romance borders of Chrétien de Troyes to the East. Unlike Arthurian heroes in twelfth-century French narrative who "were not concerned with travel to a specific place so much as proving themselves or learning the lessons of chivalry," the heroes of Italian romance and epic now had a specific "set of itineraries and endpoints toward which action is newly driven" (13–14). To borrow Boiardo's words, "Lunga è la istoria, ed il camin lontano" ("The story's long, the voyage far"; *Orlando innamorato* 2.9.48).

Late-medieval and early modern Italian cartographic documents echo many of the geographic references in Italian epic and provide a powerful visual entry point to the genre's energetic narratives. This essay will explore key examples of cartographic production between roughly 1350 and 1540 and will suggest ways in which classes can use maps to help guide students' interactions with Maria Matteo Boiardo's and Ludovico Ariosto's geography.

## Historical Context for a Cartographic Approach

A cartographic approach to teaching Italian epic literature makes sense from a historical perspective. Poets and readers traveled virtually with maps, using imagination and contemplation, an acceptable alternative to arduous journeys. Because of intensifying trade with the East during the late Middle Ages and rumors of great riches, audiences were curious to see maps and to read and hear epics featuring circuitous voyages and exotic peoples (see Friedman and Figg). To introduce students to the East in the European imagination, I assign reading from Paul Freedman's *Out of the East*, a fascinating account of the spice trade, John Friedman's *Monstrous Races in Medieval Art and Thought*, or translations of the letter of Prester John (Ullendorff and Beckingham; Silverberg). Susan Conklin Akbari's *Idols in the East* is also useful for this objective. The reality of treacherous travel by land and sea figures prominently in many Italian epics. Difficult sea journeys, including Rodamonte's crossing of the Mediterranean (*Orlando innamorato* 2.6) or Ruggiero and Dudone's storm at sea (*Orlando furioso* 2.41), occur frequently enough to merit discussion of their role in narrative structure and development. How does interrupted travel throw narration off course? Advanced readers of French might explore Raffaele da Verona's Franco-Italian *Aquilon de Bavière*, which structures its narrative premise—the concealed identity of the protagonist—around a seafaring tragedy. To contrast with the more circuitous journeys in the previous works, I use the British Library's digital facsimile of Matthew Paris's itinerary map to the Holy Land, discussing travel as a string of linear points.[1]

The dangers of travel piqued the curiosity of readers and poets, who opted for imaginary voyages with maps. Ariosto famously expresses his reluctance to venture out: "e tutto il mar, senza far voti quando / lampeggi il ciel, sicuro in su le carte / verrò, più che sui legni, volteggiando" ("Without ever making vows when the heavens flash with lightening, I will go bounding over all the seas, more secure aboard my maps than aboard ships"; *The Satires* 3.65–66). Evidence suggests then that maps were narrative instruments, providing a network of imaginary itineraries through a system of visual cues. Epic texts confirm the strong affiliation between map and text, and for this reason students can productively read epic as textual cartography (see Cachey). Students might think about how a nonlinear voyage across a map may resemble Boiardo's and Ariosto's narrative turns.

With a cartographic approach to Italian epic, students should understand that text and image in medieval scholasticism are inseparable. Roger Bacon explains, "And here not only is there necessary a depicting and a representation of the places, but also a narrative of those things which must be depicted; for neither suffices" (1: 328). Furthermore, students should understand that modern geography is anachronistic when considering premodern cartography. History was understood spatially and space textually. For this reason, maps often accompany histories of the world as visual reiterations of the text, and, in this way, students can understand Brunetto Latini's *Li livre dou Trésor* as a textual *mappa mundi*. The medieval notion that text and image are inseparable serves as a productive base for discussing cartography, epic, and the representation of geographic knowledge.

## Reading Medieval and Early Modern Maps

Far from a primitive representation of the Earth, the medieval *mappa mundi* is an intricate system that students must learn to decipher.[2] I devote a day or two of discussion to the cartographic principles of medieval and early modern cartography, using several resources to bring medieval maps into focus. For the student who would like to examine many map sources and understand broad traditions, Evelyn Edson's *The World Map* provides a useful cartographic survey. Also, sections of Christian Jacob's *L'empire des cartes* is a stimulating introduction to map theory (for the English translation, see *The Sovereign Map*). P. D. A. Harvey's *Medieval Maps* remains a reliable general introduction, as does J. B. Harley and David Woodward's *The History of Cartography*.[3] Naomi Reed Kline's *Maps of Medieval Thought* focuses on a detailed interpretation of the Hereford world map, illustrating the hermeneutic nuance of medieval *mappa mundi*. I devote some time to discussing the orientation of medieval maps: Why would medieval *mappa mundi* have an east orientation? Does cartographic orientation reflect the worldview of the map's creators? The instructor can tie this question to imagining the East and the representation of biblical and mercantile spaces. Finally, and specifically related to Italian epic, Jo Ann Cavallo's *The World beyond Europe in the Romance Epics of Boiardo and Ariosto* is a compelling example of how Boiardo's and Ariosto's respective ideologies can be interpreted through their expression of epic geography.

Besides medieval *mappa mundi*, there are two other important cartographic traditions: portulan charts and the Ptolemaic system. Although there is little evidence that they were used on ships, portulan charts were likely linked to navigation and trade, used in tracing the contours of shorelines and harbors (see Harvey 39–45). The Bibliothèque nationale de France (BnF) digital facsimile of the thirteenth-century Carta Pisana portulan chart helps students understand that medieval technology allowed for very recognizable and accurate outlines of the Mediterranean. The BnF's digital exhibit of maritime maps provides many more beautiful examples.[4] When portulan charts are presented alongside the contemporary *mappa mundi* tradition, students understand that medieval geographic space consisted of a range of metaphoric and pragmatic modalities.

Second, a basic understanding of Ptolemy's role in early modern cartography is critical. After Jacopo Angeli da Scarperia's 1409 translation of Ptolemy's *Geographia* disseminated the work to Florentine society, humanist scholars and epic writers like Andrea da Barberino immediately began to incorporate the Ptolemaic system into their maps, studies, and texts (see Edson 114–40). Ptolemaic thought, however, must not be presented to students as a rediscovery, since these concepts were never completely lost through the Middle Ages (Dalché, "Le souvenir"). Furthermore, the student should keep in mind that medieval travel accounts (especially Marco Polo), medieval geographic constructs (mostly inherited from classical geographers), and medieval cartographic legend (especially Prester John) persisted in various forms well into the sixteenth century.[5]

For teaching the medieval *mappa mundi*, the Psalter world map, the Ebstorf map (extant only in facsimile since the original was destroyed in 1943), and the Hereford map are the most comprehensive. I have students work together in small groups to locate on a medieval *mappa mundi* a list of features that I will later use in discussion (the Tana river, the Red Sea, Tabrobana, Cathay, etc.).

The 1375 Catalan map by the Jewish Catalan cartographer Abraham Cresques is one of the most intriguing cartographic productions of the late Middle Ages, and, because of a stunning high-resolution facsimile available through the BnF's Gallica database, this example works especially well for teaching. Not only does this text depict the travels of Marco Polo, it also features the kingdom of Prester John and the wealthy West African ruler Mansa Musa.

One of the most celebrated examples of late medieval cartography is Fra Mauro's 1450 world map. The map displays Arab influence through its south orientation, which can be linked to the discussion on cartographic orientation. Besides being an incredibly rich resource for understanding the fifteenth-century cartographic imaginary, the map happens to be one of the most readily accessible. Piero Falchetta's edition provides English translations alongside the original Venetian language inscriptions. Falchetta's work makes the map valuable to a spectrum of student audiences, from undergraduates with limited knowledge of Italian to graduate students who read the original text. This publication also includes a CD-ROM facsimile. Additionally, the University of Michigan's online exhibit *Maps and Map-making in India* includes a section on Fra Mauro, with a high-resolution image of the map inside a navigation tool.[6]

Perhaps most interesting for the study of Boiardo and Ariosto is the Catalan Estense world map, first documented in the 1488 library inventory of Duke Ercole d'Este (see Bini). This map includes many regions associated with the characters of the *Innamorato* and *Furioso* and, together with a cartographic analysis, the instructor might assign Murrin's reading of Falerina's garden in *Allegorical Epic* (53–85). To access this map, students can turn to Bini's 2004 CD-ROM edition.

Finally, to give students a non-European perspective, I introduce the work of Muhammad al-Idrisi, a twelfth-century Arab geographer known to the West as *Geographus Nubiensis*, "the Nubian geographer." I ask students to look for similarities between the sixteenth-century copy of al-Idrisi's *mappa mundi* and the Fra Mauro map, noting specifically the south orientation. Al-Idrisi, in the introduction to his work *Kitab nuzhat al-mushtaq fi'khtiraq al-'afaq* ("The pleasure of him who longs to cross the horizons"), indicates that Ptolemy was one of two sources (Levtzion and Hopkins 104–31). Al-Idrisi created this work, known to the Latin West as the *Tabula Rogeriana*, in 1154 for the court of Roger II in Palermo.[7] Not only do these maps provide a useful approach for reading non-European spatial representation, they also reveal the common Ptolemaic foundation for Arab and European cartography.

## Cartography at Court: Marco Polo, Boiardo, Ariosto

Geography was a vibrant topic at the Estense court in Ferrara, the cultural milieu of Boiardo and Ariosto.[8] Geographic study was a valued component of Duke Ercole's education, a passion kindled by the family's love for travel. In 1413, Niccolò III traveled to the Holy Land, and later, in 1440, his son Meliaduse made the journey. Ercole I wanted to show his son

Alfonso the world ("fargli veder il mondo"; "[h]ave him see the world") as part of a princely education (Bertoni 147n3).[9] The young Alfonso and the courtly poets did not need to travel far to discover the world; the library inventories of 1467, 1488, and 1495 reveal a sizeable collection of geographic and cartographic works.

A margin note to the 1488 inventory shows the Catalan Estense map, referred to as "uno mapamondi in una guaina grande de cuoio" ("a *mappa mundi* in a leather casing"; Bertoni 261). The 1467 list includes the geographic works of Paulus Orosius, Pomponius Mela, and Petrarch's *Itinerarium ad sepulcrum Domini*. The 1495 inventory includes Ptolemy's *Cosmographia*, an unidentifiable *India per Ludovico de Mario de le sue cose mirabile*, a copy of Strabo, and three copies of Pliny (Bertoni 235–52). Finally, Marco Polo's travels, an ever-popular text, circulated among courtly readers. The 1495 catalog lists a "Marcopollo in latino," and a record from 1457 indicates that the Contessa Strozzi borrowed a Marco Polo: "M.[a] Contessa de Stroza have uno marcopollo" ("The Countess of Strozzi has a copy of Marco Polo"; Bertoni 56). Another record, from 1489, reveals that Ercole asked that a copy of Marco Polo be taken to his office for study (Bertoni 19).[10]

Indeed, Marco Polo's *Devisement du monde* enormously impacted both cartography and epic and is regularly cited in both.[11] The instructor may have students compare ocular and third-person testimony between the prologue to the *Devisement* ("Pour ce metrons nous les choses veues pour veues, et l'entendue pour entendue" ["We shall report things seen as seen, and things heard as heard"]; Polo 117; my trans.) and Fra Mauro's treatment of the same problem in his map inscriptions ("ho solicitado verificar la scriptura cum la experientia . . . praticando cum persone degne de fede, le qual hano veduto ad ochio quelo che qui suso fedelmente demostro" ["So I say that in my own day I have been careful to verify the texts by practical experience, . . . frequenting persons worthy of faith, who have seen with their own eyes what I faithfully report above"]; Falchetta 699). While exploring the maps, students formulate Marco Polo's influence on the cultural circles of Boiardo and Ariosto.[12] They can then interpret what this means in the context of the *Innamorato* and *Furioso*.

There are many ways students can use the cartographic principles surveyed above to discuss space and geography in Boiardo and Ariosto. First, students may focus on specific geographic regions. Boiardo's Cathay makes for interesting discussion, as does the dominant presence of the Caspian Sea.[13] Cathay lies two hundred days beyond the Tana (*Orlando innam-*

*orato* 1.1.26), the cartographic barrier separating Europe from Asia. What then does it mean that Angelica and Albraca lie beyond this boundary in Asia, a region that traditionally orients the *mappa mundi*, and that is associated with trade, wealth, and marvels? Much of the narration involves the Caspian Sea and, as Murrin notes, European travelers would seldom stray into these lands. With these regions still uncharted, "the poet could therefore create various marvels for these places" (*Allegorical Epic* 76). What version of the Caspian would Boiardo have seen on the Catalan Estense map? Where does Boiardo locate his marvelous creatures, and how do these locations impact the narrative? What does it mean to return west to Charlemagne's Paris? How is power mapped textually and cartographically? What is the geographic importance of the poem's two urban poles, Paris and Albraca? Many of these questions are of course also valid for the *Furioso*, and students could compare the two epic geographies.

As a final thought, students might examine the role of sea crossings (as discussed above) and sea monsters in both the *Innamorato* and *Furioso* (see Van Duzer, *Sea Monsters*). Although Olaus Magnus's Carta Marina was created later than Boiardo or Ariosto (1539), it nonetheless gives an idea of what sea travel meant to readers of epic.[14] The instructor can pair the Carta Marina with Ariosto's *canti* on Angelica in the Hebrides (*Orlando furioso* 1.8–10) or with Astolfo's disappearance on the back of a whale (*Orlando innamorato* 2.13; *Orlando furioso* 1.6).[15] Discussion on this topic might consider how Boiardo and Ariosto use cartographic margins, including water, as a site for marvelous events and beasts (see Van Duzer, "*Hic sunt dracones*").

I hope the cartographic sources and traditions surveyed here will give instructors persuasive visual resources to lead students to stimulating interpretations of Italian epic, including the *Innamorato* and *Furioso*. The maps presented here have always fascinated my students and have provided a powerful visual medium through which to explore Boiardo's and Ariosto's epic realms.

## Notes

1. See the appendix, Digital Map Sources, below.

2. For an analysis of modern perceptions of premodern cartography, see the first three chapters of Dalché, *L'espace géographique*.

3. The volumes are available at www.press.uchicago.edu/books/HOC/index.html.

4. For the BnF collection of maritime maps, see gallica.bnf.fr/html/cartes/cartes-marines-sur-parchemin.

5. Prester John appeared on maps as late as the seventeenth century. See the 1603 copy of Abraham Ortelius's "Presbiteri Iohannis, sive, Abissinorum Imperii descriptio" in Princeton's online exhibit: libweb5.princeton.edu/visual_materials/maps/websites/africa/maps-central/central.html.

6. See www.lib.umich.edu/online-exhibits/exhibits/show/india-maps/early-maps.

7. For a modern consolidation of the *Tabula Rogeriana* map panels, see daten.digitale-sammlungen.de/~db/bsb00007098/images/.

8. Doroszlaï provides the most thorough analysis of Ariosto's use of Marco Polo and cartographic traditions.

9. Translations of Bertoni are my own.

10. For a discussion of the Este family and the East, see Cavallo, *World* 10–13.

11. Marco Polo is visually cited in both the Catalan Atlas and Fra Mauro's world map. For understanding the diffusion of Marco Polo, see Gadrat-Ouerfelli.

12. For a discussion of Fra Mauro's use of Marco Polo, see Cattaneo; S. Davies. For Boiardo's use of Marco Polo, see Bregoli Russo.

13. See gallica.bnf.fr/html/cartes/cartes-marines-sur-parchemin.

14. For Olaus Magnus's Carta Marina, see www.wdl.org/en/item/3037/.

15. Stories of the aspidochelone, a legendary sea creature often mistaken for an island, are frequent in classical and medieval literature. In *Historia naturalis* 9.4, for example, Pliny tells of sailors landing on an island only to discover it is a whale. In the medieval *Navigatio Sancti Brendani Abbatis*, a similar creature is called Jasconius.

## Appendix

## Digital Map Sources

"The Carta Marina" (Laféry edition of 1572). Library of Sweden, shelfmark KoB 1 ab (www.wdl.org/en/item/3037/)

"The Carta Pisana." BNF, Dép. des Cartes et Plans, Res. Ge. B1118 (gallica.bnf.fr/ark:/12148/btv1b52503226n.r=carte+pisane.langEN)

Cartes marines sur parchemin, Bibliothèque nationale de France (gallica.bnf. fr/html/cartes/cartes-marines-sur-parchemin)

"The Catalan Estense map." Modena, Biblioteca Estense Universitaria, C.G.A.1 (nla.gov.au/nla.map-vn1600394)

Cresques, Abrahams. "The Catalan Atlas." BNF, Dép. des manuscrits, Espagnol 30 (gallica.bnf.fr/ark:/12148/btv1b55002481n)

"The Ebstorf *mappa mundi*" (www.uni-lueneburg.de/hyperimage/EbsKart/start.html)

"The Hereford *mappa mundi*" (www.themappamundi.co.uk/)

Higden, Ranulf. *Polychronicon*. British Library, Royal 14 C IX ff. 1v-2. (www.bl.uk/catalogues/illuminatedmanuscripts/ILLUMIN.ASP?Size=mid&IllID=43424)

al-Idrisi, Muhammad. *Tabula Rogeriana*. BNF, Dép. des manuscrits, Arabe 2221 (gallica.bnf.fr/ark:/12148/btv1b6000547t/f1.image)

al-Idrisi, Muhammad. "World Map." Oxford Bodleian Library MS Pococke 375 (bodley30.bodley.ox.ac.uk:8180/luna/servlet/view/all/what/MS.+Pococke+375?sort=Shelfmark%2Csort_order)

Paris, Matthew. "Pilgrim Itinerary from London to Jerusalem." British Library Royal MS 14 C vii (www.bl.uk/onlinegallery/sacredtexts/mparis.html)

"The Psalter Map." British Library MS Add. 28681 (www.bl.uk/manuscripts/FullDisplay.aspx?ref=Add_MS_28681)

**Karina F. Attar**

# Muslims in the Novella and Romance Epic Traditions

This essay presents ideas for teaching representations of Muslim-Christian encounters in Italian novellas and romance epics in the context of an upper-level course for Italian majors. By discussing the philological, literary, sociocultural, and historical contexts that contributed to the representation of interfaith encounters across both traditions, students can address questions such as, How do the contexts of travel, conversion, slavery, and war inflect portrayals of Muslim protagonists? How did authors writing at different times and in different genres engage contemporaneous social anxieties about real and imagined contacts with Muslims? What rhetorical strategies and cultural fantasies did novellas and romance epics exploit in fashioning Muslim protagonists who share values, blows, and intimacy with their Christian counterparts?

In the first class meeting, it can be helpful to present to students brief excerpts—a sentence fragment, a verse—that include some of the terms they will encounter in readings: *arabo* ("Arab"), *nero* ("black"), *macometani* ("Mohammedan"), *moro* ("Moor"), *pagano* ("pagan"), *saracino* ("Saracen"), *turco* ("Turk"). The designation *Muslim*, which rarely appears in medieval and early modern texts, often inadequately stands in for these various terms in scholarship on this topic (including in this essay, for it is a generalization difficult to avoid using). Introducing these terms at the outset gives students the opportunity to learn about the historical, cultural, and ideological factors behind their presence (or absence) in different texts and periods. Excerpts that regularly provoke debate among my students include "un moro turcho e saraino" ("a Turkish and Saracen Moor") from Lodovico Carbone's fifteenth-century *Facezie* ("Jokes"; or "Witticisms") (69) and "uno Spagnuolo o Iudeo, o al tutto Pagano" ("a Spaniard or Jew, or entirely pagan [man]") from Franco Sacchetti's late-fourteenth-century *Trecentonovelle* ("Three Hundred Tales") (380). Such conflations of identity categories to describe a single protagonist alert us to the texts' often porous and unreliable use of nomenclatures and can facilitate a broader conversation about the accuracy and relevance of national, religious, cultural, ethnic, and geographic identifiers both then and now.

Two relatively simple homework assignments can follow this discussion: (1) In pairs or small groups, students consult and take notes on the entry for one or more of these terms in the *Grande dizionario della lingua italiana* ("Great Dictionary of the Italian Language") and discuss them at the next class meeting; (2) Using the IntraText Digital Library (intratext.com), which provides lexical hypertext concordances, students tally how often the terms appear in the *Innamorato*, *Furioso*, and *Liberata*, as well as in Giovanni Boccaccio's *Decameron* and Sacchetti's *Trecentonovelle*. Students can also search for terms by downloading Matteo Bandello's *Novelle* ("Novellas") and Masuccio Salernitano's *Novellino* as PDFs at *Biblioteca della Letteratura Italiana* (www.letteraturaitaliana.net/index.html). It is also worth delaying the second activity until students have encountered a broad variety of portrayals of Muslim protagonists. Students can then expand their search, looking for both vilifying and praiseful labels, including "barbaro" ("barbarous"), "cane" ("dog"), "mostro" ("monster"), "gentile" ("courteous"), "magnanimo" ("magnanimous"), and "valoroso" ("valorous"). Students can also consider narrative and historical contexts in greater depth: Who speaks these labels, the author, narrator, or a Christian protagonist? Are the same terms also applied to Christian protagonists, and if so by whom? Are individual Muslim figures branded both negatively and positively at different points in the texts? How do the social class, military rank, geographical provenance, gender, or religious conversion of Muslim protagonists modulate the vocabulary employed to describe them?

An engaging point of departure for the primary readings is to discuss Boccaccio's three novellas of Christian-Saracen liaisons in the *Decameron* (c. 1350)—the tales of Alatiel (2.7), Alibech (3.10), and Gerbino (4.4)—alongside the intercalated "novella" of Isabella and Zerbino that Ludovico Ariosto partly fashions from them in *Orlando furioso* (cantos 13 and 24). Since both Boccaccio and Ariosto creatively adapt motifs from chansons de geste and novellas, students can explore these narratives as products of a cross-cultural fertilization between genres. These stories also dramatize the perils and delights of traversing religious, cultural, and geographic boundaries across the Mediterranean region, including captivity, sexual experience, and the (potential) loss of country, kin, honor, or life. In addition, by viewing the four heroines as variations on the trope of the Muslim woman who desires and is desired by a Christian man, we can approach their tales as fantasies of cultural assimilation and appropriation. Students might compare Isabella's voluntary religious conversion and journey to a convent near Marseilles, which are facilitated by a hermit (*Furioso* 24.88–92) with Boccaccio's subversion of Christian catechism in the hermit Rustico's "devil" (*Decameron* 3.10) and the fabricated convent devoted to "Saint Stiffen-in-the-Hollows" ("san Cresci in Valcava"), also purportedly near Marseilles (2.7). Zerbino's death (*Furioso* 24) and Isabella's martyr-like demise (*Furioso* 29) can similarly be read side by side with the executions of the princess of Tunis and the king of Sicily's grandson (*Decameron* 4.4).

While romance epics feature numerous Muslim heroines in martial and amatory roles, in the post-Boccaccian novella such figures are singularly rare. Giovanni Sercambi's *Novelle* (c. 1390–1402) includes a significant variant of the *inclusa* motif (wherein a woman is locked up by her husband or father): in tale 144, the sultan of Babylon (Cairo) jealously confines his wife Lavinia (daughter of Kublai Khan) to a tower. Enticed by reports of her beauty, the Genoese Antoniotto sails across the Mediterranean, seduces Lavinia, and—through a subterfuge that includes camouflaging her as an Italian—absconds with her back to Genoa. Students might examine how Sercambi calls attention to the couple's cultural and religious difference: Antoniotto teaches her "a parlare al modo d'Italia" ("to speak in the manner of Italy"; 1211), Lavinia—in a passage that recalls Alatiel's dancing in the Alexandrian style (*Decameron* 2.7)—performs "una danza al modo turchiesco" ("a Turkish-styled dance"; 1213), and, on boarding the galley to Genoa, Antoniotto entrusts "il soldano a Macometto e loro a Dio" ("the sultan to Mohammed and them to God"; 1217).[1]

Romance epics likewise repeatedly point to differences of dress, custom, language, and faith. In Matteo Maria Boiardo's opening setting for Charlemagne's tournament, for example, the King sat

> [s]opra una sedia d'ôr . . . alla mensa ritonda
> Alla sua fronte fôrno e Saracini,
> Che non volsero usar banco né sponda,
> Anzi sterno a giacer come mastini
> Sopra a tapeti, come è lor usanza,
> Sprezando seco il costume di Franza.
>
> on a gold throne at his Round Table.
> In front of him were Saracens
> who had no need of bench or couch;
> instead, they lay full length like hounds
> on carpets, as they always do,
> scorning the customs Frenchmen use. (*Orlando innamorato* 1.1.13)

Later in the poem, we learn of the limits of Moorish armor:

> Non avea intorno pezzo di metallo,
> Perché era armato pure a quella usanza,
> Moresca, dico, essendo Genoese:
> Ma con la fede avea cambiato arnese.
>
> No metal plates protected him
> whose panoply was made in Moorish
> fashion. Although from Genoa,
> he'd changed his arms with his religion. (3.6.17)

We also find numerous appeals to Apollino, Macon, and Trivigant, the imaginary trinity of deities ascribed to Muslim worship in medieval texts (including 1.18.9, 1.20.54, and 2.1.59). In the *Furioso*, Orlando passes for a Saracen as he searches for Angelica in the enemy camp:

> e ben lo potea far sicuramente,
> avendo indosso l'abito arabesco;
> ed aiutollo in questo parimente
> che sapeva altro idioma che francesco,
> e l'africano tanto avea espedito,
> che parea nato a Tripoli e nutrito.
>
> The surcoat of an emir which he wore
> Made this less hazardous for him to do,
> And in his quest it helped him furthermore

That other languages than French he knew.
He spoke the Arab tongue so fluently
Men deemed him born and bred in Tripoli. (9.5)

Evoking Boccaccio's Alatiel, who falls prey to Pericone's sexual advances because she is drunk and unaccustomed to wine, Ariosto describes Rodomonte as enjoying his first taste of wine so much that he berates his own faith and gets drunk before beheading Isabella (29.22). In Torquato Tasso's *Liberata*, the Franks can follow Alete's embassy from the king of Egypt because they "han già il sermone appreso / de la Soria" ("had by now well sped / in learning Syrian"; 2.61), and Clorinda reminds Aladino that Islam forbids idolatry when she condemns Ismeno's theft of a statue of the Virgin Mary (2.50).

A striking novella of Christian-Muslim love that partly evokes Sercambi's 144th narrative is the opening tale of Agnolo Firenzuola's *Ragionamenti*, from 1525 (Firenzuola, *Le novelle* 9–199): a Tunisian noblewoman falls in love with Niccolò, a Florentine nobleman sold as a slave to her husband, and escapes back to Italy with him. Two portions of the novella underline cultural, social, and religious difference from the protagonists' perspective: first the Tunisian woman dismisses her fears about loving Niccolò by asserting the equal merit of all men regardless of cultural or geographical origin, social status, and religious faith; then Niccolò persuades her to escape with him by arguing for the cultural and religious superiority of Christian Florentine society over an uncivilized and hostile Muslim Tunisian world. The contrast between Niccolò's reductive xenophobia and the heroine's tolerant relativism reflects tensions between orthodox and heterodox worldviews particular to sixteenth-century Italy. Firenzuola's novella is also a stimulating counterpoint to the more genuine conversions of Fiordelisa (*Innamorato* 1.17.37), Marfisa (*Furioso* 38.18–23), and Clorinda and Armida (*Liberata* 12.65–69 and 20.136, respectively).

Novellas that narrate the coupling of Muslim male and Christian female protagonists elaborate a broader variety of character types and scenarios. Salernitano's *Novellino* (1475), a collection composed after Constantinople fell to the Ottoman Turks in 1453 and in the hierarchized world of Aragonese Naples, includes three novellas (22, 24, and 25) that recount sexual liaisons between Italian women and their black Moorish slaves, underscoring the transgression of religious, cultural, ethnic, and social boundaries as well as the physical and verbal violence Christian male protagonists use to restore their honor. While such pairings do not appear in romance epics (and students might be invited to consider why), Salernitano's stereotypes of barbarity and monstrosity that cast the women and Moors as extreme threats to social order and morality recur in the portrayals of numerous Saracen warriors: King Grandonio of Morocco is "il cane arabïato" ("that mad dog"; 1.2.49) and King Trufaldino of Baghdad is "Quel falso cane de Dio maledetto" ("a false dog cursed by God"; 1.21.4) in the *Innamorato*; the Tartar king Mandricardo is "il crudel barbaro" ("that [cruel] infidel"; 14.37) in the *Furioso*; and the Circassian mercenary Argante is, in the *Liberata*, "il feroce pagan" ("the ferocious pagan"; 7.89). Comparative studies of such passages suggest continuities in formulaic notions about Muslim identity across time, genres, and narrative scenarios, even as the texts include flattering depictions, such as the *Innamorato*'s Iroldo and Prasildo (also from Baghdad) and the examples of magnanimity described below.

Two novellas that present more favorable versions of this coupling are Giovambattista Giraldi Cinzio's *Hecatommithi* 3.7 (1565), which served as the source for Shakespeare's *Othello*, and Bandello's *Novelle* 4.12 (1574). Both narratives can be read as variants of the motif of unjustly accused wives and correlated with Zinevra's novella in the *Decameron* (2.9) and the episode about Zerbino's sister Ginevra (*Furioso* 4.57–6.16). Bandello's novella joins the tradition of miracle narratives (here based on legends about the union of a Tartar king and a Christian Armenian princess) and concludes with the conversion of the king and his entire nation. This story can be juxtaposed to the dynastic union between Ruggiero and Bradamante in Boiardo's and Ariosto's poems, as well as the wholesale conversion of Armenia, precipitated by the neophyte Fiordelisa, in the *Innamorato* (2.27.35).

Although there is no shortage of gory violence in the novella tradition, armed conflicts function almost exclusively as background. Take, for instance, the Crusade context in *Decameron* 10.9, the description of conflict and trade between Christian and Muslim corsairs that opens Salernitano's *Novellino* 22, and the Venetian-Ottoman war that frames Giraldi's *Hecatommithi* 3.7. Conversely, Christian-Muslim battles and duels are central components of romance epics, which often dwell on the bloodiest details of injury and death. Students can discuss possible explanations for this divergence, including the fact that novellas tend to be more domestic in scope, while romance epics are grounded in the history of Christian-Muslim enmity. Within single novellas, however, passages often evoke the battles of romance epics, such as Gerbino's storming of the Tunisian ship carrying his beloved in *Decameron* 4.4.

Conflict also opens the door to mutual magnanimity and expressions of chivalry in both genres. The *Decameron* novella of Saladin and Torello (10.9) is a well-known example. Salernitano's *Novellino* includes two less studied but no less striking tales. In novella 46, King Alfonso of Portugal captures the Arab military captain Molefes after conquering Arzil (Asilah). What begins as a narrative of territorial conquest turns into a negotiation for Molefes's release, mediated by his eloquent and fearless mother. In novella 48, Catalan corsairs capture Malem, the King of Tunis's son, and sell him as a slave to Guidotto, a nobleman of Pisa. Guidotto sets him free only to be captured in turn by a Moorish galley and find himself serendipitously in Malem's service. Unlike Saladin and Torello, Guidotto and Malem explicitly discuss their adherence to their respective faiths. Their tale is thus apt for comparative analyses with *Decameron* 1.3 (Saladin and Melchisedek) and with Boiardo's creative imitation of this pattern in the conversation between Orlando and Agricane that interrupts their duel (*Innamorato* 1.18.36–54) and the latter's conversion in extremis (1.19.12–16). While Malem is not prepared to renege his religion, the novella concludes with a fantasy of cultural assimilation: Guidotto returns to Pisa with Malem's sister as his newly converted bride.

In romance epics, magnanimous acts occur more often in truces or even military alliances that run counter to religious fealty. In *Innamorato* 1.3.78–81, for example, Orlando requests a truce so he may pursue Angelica. Feraguto initially refuses, but then himself asks Orlando to defer their duel so that he may help his uncle, King Marsilio, fend off Gradasso's attack on Spain (1.4.11–12). Charlemagne, who had already gone against literary tradition in the poem's first canto by opening a Pentecostal joust to both Christian and Saracen knights, barring renegades (1.1.9), explicitly sets religious difference aside when Spain is threatened ("Dico che, se Marsilio è saracino, / Ciò non attendo" ["Marsilio is a Saracen: / that does not matter"]; 1.4.14), citing as grounds for supporting the Spanish king not only France's national security but also his neighborly and kinship ties to Marsilio (1.14–16). In the *Furioso*, Ferrau's and Rinaldo's quest for Angelica inspires them to suspend their duel and ride the same steed in her pursuit: "Oh gran bontà de' cavallieri antiqui! / Eran rivali, eran di fé diversi, . . . e pur per selve oscure e calli obliqui / insieme van senza sospetto aversi" ("O noble chivalry of knights of yore! / Here were two rivals, of opposed belief, . . . Yet to each other no resentment bore. / Through the dark wood and winding paths, as if / Two friends, they go"; 1.22). Such episodes show students how chivalry can eclipse religious difference.

There are more Muslim-Christian encounters in the novella and romance epic traditions than this essay can survey. Instructors can find additional examples in secondary readings that might supplement lectures, accompany primary readings, and aid students in drafting research papers. These might include, among others, Robert J. Clements and Joseph Gibaldi's *Anatomy of the Novella*, particularly the section titled "Nationalism, Patriotism, Xenophobia, Racism" (109–21); Michael Papio's *Keen and Violent Remedies*; Janet Smarr's "Non-Christian People and Spaces in the *Decameron*"; Gloria Allaire's *The Italian Novella*; Sergio Zatti's *The Quest for Epic*; Jo Ann Cavallo's *The World beyond Europe*; and my articles "Muslim-Christian Encounters in Masuccio Salernitano's *Novellino*" and "Genealogy of a Character: A Reading of Giraldi's Moor."

Instructors interested in adapting the content discussed here for survey courses on Italian literature in translation will find excellent suggestions for editions of romance epics in this volume. The few available translations of post-Boccaccian novellas are very dated and so bear the occasional error and lack the critical apparatus of present-day praxis (Taylor's "Cinthio's Tale of the Moor of Venice" [1855], the anonymously translated *Tales of Firenzuola* [1889], Payne's *The Novels of Matteo Bandello* [1890], Waters's *Salernitano's Novellino* [1895], and Steegman's *Tales from Sacchetti* [1908]). It is nevertheless worth acquainting students in survey courses, who typically might only read selections from the *Decameron*, with some of these provocative and largely understudied works from the later tradition. The texts outlined in this essay can also supplement the discussions and reading lists of interdisciplinary courses on medieval and early modern representations of race, gender, religion, and sexuality.

Most recently, I included some of these texts in a course that bore the same title as this essay, Muslims in the Novella and Romance Epic Tradition (my iteration of my department's Writing about European Literature and Culture course designation, itself an iteration of College Writing 2, a writing-intensive course required for all undergraduates). Alongside more traditional assignments, I paired students for a creative project in which they adopted the voice of an author on the syllabus and rewrote a Christian-Muslim encounter as either a novella or romance epic episode. Students were free to develop a more verisimilar or fantastic storyline (or a little of both) and to borrow motifs and protagonists from any text on the syllabus. The assignment allowed students to engage collaboratively outside the conventions of academic writing with some of the narrative patterns and phraseologies they had encountered. My students enjoyed working together creatively and produced compelling variants on stories of medieval and early modern cross-cultural contact.

## Note

1. Translations are mine unless otherwise noted.

**Allison DeWitt**

# Digital Approaches to the Italian Romance Epic in the Classroom

> *I drew a pencil line to trace Astolfo's eastward voyage in pursuit of Orlando, and the impetuous sweep of that curve seemed to reflect Astolfo's personality and at the same time to symbolize the particular pleasure of reading this romantic epic.*
>
> — *Orlando innamorato* (Charles S. Ross trans.)

When faced with works of literature as complex and detailed as the *Innamorato* and *Furioso*, most students will devise a chart or apparatus to track all the fictional information that helps them understand the narrative. In the above quotation, Charles Stanley Ross reflects on his own experience drawing a map on the walls of his room and how the experience helped him understand something new about the literary work. Given the highly geographic nature of the romance epic, the impulse to map the crisscrossing journeys, exotic locations, and characters' origins is not surprising. With the technologies and tools available today, students are no longer limited to maps taped to the wall or sketched in notebooks.[1] However, it is not enough to merely ask students to plot points on *Google Maps* or create spreadsheets of important references. The inclusion of digital tools in the Italian romance epic classroom requires forethought and planning on the part of the instructor. This paper will discuss considerations that go into incorporating such a project as well as the numerous benefits afforded by the inclusion. Such projects help students gain valuable skills for understanding and working with data and make them more comfortable learning and using new technologies. The questions and considerations involved help students apply critical thinking and analysis to digital tools and methods, a useful mode of thinking that will extend beyond the semester's work. The final product shows students the results of their intellectual labor in a format that can be shared with their peers as a learning resource.

Before choosing an exciting new tool and having students create extensive data sets on top of their other assignments, we must carefully consider the class's learning objectives, how the digital can enhance these objectives, and how the digital can become a key part of the intellectual inquiry. Each step of the project helps students engage with the text in a completely new way: drawing out specific references, categorizing them for digital use, and analyzing the results of the data they input. Since the project's aim is not the end result but rather each step of the process, we must be aware of the work involved throughout the semester and give students credit for all tasks completed, even when they seem tedious.

Although students will need to complete simple but time-consuming tasks, it is important to balance this digital work with time for reflection and discussion of both the literature and the project. Before students can digitally map the geography or narrative of the text, they need to formulate detailed questions about the nature of spatiality and narrative.[2] In any class on the romance epic students will already be considering the work's use of geography and thinking about the narrative functions of different spaces. The romance epic is highly locational; creating a timeline of the story and mapping its locations are almost comparable tasks. Each of the *Innamorato*'s three books begins with a new king of a different geographic region heading toward Paris. The movements of Matteo Maria Boiardo's characters sketch a map of Boiardo's world, while the narrator also directs the reader's attention to different places on the map when he shifts from one character's story to another's. There are many moments when the narrator tells the reader that the plot will leave one group of characters where they are (fighting a battle, traveling, etc.) and pick up with another group literally where we left them.

Considering literary texts from a geographic lens is not something particularly radical when we consider the ways these texts function in the world. In *Geocriticism: Real and Fictional Spaces*, Bertrand Westphal maintains that "literature is already playing the game: texts have always looked at geography and at ways of representing human spaces" (32). This is not merely true for literary works focused on geographic spaces and journeys. Robert Tally argues in *Spatiality* that "the very idea of *plot* is also spatial, since a plot is also a plan, which is to say, a map" (49). Students could come to these realizations just through reading and discussing, but it takes a different skill set to show these realizations using digital tools. Once they have mastered a critical conception of spatiality and narrative, they analyze their own roles as they mine data from the text and manipulate it into different forms.

In the preface to his translation of Westphal's *Geocriticism*, Tally argues that "[a]ll writing partakes in a form of cartography, since even the most realistic map does not truly depict the space, but, like literature, figures it forth in a complex skein of imaginary relations" (x). In devising and creating a digital map, students become mapmakers of a new text of references. The concept of writer as mapmaker is central to literary cartography, but creating a digital map asks students to be self aware and critical of their own role in the production and analysis of information. Calling the text's references "data" and entering them into a tool that automatically arranges them could give students the sense that there is something inherently real or true about the digital analysis. In fact, the digital merely gives us new ways of looking at the same information and prompts questions that a standard reading might not have revealed.

There are many themes that students could explore in a standard course paper, but in order to go beyond a simple spatial discussion of the text, they require a new tool kit that allows them to interact with this data in multiple ways. Franco Moretti, the famous theorist of distant reading, has explained the importance of the literary map: "You choose a unit . . . find its occurrences, place them in a space . . . or in other words: you *reduce* the text to a few elements, and *abstract* them from the narrative flow, and construct a new, *artificial* object. . . . And with a little luck, these maps will be *more than the sum of their parts*: they will possess 'emerging' qualities, which were not visible at the lower level" (53). Before the map has even been created, it is a valuable exercise to ask students to agree on a unit, debate what constitutes an occurrence, and decide how best to place these in a space. This initial conversation already gets students thinking about questions of reading and interpretation and how their digital interventions can uncover new ideas as well as how to make their categorization most effective.

One unit that students might map could be each character's place of origin in the epics of Boiardo and Ludovico Ariosto. If the course is not focused on developing technological aptitude, the project could be as simple as having students drop points on a group *Google Map* throughout the semester as they read. If creating, for example, a map of characters' origins in the *Innamorato* and the *Furioso*,[3] students might color code the characters, highlighting Christians as yellow, Saracens and pagans as green, and fantastic creatures as blue. This map would help students extract key pieces of information from the texts, while also posing further questions for research. Students might immediately see that Christian characters are outnumbered by Saracens, pagans, and magical beings. They might also notice the density of characters coming from North Africa and Spain and the Eastern origins of all fantastic beings. However, these observations beg further questions. Where are these characters at the end of each epic? What would a consideration of their travels tell us? What other locations are important to the story, even if they are not any character's place of origin?

Not only does visualizing the data allow for a different understanding of the text but even such a technologically simple project prompts questions about the digital medium itself. What effect does *Google*'s standard GIS backdrop have on our relationship to these early modern (sometimes fictional) place references? What aspects of our literary analysis are not represented in this map? How much can truly be shown in a map, and what needs a deeper explanation?

Obviously, such a map is not intended to be viewed in a screenshot. The advantages of digital mapping are that students can zoom in and out and play around with the locations. Ranaldo and Orlando have a fairly specific place of origin, which students can explain in a note accompanying the map point. However, since the map requires a dropped pin for each character, it is impossible to see just by looking that Orlando is from a very specific place, while other characters are just from Spain. Other places, like Brandimarte's birthplace in the Isole lontane, are much more debatable, and although this can be explained in a note, the map does not capture the amount of interpretation that went into deciding where to drop Brandimarte's marker.

This project is a low-stakes example of integrating technology into an existing course on the romance epic. It does not require students to learn many new skills beyond what they most likely use in their daily lives. However, it also does not create a carefully curated data set drawn from the text or a final product that could be widely disseminated as a teaching and learning tool.

A significant benefit of more involved digital projects is their potential for long-term growth as well as the creation of long-lasting resources. In creating more detailed digital projects, students engage with the humanities in new ways and gain both conceptual and practical skills to apply such a methodology more broadly. The ultimate result is the creation of visualizations, data sets, and new tools that can help other students understand various aspects of the epic as well as assist future scholarship. Through the creation of these resources students will see the relevance of their work, learn valuable new skills, and benefit from the work of their peers.

However, not all the questions raised by the creation of the *Google Map* are solved by more advanced digital tools. In some ways, using tools specifically created for digital humanities projects allows students more freedom to introduce nuance and explore a variety of representations. But some aspects of mapping literary texts are inherently problematic. A literary geographic reference can be vague or fragmentary, but a digital map requires an exact coordinate or polygon for representation. As mentioned above, a character can be from Spain, but it is just as inaccurate to drop a point anywhere in the country as it is to indicate the entirety of Spain as their place of origin.

It is also possible that an author's use of a place differs greatly from the real-world place. An author may introduce a castle into a known city, but if the castle is fictional it is hard to indicate it on a GIS map based on actual geography. Additional considerations come into play for scholars of early modern texts. Questions of spelling and nomenclature can make it difficult for us to understand exactly what place the author was referring to hundreds of years ago. Changes in borders, measures of distance, and names of places often require the modern mapmaker to first gain a strong understanding of early modern geography before being able to identify the significance of even a simple reference. And of course there is always the issue of using twenty-first-century software and modern ideas of cartography to represent spatial knowledge that was based on a different understanding of the world.[4]

The growth in digital humanities projects has resulted in the creation of many easy-to-use tools that address the challenges of mapping literature as well as the deficiencies of *Google Maps*. Tools for narrative mapping such as *Neatline* (neatline.org) or *Story Map* (storymap.knightlab.com) allow students to go beyond a map of coordinates. Alongside geographic points, they can include images, links, and timelines. They can use an image as a background rather than a standard GIS display, and a copy of the text could accompany the map of the characters' travels. Unlike the *Google Maps* exercise discussed above, here students would need to create a data set of references mined from the text to work with these digital mapping tools. While this means more work for the students, understanding how data works and how to create and maintain data sets is a useful skill, and the workload, if divided among groups of students, could still be kept quite manageable. A project that contains so many potential components could be a great opportunity for collaboration, as different students could be responsible for geographic data, images, text, or timeline.

The *Furioso Atlas* is a wonderful example of a *Neatline* project that represents the romance epic. While this project is too complex to complete in a semester, it shows students what is possible and could help them think through their own smaller projects on the genre. The atlas uses a scan of Martin Waldseemüller's 1507 world map alongside a highlighted copy of the text. The user can either follow the lines of a character's journey on the map or select place names in the text in order to jump to their corresponding placement on the map. Daniel Leisawitz, the map's creator, states the aim of the atlas in terms that could help students conceptualize the goals of their own projects: "It is our hope that by reelaborating Ariosto's poem in spatial terms, we may better understand the interaction of the real and the imaginary in the poetic text as patterns and meanings emerge which have heretofore gone unnoticed."

*TimelineJS* is another tool created by Esri, the developers of *Story Maps*. It is purely for creating narrative timelines, and while it does not include a map as the organizing principle, it can include other media (images, videos, recordings) as well as links. This tool would particularly help students draw out the chronology of an often-shifting narrative and would allow them to explore or represent events through the inclusion of artistic representations or staged performances of a scene. A timeline could examine the chronology of the epic tradition itself or a character's development over time and a variety of texts.

The various romance epics use and expand on many of the same locations and characters, and we can learn much by studying these repetitions and rewritings. Tally maintains that "genre is itself a sort of map, since the generic parameters help to establish the projected 'world' of the story" (*Spatiality* 55). Here is another contention about narrative that succinctly describes a key aspect of the Italian romance epic. Writing within such a rich and long tradition and for an audience already familiar with the details, each epic author was obliged to include certain characters and refer to their earlier exploits. Although the characters have appeared in previous epics, new authors play with their reputations or rewrite their exploits in order to fit them into their personal narrative scheme. An analysis of these reuses and rewritings could pose fruitful questions and uncover new realizations about the tradition.

Another tool that would be particularly useful for considering the epic tradition, a manuscript tradition, or the development of certain characters, is *Palladio* (hdlab.stanford.edu/palladio/). It is an NEH funded project developed at Stanford and inspired by the Mapping the Republic of Letters project, which examines networks of knowledge between 1500 and 1800 (republicofletters.stanford.edu/). Students would need to create a detailed data set for upload to the site, but then the tool provides multiple modes of exploring and visualizing the data. A project using *Palladio* would not result in a shareable Web site like *Neatline* or *Story Map*, but if the project's goal is for students to continually play with the data, ask new questions, and try out different visualizations, it is less important for them to create a polished final product.

This essay has just touched on a few of the existing digital mapping tools. The available resources and the services they offer are constantly changing, particularly as more scholars become interested in addressing the difficulties of effectively mapping literary references. Ultimately, the key to integrating a successful digital mapping project into the romance epic classroom relies on creating well-thought-out learning goals, balancing digital tasks with humanist reflections, and continually assessing student learning and the manageability of assigned tasks.

## Notes

1. See Presner and Shephard for a discussion of the development of digital humanities mapping and an overview of projects and tools.

2. When reworking or formulating learning goals for a digital assignment, it is useful to consider Bloom's taxonomy, which shows that students must understand before they can apply and analyze before they can create (cft.vanderbilt.edu/guides-sub-pages/blooms-taxonomy/).

3. This information comes from the table "Names and Origins of Fictional Characters" in Cavallo, *World* 263–66.

4. These considerations have been adapted from those discussed by Reuschel and Hurni; Piatti and Hurni; and Wrisley.

# Part VI

# Beyond the "Three Ferrarese Crowns": The Italian Romance Epic in Translation

**Andrea Moudarres**

# Margutte's Pupils: The Ethics of Laughter in Pulci's *Morgante*

In *cantare* 18 of Luigi Pulci's heroicomic poem *Morgante*, the titular hero encounters Margutte (18.112–13), a half-giant of dubious parentage, monstrous features, and appalling moral credentials. As Margutte himself proudly details in a mock-confession modeled in part after the Nicene Creed (18.115–18), he has been a relentless sinner since the moment of his conception: "io fu' cattivo insin nell'uovo" ("Even in my mother's womb I was perverse" 18.141.8).[1] Throughout his life, he has shown his natural talent as a thief and a pimp as well as an irresistible inclination toward gluttony (18.115–42). The only sin that Margutte has never committed is treachery (18.142), as he tells Morgante perhaps with a nod to the moral structure of Dante's *Inferno*, where treachery is punished in the lowest circle of hell. Margutte's confession marks the beginning of one of the most hilarious and ribald episodes of the *Morgante*. While it would be tempting to focus exclusively on the comic verve of Margutte's and Morgante's adventures, which unfold over roughly 240 ottave between *cantari* 18 and 19, this essay proposes a teaching strategy that integrates the analysis of the most irreverently funny aspects of the Margutte episode with what could be described as the episode's ethics of laughter—the subversive ethical dynamics set in motion by Margutte's and Morgante's playful feats.[2]

The proposed reading assignment is intended to take two or three weeks (and a total of four or five meetings) in an undergraduate seminar either on fifteenth-century Florence, alongside texts such as Angelo Poliziano's *Stanze* and a selection of Lorenzo de' Medici's poems, or on Italian Renaissance epic, together with excerpts from works ranging from Matteo Maria Boiardo's *Orlando innamorato* and Ludovico Ariosto's *Orlando furioso* to Torquato Tasso's *Gerusalemme liberata*. The course, whose enrollment would preferably not exceed twenty students, could be conducted in English or in Italian. I should note that, considering the limits of this essay, I will not dwell on the remarkable linguistic challenge that a work such as the *Morgante*—written in a vernacular rich with colloquialisms and proverbial expressions rooted in the popular culture of fifteenth-century Florence—poses even to the most advanced students of Italian.

In introducing Pulci's *Morgante* to an undergraduate class, it seems necessary to contextualize the political and cultural history of quattrocento Florence, particularly the tensions among some members of Lorenzo de Medici's circle of intellectuals (including Marsilio Ficino and Luigi Pulci) and about the Medici family's interest in the carnival. The dearth of English studies on Pulci means a professor teaching the course in translation must lecture on the information needed to contextualize the *Morgante* and rely on one of the works dedicated to Renaissance Florence, even though it may not specifically address Pulci's contribution to his city's cultural production.[3] Students who are highly proficient in Italian can also benefit from the research of Alessandro Polcri and Alessio Decaria, two scholars who have recently investigated in great depth Pulci's often polemical engagement with other protagonists of Florence's intellectual life.[4] Moreover, excerpts from Mikhail Bakhtin's introduction to his *Rabelais and his World* (1–58, especially p. 9) can provide a suitable theoretical starting point for a productive discussion on the carnival as a cultural phenomenon that radically upends society's traditional hierarchies. Given Lorenzo's role as Florence's de facto ruler, his significant accomplishment as an author of *canti carnascialeschi*, and his patronage of artists and writers such as Pulci, I find it beneficial to propose and provoke questions regarding the carnival's political uses and to point out its relation with the sacred. My main goal in illustrating the interplay of the carnival with the political and religious life of a community, and of Florence in particular, is to offer a clear example of a ludic event (or series of events) with eminently serious implications. It is in this light that I would like to examine the Margutte episode.

Before turning to the *Morgante*, however, let us first imagine a hypothetical scenario: in the crime section of a local newspaper we read that two men entered a bed and breakfast and, after robbing the owners, terrorized them and destroyed their property; the two perpetrators are still on the loose. How would we react to such a piece of news? It is probably safe to assume that most of us would respond with a combination of horror and dismay and with the hope that the police quickly apprehend the criminals. What might alter this most natural reaction? One possible answer: play. As it happens, this scenario does not significantly differ from the scene on which I would like to focus in the following pages: Margutte's and Morgante's encounter with an innkeeper, whose name—"il Dormi" ("the Sleeper"; 18.169)—leaves little hope for his good fortune. It is not only the self-described paragon of sin, Margutte, who abuses il Dormi's foolishness and helplessness but also the good giant, Morgante, who in the first part of the episode repeatedly strikes the innkeeper with his bell clapper. The innkeeper's fault consisted of offering an inadequate meal to the ravenous giant and of pointing out, somewhat curtly, the impossibility of finding more food at night:

> Rispose l'oste: "Mangi delle ghiande.
> Che vuoi tu ch'io provvegga, or ch'egli è sera?"
> e cominciò a parlar superbamente,
> tal che Morgante non fu paziente:
> comincia col battaglio a bastonare;
> l'oste gridava e non gli parea giuoco.
>
> Th' innkeeper answered, "Acorn let him eat.
> Where do I go for something else? It's dark."
> His tone of voice was full of arrogance:
> Morgante lost his patience all at once.
> His clapper he began to use on him,
> and the innkeeper did not like it much. (18.151.5–18.152.2)

The scene's humor derives mainly from the hyperbolic contrast between the giant's strength and the innkeeper's weakness, although what makes the scene playful to the reader is exactly what, as Pulci notes with litotes ("non gli parea giuoco"), is not playful to the poor innkeeper. The perceived lightheartedness of the passage masks a power relationship in which the victim's suffering is barely registered. Unsurprisingly, though, Morgante's beating is only the first of the innkeeper's woes. After consuming more than enough food to feed an entire village for a month (18.159.7–8), Morgante takes his leave and goes to sleep, whereas Margutte continues his inglorious deeds. The half-giant moves stealthily through the inn while everyone is asleep, stealing the little money that il Dormi and his wife had saved, all the supplies left after the previous evening's feast, and a camel to carry the stolen goods (18.176.3–4). Then, for good measure, Margutte sets the inn's barn on fire (18.176.7–8). When our two "heroes" leave the hostel, Morgante reacts to Margutte's account of his theft with an uproarious laughter (18.182.1–2).

There is nothing in the events I just summarized to ostensibly suggest that the reader should not cheer Morgante's and Margutte's gleeful roguishness. After all, what should really matter is the prank's goliardic tone, not the innkeeper's well-being. But is that actually the case? To be sure, the remainder of the episode abundantly shows that Morgante's colossal hunger and his readiness to sate it with his bell clapper remain the comic foci of this section. There are at least four vignettes between *cantare* 18.188 and 19.97 in which Morgante ruthlessly (and hilariously) devours his meals, including a giant turtle and an elephant, ably prepared by Margutte, who in turn (perhaps deservedly, given his earlier misdeeds) is left nothing but a few crumbs. In each of these scenes Morgante's boisterous laughter—or that of Florinetta, the girl our two protagonists rescued from a dreadful predicament (19.4–52)—accompanies Margutte's displeasure (18.196, 19.64, 19.70, and 19.87). It seems, nevertheless, that beneath the inn episode's indubitable comic force lies a less lighthearted, possibly even disturbing, undertone, an undertone that is not unique to Pulci's comedic style but that in fact typically informs much literature of play.

As is also often the case in Boccaccio's *Decameron*, a text to which the *Morgante* is indebted, play can become an effective instrument of ethical manipulation, whereby the author artfully inverts conventional standards of compassion. A rather large set of novellas in the *Decameron*, including those of the seventh day, is built around the motif of the *beffa*—that is, a trick or a joke played at the expense of one or more credulous individuals.[5] Among the best known of the *Decameron*'s *beffati* ("pranked individuals") is certainly Calandrino, a Florentine painter who appears in four novellas (8.3, 8.6, 9.3, and 9.5). In each of these stories he is pranked by his friends Bruno and Buffalmacco, who lead him to believe, among other things, that he is invisible (8.3) and that he is pregnant (9.3). A sound beating provides the proverbial icing on the cake in most of these pranks: for instance, while in 9.3 Calandrino beats his wife, in 9.5 the roles are inverted. The helplessness of characters such as Calandrino in the *Decameron* and il Dormi in the *Morgante* test the boundaries between comedy and cruelty, for the reader's likely impression is that, although they are not ascribed any particular guilt and do not present any irredeemable moral flaw, their gullibility warrants the ills that befall them, and the logic of this kind of play exacts the presence (perhaps the sacrifice) of a laughable victim whose suffering is never tragic. Contrary to what is likely in a story that does not gravitate around a *beffa*, readers are nearly complicit in the text's act of violence—physical, psychological, or both—insofar as they are subtly induced to feel no sympathy for the victim or even to rejoice at the perpetrators' violence, as we have just seen with Morgante and Margutte.

But why do we not feel sorry for the victim of a *beffa*? What psychological mechanisms does a storyteller exploit to make us perceive cruelty as amusement? These are only two questions that can fuel a discussion of the Margutte episode by challenging students' assumptions about what generates compassion for the weak and, more broadly, about their understanding of the line between good and evil. Furthermore, if a play can prove such a powerful rhetorical tool in subverting (presumably) established ethical principles, under what other circumstances can it be employed? For instance, could a modern society justify political violence aimed at purging an alleged internal threat when the violence is under the guise of a cathartic or even ludic ritual? Modern pop culture—including highly successful novels turned into films such as *A Clockwork Orange* and *The Hunger Games* trilogy, in which violence and entertainment go hand in hand—provides interested instructors a vast repertory of visually powerful materials that can resonate with twenty-first-century students, helping them gauge the differences and the similarities between our time and Pulci's.

It would of course be mistaken—not to mention counterproductive to the mood of the class—to reduce the *Morgante* to a rather grim allegory, political or otherwise, glossing over its exuberant comic vitality. In fact, precisely because of this vitality, the *Morgante* also offers the opportunity to examine comedy's frequent, though by no means exclusive, rhetorical tropes (for example, irony, parody, and witty riposte). As I have tried to show in this essay, however, it would be equally mistaken to teach Pulci's text as a mere divertissement and as if it did not present a wide range of profound ethical questions. It is not a coincidence that the last two *cantari* of the *Morgante* describe Orlando's rout of the Christian forces in the Battle of Roncevaux, the subsequent revenge inflicted on the Moorish troops, and the execution of the traitors Marsilio and Ganelon. Pulci himself, at the beginning of *cantare* 27, addresses the Lord, noting that his poem might be on the verge of turning into a tragedy : "s'altro aiuto qui non si dimostra, / sarà pur tragedìa la istoria nostra. // Ed io pur comedìa pensato avea / iscriver del mio Carlo finalmente" ("Unless greater help comes down to me, / this tale of ours will soon be tragedy. // And yet I had first thought I would write / about my Charlemagne a comedy"; 27.1.7–27.2.2). That Margutte dies bursting from laughing too hard at a trick played by Morgante (19.145–50) simply confirms that play can be deadly serious.

## Notes

1. Unless otherwise noted, Italian quotations of *Morgante* are from the Ageno edition (1994), and the English is Tusiani's translation.

2. For the theoretical perspective adopted in this essay, I am particularly indebted to Bakhtin, *Rabelais*; Huizinga, *Homo Ludens*; Mazzotta; and Turner.

3. A useful, albeit not entirely convincing, essay in English on Pulci is Lèbano, "Luigi Pulci and Late Fifteenth-Century Humanism."

4. See Polcri 5–66; Decaria, *Luigi Pulci* 116–38, 209–36; as well as Decaria's introduction to Pulci's *Sonetti extravaganti*, ix–xxxix.

5. On the *beffa* in the *Decameron*, see Mazzotta, 66–67, 186–212.

**Stefano Gulizia**

# Folengo's *Baldus* and *Orlandino*

Instructors can include Ann E. Mullaney's accessible translation of Teofilo Folengo's *Baldus* in both graduate and undergraduate courses in the Italian Renaissance.[1] The work, however, is well suited to many other types of upper-division courses, such as comparative surveys of Western epic, seminars of women studies that address comedy and misogyny, history courses on religious heterodoxy in areas that include the Serenissima and the Po Valley, or even a syllabus highlighting the role of food, dance, and other folkloric materials. Finally, its exuberant versatility and deep response to visual sources makes Folengo's *Baldus* particularly helpful in introducing art history students to the self-fashioning of Mantua as an alternative Rome during the years of Andrea Mantegna and Giulio Romano. In fact, Folengo's epic set pieces offer an original and self-assured reading, on grounds of sheer size and originality, for any course involved with the artistic and literary production of Northern Italian courts in the sixteenth century.

Typically, instructors following any of the options listed above could dedicate a single class, or perhaps two, to the *Orlandino*, a smaller chivalric poem written in 1526 and signaling, at once, Folengo's embrace of the vernacular in the coalescing *questione della lingua* ("language question"), his arrival in Venice, and his temporary leave from the Benedictine order. Instructors can use the *Orlandino* to show students how Folengo enters into dialogue with such contemporary authors as Matteo Maria Boiardo, Luigi Pulci, and Ludovico Ariosto through literary parody. I think it is crucial for every student to have a sense not only of the social and political contexts but also of the history of ideas that made these works possible: like Folengo, all epic and chivalric authors use a combination of humor and aestheticism, revisit old stories, and are engaged in an unending conversation with their predecessors. In this essay, I examine short and specific passages from Folengo's major work, the *Baldus*, adhering strictly to the articulation of its plot, which is neatly anchored around three events—a municipal epic (books 1–10), with the *Orlandino* framed as a theoretical counterpoint; a Lucianic voyage (11–20); and a descent to hell (21–25). My demonstration emphases Folengo's potential for teaching the cultural spaces of the Renaissance city and the sonic dimension of the piazza.

## *Baldus* 7.8–748

Among the possible books of the *Baldus* to assign, book 7 stands out. This book presents a set of related narratives that radiate with centrifugal force across the entire macaronic corpus of Folengo—namely, the panic function of dances and weddings as well as the disconcerting sexual frenzy of Mantuan youths and girls during a carnival season or other rustic entertainments. Folengo is inevitably drawn to the marvelous potentials of a Brueghelian, trompe-l'oeil-embroidered narrative involving peasant mockery and abandonment, but rarely as in book 7 has he been able to attain his goals with such spectacular effects and a distinctively macaronic sensibility. And what gives this book its ultimate unity, literary and folkloric, is the decision to anchor the narrative around Cingar's trick at the expense of a hapless and dim-witted local farmer, with the telltale name of Zambellus.[2] The plot moves, as it were, in concentric circles. Baldo is in prison, and his companion meditates on how to free himself and avenge his honor. Cingar first convinces the older Tognazzo that pretty Berta is in love with him and promises to do all in his power to favor their union (7.21–79; 167–71); then Cingar instructs Berta on how to feign flirtation and accompanies her to the communal dances (7.202–11; 212–82) while also plotting the ruin of the arrogant Zambellus. This last scene culminates with Cingar's successful attempt to sell at the marketplace a barrel of shit covered with honey

(7.461–532) and his final threats to the city's gullible apothecary (7.657–69) that turn out to be instrumental to leaving the jail.

Book 7, a decisive moment in Folengo's *Baldus*, proceeds with a combination of flashbacks, reported direct speech, and virtuoso set-pieces of a more descriptive intent. Students new to Folengo are immediately struck by the savage comedy enacted by the wily Cingar, which is magnified by woodcuts of the 1521 printed edition depicting the beatings of Zambellus,[3] but students can also be led to a more sophisticated awareness of the text's anthropological genealogy and literary predecessors. In addition to providing a proximate model for Tognazzo, as Massimo Scalabrini has demonstrated ("Contadini e mostri"), Polyphemus's lament in the bucolics of Theocritus, and its humanist imitations, is what Folengo kept in mind during this protracted pastoral incident. Tognazzo's foolish praise of his own virtues is especially indebted to the Greek author (7.132–34). Not unlike Torquato Tasso's version of pastoral, which similarly emphasizes the economic and almost utopian viability of a life in the fields, Folengo exploits the ambivalence between old age and youth to reframe the topical early modern contraposition between *urbanitas* and *rusticitas*, or city life versus country life. In conclusion, by studying *Baldus*'s book 7 as a stand-alone piece, students follow Folengo in revisiting a nexus of persistent peasant representation (and so paradoxically redeeming the European chivalric import of the adventure from a seemingly municipal and isolated position). Folengo's repetition of rustic comedy and tricks allow readers to recognize a character they have met elsewhere—in folklore or in Boccacio's *Decameron*, for instance—and to appreciate the play of similarities and differences that enables the invention of tradition.

## A Longer Chivalric Digression: The *Orlandino*

At 4,752 verses (eight books of vernacular octaves), Folengo's *Orlandino* is both the most eccentric and the most conservative product of his literary career. The very nature of the poem, an energetic take on the tale of Roland that is disproportionally focused on the hero's childhood,[4] reflects its author's perspective at a precise moment in time, in the mid-1520s, when he had left the Benedictine order and joined the ranks of the Venetian polymaths and writers-for-money. Although short-lived, Folengo's defection met with immediate success, as signaled by the quick publishing of two consecutive editions of the *Orlandino* in 1526.[5] At the same time, this narrative is only funneled through a somewhat convoluted mirroring device:

the poem is neither written nor read by Teofilo himself but by his fictional alter ego, Limerno Pitocco (literally, Merlin the Mantuan beggar). As a liminal figure between manuscript production and the economy of the book trade—parallel, in this, to other characters in Folengo's works, such as the singer Zoppino or the Roman Pasquino (*Baldus* 23)—this Mantuan street peddler offers great advantages to those teachers interested in the ephemerality of the public sphere or willing to contextualize a chivalric poem as a vital source of communication history. In this light, the materials of a homework assignment can be organized into spaces of arrival and distribution in an urban environment like a piazza and into strategies of authentication mediated by early modern charlatans, as in the episode of Turpino, near the opening of the *Orlandino* (1.21–22), which openly discusses the role of apocryphal literature in the Italian epic.

On the one hand, then, the poem's closeness to a layered chivalric intertext (while ostensibly refusing its consolidated technique of *entrelacement*, at 1.16) allows it to be taught as following many conventions established by Boiardo, Pulci, and other epic writers of the Italian quattrocento. On the other, however, a few glaring differences undermine its documentary value and its alleged dependence on the formulas of the oral tradition. Not only is it hard to situate the low comedy of the Bakhtinian carnival in the poem, but, as Maria Cristina Cabani has cogently argued, the use of acrostics and other reading devices ultimately make the *Orlandino* a bookish object ("L'*Orlandino* di Folengo"). All in all, the best framework for students is one that places Folengo's poem in response to both the *Baldus* and *Orlando furioso*. Of the larger macaronic work, the *Orlandino* recaptures, not without a sense of closure, the double aspects of mock-heroic romp across the Po Valley (4.73, 7–8, with the rhyme of *pantano* with *villano* ["bog"; "peasant"]) and its overall melancholic disposition (1.65, 7–8, with the opposition of *platonico* and *malenconico* ["Platonic"; "melancholic"]).[6] As for Ariosto, Folengo's poem appeared right after the first two versions of the *Furioso* and right before the third redaction, which would make it a fundamental grammatical revision in accordance with Pietro Bembo's rhetoric. The paradoxical result of Folengo's position vis-à-vis Ariosto, in short, is one of admiration without imitation (Capata 29).

Fewer Renaissance texts offer a richer or more direct peek into the writer's atelier than the *Orlandino*, with its repeated references to Federico Gonzaga's court life and milieu (a similar argument could be made of Pietro Aretino's *Marfisa Bizzarra* (1526), another chivalric poem dedicated to Federico). In book 3, Folengo signals in the middle of a tournament (16–21) the poetic genealogy of Dante and Petrarch from Virgil, and the legacy of the Mantuan Homer, in an interpretation of trecento writers as understood through the explicitly philosophical sign of Saturn; in another passage (6.29–30), Folengo interrupts a great clash (*conquasso,* a chivalric term validated by Antonio Berni) to recall the literary trophies of Mantua. In sum, the *Orlandino* can be a parodic point of entry into the ways of court and techniques used to move up the greasy rope of court favor—techniques known to Renaissance analysts or modern sociologists specializing in network theory. Unsurprisingly, since the poem's inspiration is ascribed to the aftermath of the author's split from the Benedictine monks (*indignatio fecit* ["product of fury"], an expression borrowed from Juvenal's *Satires*), its frequent tone of bitter scorn unlocks the intellectual tools of public life already discussed by Florentine humanists like Leon Battista Alberti and Pulci. Folengo's declared allegiance to Pulci may suggest a new way of looking beyond mockery at the development of chivalric epic in Northern Italy; in other words, Folengo's alignment with Pulci demonstrates how deeply, proudly, and consciously anachronistic the *Orlandino* really is as a chivalric project. Other features that present Folengo as a competent reader of court life are statements like 7.58, where the fantastical comparison of the author's brain (*mio cervello assai lunatico* ["my scattered brain"]) with abstract geometry or pure grammar displays a sort of pre-Galilean recognition of the cosmological style. When Giordano Bruno tried his hand at vernacular dialogues, his Copernical language looked back at Folengo and the *Orlandino.* Finally, Folengo's description of a courtly entertainment, which turns a staple of every romance into an erudite digression on reeds and instruments (4.26), depicts a continuing preoccupation with music and the sonic dimension of epic poems—already explored in the *Baldus.*

## *Baldus* 12.400–585 and 13.6–415

With book 11 of the *Baldus,* sustained by mythological exempla and sharply divided from the rest of the narrative by a classical *proemio al mezzo* ("proem in the middle"), Folengo considers how best to fit the Renaissance template of curiosity and wandering. The plot is largely taken up by a voyage at sea. And the tone is more or less in conformity with the Apuleian tradition of antiquity, with its multifarious, Lucianic, or Boccaccian (and by extension, Mediterranean), offspring. Given the printed diffusion, in Venice and beyond, of such books, that Folengo should use this section of the *Baldus* to write surreptitious messages to users of the book trade is of paramount importance. After all, if the narrator's unusual geographic perspective creates artificial suspense around what remains at times an extremely familiar story, readers as well discussed the rationale of his choices and the resulting ambivalence, within such philosophical fiction, between epic and novel. In particular, the business of genre stirred a remarkable reflection in Anton Francesco Doni's *La Libraria*, printed in 1557 by the Venetian firm of Giolito. In a canon of over fifty chivalric texts, extending to the anomalous *Morgante* by Pulci, Doni excludes the *Baldus* and includes the *Orlandino*.

Doni's reluctance, which offers upper-division courses many opportunities to reflect on the epic's role in Renaissance poetics and to expand the history of heroicomic poetry through theorists like Giraldi Cinzio and Alessandro Tassoni, makes perfect sense once one sees in detail Folengo's compressed allusions and verbal echoes of the *Baldus*. The second section of Folengo's poem, moreover, touches on alchemical materials and uses the constellations and the rising or setting of stars to produce Folengo's own ludic version of changing seasons and the passing of time; in fact, the longer sequence at the beginning of book 13 (in Cingar's mouth) is a veritable macaronic lesson in astronomy. This episode has invaluable classroom potentials. One model is offered, of course, by the long tradition of Latin didactic poems and the etiological myths in collections such as Ovid's *Fasti*. Folengo's proximity to this development is evident at 13.202: *machina mundi* ("machinery of the world") is a nod to Lucan, and in the following line the expression *dentata menat moles diversa rotarum* ("driven by a complicated mass of cogged wheels") conflates the Ovidian beginning, *rudis indigestaque moles* ("a shapeless mass"; *Metamorphosis* 1.7), with the Aristotelian theory of the spheres. Folengo's diction here is both impeccably classical and deeply macaronic (as with *pirlare* and *rotolatio* ["tumbling down"]),[7] while this book still follows the chivalric idea of marvel and wonder at the heavenly pounding of the hammers. Teaching this outstanding astronomical excursus also allows students to situate the *longue durée* of popular and folkloric prognostication (Martin 13–19), which moves from Folengo's *Baldus* to Rabelais and to the early Paduan observations of Galileo, in particular the *Dialogo de Ceccò di Ronchitti*. In other words, the instructor can draw attention to the relation between Folengo and the Aristotelian tradition in vernacular and Latin across the Veneto region, and focus profitably on the well-documented fusion of chivalric and cosmological styles in sixteenth-century Italy (Reeves 101–35).

What binds these themes is Folengo's tapping into sonic effects. The narrator says a murky tempest is making the ship groan and the heart tremble. This idea is sounded out as a fearsome leitmotif throughout the long sequence (for instance in the Apuleian *tremebundus* at 12.551, referring to the ship's pilot). The only difference is whether Folengo uses dialectal resources, as in *querza*, *spazzatum*, and *brancaverat*, or whether he relies on Virgil's high-voltage rhetoric: here line 546 is underlined by a cosmic idea (taken from *Georgics* 1.511) and effectively constructed by combining the epic diction *acerba* (always tragic in the *Aeneid* and in the hexameter's second position at 9.794 and 12.398) with the clause *per undas* (6.370 and 7.299). Folengo tends to repeat himself, but aside from that, this example illustrates his macaronic aesthetic in action as well as in words, demonstrating how novelistic digressions can coexist with epic pretensions.

## *Baldus* 25.1–174 and 25.462–569

It begins with chaos, as in Ovid, or it ends with chaos, like here. That is because at the end of a curricular activity on the *Baldus*, any anthology taken from the infernal and final portion is likely to prove purposely insufficient as context for the poem's ending. If the descent to hell is a trial for sustained epic ambitions, do the hundreds of stories and the disparate genres contained in books 21–25 really constitute a singular work, an aesthetic whole on a par with Virgil's achievement in the *Aeneid* or with Dante's *Inferno*? And why does Folengo actually set a gold standard for the literary sweep of his indecorous transgressions here, as opposed to in other sectors of his vast poem? A teacher's decision to include or exclude nocturnal segments from Baldus's underworld narrative derive from an evaluation of the students' knowledge of either classical or sixteenth-century traditions: the segments can precede the epics to which they aspire or be placed side by side with the texts they have helped to form, including Giordano Bruno's Italian dialogues. Indeed, the initial chaos and confusion notwithstanding, it would always be preferable for any class to read the poem without detailed annotation rather than, as in some undergraduate surveys of Renaissance literature, an abundance of annotation without the poem.

The relative advantages of assigning book 25 are less about absolute quality, versatility, and adaptability than about thematic coherence. The book brings to the fore two large and simple patterns—one related to the fight against Tisiphone, which culminates with a visit to her council, and the other centered on the house of Fantasy, an apocryphal Aristotelian locus where grammar is suspended and dialectical arguments are flying around the chivalric paladins. Folengo's invention, which is set aside by sonic markers (*silenti / murmure* at 25.476–77) and notations of logic (the *ordine confuso* ["confused order"] of 25.478), can better articulate a Benedictine's polemic against Scholasticism for the instructors who had followed the previous engagements of the poem with Paduan academic Aristotelianism. Moreover, since in the house of Fantasy the labor of walking is lifted upward, and Folengo pays special attention to the rushing and floating of the bodies, this episode also increases the range of approaches for teaching the historical construction of gender roles and embodiment in classical and postclassical treatments. Folengo's humor, complexity, and vivid imagery—as with the heifer bitten by a horsefly that sets book 25 in motion (line 6)—reward the student who attends to the details of the *Baldus*'s underworld. In sum, if Folengo's bombastic imitation of Dante and Virgil is a key to understanding his fortunate European diffusion, it is primarily through sound that students can best appreciate what a formidable reader he was of court life in sixteenth-century Italy.

## Notes

1. It is available in two volumes of the I Tatti Renaissance Library series; see my review in *Renaissance Quarterly*.

2. The Italian word *zimbello* marks a kind of scapegoat, whose desires are invariably denied and crushed by the community.

3. For the role of these woodcuts in the book trade, see Gulizia, "Scaffolding Folengo."

4. One of the best commentaries on the importance of the *enfances* and the anthropological vitality of childhood in Folengo is Scalabrini, *L'incarnazione del macaronico* 19–82.

5. The first is with Gregorio De Gregori's typography, the second with the brothers Sabbio.

6. Marco Faini uses melancholy as a cipher for Folengo's work at large (127–65).

7. Both of these are Folengo's neologisms, inspired by the Milanese language.

Julia L. Hairston and John C. McLucas

# Teaching Tullia d'Aragona's *Il Meschino, altramente detto il Guerrino (The Wretch, Otherwise Known as Guerrino)*

## From Preface to Poem

Tullia d'Aragona's thirty-six-canto epic *Il Meschino, altramente detto il Guerrino* offers exceptional opportunities for teaching issues of gender, otherness, authorial intention, literary tradition and register, and the epic quest for identity. The poem recounts the wide-ranging adventures of a virtuous young man in search of his parents and the truth of his origins, a search that leads him into experiences military, sexual, and spiritual, in this world and in others. The poem figures as the crowning achievement in a literary career already distinguished by a prose dialogue and verse collection, both published by Gabriele Giolito in 1547.[1] D'Aragona likely began composing the *Meschino* in Florence before 1547, as attested in a sonnet by Benedetto Arrighi included in her choral anthology, but it was only published in 1560 by Giovan Battista and Melchior Sessa in Venice, four years after her death, and likely edited by Girolamo Ruscelli, who sought the copyright (*privilegio*) from Venetian authorities.[2]

Echoing Boccaccio's introduction to the *Decameron*, d'Aragona's prose preface signals her explicit intention of offering a morally edifying story for women through poetry, about which she claims: "il verso, il quale non è alcun dubbio che molto più diletta, molto più vagamente si legge, molto più efficacemente fa impressione ne gli animi nostri, e molto più lietamente ci lascia la forma sua nella memoria, che le prose non fanno" ("There is no doubt that verse is much more delightful than prose, is much pleasanter to read, makes a much more effective impression on our spirits, and leaves a much happier trace of its form in our memory").[3] The author's emphasis on the importance of verse echoes earlier, similar comments in the dedication of her *canzoniere* (*Poems and Letters* 62–64). In the preface to the *Meschino*, d'Aragona claims to base her text on a Spanish prose original, yet she does not identify the author, who also remains unnamed in most fifteenth- and sixteenth-century printed editions. Close comparative reading reveals that her source text was a Tuscan romance of the same name by Andrea da Barberino, although in many instances d'Aragona diverges from her source to develop her characters' emotional lives more fully.[4] The adventures of Guerrin Meschino—the hero is called both by his baptismal name, Guerrino, and by the sympathetic epithet *il Meschino* ("the Wretch") given him in infancy—remained popular throughout the centuries, spawning a comic book series in 1917, a film by Pietro Francisci with score by Nino Rota in 1951, as well as—more recently—a novel by Gesualdo Bufalino in 1991.[5]

The preface provides interesting reflections on the function of literature. D'Aragona elaborates on the pleasures of reading and how it releases the reader (male or female) from other cares. She also emphasizes its independent nature and the relative ease with which one might adopt it: "Là ove nel leggere, noi possiamo da noi stessi governarci a tutto voler nostro, soli, accompagnati, poco, molto, senza spesa, senza pericolo, senza danno, senza travaglio, ma con piena satisfattione, e contentezza di noi medesimi" ("In reading, on the other hand, we can direct ourselves independently, following our own will entirely, whether alone, in company, briefly or at length, without expense, risk, harm, or fatigue, and to our own full satisfaction and happiness").

The preface also highlights how the author contextualizes herself in the literary tradition of ottava rima. Her observations on style and lexicon would fit aptly in a course in Italian that considers linguistic register:

> Et havendo considerato e inteso da molti giudiciosi la diversità de gli stili in quei libri d'ottava rima, che fin qui si son visti, trovai, che alcuni vanno tanto serpendo a terra, che ogni animo non del tutto basso si sdegna pur di vederli, non che possa dilettarsi a leggerli. Altri all'incontro havendo aspirato a quasi piacer solo a i dotti, si sono alzati tanto, che non solamente, a i mezani, e principalmente alle donne, ma anco a i

> dotti stessi danno in molti luoghi da fare per farsi intendere, e si veggono ad ogn'ora commentatori, et espositori sopra di loro, come nelle leggi, e nella filosofia. Là onde io ho procurato di tenermi con quei che han seguita la via di mezo, sì come è stato il Pulci principalmente, e 'l Boiardo, e il Mambriano. I quali ancora non son restata di far pruova d'avanzare in quelle cose, che in quanto allo stile, per haver la facilità, e la vaghezza insieme, mi son parute opportune.
>
> I considered and learned from many men of sound judgment that there is a great variety of style in books written heretofore in ottava rima. I found that some crawl so low on the ground that any not entirely degraded spirit would scorn even to see them, let alone take pleasure in reading them. Others, by contrast, have aspired to please almost exclusively the most learned readers, and have taken on such a lofty style that not only moderately educated people, and women in particular, but indeed even learned men themselves must struggle to understand some passages in them, and they require technical commentary and exposition as if they were legal or philosophical texts. Thus I have chosen to take my place among those who have followed the middle path, especially Pulci, Boiardo, and Mambriano; yet I have not hesitated to attempt to surpass them in certain things where I have thought it appropriate, such as combining ease of reading with charm in my style. In my language, too, I have decided not to follow that of a single province, but that of our whole Italy, which is spoken in common by distinguished persons of good judgment.

D'Aragona's lexical preferences diverge from the norms dictated by Pietro Bembo, from an earlier literary benefactor, Benedetto Varchi, and, in part, from her own poetry. But different genres require different styles and lexicons.

Many students will readily recognize d'Aragona's sources from classical antiquity, Dante, and Ludovico Ariosto: the Sibyl, despite her Virgilian pedigree, is a wicked enchantress similar to Ariosto's Alcina, and Meschino's visit to the Purgatory of Saint Patrick is described in terms consciously reminiscent of Dante. The protagonist, Guerrino, born Christian and of noble blood, captured in his infancy by pirates, sold as a slave in Constantinople, and brought into the service of the emperor, eventually departs in search of his parents. During his quest, he finds himself occasionally waging battle for Muslim rulers (including the king of Solta, who propositions him) and journeys widely throughout Muslim lands, before finally arriving at Mecca, where he visits the tomb of Mohammed. His own Christian faith clearly does not waver; however, he does feel pressed at times to be laconic or, more rarely, to dissemble. The poem's representations of Islam evince perspectives that derive in part from the Counter-Reformation but also from polemics in act since the fifteenth century, if not earlier. Yet Guerrino also offers anthropological descriptions of Islam and its mores that are occasionally based on his sense of reason and humanity. In canto 13, lines 69–72, he questions the Islamic doctrine of gaining paradise through martyrdom but nonetheless comments that "ben c'havea gran dispiacere / veder sì tristamente persa quanta / vedea generation, ch'è pure umana / per fede sì bestiale e sì villana" ("he was very sorry to see as great a generation as he was seeing so sadly lost through their bestial, villainous faith, for they are still human"). Such reflections will certainly provoke classroom discussion.

The narrator frequently mimes the persona of a male minstrel poet, with occasional although striking exceptions when the author's own gender is foregrounded in asides. This suggests another perspective from which the text might be taught—that of women's literary history: Tullia d'Aragona's *Meschino* (1560) serves as the starting point for courses on the Italian epic tradition by women authors, as her poem heralds Moderata Fonte's *Tredici canti del Floridoro* (1581; *Floridoro, A Chivalric Romance*), Margherita Sarrocchi's *Scanderbeide* (1606; *Scanderbeide, The Heroic Deeds of George Scanderbeg, King of Epirus*), and Lucrezia Marinella's *L'Enrico, overo Bisantio acquistato* (1635; *Enrico; or, Byzantium Conquered, A Heroic Poem*), all now available in English translation.[6]

## Teaching *Il Meschino* in an Italian-Language Literature Survey Course

Teaching portions of the *Meschino* in Italian as part of a literature survey course has proven rewarding and entertaining. So far, I have taught it only twice, as an almost-forgotten work by a lesser-known author, in a course largely dedicated to a dizzying *più belle pagine* ("finest pages") parade of masterworks from the thirteenth through the sixteenth centuries. D'Aragona was the only woman, with the exceptions of the *Compiuta Donzella* ("Learned Damsel") and Vittoria Colonna (each represented by a single lyric), included in the course syllabus, though future iterations will include a broader selection of lyrics by Renaissance women. Including selections from the 28,000-line *Meschino* already constitutes a sexual-political and curricular statement, because no other book of remotely comparable length by a woman exists in Italian in the course's time frame. With an English translation of the entire poem forthcoming, I believe that d'Aragona's magnum opus will assume its rightful place as an extraordinarily ambitious contribution to the Italian epic tradition by a woman author. I fully expect it to become a standard component in syllabi of courses on women's literature, Renaissance epic, cinquecento, and the narrative of self-discovery, as well as the culminating work in courses dedicated entirely to d'Aragona.

Students normally take the survey course after completing three full years of Italian language study, though I have admitted some with less. I include passages of d'Aragona's epic between readings from Ariosto and Torquato Tasso. The course ends with the *Liberata*, so that students read this text not only sandwiched between literature of the highest prestige but also at their own most fluent level of reading and discussing preunification Italian. Earlier in the semester, they had grown accustomed to reading the *stilnovisti* (the school of lyric poets preceding and including the young Dante), Petrarch, Boccaccio, Machiavelli, and Castiglione. While I had expected to offer students my draft translation of the *Meschino*, I found that they had no need of it—an interesting demonstration of d'Aragona's relative legibility. Students also were able to discuss literature somewhat fluently in Italian, and to recognize features typical of the Italian epic romance tradition—classical references, the Carolingian cycle, sorcery, Orientalism, and so on. Having based my own assessment of the book on the sometimes exasperating experience of translating it, I was cheered, perhaps even surprised, by students' generous and enthusiastic reactions.

The first major decision was how to present the text. Since its original appearance in 1560, there has been no other edition, as far as we know, until 1839, and none since.[7] The relationship of these two texts, however, is not entirely clear. Francesco Zanotto, the editor of the 1839 version, seems to follow the editio princeps precisely, merely correcting minor typographical errors, and I accepted almost all such corrections in my translation. Yet a riddle remains regarding the arguments that introduce each of the thirty-six *canti*: those in the 1839 edition bear no relation to the originals. Moreover, the original arguments are in prose whereas those of the latter edition are single octaves. In one instance, too, Zanotto aggressively rewrote a line from the first edition; the original violates the rhyme scheme, and he seemingly corrects it by altering the words but not the sense.[8] These two elements raise the question of whether Zanotto consulted a different edition that is no longer extant.

Without a modern edition, I had originally intended to teach from photocopies of the 1839 version because its typographic appearance is quite similar to books today. The font is familiar and modern, and the edition does not replicate, for example, some formatting choices of the original's printers that are strange to modern eyes: setting the arguments so that the lines taper to a large V on the page or printing words in each canto's proem in all-capitals. Citing from the 1839 edition is also simpler because it numbers the octaves, whereas the 1560 does not. Ultimately, however, I opted to use photocopies of the 1560 princeps. This was the base text for my own translation work, and I wanted students to experience the puzzles and pleasures it affords. They found the decipherment of the antique text exciting, and the extra effort underscored the lack of a modern edition. The italic cursive font is attractive, and students got a paleographic thrill from navigating the conventional use of *V* and *u* in early modern writing and printing. This practice is thrown into relief in the *Meschino*'s first edition by the capitalization of each line's first word—for example, *Vmana* (capitalized as the first word in 12.59.2) versus *Vergine* later in the same line or *qual* versus *ti uanti*, both appearing in 12.60.6. Likewise, students quickly mastered the long *s* and the ligatured double *ss* (the latter, incidentally, is not always used by the typesetters; they often simply place one long *s* after another). They found it entertaining to learn to distinguish, for instance, *falso* and *salso* and to recognize in such a case that *falfo* isn't a word.

My second decision was which passages to assign. In an introductory survey course, crowded with canonical masterpieces, I wanted to limit the *Meschino* to a single week. I limited the selection to fewer than a hundred octaves out of the poem, plus a few lines from the elegant prose preface, *A i lettori* (discussed below). The passages were chosen more to present certain issues and authorial preoccupations than to summarize the sprawling plot. Students read the proem to the epic, 1.1–8; the first three octaves of canto 3, in which the ambiguous gendering of the author and narrator is most vivid; part of canto 23, in which the African princess Rampilla murders her brother for love of Guerrino and then kills herself when he rejects her; and selections from 23 to 26 which describe Guerrino's yearlong sojourn with the Sibyl, including her relentless and futile attempts to seduce him. These passages highlight d'Aragona's complex and creative literary gender play. Dynamic and fluid presentations of gender in selections from Boccaccio, Castiglione, Ariosto, and others had already been topics of discussion in the course, and the students knew with no prompting that the participation of a woman author in this centuries-old discourse would be intriguing. D'Aragona's status as a celebrity courtesan with an illustrious literary career made the importance of gender issues self-evident to the class, and I showed how d'Aragona often wove sophisticated reflections on sexuality and gender into her rather conventional romance source. This includes an emphasis, original to her, on her young hero's beauty and vulnerability, particularly as he is objectified by the desire of powerful and unscrupulous women. The male narratorial persona d'Aragona usually adopts, and her stated moralizing objectives, also lend paradoxical depth to a woman author's stock expressions of disapproval for women's seductiveness and guile.

I showed students a few sentences of *A i lettori* in which the author discreetly alludes to her own past life and the potentially deleterious effects reading may have on impressionable young women. In this passage she also states her delight in finding a Spanish prose source (see Hairston's comments on sources, above)—"tutto castissimo, tutto puro, tutto Cristiano" ("all most chaste, all pure, all Christian"). I have students read the following:

> Io adunque, la quale ho ne' primi anni miei havuta più notitia del mondo, che ora con miglior senno non vorrei haver havuta, e la quale in me stessa, e in altre molte ho veduto di quanto gran danno sia ne i giovenili animi il ragionamento, ma molto più la lettione delle cose lascive, e brutte . . . trovai finalmente, che *Morganti*, *Ancroie*, *Inamoramenti d'Orlando*, *Bovi d'Antona*, *Leandre*, *Mambriani*, e finalmente l'Ariosto stesso non mancavano di questo gran vitio di contenere in essi cose lascive, e disoneste, e indegne, che non solamente monache, donzelle, o vedove, né maritate, ma ancora le donne publiche se gli lascino veder per casa.[9]

> I, who in my earlier years had more experience of the world than now with more mature consideration I would wish to have had, and who have seen in myself and in many other women what great harm can be done to youthful spirits by discussing and, even more, reading lascivious and ugly things, . . . still found that *Morganti*, *Ancroie*, *Innamoramenti d'Orlando*, *Bovi d'Antona*, *Leandre*, *Mambriani*, and finally even Ariosto himself were not free of this great vice of containing material lascivious, dishonorable, and unworthy for any woman—not only nuns, maidens, widows, and married women, but even "public women"—to allow these books be seen around their houses.

This authorial goal merits as much consideration as the prefaces to the *Decameron* or the *Libro del Cortegiano*. The self-referential freight of these lines accords closely with other public documents about her decision to regain "the lost path of virtue."[10] I encouraged students to read this passage not merely as confessional but rather or also as a strategy of self-presentation. I also presented the historical and ecclesiastical context of Rome's courtesan culture and the expected public stance of the *pentita* or *convertita*. It was obvious to students that the narrator's voice throughout the *Meschino*, though markedly less prominent and perverse than Ariosto's, was, like his, generally that of a minstrel of unmarked or masculine gender. This narrative "I" adopts a pietistic and uplifting tone in each canto's proem, fully consonant with d'Aragona's stated goal of producing a morally edifying tale suitable for the eyes of all ages and genders. With both the high moral tone and the narrator's masculine gender clearly established by the proem to canto 1, we moved directly to the very surprising proem to canto 3:

> Mi preme sí l'amore, e la pietade
> di non lassar questo principio perso,
> poi ch'io l'ho fatto, benché sien le strade
> mal trovate da me del bel dir terso;
> ch'io son disposta insanguinar le spade,
> romper le lance, e mostrarmi converso
> in huomo ardito, ancor che donna io sia
> onde torno a seguir l'istoria mia

> Love and piety so inspire me not to abandon this beginning, now that I have started, even though it was difficult for me to find the paths of elegant speech, that I am determined to bloody swords, break lances, and show myself changed into a bold man, though I am still a woman; and so I return to pursue my story.

It is striking and artful to place the masculine *converso* in the emphatic rhyme position, flanked by two unambiguous feminines, *disposta* and *donna*—the signature of a protean, polymorphous narrator and a confident stylist.

This example, which I consider some of the most successful and original verse in the book, helped me understand the students' positive reactions in other places. In a survey course, one goal is to help students appreciate the literary art of canonical authors. Earlier in the semester the class learned to savor the legendary stylistic refinements of the *tre corone*—the so-called three crowns of fourteenth-century Tuscan literature: Dante, Petrarch, and Boccaccio—among others. In the light of this, I was both gratified and taken aback that students defended d'Aragona's versifying even when I saw it as less polished than that of better-known authors. For example, I am genuinely surprised that d'Aragona rhymes *vero* with itself in the poem's first octave. Students had learned the *rima equivoca* in Ariosto and noticed that d'Aragona does not vary the meaning of the rhyme word. When I suggested that the repetition of so simple a word might have been a placeholder d'Aragona would have eliminated in revision, students argued that it was an emphatic declaration of authorial truthfulness from the outset. I also took one octave (10.45) out of context to show what I considered inexpert repetition—the use of the simple noun *cam[m]in* three times in five lines. Students again defended the author, seeing the repetition as vividly underlining the thematics of the journey and quest.

Guerrino's sojourn with the Sibyl contains significant discrepancies between d'Aragona and her source, though as always, she closely follows it overall. In her description of the Sybil, d'Aragona expatiates much more than the author of *Il Guerrin Meschino* on her sensual physical attractions and seductive wiles. D'Aragona expands greatly on Andrea's brief and conventional *blason* in passages such as 25.52–60. The following two portions of that section attracted particular comment:

> Non è, non è per certo quel che leghi
> l'huomo, com'alcun dice, la pazzia;
> ma l'incanto d'amor, d'amor l'incanto
> ci dà sì breve riso, e lungo pianto.
>
> . . . . . . . . . . . . . . . . . . . . . . . . . . . . . . . . . . . .
>
> se fusse, Amanti, in libertate vostra
> di godervi bellezze sì stupende,
> forse terreste Guerrin sciocco e lieve,
> non pensando al gran danno, e 'l piacer breve.

> Madness is not, no, it is not the thing that binds men, as some say, but rather the enchantment of love, love's enchantment gives us such brief laughter and such long weeping. . . .
>
> If it were in your power, lovers, to enjoy such amazing beauties, you might perhaps consider Guerrino foolish and petty, not taking into account the greatness of the harm and the brevity of the pleasure. 25.54.5–8, 25.60.5–8)

In these philosophical ponderings on love and attraction, in which the author invites the reader to identify herself or himself with the protagonist, we may recognize the d'Aragona who wrote the Neoplatonic *Dialogo della infinità d'amore*. In her brief analysis of *pazzia*, she might also be said to have accomplished the world's most concise gloss of Ariosto—an insouciant touch of intertextual bravura which students recognized immediately. The judgment implied in the narrator's depiction of the Sibyl is perplexing and contradictory and prompted interesting classroom conversation. The narrator overtly admires Guerrino's pious resistance to the temptress's wiles; he is the virtuous hero of a self-consciously high-minded book, and like it, he is *tutto castissimo, tutto puro, tutto Cristiano*. The *Guerrin Meschino* makes clear the same moral, but the male author dedicates many fewer lines to the Sibyl's powerful attraction. By expanding greatly on the potency of women's allure, d'Aragona both articulates requisite disapproval of a pagan sorceress's attempts on the hero's virtue and celebrates the nearly irresistible power of female beauty. The feminist implication of such passages is complicated and subtle.

These brief glances into d'Aragona's sprawling epic were not enough to give students any sense of its scale, variety, or density of incident. They did suffice, however, to acquaint students with the idea that women of the cinquecento began to assert themselves in the literary realm with original and weighty publications. It pointed to the rich pleasures of less famous works in Italian epic and chivalric romance. Perhaps an even greater tribute to d'Aragona is that students found the few pages we studied to be unusual, accomplished, forceful, and entertaining.

## Notes

Julia L. Hairston wrote the first section of this essay; John C. McLucas wrote the second.

1. See d'Aragona, "Dialogo" for the modern Italian edition and see d'Aragona, *Dialogue* for the English translation. The choral anthology is available in a dual language edition, d'Aragona, *Poems and Letters*.

2. See poem 110 in d'Aragona, *Poems and Letters* 242–44. For further reflections on issues related to the composition of the *Meschino*, see Allaire, "Tullia d'Aragona's *Il Meschino*." For use of the term "choral anthology," see Hairston 164–66. See also Procaccioli 313 and fig. 2B.

3. This essay quotes from the 1560 publication of *Il Meschino*; translations are by John C. McLucas. A published version of d'Aragona's preface by Elizabeth Pallitto is available in d'Aragona, *Sweet Fire* 99–103.

4. The critical edition of the prose text is Andrea da Barberino, *Il Guerrin Meschino*. An English translation of d'Aragona's *Meschino*, edited by the authors of this article, is forthcoming from The Other Voice in Early Modern Europe series and annotates the additions original to d'Aragona.

5. Another approach to teaching this text might be a transhistorical view of the protagonist, inserted into a course on other literary heroes such as Ruggiero or Angelica and using literary, visual, and musical sources.

6. Oddly enough, or not, English translations of these works are more readily available than modern editions in Italian. For a modern Italian edition, only the works by Fonte and Marinella are available: see Fonte, *Tredici Canti* and Marinella, *L'Enrico, ovvero Bisanzio acquistato.* Sarrocchi's *Scanderbeide* is available in a 1701 edition online. The English translations—the first complete and others abridged—are: Fonte, *Floridoro*; Sarrocchi, *Scanderbeide: The Heroic Deeds*; and Marinella, *Enrico; or, Byzantium Conquered.*

7. For digitized versions of the 1560 and 1839 editions, see the Italian Women Writers Web site at the University of Chicago, www.lib.uchicago.edu/efts/IWW/.

8. At canto 34.61. The original line 6, "Ma ora di narrar fatt'ho pensiero," creates an irregular rhyme scheme of *ababaacc*; the apparent editorial emendation to "Ma ora a narrar torna il mio lavoro" corrects the rhyme without significantly changing the sense.

9. Students noticed that Ariosto alone is mentioned by name, not by the title of his book.

10. See d'Aragona's sonnet to Pietro Bembo in *Poems and Letters* 82–84, where she alludes to "la strada di virtù smarrita."

**Julia M. Kisacky**

# Teaching Moderata Fonte's *Floridoro*

*Tredici canti del Floridoro* ("Thirteen Cantos of Floridoro"), by Moderata Fonte (Modesta Pozzo, 1555–92), originally published in 1581, is the first original Italian chivalric poem written by a woman. Though long a genre popular with women readers, only a few women authors overcame the challenges it posed for them and published their own chivalric works.[1] These works have received increased critical attention in the past few decades, enriching our understanding of Italian culture in this period.

The *Floridoro* is available both in Italian and English translation. The original Italian version is available on the Web through the University of Chicago Library Italian Women Writers project. A modern edition in Italian, *Tredici canti del Floridoro*, was edited by Valeria Finucci and published in 1995, with modernized spelling and punctuation as well as the addition of stanza numbers. Finucci and I followed the same numbering scheme in our 2006 translation, *Floridoro: A Chivalric Romance*. The translation includes an appendix with eighty pages of a modernized transcription of the book's high points, providing a limited exposure to the Italian version.

I have twice taught the *Floridoro* in English in a single seminar meeting. These seminars, called honors colloquia, are organized by Baylor University's honors program for undergraduate honors students. Faculty members volunteer to teach a seminar on a book they choose and then grade students on their participation and papers. Students select the colloquia they prefer, resulting in a small class of about eight to twelve students. Consequently, while the students were at least curious about the *Floridoro*, they had no reliable background in the chivalric tradition or Italian literature. Indeed, the Baylor University honors program expects that "the Colloquium courses prompt [students] to engage content and to ask questions about materials that are in some cases far removed from their own disciplinary homes" ("Honors Colloquium").

For the seminars, we read extensive selections (around 260 pages) from the poem. I omitted lengthy encomiastic, descriptive, or historical passages; we concentrated on the presentation of characters and themes. Specifically, I assigned cantos 1–2 (all); canto 3 (octaves A[rgument]–50, 70–76); cantos 4–8 (all); canto 9 (octaves A–60); canto 10 (octaves 36–95); canto 11 (all); canto 12 (octaves A–4, 83–86); canto 13 (octaves A–4, 35–70).

My introductory lecture started with the author's biography and the significance of her pen name. She "jettison[s] . . . the timid 'Modesta' for 'Moderata,' with its connotations of self-regulation through reason" (Cox, "Moderata Fonte" 5) and replaces "Pozzo" ("well") with the more active image of "Fonte" ("fountain" or "spring").[2] I proceeded with a sketch of the genres involved: the contrast between epic and romance, the strong influence of classical literature in Italy, the popularity of chivalric literature since medieval times, and the boldness of Fonte's choice of this especially masculine genre. I also read aloud a brief excerpt of the Italian version to show students that only in the original language could they hear the poetry's rhythm and rhyme.

Most of the class was devoted to discussion of literary topics. Colloquium students are encouraged to prepare their own questions for discussion, in addition to the following two discussion topics provided in advance:

The representation of men and women, e.g., their status, abilities, and characters. I cautioned students that the narrator's comments and foreshadowing would be helpful but would not give all the answers.

The theme of friendship. The topics of gender relations and women's status are clearly fundamental to Fonte's writings, but friendship is another prominent theme and intertwines with gender questions in complex and interesting ways. For instance, Fonte's explicit examples of friends are male (e.g., Floridoro and Filardo, Silano and Clarido); though female characters do help each other, we see no

> pairs of formally acknowledged women friends in the poem. In a course where more time could be devoted to Fonte, this topic could be fruitfully expanded by referring to her later work, *The Worth of Women* (*Il merito delle donne*). Here, when Fonte lists exemplary friends, they are the usual males from the literary tradition—despite the interlocutors having just agreed that men make inferior friends and that women befriend each other faster than men (*Worth* 123–28; *Merito* 76–80). But the dialogue also contains examples of female friendship in the seven interlocutors themselves. Moreover, these ladies of varying ages and conditions joke with, tease, play with, advise, and educate each other, displaying relationships of a much less hierarchical nature than those presented in the *Floridoro.* Fonte finds true women friends not in the chivalric literary tradition but in her contemporary Venetian society.

Students were required to write a seven- to eight-hundred-word essay. Since the *Floridoro* is formally unfinished, readers inevitably wonder how the various plotlines might be continued and resolved. In one seminar I therefore assigned a creative and analytical essay asking students to explore how Fonte might have concluded or continued one of various plotlines, specifically Risamante and Biondaura's struggle over the kingdom of Armenia, the magical trial and prison at the Castle of the Garland, Raggidora's imprisonment by her rejected suitor Lideo, the developing power imbalance between the newlyweds Risardo and Odoria, the adventures of the former queen of Phrygia and her son after their release from seclusion, the fated abandonment of Circetta by the manipulative Silano, the prophesied reunion of true lovers Nicobaldo and Lucimena, the deeds of the unproven hero Floridoro and his beloved Celsidea, or the vengeance promised by Marcane.

The other seminar's essay topic was a comparison of characters who are rulers. As with almost any thematic topic, this allowed for a discussion of gender roles, since some of the rulers are female. Students were invited to use the following questions as a springboard but were not obliged to answer them all. My directions read:

> Choose two to four characters from the list below and compare them as rulers. Who is a good, bad, or middling ruler and why? How can we tell what constitutes a good or bad ruler? Remember that the narrator may not always say what the author thinks. What is the purpose of any inconsistencies between the narrator's description of a character and that

character's actions? What can we tell about Fonte's understanding of courts? Do gender, religion, or culture make a difference?

List of characters: Aclide, king of Phrygia; Acreonte, king of Persia; Agricorno, emperor of Thrace; Algier, king of Sparta; Biondaura, queen of Armenia; Cleardo, king of Athens, high king of Greece; Cloridabello, king of Babylonia; Dacia's queen; Macandro, king of Parthia; the pygmy king

At the undergraduate or graduate level the *Floridoro*, whether in excerpts or complete, could easily constitute a one- or two-week segment in courses about chivalric or epic literature, Renaissance studies, women authors, or women's studies. In a course focused on gender studies, students might read selections that showcase the warrior heroine Risamante, in conjunction with passages from *The Worth of Women*. In this way, excerpts of Fonte's youthful *Floridoro*—with its proto-feminist portrayal of male and female characters having adventures in an imaginary ancient setting—could be juxtaposed with her later direct reflections on contemporary Venetian society, thus showing both continuities and development in Fonte's thought. The fact that Risamante's quest pits her against her twin sister, Biondaura, who had a more traditional feminine upbringing, should give rise to fruitful discussions. Nor is the poem devoid of pro-woman statements. Through the centuries the most cited passage has been the proem to canto 4, where Fonte argues that women's limitations "come not from women's nature but from patriarchal culture" (Finucci, "Moderata Fonte" 23), that is, their restricted education. Gender concerns also profoundly influence Fonte's depictions of friendship, family relations (e.g., Risamante's biological vs. adoptive parents, Circetta's upbringing), various types of love, and madness (Circe), themes that would also be of interest in a more general Renaissance studies course.

The eighty-page modernized Italian transcription in the appendix of the *Floridoro*'s translation can remind students of the original Italian verse. It could also provide undergraduate language students with the opportunity to learn about poetic vocabulary and syntax without the added difficulty of antiquated orthography, punctuation, and abbreviation. If more advanced language students wish to read excerpts, this selection could guide them in accessing the scanned 1581 edition online.

One could also profitably study the character of the sorceress from among Fonte's variations on traditions. Fonte's major sorceresses are the mythic Circe, rewritten "to valorise female achievement in the context of a universal story, to tell the other side" (Kolsky 171), and her daughter Circetta, the guileless, virginal "victim . . . of the wiles of the calculatingly flirtatious [knight] Silano" (Cox, "Women" 143). In this context I would assign as a supplemental reading a pertinent selection from *The Worth of Women*, which describes the pattern of error followed by women who fall in love with deceitful men (*Worth* 121; *Merito* 75), an error committed by Circe and repeated by Circetta. In addition I would assign Petrarch's sonnet "Erano i capei d'oro a l'aura sparsi" ("Her golden hair was loosed to the breeze"; 192–93, poem 90), which is alluded to both in this theoretical passage and in the poem with reference to Circetta (*Floridoro* 5.28).

Discussions of other modifications to literary traditions might include the night raid, which in the *Floridoro* becomes an attempted kidnapping by the king of Persia and his brother, targeting the virgin daughter of their host; the parallels between Risamante and both Bradamante and Ruggiero from the *Orlando furioso*; the shipwrecked knights, in this case, Silano and Clarido, the ship's only survivors because they claim the lifeboat first and fight off other would-be passengers; and the novella, here the one recounted by Nicobaldo in canto 6 about two young lovers' timid struggles against authority. Regarding this last topic, students familiar with the *Decameron* will quickly recognize the more ladylike style of Fonte's tale, as is to be expected from a respectable young woman author of the era, and may then analyze the tale's observations about patriarchal society. In addition, the characteristics of the *Floridoro*'s male characters, particularly the heroes, make an interesting contrast to those of Fonte's predecessors.[3]

To study the *Floridoro* in a fully interdisciplinary context, one could invite colleagues from other departments to discuss aspects of the poem outside one's own area of expertise. For example, I would arrange for a lecture on tourneys, a historical introduction about Venice and the significance of the battle of Lepanto, as well as a lecture on art so that students could see the sort of fresco cycles, sculpture, and architecture that embellish the poem's world.

Assignments could include a mixture of papers, projects, and presentations, with creative options, in addition to more traditional tests. I would include options such as an artistic rendering of fictional settings described by Fonte, for example, the temple of Apollo in cantos 9–10; illustrations of scenes; research into Renaissance dances, banquets (e.g., canto 11), or fashion; and further historical background, for instance on the poem's dedicatees, Bianca Capello and Francesco I de' Medici.

I sincerely hope that the *Floridoro* can be more widely integrated into the undergraduate and graduate curriculum as a valuable and enjoyable addition to our knowledge about this remarkable author and her contribution to the chivalric tradition.

## Notes

1. To learn about challenges in Fonte's life, see the brief biography written by a contemporary who knew her well, the Venetian notary and writer Giovanni Nicolò Doglioni. Doglioni's "Vita della Sig.ra Modesta Pozzo de' Zorzi, nominata Moderata Fonte" ("Life of Moderata Fonte") was published with the first edition of *Il merito delle donne* in 1600 and again with Adriana Chemello's 1988 edition. Virginia Cox likewise included a translation of it in her 1997 edition and translation of *The Worth of Women.* On the genre's challenges for women writers in general, see Cox, "Women"; Kolsky; Finucci, "Moderata Fonte"; and Malpezzi Price 31–32.

2. For more discussions of Fonte's pseudonym, see Finucci, "Moderata Fonte" 5; Malpezzi Price 30.

3. In short, the *Floridoro*'s relatively positive male characters have traditionally feminine characteristics. See Finucci, "Moderata Fonte" 14–33; Kolsky 177–81; and Malpezzi Price chs. 5–6.

**Maria Galli Stampino**

# Naming the Enemy: Linguistic Slippery Slopes in Lucrezia Marinella's *Enrico; or, Byzantium Conquered: A Heroic Poem*

One of my central concerns in teaching undergraduate students is to make them aware that how we express ourselves is as important as what we say. Connecting literary texts to their contexts and to other horizons is one important way we can create a transformative learning experience for our students: we help them dispel the notion that the past is foreign and different, and that what is normal to our culture is immediately understandable and devoid of hidden meanings. I remember facing my students' enthusiasm for the story and special effects in the 2006 movie *300*, which recounts the battle of Thermopylae pitting Leonidas against Persian invaders. I went nowhere when I tried to explain the way the two fighting bodies were presented (disciplined, aggressive, principled on the one side; lustful, bejeweled, bloodthirsty on the other) in relation to the contemporary geopolitical situation (a then three-year-old war in Iraq and the unease around Muslim communities in the United States after 9/11, just to name two). They were not (yet) able to go beyond the surface.

As Julius Taranto and Kevin J. H. Dettmar have remarked, good humanities teaching "take[s] something that's confusing and complicated for students and simplif[ies] it to the point where students have their bearings." Good professors, moreover, "teach the text again, but this time show their subtleties and depths. They start bringing out the reasons that the text looked complicated in the first place—because it is." As I indicate in what follows, Lucrezia Marinella's 1635 *Enrico; or, Byzantium Conquered: A Heroic Poem* offers some clear examples of linguistic and representational slippages that allow instructors to simplify and then complexify, as Taranto and Dettman suggest.[1]

My approach is built on the belief that, as Sergio Zatti has written, the epic as a literary genre might now be dead, but its mode lives on.[2] Literary epics are typically the expression of the "momenti primi e fondanti di una coscienza indivisa" ("earliest, foundational moment of an undivided self-perception"; *Il modo epico* 5). As such, they resurface in response to a real or perceived threat to a way of life or culture. The outward difference between a text penned in the first half of the seventeenth century in Venice and a twenty-first-century movie (for example) is thus tempered, and ideological points of contact between them become more visible and therefore teachable.

Approaching any epic text with a keen appreciation for the crucial juxtaposition between the present and the past and between different cultures allows students to tease out the representational and rhetorical strategies at work. In the case of *Enrico*, Marinella follows in a long-standing tradition that goes back to Virgil, contrasting the (good) Trojans to the (untrustworthy) Greeks for reasons connected to the geopolitical situation in Augustus's times (Stampino 20–21).[3] Marinella wrote her poem following the (literary and theoretical) example of Torquato Tasso's *Gerusalemme liberata* and its later reworking, *Gerusalemme conquistata* (published in 1581 and 1593, respectively). The cultural and religious horizon in which both early modern authors worked was strongly marked by the Counter-Reformation, or Catholic Reformation, a movement of "great international revival that occurred within the [Catholic] Church between the late fifteenth and early eighteenth centuries" and that also included "prohibitionary measures . . . designed to combat Protestantism" (Lampe and Soergel 308).

Tasso took the First Crusade as his topic, aiming to present his fellow Catholics with examples of positive behavior and overcoming temptation, goals that were placed in juxtaposition with the so-called infidels—to wit, the Muslims holding Jerusalem. The crusaders (those soldiers who had literally and figuratively taken on the cross, like Jesus, and whose armor was therefore adorned with its image in the front and back) fought against the latter to achieve the religiously meaningful task of reconquering the holiest city of Christendom.[4] Marinella chose instead historical events more relevant to Venice, her city: *Enrico* concerns the Fourth Crusade, an anomalous expedition carried out between 1202 and 1204, in which Christian troops (largely coming from what we now call France, Belgium, the Low Countries, Germany, Austria, and Venetian lands in northern Italy), led by doge Enrico Dandolo, laid siege to and conquered first Zadar (on the Dalmatian coast) and then Constantinople, without ever reaching Jerusalem. Here lies the assumption that makes any slippage possible: for Marinella's contemporary readers, Constantinople was a constant threat to coastal and continental European lands and, as the seat of the Ottoman Empire, the ideological enemy of choice; its reputedly general Muslim religion was juxtaposed to the Christian one. Yet the Turks conquered so-called Constantinople only in 1453; what Marinella's poem conveniently leaves out is that the crusaders laid siege to and conquered a Christian city; in fact, many did so while excommunicated.[5]

Within this ideologically based comparison, *Enrico* can be fruitfully utilized in a variety of pedagogical settings. Although my own course provided an introduction to the tradition of the epic in Western literature (a course in English that borrowed its title from David Quint's 1993 seminal work *Epic and Empire*), my remarks could be adapted to an overview of Western culture or civilization, to an early modern cultural history class, or to a survey of Italian texts, whether in Italian or in translation, to which issues of identity, Italian-ness, and relationships with others are central.

Focusing students' attention is paramount while reading epic poems, as these tend to be lengthy and entail complex plots. It is typically necessary to switch between macro- and micro-level attention, recalling the plot, character traits, and context, and engaging in close readings, fundamental to unearthing textual "subtleties and depths," to go back to Taranto and Dettmar's felicitous phrase. Recalling the us-versus-them stance pervading *Enrico* and the general epic mode, the way Marinella presents the crusaders' enemy can focus our attention on tropes, metaphors, similes, and other textual strategies. Early in the poem, as Enrico Dandolo acknowledges that conquering Byzantium would help the intended goal of the expedition, he uses ambiguous terms to describe the crusaders' immediate enemy: "this unfaithful people, enemy to the heavens and a heavy plague on men, a people who despise Christ's shepherd, do not harbor true faith, and do not fear God" (1.68.1–4). Marinella's most attentive readers would understand that "this unfaithful people" could also depict the enemy as Orthodox Christians, who did not recognize papal supremacy; the temptation to conflate them with "the Turks and the Moor" (1.68.8), against whom the crusaders would turn next, however, is undeniable.[6] Students can also understand that Marinella deliberately uses a covert rhetorical strategy to advance her ideological agenda; in other words, we in the twenty-first century could be taken in as much as her intended seventeenth-century audience.

To reinforce the difference between crusaders and enemies, Marinella stresses different behaviors. For example, when under duress or faced with military disaster, three main characters on the Byzantine side blast God with blasphemies: Alessio, the city's illegitimate ruler (18.48.7–8); Esone, a practitioner of black magic and Alessio's counselor (25.1.5 and 7); and Oronte, a fierce fighter from Hyrcania (27.49.1). Their utterances contrast with one of Enrico Dandolo's speeches to his troops, significantly not far removed from Alessio's curse; in canto 19, the doge rouses them to battle, assuring them that "Né 'l Ciel vorrà che 'l popolo malvagio / Noi sua parte miglior conculchi e prema" ("Heaven will not want that evil people to defeat and crush us, his better part"; 19.17.3–4). If the two people believe in two different gods, then one of them is true, and the other is necessarily a false idol; implicitly, "we" are Christians and "they" are infidels or Turks.

Throughout the poem, Marinella scatters elements that sharpen another difference between crusading and Byzantine leaders: the former fight because of a (religious) principle, the latter for power and self-fulfillment. Faced with a loss in a naval battle, Alessio is upset and angry at heaven:

> Alessio intanto freme, innalza al cielo
> D'ira infette le luci e di veleno,
> Ch'è perduta la classe e d'aspro telo
> Ferito il capitano onde vien meno.
> Travaglio, rabbia e timoroso gelo
> Fiedono a prova infellonito il seno,
> E qual leon sdegnoso al vivo offeso
> Passeggia alteramente d'ira acceso.

> [He] shook and turned his eyes heavenward; he was infected with wrath and poison because he had lost his fleet and his captain, wounded by a sharp weapon, was out of commission; fights, anger, and fearful coldness vied to wound his evil chest, as he paced haughtily, lit with wrath, like a disdainful lion injured to the quick. (8.34)

The simile of the hurt lion, the repetition of "wrath" ("ira" in the original), and the effective characterization of Alessio's eyes lifted toward heaven all indicate that his primary concern is himself and his hold on power. There is no expression of distress for the fate of his captain, only annoyance that he is "out of commission" ("vien meno" in the original).

Other Byzantine rulers are pusillanimous and flee before danger and military loss: their attitude is in sharp opposition to devoted crusading fighters. Among the latter, the priest (or monk) Egidio fights and dies foretelling Byzantium's capitulation:

> Parea, mentre moria, così dicesse:
> "Ancorché agli occhi altrui m'involo e celo,
> Nulladimen vedrò nel Cielo amando
> Bisanzio preso e 'l fier Mirtillo in bando"
>
> As he died, he seemed to say: "Although I remove myself and hide from other people's eyes, still from heaven I will see and enjoy Byzantium captured and harsh Mirtillo banned." (26.60.5–8)

The fact that he appears only in this episode underscores his uselessness in the plot and, conversely, his ideological import. This, too, bears stressing to students, as it is a feature in many types of texts. The same is true of the Frankish crusader Novellone, whose courage Marinella even more explicitly ties to his knowledge of the future:

> Dell'Isola di Francia, che s'intende
> Del regno il centro, Novellone uccide,
> Novellon sacro a Dio, che dal Ciel prende
> Fuoco divin, di Grecia il fin previde
> E di sua morte il giorno, né s'astenne
> Dalla pugna, però, ma in guerra venne.
>
> Novellone from the Island of France . . . was sacred to God, and thanks to a divine fire he had foreseen the ending of Greece as well as the day of his death. Still, he came to war instead of staying away from it. (27.15.3–8)

The devout Rainiero, after killing Araspe in single combat, is nursed back to life by the hermit Criso; in canto 16, as he lingers between life and death he has an allegorical vision in which a lion (St. Mark, patron saint of Venice) and a virgin (Venice herself) beg Mary for her support in peace and war. Marinella dubs him "warrior for Christ" ("guerrier di Cristo") twice (16.25.1 and 16.96.8), thus bracketing this important episode with an explicitly ideological phrase. For those teaching the poem in Italian or referencing its original, it would be important to note that Marinella utilizes "Cristo" in rhyming position. In the second of the recurrences, "Cristo" rhymes with "acquisto" ("conquer"), a reference to the poem's title and, as I have noted elsewhere (Marinella, *L'Enrico* 383n12), a meaningful term in relation to epic narratives pitting Christians against the infidels. In sum, while those fighting on the Byzantine side are ready to curse God and only interested in personal safety or gain, the crusaders eagerly followed God's will, full of abnegation, offering positive examples of individual behavior. Marinella uses word choice and character description to emphasize these differences; readers must pay attention to these features to be alert to Marinella's ideological goals.

Attending to Marinella's words and to the ways she uses them builds a pedagogy that makes students aware of the connections between cultural and ideological contexts on the one hand and textual strategies on the other. The sheer number of negative behaviors that Marinella attributes to the Byzantines invites her readers to associate them with their own contemporary enemy par excellence. Adding a few stereotypical traits, such as softness and cowardice, advances her rhetorical, ideological, and political goals.[7] Her talent in her poetic form and the poem's very length make us lose sight of the fact that Enrico's Byzantine enemy was not the same as her contemporary one. These traits should be underscored to our students, who may be taken with the surface and lack the tools to explore other messages, implicit or not, of any type of text. Connecting *Enrico* to other literary traditions and historical realities (classical, medieval, early modern, modern, or contemporary) illustrates the malleability of rhetorical tropes, phrases, and situations in the epic mode. At a time when discussions abound concerning the difference between a refugee and a migrant, resulting in substantial legal implications, reading (and rereading) *Enrico* with a keen eye for monikers and descriptions is a valuable lesson in the power of words.

## Notes

1. Translations of *Enrico*, except where noted, are drawn from my 2009 edition and translation of the text; translations of all other works are mine.

2. Zatti defines "mode" as "quel principio organizzativo dell'immaginario letterario che si concretizza storicamente nei singoli generi" ("the organizing principle of literary imagination that finds concrete historical realization in genres"; *Il modo epico* 5).

3. Depending on the historical span in which *Enrico* is taught, Virgil's anti-Eastern position could be connected with Herodotus's stance against Persian invaders, for example, and with pervasive Orientalizing tendencies in Western literature.

4. Tasso's *Allegoria della Gerusalemme liberata* would be an interesting text to pair with Marinella's in a class concerned with early modern epics or the Italian literary tradition. Its text is easily found online, for example in Amedeo Quondam's authoritative edition for *Lexis progetti editoriali.*

5. The pope excommunicated the Crusaders for laying siege to a city (i.e., Zadar) belonging to a Christian ruler who had also taken the cross. See Stampino 19–20 for more details and for the reasons why it mattered. Basic information on the Fourth Crusade is in the *Wikipedia* entry ("Fourth Crusade"). There are many resources online to help students contextualize the so-called fall of Constantinople; *Wikipedia* has helpful maps ("Fall of Constantinople").

6. There is one additional nod to the Crusaders' intended enemy; early on, the text passingly references the fact that the illegitimate emperor Alessio sends a general, Dioro, to the Sultan to ask for military help (2.53.5). It is noteworthy that Jerusalem is mentioned only three times in the poem: twice in canto 1, in connection with the debates about where to send the crusading ships (1.63.8 and 1.71.7), and once in canto 21, when Erina and Venier observe the world from her flying chariot (21.58.3). This reinforces the observation that the poem later depicts Jerusalem as simply a city noticed from on high, among many others, and not a chronologically subsequent (but ideologically fundamental) goal for that expeditionary force.

7. I have argued elsewhere that Marinella utilizes the poem to advocate for a more aggressive political stance against the Ottoman Empire: see Stampino 11–13.

# Part VII

# Renaissance and Early Modern European Literary Contexts

**Charles S. Ross**

# The Italian Romance Epic and English Renaissance Literature

Both episodic and teleological—meaning there is goal or end point to the story—the Italian romantic epics of Matteo Maria Boiardo, Ludovico Ariosto, and Torquato Tasso repackaged the classics of Homer, Virgil, and Ovid for the English Renaissance. They were also intermediaries for the tales of magic and love in French (including Anglo-Norman) Arthurian romances and stories about the wars and rebellions of Charlemagne and the twelve peers of France. The *Orlando innamorato*, *Orlando furioso*, and *Gerusalemme liberata* each in its own way also contributed a blend of Boccaccian novellas, biblical echoes, and wry Italian spirit and musicality unmatched in earlier literature.

Major writers like Edmund Spenser and John Milton who knew the Italian romance epics well also followed their handling of classical mythology, particularly their common resort to Ovid's *Metamorphoses.* Philip Sidney in his *Arcadia* (1590, 1593) and Shakespeare, whose knowledge of Boiardo, Ariosto, and Tasso was less direct, inherited the Ovidian and Petrarchan tradition of treating love, which developed into Neoplatonism, as in the fourth book of Baldassare Castiglione's *The Courtier* (1528, translated by Thomas Hoby in 1561), where an attraction to beauty is seen as a first step toward spiritual transcendence.

As individual works of art, the Italian epic romances maintain a charged mood of characters, objects, and landscapes. They are worth teaching in full, in a course by themselves, and students of the English Renaissance will want to refer to John Harington's *Orlando Furioso* (1591), which includes extensive commentary on the nature of poetry and allegory, and Edward Fairfax's *Jerusalem Delivered* (1600), which captures the darker overtones of Tasso's imagination, suited to the growing specter of witchcraft that haunted the English imagination.

The more practical problem is teaching how the romance epics look forward to works that openly acknowledge their debt to these poems and those that merely benefitted from their extraordinary achievement. Each of the three crowns of Ferrara (as Boiardo, Ariosto, and Tasso are known because of their patronage by the Este family) exerted its influence on the English Renaissance (as did the Ferrarese collector of prose tales and romance theorist Giovambattista Giraldi Cinzio, whose *Hecatommithi* gave Shakespeare the source stories for *Othello* and *Measure for Measure*). "'Influence' is too weak a word for the relation which exists between the Italian epic and *The Faerie Queene*," C. S. Lewis wrote. "To fight in another man's armour is something more than to be merely influenced by his style of fighting" (*Allegory of Love* 304). Lewis is thinking mainly of Ariosto, but others have argued that much of the vitality of Milton's Satan can be traced to Boiardo's endless pursuit of Fortune.[1] Recently Barbara Brumbaugh has shown that the character Tancredi, who tragically kills Clorinda in one of the most famous passages of Tasso's poem, is probably the source of the equally heroic but flawed Amphialus in Sidney's *Arcadia*.

The usual solution to the length of the Italian romances, probably the only one pedagogically possible, is to use selections, an approach that allows teachers to vary the Italians' cantos, Spenser, and the plays of Shakespeare from year to year. For example, Spenser directly translates Tasso's *Jerusalem Delivered* 16.14–15 for the carpe diem lay that is heard at *Faerie Queene* 12.74–75, while Sir Guyon's boat trip to the Bower of Bliss in *Faerie Queene* 2.12 parallels Carlo and Ubaldo's mission to rescue Rinaldo from the charms of Armida. Ariosto's completion of Boiardo's unfinished story and Tasso's constant tinkering with his masterpiece until reducing it to the form known as the *Gerusalemme conquistata* provide another link between the Italian romances and English writers in literary history, because Spenser's endless romance was also incomplete.[2] (He projected another six if not twelve more books of the *Faerie Queene* before he died in 1598 in the aftermath of Tyrone's rebellion in Ireland.)

In a famous passage in *Paradise Regained*, Milton shows he has read Boiardo by referring to the battle of Albracca (Albracà) in the *Innamorato*, fought by Agricane against Angelica and her father, King Gallaphrone:

> Such forces met not, nor so wide a camp,
> When *Agrican* with all his Northern powers
> Besieg'd *Albracca*, as Romances tell,
> The City of *Gallaphrone*, from thence to win
> The fairest of her sex, *Angelica*,
> His daughter, sought by many Prowest Knights,
> Both *Paynim*, and the Peers of *Charlemagne*. (3.337–42)

Tasso's particularly impious Argante, who fights the Christian hero Tancredi, provides a source for Sidney's equally impious Anaxius, who fights Pyrocles in the last scene Sidney wrote before he was killed at Zutphen in 1586, leaving his revision of the *Arcadia* unfinished.

My experience is that teaching the Italian epics can be done in several ways, despite their length. Boiardo, especially book 1 plus the allegorical sections of book 2 (Falerina, Morgana) and the famous meeting of Ruggiero and Bradamante in book 3, can be included in a course on great narratives (one of the standard offerings at Purdue University), to be read right after Homer's *Odyssey* and before moving to Madame de Lafayette's *The Princess of Clèves*, Jane Austen's *Sense and Sensibility*, and Charles Dickens's *Great Expectations*.[3] As for Ariosto, although the complete *Furioso* works best in a graduate course on Spenser, portions of the poem can be included in undergraduate courses on Arthurian romance. I like to use the custom of the castle motif to discuss how romances think about the other (see Ross, *Custom*). Thinkers including Montaigne wondered at the power of custom to justify various behaviors, including how different societies treated and defined women's rights. The motif goes back to Chrétien de Troyes's Arthurian romances and is characteristic of the *Lancelot* cycle. A traveling knight who wants lodging must joust a local defender of the custom of the castle. The point, however, is not a display of prowess but an indirect commentary on the lady's role in the castle, which can vary from dutiful daughter to the jealous fiend in Boiardo's Castle Cruel episode (*Orlando innamorato* 1.8.26–1.9.35). Ariosto presents a woman's rule when Marfisa rearranges the misogynistic laws of King Marganorre in *Furioso* 37. And Spenser sexualizes and, unusually, questions the trope when Britomart defeats the custom of Malecasta's castle but later finds the lady entering her bed. The moral of the episode is that Britomart can defend herself against everything except being looked at (only Gardante draws blood, "Which did her lilly smock with staines of vermeil steep," *Faerie Queene* 3.1.65).

A very manageable approach to teaching Italian epics is through Shakespeare. An artistic sensibility as well as motifs of love and fantasy connect Boiardo to *A Midsummer Night's Dream*, both drawing on Apuleius's *Golden Ass.* Orlando in *As You Like It* is named after Ariosto's hero and the play's setting in the Forest Arden recalls Arden Wood, where Boiardo locates the marvels of Merlin, as well as the family holdings of Shakespeare's mother, Mary Arden. Boiardo creates an early version of what Northrop Frye identified as the green world in Shakespeare, places like Arden or Belmont in *The Merchant of Venice* where urban issues are seen from a new perspective and sorted out before characters troop home, newly enlightened (182–84).

Shakespeare knew Ariosto as the author of the play *I Suppositi*, which provides the Lucentio plot in *Taming of the Shrew* (see Ross, "Ariosto in Prose"). He also knew *Orlando furioso*, at least Harington's translation, for the tale of how Ginevra is falsely calumniated by those who claim to see her making love in a window, a scene that provides a source for Hero's similar troubles in *Much Ado About Nothing* (pronounced "noting" in Shakespeare's time and so directly commenting on false seeing).

Shakespeare's problem plays such as *Measure for Measure*, as well as *Hamlet*, line up with Tasso's post-Reformation sensibility, as Louise George Clubb has argued (65–89, 191–203). The influence is probably indirect, yet Shakespeare thought about how to bring politics and the nature of kingship into his plays, and he read *The Faerie Queene*, where the veiled praise of England's queen imitates the Italians' flattery of the Este but also their covert criticism. Spenser acknowledges his debts to the Italian romantic epic and spells out the issue of political allegory in his *Letter to Raleigh*, where he explains his intention to follow the example of Homer and Virgil and to make King Arthur the model of a "good governour and a vertuous man" (715). He goes on to point out the long tradition, that "Ariosto comprised them both in his Orlando: and later Tasso disservered them againe, and formed both parts in two persons, named, that part which they in Philosophy call Ethice, or vertues or a private man, coloured in his Rinalado: The other name Politice in his Godfredo."[4] In either case the poet must speak to power without losing his head.

Not unrelated to politics is the ever-popular image of Fortune that flourishes in the Italian writers and the English Renaissance. When Machiavelli in *The Prince* (ch. 25) warned Lorenzo de' Medici that Fortune is a woman and therefore must be beaten (Machiavelli, *Chief Works* 92), he was coarsening a long history of poetic illustrations of her powers. Dante chose Fortune as the tutelary deity of Earth (as Mars is for the red planet and Venus for Venus), because beneath the moon, things change.[5] The image of Fortune's wheel is at least as old as Herodotus's *Histories* (which Boiardo translated) and famously shows up when Arthur, the night before Mordred kills him, dreams he rides it to the heights and therefore the only way to go is down (1.207).[6] Boiardo has Orlando pursue Fortune through her underworld and finally grab her by the forelock, the proverbial way of catching her before she turns the bald side of her head to a man (*Orlando innamorato* 2.8–9). The image can be found as early Chrétien's *Percival* (c. 1180).[7] In *Hamlet*, Shakespeare captures the creakiness of both the wheel and the goddess as the second-rate players who perform at Elsinore give Hamlet a sample of their provincial wares by recounting the fall of Troy. The "whiff and wind" of Pyrrhus's sword is enough to knock over old King Priam. Before the final blow Pyrrhus pauses, his sword aloft, "as we often see, against some storm, / A silence in the heavens, the rack stand still, / The bold winds speechless, and the orb below / As hush as death" (2.2.483–87), before the melodramatic climax:

> Out, out, thou strumpet Fortune! All you gods,
> In general synod take away her power!
> Break all the spokes and fellies from her wheel,
> And bowl the round nave down the hill of heaven
> As low as to the fiends! (494–98)

Although best suited for advanced research projects, again because of plot complexities, discussions of Renaissance women should not overlook the Italians. Sidney's princesses Pamela and Philoclea, Spenser's Britomart, Shakespeare's great female characters such as Rosalind, and even Milton's Eve are largely influenced by the women warriors of the romantic epic—Fiordelisa, Bradamante, Marfisa, Clorinda—as well as the incomparable enchantresses Angelica (Boiardo and Ariosto) and Armida (Tasso). Fiordelisa's loyal pursuit of Brandimate in the *Orlando innamorato* is a forerunner of, if more charming than, Helena's pursuit of Bertram in Shakespeare's *All's Well That Ends Well.* Shakespeare's bed trick in that play is less erotic than Boiardo's love scene, which is set against the turmoil of the battle of Albracca:

> Sei volte ritornarno a quel danzare,
> Prima che il lor desir ben fosse spento;
> Poi cominciarno dolce ragionare
> De' loro affanni e passato tormento;

Il fresco loco gli invita a posare,
Perché in quel prato sospirava un vento,
Che sibillava tra le verde fronde
Del bel boschetto che li amanti asconde.

Six times they went back to that dance
before their passion was extinguished.
Then, talking softly, they began
to tell of trouble, torments past.
The cool glad beckoned them to rest,
as a breeze rose and whispered over
that meadow, breathing through the leaves
that hid the lovers in the grove. (*Orlando innamorato* 1.19.63)

Not only loyal and loving, Fiordelisa can instruct knights on how to avoid traps, escape enchantments, and behave like virtuous gentlemen. Her literary descendant is Shakespeare's Rosalind in *As You Like It*, who teaches tongue-tied Orlando to treat her as a complex person when she appears to him as a woman disguised as a man who pretends to be a woman teaching him the art of love. Shakespeare's reading of Ariosto is signaled in his changing the name of the hero in his source, Thomas Lodge's *Rosalynde: Euphues' Golden Legacy* (1590), from Rosader to Orlando.

The only real female warrior in Shakespeare is Joan of Arc in *1 Henry VI*. Her burning as a witch can introduce an undergraduate class to the sixteenth century's darkening of superstition. In 1482 Boiardo could still regard the devil as a comic figure. When the magician Malagigi (Malagise) calls his demons to the field and turns them into warriors, Boiardo's narrator comments:

Quella battaglia orribile e infernale
Che io ve ho contata, e piena di spavento,
Me piacque sì che, s'io non dico male,
Mirarla in fatto avria molto talento,
Sol per veder se il demonio è cotale
E tanto sozzo come egli è dipento,
Ché non è sempre a un modo in ogni loco:
Qua maggior corne, e la più coda un poco.

That terrible, demonic war,
that horror I described before,
pleased me so much, I wish I'd seen—
if I may say so—the real thing.

> that way I'd see if Satan is
> as ugly as he's pictured when
> portrayed in different places, here
> with larger horns, with more tail there. (*Orlando innamorato* 2.23.1)

Even Brunello, Boiardo's version of the dark imp of medieval folklore, is a comic figure.[8] But Ariosto demonizes him, as he does Angelica.[9] Tasso's personal paranoia finds its way into his poem, and Spenser inherits the dark tradition when Archimago calls up his demons to infect Redcrosse's sleep in the first canto of *The Faerie Queene.* Shakespeare's Mercutio is amusing if not pornographic when he seeks "To raise a spirit in [Romeo's] mistress's circle / Of some strange nature, letting it there stand / Till she had laid it and conjur'd it down" (*Romeo and Juliet* 2.1.24–26). Both Romeo and Juliet believe in ghosts and live in a world of portents and planetary influences that we may want to regard as tragic images of fate but that are better understood as strong superstitions that grip the characters' imaginations.

Each of these approaches to appreciating poetry is far preferable to defining the European Renaissance as a period of protocolonialism rather than an artistic rebirth. *The Norton Anthology of World Literature* (3rd ed.) unfortunately offers only a meager portion of the *Furioso*, dwarfed by *Don Quixote*'s many pages, with no literary context or understanding of the relation between medieval French culture and its Renaissance Italian and English counterparts. Boiardo knew from Herodotus the history of conflicts between Europe and Asia. If the world was a wider place by the time Ariosto published the *Furioso* in 1516, the same lessons of war and peace can be learned from reading about the clashes of civilizations in the romantic epic, rather than ignoring them. Just as the Greek cities fought among themselves during the Persian invasions, Ferrara and Rome eyed each other suspiciously in the Renaissance, as did Catholic Spain and Protestant England, whose struggles form the backdrop to *The Faerie Queene* and *Paradise Lost.* But there are internal conflicts as well. Spenser lived in Ireland, and when Milton aligns his epic poetry with "the anti-Virgilian, anti-imperial epic tradition of Lucan" (Quint, *Epic* 326), he is putting a republican face on a tradition of poetic, artistic distancing from worldly politics that gives such a strong binary tension to the form of the Italian epic romance. The pastoral retreat illustrated by Fiordelisa and Brandimarte's love-making or Erminia's truancy in the *Liberata* shows up when Spenser's Sir Calidor watches the Graces dance to the tune of Colin

Clout on Mt. Alcidale, before he must resume his quest for the Blatant Beast (*Faerie Queene* 6.10.16).

Spenser never writes an epic battle scene into his *Faerie Queene*, and Shakespeare's battles are usually off-stage or represented onstage by a few soldiers or messengers. But warfare is deeply engrained in the Italian poems, from Boiardo's armies seesawing across the plains below Albracca to Ariosto's tightly organized battle of Paris and Tasso's siege towers besetting Jerusalem. Individual combats in Boiardo and Spenser advance the stories and distinguish individual personalities and themes, although Ariosto has a better eye, and Sidney the best of all, for he was an aristocrat who studied horsemanship and fencing. Even as the Italians and English writers clung to the chivalric world (the way Lewis does in the Narnia tales), the illusion of that world is broken by Cimosco's arquebus in the *Furioso.* This weapon was based on Alfonso d'Este's two cannons that swept the field at Ravenna in 1515 (*Orlando furioso* 14.1–9), one named La Diavola and the other Giuliana because it was cast from a recycled bronze bust of Pope Julius II. Eventually Orlando buries the evil engine in the ocean, and Milton borrows the idea for the war in heaven in *Paradise Lost*, where the demons use it but then lose it:

> Th'invention all admir'd, and each, how hee
> To be th'inventor miss'd, so easy it seem'd
> Once found, which yet unfound most would have thought
> Impossible; yet haply of thy Race
> In future days, if Malice should abound,
> Some one intent on mischief, or inspir'd
> With dev'lish machination might devise
> Like instrument to plague the Sons of men
> For sin, on war and mutual slaughter bent. (6.498–506)

Gunpowder forever separates our world from the books of chivalry that drove Don Quixote mad—although the barber and the village curate recognized the preeminence of Boiardo and Ariosto when they burned his books. From our distance, and from the perspective of world literature, the Italian epics and the English Renaissance help bring the tradition of Virgil and Rome to the modern American classroom. Milton, with his Christian theme of salvation, claimed to write of "Things unattempted yet in Prose or Rhyme" (*Paradise Lost* 1.16). But Ariosto had made the same claim (*Orlando furioso* 1.2) about the effects of love on Orlando. And Ariosto knew very well the debt he owed Boiardo's imaginative synthesis of literary traditions, for the boast occurs twice in the *Innamorato*, once when Boiardo calls the battle of Montalbano "La più stupenda guerra e la maggiore / Che racontasse mai prosa né verso" ("The largest, most amazing war / attempted yet in prose or rhyme"; *Orlando innamorato* 2.29.1), and again when he doubles down a canto later after Agramante has led all of Africa to join the Spaniards opposed to Charlemagne: "La più fiera battaglia e sterminata, / E la più orrenda e più pericolosa / Che racontasse mai verso né prosa" ("the largest and the fiercest fight, / the most perverse and perilous, / that verse or prose have ever told"; *Orlando innamorato* 2.30.1). The debt of the greatest English Renaissance poets to the Italian romantic epics may be diffuse, but it is palpable and even at times intense.

## Notes

1. See Quint, "The Fortunes of Morgana"; and Nohrnberg, "Orlando's Opportunity."

2. The idea that the epic form has an end point while romances tend to wander or err, with a pun on knights errant, animates Nohrnberg's *The Analogy of* The Faerie Queene; Parker's *Inescapable Romance*; and Quint's "The Figure of Atlante."

3. A kind of bildungsroman theme connects these works to the classics; see Cavallo and Ross, "Teaching the *Innamorato.*"

4. Spenser's *Letter to Raleigh* came at the end of the 1590 edition of *The Faerie Queene* and was moved forward in the 1596 edition.

5. See Dante's *Inferno* 7 and, for a discussion, Lewis, *Discarded Image* 82.

6. Boiardo translated a substantial portion of Herodotus from Lorenzo Valla's Latin; see Murrin, *History and Warfare* 248–54 (appendix 2, "Boiardo's Translation of Herodotus").

7. "Ha! Perchevaux, Fortune [est] cauve / Detriers et devant chavelue" ("Ah, Percival! Fortune is bald behind and forelocked in front"; 136 [lines 4645–46]); see also halfway through the movie version directed by Eric Rohmer, which is what I use to introduce English literature classes to the Holy Grail story.

8. Cervantes has Don Quixote remember how Brunello steals Sacripante's horse from under him (2.4; *Orlando innamorato* 2.3.30–40).

9. For a complete guide to Ariosto's changes to Boiardo, see Cavallo, *Romance Epics.*

**Phillip John Usher**

# A Painting of Trojans / A Map of America: Early French Reactions to Ariosto

The influence of Ludovico Ariosto's *Orlando furioso* in early modern French literature was both vast and varied (Cameron, *Influence* [1930] and *Influence* [1933]; Cioranescu; Keyser). To illustrate this, we might recall how Joachim Du Bellay, in his Petrarchan *Olive* (1549–50), imitates Ariosto's portrait of Alcina, while in the *Regrets* (1558), that same Circean sorceress embodies the seductive horror of Rome (poems 87–92) (Lupton). Or we might think of France's first career tragedian, Robert Garnier, who authored a tragicomic *Bradamante* (1582) that transformed Ariosto's story of a battle between Christians and Muslims into a nationalistic account of France's Wars of Religion between Catholics and Protestants (Usher). Many other examples suggest themselves, for Ariosto also influenced Pierre de Ronsard, Jean-Antoine de Baïf, Amadis Jamyn, Etienne de la Boétie, Philippe Desportes, and countless others. As might be expected, his influence was nowhere stronger than in epic. Now, it is likely that many undergraduate students will first read the *Orlando furioso*, or extracts thereof, in courses that emphasize and explore continuities between national literary traditions, but that can indeed be a challenge—the works are generally long and frequently complex. Such courses might be of the so-called great-books variety or else be more focused with titles like Epic

Travel or Early Modern Epic. Such courses are quite common, and students might feel anxious when first glancing at such ambitious reading lists. The purpose of this article, therefore, is to discuss one pedagogical approach to help students reflect on some points of contact between Ariosto's Italian epic about a French knight, first translated into French in 1543, and French epics written around the same time. While French epics do not hold the canonical status of the *Orlando furioso*, the *Lusiads*, or the *Faerie Queene*, that is largely the result of nineteenth-century critical paradigms: French Renaissance authors were not only very intent on creating a national epic, but they also produced approximately two hundred of them. I will focus in particular on the use of projected images (a painting and a map), as starting points for classroom discussions about two French Renaissance epics and their possible connections to, or differences from, the *Orlando furioso*.

## Against Fevered Reveries

The course of literary history, especially the bungled opinion pieces of Sainte-Beuve that also goaded Proust to write his masterpiece, means that much of sixteenth-century French literature was essentially erased—but from the perspective of sixteenth-century France, Ronsard's unfinished *Franciade* (1572) was considered an epic capable of standing up to Ariosto's *Orlando furioso*. In it, Ronsard saves from the Homeric flames of the Trojan War a son of Hector called Astyanax, Skamandrios, and then Francus in order to make him the ancestor of the French. Ronsard borrows his general structure from Virgil: just as Aeneas escapes from Troy, lands in Carthage where he falls in love with Dido, then continues, at Mercury's prompting, his travels in order to found Rome, so the Trojan Francus sets out from Buthrotum, arrives in Crete where two women fall in love with him—at least proleptically in book 1—before he is sent to found Paris and France. The poem's last book features a long prophecy detailing the kings of France, right up to the current king, Charles IX.

French readers first heard of Ronsard's project in the 1550s but had to wait until 1572 for the publication of the first (and only) four books. It was an immediate success, leading to several new editions over the coming years—and indeed even to the publication of pirated editions in Antwerp and Turin (Rouget 42–45). As one critic put it recently, it is "historically incorrect" to argue—as many have—that the poem was not a success (Ternaux 117). The *Franciade*'s centrality to a (sixteenth-century) view of the French Renaissance canon would be reason enough to put it into dialogue with the *Orlando furioso* in an undergraduate class. That dialogue proves even more essential and rich when we recall that the *Franciade* imitates Ariosto's text at various points and that in the *Franciade*'s preface (and elsewhere) Ronsard excoriates his Italian predecessor. Comparing the two epics can open up a vast array of useful discussion topics, from microtextual questions about style and influence to bigger questions about canon formation and national identity in the early modern period.

One interactive way to introduce Ronsard's *Franciade*, and specifically its conflicted relation to Ariosto's text, is to focus a first class on the two texts as specifically *romance* epics. A useful starting point might be the projection and discussion of a painting by Toussaint Dubreuil, *Hyante et Climène à leur toilette*, which brings out precisely that.[1] Realized for Henry IV's new castle at Saint-Germain-en-Laye, the image and the verses it illustrates linger on details of hair and clothing, rather than on plot or epic telos. It depicts the two women who fall for Francus: Clymène will die; Hyante will live to prophesy France's future kings. With the painting projected, and before introducing the *Franciade*, the instructor might ask students who they think the various characters are, what role they might play in an epic (why two not one love interest?), and especially how the scene is depicted.

At this point, students can read out the short extract from the *Franciade* on which Dubreuil's painting is based:

> . . . du jour la lumiere sacrée
> Dedans la chambre estoit par tout entrée,
> Quand ces deux sœurs, ainçois ces beaux printemps
> Sortent du lict : ils demeurent long-temps
> A leur peigner, atiffer, et à faire
> Par le mirouer ung visage pour plaire:
> En cent facons ils tordent leurs cheveux
> Ondez, crespez, entrefrizez de nœuds,
> Et d'un long art mille beautez s'attachent:
> Puis teste et col d'un guimple elles se cachent,
> Qui bien plié jusqu'aux pieds leur pendoit.

> . . . the sacred light of day
> Entered the room from all directions.
> These two sisters—no: these fine springtimes—
> Rise from their beds. They spend much time
> In front of the mirror, combing their hair,

Adorning themselves so their faces will delight.
In hundreds of ringlets they curl their hair
Into waves and crinkles and knotty flourishes.
With patient art they dress in a thousand fineries.
They hide face and neck with wimples
That hang in folds down to their feet.
Their white faces now
Glowed like rubies. (3.129–41)[2]

Students could discuss how the verses resemble (or not) descriptions of (for example) Ariosto's Angelica, then more generally the aesthetics of love in the *Furioso* and the *Franciade*, the presence and role of female characters in both, and other related topics. Moments where Ronsard directly imitates Ariosto could then be read and discussed, to explore what Ronsard borrows (a theme, a simile, a specific word, etc.), as well as whether the borrowing is translation or creative imitation (and what the difference is).[3] Students might then compare Ronsard's traceable debt to Ariosto with what Ronsard says of Ariosto in the preface. Rather than have students read out extracts of the preface in class, they might read it at home and think about Ariosto's role therein—and especially what they make of Ronsard's statements given their own reading of the *Furioso*. Ronsard's central appreciation of Ariosto is as follows: "[The epic poet] must not . . . forge fantastical poetry like that of Ariosto—its limbs are sometimes quite fine but the body is false and grotesque, more closely resembling the prolonged and fevered reveries of a madman than the writings of a sane individual" (3–4). Follow-up questions could unpack what is (or is not) false and grotesque about the *Furioso*, why Ronsard might have thought of the poem in such a way (in comparison with his own style). Further discussion could turn productively on Ariosto's place in Ronsard's bigger argument in the preface, on the topic of verisimilitude. Ronsard seems to agree fundamentally with Ariosto's privileging of poetic fiction over historical accuracy in matters of epic poetry—only he sees Ariosto as going too far.

## Not-Rodomont

A particularly exciting moment in the French reception of the *Orlando furioso*, and which has great potential for lively classroom discussion, is a short epic poem or epyllion written by Marc Lescarbot in the first decade of the seventeenth century. Titled *De la défaite des Sauvages Armouchiquois* (*The Defeat of the Armouchiquois Savages*), the poem is among the first

French verse in any genre to be based in a direct manner on lived experience in the New World. Perhaps written on a ship as its author sailed back from Canada to France, the poem ostensibly promotes French colonial efforts to a hesitant king and country. The poem's hero is however not a European but a Souriquois Indian called Membertou, who is defined specifically as a non-Ariostan hero. Projecting a very specific map of early modern Canada[4] can lead students into productive discussion of the relation between the *Furioso* and the *Défaite*, about their different local and global cartographies of the Old and New Worlds, as well as about the contrasting ways in which notions of here and there, us and them, define and redefine heroism.

Rather than announce this as a map of (part of) Canada, the instructor might first ask students to rise from their seats in order to look at the projected map. Leading questions might include the following: Which part of the world does this show? In what century? Was it drawn for anyone in particular? Does it bear traces of any political projects? What kinds of things are represented on the land? And what do we see in the sea? These and other leading questions will open up the map onto the general context of France's colonial presence in Canada in the early seventeenth century, specifically under the patronage of Henry IV whose arms, signaling him as King of France and of Navarre, are featured in the top left-hand corner of the map (three fleurs-de-lys on the left and a set of connected chains on the right). The sea monsters, which will surely attract smiles or raised eyebrows, might be used to start a discussion about the fears and hopes of European travelers, how they worried about being shipwrecked, and subsequently about the likely consequences of such hopes and fears on the relations between Europeans and non-Europeans. A further and productive line of discussion would focus not on the pictorial elements but on the words printed on the map, even if students do not know French. Armed with the simplest of print or online dictionaries, students would likely uncover the following: "La Terre Neuve" (Newfoundland), "Canada Montagnais" (mountainous Canada), "Golfe de Canada" (Gulf of Canada). But even more crucially, they would probably stumble on terms not in the average French-English dictionary, especially toponyms like "Hochelaga" (Montreal) and "Chouacoet," as well as the names of several Native American tribes ("Iroquois," "Armouchiquois," "Souriquois," and "Etechemins"), which students may or may not recognize. Discussion can stress the French presence in the New World and the way the map betokens both a European style of mapping and images and words that clearly belong to the American context and Native American languages.

With this discussion still in mind, the instructor might next explain that the map was first printed in a book called the *Histoire de la Nouvelle-France* written by Marc Lescarbot, a historian who was also an epic poet. The instructor can announce the spot marked "Chouacoet" as the location where a short epic written by Lescarbot took place. Before looking at the poem, students might propose possible epic stories that would be appropriate to this location and the context derived from discussion of the map. Without too much prodding, students may well suggest that the poem could entail a confrontation between Europeans and Native Americans. Discussion would then profitably turn to how this confrontation is similar to, or different from, the kinds of confrontation that populate Ariosto's work. At this point, a new slide could project a smaller version of the map and the first five lines of *La Défaite des Sauvages Armouchiquois*:

> IE ne chante l'orgueil du geant Briarée,
> Ni du fier Rodomont la fureur enivrée
> Du sang dont il a teint pre[s]que tout l'uniuers,
> Ni comme il a forcé les piuots des enfers.
> Ie chante MEMBERTOV . . .
>
> I sing not the pride of that giant Briareus. Nor do I sing the drunken fury of proud Rodomont with which he stained the whole universe in blood, nor how he forced open the doors of the underworld. I sing of Membertou. (my trans.)

In a great-books class, as well as in comparative courses focused on the history of epic, students will surely recognize the formulaic epic beginning. Asked to compare Lescarbot's opening with those of the *Aeneid* ("Arma virumque cano . . ."; "Of arms and of men I sing . . ."; my trans.) and of the *Furioso* ("Le donne, i cavallier, l'arme, gli amori, / le cortesie, l'audaci imprese io canto"; "Of ladies and knights, and of arms and love I sing / Of courtesies and of many daring feats"; my trans.), students will identify the formal similarities but also the primary singularity of Lescarbot's text, namely that it defines its subject negatively. The specific disalignment vis-à-vis the *Furioso* should become the focus of conversation, as a textually rooted way of discussing a whole host of issues. A first topic would be why Lescarbot wants to avoid singing of proud Rodomont, the King of Sarza and Algiers, champion of the Saracens. Students could be asked why such a hero—or someone like him—would not be adaptable to a French poem set in the New World or to the political context shaped by Henry IV's sponsorship of colonial projects. Still focusing on the opening lines, emphasis could be effectively placed—typographically, sonorously—on the opposition between "Rodomont" and "Membertov," the first name recognizable, the second likely unknown, and both clearly belonging to two different linguistic traditions.

If such preliminary discussions took place in a first class on Lescarbot, a second and final class would be a more productive time for discussing the rest of the *Défaite*, which tells of how Membertou, a Souriquois Indian and ally of the French, helps the French defeat a tribe of Armouchiquois Indians. For this second class, students could read passages from the *Orlando furioso* concerning Rodomont to show to what extent Lescarbot's claim that Membertou is not-Rodomont bears out.

Teaching Ariosto alongside roughly contemporary epics written in other countries is fairly common, in both lower- and upper-level classes, although the other works are more likely to be those of Camões, Spenser, or Milton than those of Ronsard and Lescarbot. This essay has thus attempted to suggest how images—a painting and a map—might be exploited pedagogically in the classroom, in order to help students make connections between Ariosto's *Orlando furioso* and the two French epics. The suggestions made aim to generate classroom discussion about epic literary tradition, about national claims to, and squabbles over, literary traditions, and about epic's role not just in representing but in creating the world we live in.

## Notes

1. For the painting, see the Web site of the Musée du Louvre: cartelfr.louvre.fr/cartelfr/visite?srv=car_not_frame&idNotice=1106.

2. Unless otherwise noted, all translations of the *Franciade* are from my 2010 edition.

3. See, for example, Ronsard, *Franciad* 2.1022, 3.816, and 4.1,220, as well as the accompanying notes in the English translation.

4. For example, see numerique.banq.qc.ca/patrimoine/details/52327/2244751.

**Patricia E. Grieve**

# Moorish Lovers, Moorish Invaders, and the Call to Empire: The Inspiration of Ariosto in Early Modern Spain

## Ariosto in Spain and Pedagogical Strategies

It is a commonplace of Cervantine criticism to connect *Don Quixote* to Ludovico Ariosto's *Orlando furioso.* After all, in the Sierra Morena mountain range, Don Quixote, despairing over his unrequited love of Dulcinea, overtly imitates the madness of Orlando; indeed, according to David Littlejohn, Cervantes cites Ariosto or *Orlando furioso* eighty-three times in his work (109). While Thomas R. Hart argues that Ariosto directly inspired Cervantes's use of the irony of purposeless chivalry, others point to the widespread combination of the serio-comic and the chivalric in romance, beginning with Chrétien de Troyes in twelfth-century France.[1] As is well known, Ariosto's opening lines highlight what will be a combined epic-romance tradition: "Le donne, i cavallier, l'arme, gli amori, / le cortesie, l'audaci imprese io canto" ("Of ladies, cavaliers, of love and war, / Of courtesies and of brave deeds I sing"; 1.1). Rather than rehearse the same arguments about direct or indirect influence, I propose three pedagogical strategies for studying Ariosto in Spain, which treat epic, romance, and lyric poetry. The first considers Castilian translations of *Orlando furioso* in the sixteenth century, which serve as calls to empire or what we might deem invocations or gestures to Spanish imperial aims, especially in the translation by Jerónimo de Urrea, who also translated Sannazaro's *Arcadia* and was the author in his own right of Spanish romances of chivalry. The second looks at prose romances in sixteenth- and seventeenth-century Spain, which reflect on the role of women in both conflict with Islam and the romanticizing of Muslim Spain, including the exceedingly popular *La historia de los dos enamorados Flores y Blancaflor* ("History of the Two Lovers Flores and Blancaflor") and the historical romance *Crónica del Rey don Rodrigo* ("Chronicle of King Rodrigo"), also known as *Crónica sarracina* ("Saracen Chronicle").[2] The third part of this essay addresses poetic imitations of Ariosto in Spain, specifically some that treat Angelica and Medoro's love story. In this way, we see the epic tradition, the prose romance, and poetic traditions inspired by Ariosto sharing some of the same preoccupations of the time, the interactions with and conflicts with Islam—to Ariosto, Saracens, sometimes "sarracenos," "mahometanos," "musulmanes," and, most frequently, "moros," to Spanish writers.

University and college curricula now include a variety of courses on multicultural encounters. Between Mediterranean studies writ large and Hispano-medieval and early modern Spanish studies, Spain features in the examinations of Christian, Muslim, and Jewish conflicts, as well as relatively harmonious episodes in history. I teach an interdisciplinary course titled Andalusian Symbiosis: Islam and the West; one titled Blood/Lust: Staging the Early Modern Mediterranean; which focuses on the views England, Spain, North Africa, and the Ottoman Empire hold toward themselves and one another; and other courses on medieval and early modern romance, epic and ballad, and Cervantes's *Don Quixote* and novellas. All my courses have undergraduate and graduate versions, and what I propose below could be used in both levels. One might imagine a comparative course on Italian and Spanish Renaissance epic or romance, in which Ariosto's *Orlando furioso* figures prominently, or, indeed, may be the sole focus of the course's Italian part. Some of the Spanish works I mention below exist in English translation, while others do not. Rather than propose a single course in English translation or one in which the student must know both Italian and Spanish, I suggest three subfields from which an instructor could devise a graduate or undergraduate course and decide which romance language(s), if any, a student must know to be eligible for the course.

## Renaissance Epic in Spain: Translations of *Orlando furioso* and the Aims of Empire

In the first instance, the Renaissance epic could be a single course, such as Ariosto in Spain or Renaissance Epic in Italy and Spain. There are a number of translations of *Orlando furioso* in sixteenth-century Spain. One of them, by Captain Jerónimo de Urrea, went through at least twelve and possibly as many as eighteen printings between 1549 and 1583.[3] Urrea's translation, printed in August 1549 in Antwerp by Martín Nucio's press, coincided with the arrival of Charles V, Holy Roman emperor and king of Spain (as Charles I) to the city. The translation's introduction cuts forty-seven stanzas on the House of Este's future and adds 111 stanzas on famous Spanish men and women, from King Ferdinand to Charles's son, Prince Philip, soon to be king of Spain.[4] Urrea clearly interweaves Ariosto's narrative strategies of prophecy and empire to produce a laudatory text of Spanish imperialism. In a classroom, one might have students compare these strategies and identify the ways Spanish and Italian contexts differ. The success of Urrea's work in court circles and beyond, measured by the many printings in the sixteenth century alone, not only celebrated Spain's past and its hoped-for world domination but cemented Ariosto's privilege in early modern Spain. However, while the court and reading public may have been impressed by Urrea's translation, Cervantes was not: in part 1, chapter 6 of *Don Quixote*, when the priest and the barber discover Urrea's work in Don Quixote's library, the priest declares that he won't read Ariosto in any other language than Ariosto's own, opining further that "the captain" had lost some of the valor and value of the original, which always happens with translation and especially translation of poetry.

Subsequent Castilian translations increasingly took liberties with Ariosto's text, and students can explore this by reading parts of, for example, the soldier-poet Nicolas Espinosa's loose translation of *Orlando furioso* (1555). Medieval Spanish epic invented the story of a legendary Asturian hero, Bernardo del Carpio, slayer of Roland at Roncesvalles, which links the French defeat to the foundational myths that insist that Muslims never dominated Asturias, birthplace of the Spanish monarchy, after the invasion in 711. Hence, Bernardo del Carpio was lauded as the true Castilian hero of Spain for centuries before nineteenth-century and literary histories claimed this honor for El Cid. Espinosa's work is noteworthy for being the first to introduce the legend of Bernardo del Carpio into Ariosto's *Orlando*.[5]

## War, Women, and Conversion to Christianity in *Historia de los dos enamorados, Flores y Blancaflor,* and *Cronica del Rey don Rodrigo*

By considering two themes of the romance tradition—invasion or battles and conversion that place women in prominent roles—not only do we look at some of the most popular works in early modern Spain, but we can focus on historical geopolitical preoccupations of the time. Countries of the Western Mediterranean feared the Ottoman Turkish Empire and the Barbary States. As Iberia faced ongoing concern about the Morisco problem, Spaniards feared that sixteenth-century Muslim converts to Christianity and their descendants, known as Moriscos, still secretly embraced Islam and might conspire with Muslims in the Mediterranean. Because the Morisco population was concentrated along the Mediterranean coast and the land near Gibraltar, such a collusion would leave Spain's coasts vulnerable. The Carolingian romance of the Iberian Saracen prince Flores and the sometimes French, sometimes Italian, Christian noblewoman Blancaflor along with the historical romances of King Rodrigo and the eighth-century fall of Spain to the Muslims saw numerous printings in the sixteenth century. While I have artificially separated epic and romance by first considering that the Castilian translations of *Orlando furioso* invoked Iberian expansionism and its relations to the epic and then contemplating that the prose romances represent love and conflict between Islam and Christianity, ideas of expansionism, religious and political conflict, and amorous affairs bind epic and romance in all the Spanish works. One can find examples of romance in Spanish epic translations and of military conflict and imperialism in prose romances. The Spanish examples of romance discussed here, the anonymous *Flores y Blancaflor* and Pedro de Corral's *Crónica del Rey don Rodrigo*, both place women at the center of conflict and resolution.

*Flores y Blancaflor* (c. 1532) and *Crónica del Rey don Rodrigo* (1499, 1527, 1549) share with *Orlando furioso* the historical landscape of the eighth century Muslim invasion of Spain. The sixteenth-century *Flores y Blancaflor* owes more to a lost Italo-Spanish version than to the twelfth-century French versions or even to an early Spanish chronicle-romance found in a manuscript of Alfonso X's thirteenth-century *Estoria de Espana* ("History of Spain") or *Primera cronica general* ("First General Chronicle").[6] *Orlando furioso* appeared in print in 1516 and the definitive version appeared in 1532; catalogs of early modern printings list a *Flores y Blancaflor* from

Alcalá de Henares in 1512, though I could not find it, and none of the catalogs mention having seen it firsthand. The earliest printing I found was from 1532, simultaneously published in different cities. Nevertheless, it seems likely that the Spanish version I deal with and *Orlando furioso* were first known to their respective publics in the first part of the sixteenth century, and they share 1532 as significant publication dates. *Crónica del Rey don Rodrigo* by Pedro de Corral, composed around 1430, circulated in manuscript form in the fifteenth century and then went through numerous printings beginning in 1499 and continuing throughout the sixteenth century.

Scholars of romance have noted that amorous relationships between non-European or non-Christian men and European Christian women are far less common than between Christian men and non-Christian women, which makes an interesting link between the lovers in *Flores y Blancaflor* and *Orlando furioso*'s Ruggiero and Bradamante. Flores's father has come to rule Spain after the invasion of the peninsula in 711 by North African Muslims, and baby prince Flores and baby Christian captive Blancaflor are born on the same day, grow up together, and fall in love. His parents object to the love affair and sell Blancaflor into captivity. Flores rescues her from Cairo, and during the journey home to Spain, Flores converts to Christianity at the insistence of Blancaflor. Subsequently, the entire Iberian Peninsula converts to Christianity, thereby overturning, hundreds of years earlier than the historical facts, the rule of Islamic Spain (al-Andalus). Students might be asked to question what is at stake when a Muslim man and a Christian woman fall in love and could fruitfully compare the love and trials and tribulations of Flores and Blancaflor with those of Bradamante and Ruggiero, the legendary ancestral founders of the House of Este, and the ways in which conversion, especially inspired by the love of a virtuous Christian woman, are used to create foundational myths.

Pedro de Corral's *Crónica del Rey don Rodrigo* could be compared with *Orlando furioso* in a number of ways. As I mentioned earlier, its historical setting is King Rodrigo's eighth-century Visigothic court in Toledo, on the eve of, during, and after the Muslim invasion of the peninsula. A long work, it includes numerous protagonists and relationships, amorous and otherwise. Even in a graduate class, selections from the two-volume work would be recommended, rather than an attempt to read the whole thing. In addition to Christian-Muslim conflict and the invasion of Spain, the romance contains many opportunities for comparison with *Orlando furioso*, such as its instances of prophecy, emphasis on the Visigothic kingdom as a sophisticated empire, and the king's dereliction of duty because of his obsession with La Cava, the daughter of his military leader, Don Julián. The king's rape of the daughter and the prophecy that the kingdom would fall to Muslims is the fortunate fall that leads to the emergence of a Christian hero, Pelayo. A putative relative of King Rodrigo—putative since most of this material, while treated as official history by historians well into the twentieth century, has little historical verification—fights back against the Muslims in Asturias, when a Muslim governor, Munuza, abducts Pelayo's sister. Unlike earlier medieval chronicles of the fall of Spain, Corral's historical romance is the first to blame La Cava, by focusing on the dangers of female sexuality, calling her, at one point, "fija de Satanás" ("daughter of Satan"), which becomes a commonplace in sixteenth- and seventeenth-century poems, ballads, plays, and histories. Thus, we see the tight link between women and land, in which poor La Cava is blamed for Spain's fall while military defense of Pelayo's virtuous sister allows for its restoration. Pelayo, crowned as the first Asturian king, is today considered the founder of the current Spanish monarchy.

### Poetical Treatments of Angelica and Medoro in Early Modern Spain

The third pedagogical strategy is to consider poetic forms in early modern Spain, particularly the treatment of Angelica and Medoro. The Spanish literary giants Lope de Vega Carpio and Luis de Góngora both produced poems on the subject in 1602, "La hermosura de Angélica" ("The Beauty of Angelica") and "En un albergue pastoral," sometimes called "Romance de Angelica y Medoro" ("In a Simple Shepherd's Cabin"; or "Ballad of Angelica and Medoro").[7] Lope's poem falls somewhere between an epic and a narrative poem; written in royal octaves, it comprises twenty cantos of more than 11,000 lines. Written in 1588, shortly after the defeat of the Spanish Armada, its point of departure is Angelica and Medoro in India, where they learn that the Andalusian king has willed his kingdom to the most beautiful man or woman in the world. In the blink of an eye, Angelica and Medoro are crowned king and queen of Seville, and wars and disasters soon follow. As in a number of his other works, he alludes to his own love affairs and disappointments. Góngora's interpretation of Angelica and Medoro uses the oral poetic form of the romance or ballad (sixteen syllables, assonant rhyme), and he uses his signature complex syntax and metaphors to explore a classical topos, the duality of court versus country.

At least two other significant Spanish poets wrote on Angelica and Medoro, Francisco de Aldana, who penned "Angélica y Medoro" (c. 1567), and Luis Barahona de Soto, who wrote *Primera parte de la Angélica* (1586; "First Part of the Angelica"). Aldana's poem is little known, though Aldana himself has, in recent years, become the focus of some studies in Spanish early modern poetry. Aldana wrote his poem in royal octaves (following the original), and he included it in a volume dedicated to King Philip II. There are many anonymous ballads (in Spanish, *romances*) in the second half of the sixteenth century and the first part of the seventeenth century that derive from *Orlando furioso* and in particular from the episodes involving Angelica and Medoro.

This essay has only scratched the surface of the presence of Ariosto in Spain, in translation, and in imitation. There are many more options for inclusion in courses, including the Spanish *comedias* that also treated the subject. Indeed, the difficulty is not in finding material; it is in deciding which rich works to choose.

## Notes

1. In addition, teachers may wish to consult *Approaches to Teaching the* Song of Roland," edited by William W. Kibler and Leslie Zarker Morgan, especially the chapters by Bailey and Campbell.

2. Another fruitful comparison would be the *novela morisca*, sixteenth-century romances of chivalry and love such as *Historia del abencerraje y la hermosa Jarifa* ("History of Abencerraje and the Beautiful Jarifa"), in which the Moorish lovers are celebrated and idealized for their virtues. Although there are many versions of this story, the most highly regarded is included in Antonio de Villegas's *Inventario* (1565; *Inventory*; or *Miscellany*). The appreciation for the exoticized Muslim in these stories is part of sixteenth-century Spain's fascination with Islamic culture, termed *maurophilia* by Georges Cirot. Such maurophilia contrasted with the sociohistorical reality of conflict with the Moriscos, which ended with the expulsion of the Moriscos from the peninsula between 1609 and 1614. In addition, I recommend a comparison of Ariosto with Cervantes's "The Captive's Tale," from part 1 of *Don Quixote*, an interpolated, multichapter historical romance, which recounts the battle of Lepanto in 1571 (an immensely popular topic in literature and the visual arts) and the subsequent escape to Spain of a Spanish captive in Algiers and a Muslim maiden, Zoraida, who wishes to be baptized a Christian. "The Captive's Tale" intriguingly combines historical elements of the Battle of Lepanto, in which the Holy League defeated the Ottoman fleet, with details of the Algerian slave trade and Christian captivity in North Africa into a fictional conversion romance. After detailing the sea battle, the narrative shifts to a romance between the Spanish captive and Zoraida, the daughter of Agi Morato, a rich man in the city of Algiers. Numerous English translations exist, but I recommend the translation by Edith Grossman.

3. In the 1520s, Pedro de Reinoso translated Matteo Maria Boiardo's *Orlando innamorato* into Castilian, known alternatively as *Primero, segundo, y tercer libro de Orlando innamorato* and *Espejo de cavallerias.* The history of print editions is convoluted, and scholars roundly denounce the one sixteenth-century edition that prints all three books as having changed too much of Reinoso's translation. Hence, while it could be interesting to study both Boiardo and Ariosto in Spain, in, say, a graduate course, access to Reinoso's works is partial and difficult.

4. For interesting information on all the Spanish translations of Ariosto, see Nicolopulos. Urrea's translation is generally available in libraries, but there is an excellent hypertext edition by the University of Barcelona.

5. Espinosa's *Segunda parte de* Orlando, *con el verdadero sucesso de la famosa batalla de Roncesualles; fin y muerte de los doze Pares de Francia* maintains some of Ariosto's material in order to weave Spanish glory and honor into the invented story of Bernardo del Carpio and his rout of Charlemagne's army at Roncesvalles. By "segunda parte," Espinosa means continuation, though it is more partial translation with a good deal of invention. Other sixteenth-century Castilian translations of *Orlando furioso* include those by Hernando de Alcoçer (1550), Francisco Garrido y Villena (1555; a continuation of the Roland story of Boiardo and Ariosto), and Diego Vázquez de Contreras (1585).

6. Although Alfonso X's work is from the thirteenth century, the manuscript that contains a version of Flores and Blancaflor (which also postulates that Flores and Blancaflor are the grandparents of Charlemagne!) dates from the fourteenth century. A modern edition of the 1532 *Flores y Blancaflor* is edited by Adolfo Bonilla y San Martín (*Historia de los dos enamorados Flores y Blancaflor*).

7. As far as I know, Lope's poem has not been translated into English, but there are versions accessible online. In addition to many Spanish versions, also online, Góngora's ballad is found in *Selected Poems of Luis de Góngora* (poem 22).

# Part VIII

# The Italian Romance Epic in Art, Music, and Theater

**Morten Steen Hansen**

# Ariosto in the Hands of Sixteenth- and Seventeenth-Century Artists

This essay is intended for instructors who wish to teach works of art with subject matter from the *Orlando furioso*. It assumes that there is no such thing as an illustration whose meaning is entirely contained by the text. Even a simple woodcut illustration in an early printed edition of the *Orlando furioso* can suggest an interpretation, functioning indexically, directing a reader's attention to a given episode in a canto as if it were especially significant. Rather than taking literary art as secondary to a textual source, Ludovico Ariosto's opus shall be considered as the *materia* of artists, who turned to the literary work to explore particular issues of pictorial representation that were specific to time and place.[1]

The frequency with which artists represented Ariosto's narrative poem does not correspond to the work's enormous popularity, a fact that becomes even more striking when compared to, for instance, Torquato Tasso's *Gerusalemme liberata* (1581), one of the most commonly painted poetic texts during the seventeenth century. Speculation about why more artists did not picture the *Orlando furioso* may be futile, but it is of interest that artists who did engage with the text were drawn largely to its more controversial aspects.

## Courtly Panegyric

While Ariosto's poem exemplified popular culture in premodern Italy, the work's courtly ethos accounts for its appearance in painting and sculpture commissioned by the Este in Modena and the Medici in Florence. Ariosto wrote his poem as the great ancestral fiction of the Este of Ferrara, Bradamante and Ruggiero being the family's progenitors, but only once did an artist deploy the *Orlando furioso* in a dynastic encomium addressed to that family. In honor of the 1695 marriage between Carlotta Felicita, daughter of the Duke of Braunschweig-Luneburg, and Rinaldo d'Este (named after one of Ariosto's heroes), the following year Marcantonio Franceschini frescoed the vault in the grand hall of the Palazzo Ducale in Modena (Miller). The *Apotheosis of Bradamante* pictures the warrior received by the Olympian gods to the sound of winged Fame's trumpet. Bradamante alludes to the German princess, whose expected offspring would continue the Este dynasty in Modena, the branch in Ferrara having become extinct in 1597. The fresco, though, is not predominantly biographical but speaks in broader terms of the family's eternal fame, for which Bradamante becomes a synecdoche. Strikingly, the grandiloquent decoration features no other references to the *Orlando furioso* than the heroine. The fresco reveals not only the extent to which the poem continued to be read as a glorification of the House of Este but also the difficulties presented by its many ironies, fantastic and humorous elements, and morally questionably behavior on the part of its protagonists, Ruggiero included.

## Narrative and Regional Style

The first significant monumental decoration based on Ariosto was painted by Nicolò dell'Abate around 1550 in the Palazzo Torfanini in Bologna, its surviving detached frescoes now preserved in the city's Pinacoteca Nazionale. The painter executed his works during the first critical backlash against the *Orlando furioso* (which, however, did nothing to diminish its popularity), coinciding with the first Italian translation of Aristotle's *Poetics* in 1549. As discussed by Daniel Javitch, the poet's critics found that his work failed according to Aristotelian prescriptions for epic narrative (*Proclaiming* 86–105). Dell'Abate embraced this difference by pitting Northern painterly style against the arts of Rome.

Only two of the painted walls, facing each other, are mostly intact, but originally eight scenes could be seen inside the fictive arches. In their present state the narratives begin with Ruggiero's arrival at Alcina's enchanted palace after his fight against the giantess Erfilla riding an enormous wolf, as seen in the middle ground. Both riders are now headless as a result of paint loss. His violent escape from the castle follows in the next scene. Moving toward the background, we encounter events preceding the hero's escape. The sorceress Melissa, in the guise of Ruggiero's foster father, puts him to shame because his love for Alcina has left him effeminate. Further back Bradamante and Melissa (in her original shape) stand at Merlin's tomb. On the facing wall in what likely are the two concluding scenes, Ruggiero is transported in a small boat toward the realm of the good sorceress Logistilla, the sister of the brokenhearted Alcina, whose fleet is arriving for attack. Ruggiero, however, stuns his attackers with the magical shield. In the final scene Logistilla welcomes him as the water reflects Alcina's burning ships. In the foreground can be seen a fragment of a rower in a boat, which might have included a now-lost figure of the escaping Alcina being transported away in the only boat left of her fleet.

Though critics of the *Orlando furioso* insisted that it did not qualify as epic proper, the painter seems to have insisted on the poem's modern and unclassical nature, thereby giving a different spin to the hostile readers' arguments. This in turn bore on the artist's deployment of painterly style. In the scenes with Ruggiero's arrival to and escape from Alcina's court, time is expressed spatially: what happened first in the story appears farthest toward the background. That structure is challenged, however, by the way the eye follows the images' flow, since we spontaneously see Ruggiero's catapulting from the castle as the direct continuation of the previous scene depicting his arrival. As a result, we experience the narrative of the second fresco in reverse as the gaze wanders toward the horizon, taking us backward in time. The story itself seems to be bewitched, in keeping with Alcina's realm, where nothing is what it appears to be. Like Ruggiero, initially we see the sorceress as a great beauty, though we know from the text that she is older than the sibyl, with little hair and no teeth (7.70–73). Despite the illusionism of the frescoes, the illogical proportions of figures, buildings, and landscape across the painted space lend an air of the uncanny.

Dell'Abate let the hero become increasingly marginalized. In the penultimate scene Ruggiero is the small figure on a boat, and we next see him in the background about to enter Logistilla's castle and disappear from view. The painter's strange narrative devices might be an argument for romance poetry's uniqueness and modernity, justifying its difference from classical heroic poetry as defined by Aristotle. Around the time when dell'Abate worked in the Palazzo Torfanini, the Este employee Giovambattista Giraldi Cinzio in Ferrara formulated a similar argument about *Orlando furioso*'s modernity and its independence from Aristotelian ideas (*Discorso dei romanzi*).

In the first part of the sixteenth century, a new kind of monumental narrative painting in Rome and Florence aligned itself with epic poetry. Painting in the epic style was pioneered by Raphael in the Vatican's Sala di Costantino, in which figures with a sculptural quality wearing *all'antica* costumes are placed in relief-like arrangements, testifying to the painter's antiquarian study of ancient Roman relief sculpture. In 1550 Giorgio Vasari, in the first written history of Italian art, promoted this kind of painting, which he justly identified with Rome and Florence, at the expense of painting from the Veneto, Emilia-Romagna, Lombardy, and everywhere else for that matter. Dell'Abate's narratives do not apply a Roman and Florentine sculptural and polished painterly style but shimmer with rich, North-Italian colorism, fluid brushwork capturing the airiness of leaves and feathers, transparent blue skies turning golden toward the horizon, and ephemeral reflections on water.

On the arch framing the fresco where Alcina receives Ruggiero, two gilt statues, placed on the imposts of the pillars carrying the arches, extend festoons. The left figure seems bound while the other draws him in with his finger in a homoerotic and witty commentary to the scene of seduction and enslavement below. The golden figures imitate Michelangelo's *ignudi*, the idealized nudes on the Sistine ceiling in the Vatican Palace in Rome. Michelangelo's art centered almost exclusively on the human body, paying little attention to the outdoor scenery and atmospheric effects so richly represented by dell'Abate. Michelangelo was a major proponent of the epic style. Reducing his representations of flesh to hard sculpture and making them literally peripheral to the narrative, dell'Abate argued for the superiority of Northern colorism over Roman *disegno* (meaning both "design" and "drawing") in a new type of pictorial narrative that embraced the Emilian origins of Ariosto and his romance epic.

## Florence and the *Orlando furioso*

Romance was the poetry of the marvelous. In sixteenth-century Florence the two most significant artistic interpretations of the *Orlando furioso*, by

Bronzino and Valerio Cioli, deal with the fantastic and grotesque. The poem's connection to this aesthetic is in turn tied to the criticism leveled against Ariosto's opus for lacking verisimilitude. The famous *Allegory of Venus and Cupid* by the painter-poet Bronzino from the mid-1540s, now in the National Gallery in London, takes an ironic stance to the tradition of courtly love, exemplified by the lyric of Petrarch and his sixteenth-century imitators, by using the metaphors of such poetry to depict love that is anything but chaste. The painting's girl-monster with the seductive gaze has her arms reversed, revealing her perverse nature, and she offers a honeycomb in one hand while holding the scorpion-like sting of her tail in the other. This personification of the dangers of carnal pleasure is based on Ariosto's description of Fraud (*Orlando furioso* 14.86) (Moffitt). Her presence in a painting that celebrates Tuscan poetic culture, even if ironically so, is indicative of Ariosto's status as an adopted Tuscan poet.

At the beginning of the 1560s Cioli carved for Duke Cosimo I a statue of Braccio di Bartolo titled *Morgante on a Tortoise* in white Carrara marble for the Boboli Garden in Florence. Dwarfs, considered both ridiculous and marvels of nature, were affiliated with the European courts. After having entered the service of Duke Cosimo I, di Bartolo was ironically renamed after the eponymous giant in Luigi Pulci's romance (Heikamp). It was not uncommon to name dwarfs in court service after characters from romances. Cioli pictured Morgante as the captain of Alcina's monstrous army (*Orlando furioso* 6.63), which Ruggiero encounters before the sorceress welcomes him into her palace (Maurer 129). Ariosto describes Morgante as obese, drunk, and riding a tortoise. Instead of showing him intoxicated, the sculptor portrayed the Bacchus-like Morgante parodically, with the heroic nudity of an ancient deity. Bartolomeo Ammannati's *Neptune Fountain* on the Piazza Signoria would be a Florentine point of comparison. Being portrayed naked for general amusement was among the humiliations suffered by dwarfs at the Medici court. Morgante's commanding gesture imitates equestrian statues of rulers and warlords such as the Marcus Aurelius statue on the Capitoline Hill in Rome. Morgante becomes the antithesis to Duke Cosimo I, enhancing the ruler's omnipotence.

Outside Tuscany a work in Pier Francesco Orsini's Sacro Bosco at Bomarzo speaks to the association of Ariosto's work with the marvelous. One of the statues shows the mad Orlando ripping the shepherd in two. An inscription on a wall next to the gigantic statue indicates its status as a modern equivalent to the Colossus of Rhodes (Bredekamp).

## Ariosto in Baroque Art

During the seventeenth century most representations from the *Orlando furioso* were gallery pictures, executed for the private spaces of nobility and the wealthy. In Florence in particular, paintings and statuettes based on Ariosto became popular after members of the Medici family commissioned such works for their residences. Artists typically turned to Ariosto for scenes of strong passion, erotic or violent (*Orlando in the Robber's Den*, *Rodomonte Fighting the Hermit*, scenes of attempts at raping Angelica). Among the strangest and most remarkable paintings based on the *Orlando furioso* is Giovanni Lanfranco's large *Lucina, Norandino, and the Orcus* from circa 1620, commissioned by Cardinal Scipione Borghese for his villa in Frascati and now in the Villa Borghese in Rome. Lucina is trying to escape a blind monster by dressing in sheepskin. Discovering her, the monster pulls off her hide while her lover Norandino turns in her direction on hearing her cry (*Orlando furioso* 17.56–57). Lanfranco eroticizes the representation through the soft modeling of her pale body, shadows made luminous by reflected light. In this scene Ariosto imitated Homer's tale of Ulysses and Polyphemus from the *Odyssey*, as retold by Boccaccio in his *Genealogia deorum gentilum*. Boccaccio described men covered by animal hides rather than holding onto the bellies of the animals when escaping Polyphemus. Lanfranco called attention to Ariosto's source by painting the Orcus not like the deformed monster described by Ariosto but as a giant man, recalling Homer's blinded Cyclops. Scipione Borghese was among the eager collectors of Ferrara's artistic patrimony following the death of the last duke of Ferrara, Alfonso II d'Este, in 1597. The works Borghese acquired by Dosso and Battista Dossi, Garofalo, and Scarsellino, among other Ferrarese painters, are now on display in the Villa Borghese. The relocation of large numbers of important paintings from the former duchy to Rome embodied the changed situation of power, Ferrara's relative loss of its artistic patrimony revealing its newfound identity as a province of the Papal States. The Roman fascination with things Ferrarese would have motivated the commission from Lanfranco, an artist from Parma, for a major work based on the *Orlando furioso*.

During the seventeenth century the ability of art to move the beholder emotionally became an overriding concern. This is exemplified, for instance, in a treatise by a Jesuit and a painter published in Florence in 1652 (Ottonelli and Berrettini). Of particular concern was the female nude because of its said ability to lead the beholder into sin, and the authors were at pains to define the possibility of nonlascivious nudes in art. Artists ironically addressed the difficulties in controlling responses to bodily beauty by using Ariosto in works that problematized the relations between beholding, desire, and touch. Among these are scenes with Ruggiero eagerly trying to shed his armor to rape the desperate Angelica as she recollects that the magical ring on her finger will make her invisible when placed in her mouth. In Florence the painters Giovanni Bilivert and Cecco Bravo and the sculptor Ferdinando Tacca pictured the moment immediately before she vanishes. Once Ruggiero tries to move from vision to violent touch she disappears from sight. Ariosto used the simile of the sun hiding behind a cloud to describe Angelica's invisibility (*Orlando furioso* 11.6–8). In Cecco Bravo's painting, probably from the 1640s and now in Chicago's Smart Museum, the princess resembles a crouching Venus. Her luminous body, its contours forming a curve on the left, and the soft shadow that begins to cover her reveal the artist's poetic translation of Ariosto's metaphor into painting.

Peter Paul Rubens's *Angelica and the Hermit* from circa 1626–28 in the Kunsthistorisches Museum in Vienna is based on the story of Angelica's encounter with a lecherous old hermit who practices black magic (*Orlando furioso* 8.30–50). Rubens has painted the voluptuous princess sweetly sleeping, drugged by the sorcerer who tries to rape her in her unconscious state. Despite the help of the demonic arts—a demon not described by Ariosto supports the improvised bed—the hermit remains impotent. Again the movement from visual pleasure to touch is doomed to fail.

Shortly after the publication of Torquato Tasso's *Gerusalemme liberata* in 1581, writers began to contrast the poem with the *Orlando furioso.* When Cardinal Carlo de' Medici commissioned paintings based on Ovid, Ariosto, and Tasso for his Casino at San Marco around 1621 and 1622, he and his visitors would have compared representations of the two sixteenth-century epic poems (Fumagalli et al.). Matteo Rosselli painted as lyrical pendants for the cardinal *Angelica Attending Medoro* and *Erminia Attending Tancred* (Villa Medicea la Petraia, Florence). In canto 19 of the *Orlando furioso,* Angelica comes across the wounded Medoro, a young Muslim soldier (to Ariosto a pagan), and squeezes the juice of healing herbs on his wounds to stanch the bleeding. Ariosto describes how Cupid, unable to stand Angelica's scorn for all her suitors, waits to attack her where Medoro is lying. Cupid's presence demonstrates the effect of Medoro's gaze, wounding her even deeper with the arrows of love (*Orlando furioso* 19.28). Rosselli's scene from Tasso also pictures a Muslim princess caring for a wounded warrior she loves, but this time it is a Christian prince, Tancred, participating in the First Crusade (*Gerusalemme liberata* 19.112–14). Tasso's story can be seen as rewriting Ariosto's, and it is hardly a coincidence that the cantos in which both episodes take place share the same number.

While Tancred is supported by his squire Vafrine, dressed in oriental costume because he has been spying on the Egyptian army, Erminia stops his bleeding wounds. Tasso describes how she has no medical plants but binds his wounds with her cut-off hair. The painter instead has her treat his wounds with hair not yet cut. His side wound echoes that of the dead Christ, while Erminia recalls the Magdalene, who dried Christ's feet with her hair. Erminia, like the Magdalene before her, is a figure of love converted to a spiritual purpose, and in the painting she embodies Christian charity. Their tender and pained exchange of gazes is a world apart from the languid eyes of Ariosto's lovers. Clearly two different kinds of love are portrayed in the two canvases. The one from Tasso is imbued with a Christian and moral spirit, whereas Ariosto's is not—his lovers will move on to premarital sex and then marriage before disappearing from the story. When the two paintings are compared it is easy to locate a moral lesson with Tasso on the winning side, though the situation is more complex. A scene of chaste love inscribed in a Christian context could be seen to benefit the beholder spiritually, something that could hardly be said of Ariosto's pagan lovers. At the same time, in Tasso's couple the charm, eroticism, and desirability that occur between Angelica and Medoro have gone missing in favor of the gravitas of morality. The seductive qualities, gendered feminine, had for over a century been held as crucial to a beautiful and moving pictorial style. Both ideals of seemingly incompatible love, one ruled by a mischievous Cupid and one by the Christian God, fascinated a seventeenth-century audience for different reasons. Rather than balancing each other, Rosselli's two paintings reveal a not easily resolved tension in seicento culture.

## Note

1. For Ariosto and the visual arts, see also Bolzoni, *L'*Orlando furioso *nello specchio delle immagini*; Caneparo; Lee, *Names*; and Struhal.

**Grant Herreid**

# Singing Italian Renaissance Epic Verse

> *. . . di veder questi contadini il liuto in mano, e fin alle pastorelle l'Ariosto in bocca. Questo si vede per tutta Italia. (. . . to see these rustics with lute in hand, and even the shepherdesses with Ariosto on their lips. This you may see throughout Italy.)*
>
> —Michel de Montaigne, *Journal de voyage*

We can imagine that throughout the Renaissance, epic verse was often enjoyed in vocal performance, by singers and auditors of diverse levels of society: courtly humanists intoning passages accompanied by the *lira da braccio* to gatherings of cognoscenti in the learned academies; professional singers in the courts employing artful embellishments in polyphonic madrigals, perhaps accompanied by lute or harpsichord; *cantastorie* singing for passersby in the piazza; and of course folks singing for their own enjoyment, be they swineherds in the fields, barbers in their shops, or aristocrats in their homes. For the student of epic verse, experiencing knightly exploits through song is not simply an entertaining means to understanding and replicating an important historical Renaissance practice. More important, it teaches proper scansion of Italian verse, illustrates humanist principles of oratorical delivery, and develops essential musical skills of affective ornamentation and improvisation cultivated by sixteenth- and seventeenth-century singers.

## Madrigal Settings of Epic Verse

Polyphonic madrigals are the most accessible Renaissance style of singing epic verse. In Italy composers such as Jacquet de Berchem, Giaches de Wert, and Claudio Monteverdi set stanzas of Ludovico Ariosto and Torquato Tasso for four, five, or more voices, often stringing together consecutive stanzas to present lengthy dramatic scenes. Berchem set more than ninety separate stanzas of *Orlando furioso*. Some of these settings are readily available in scholarly editions and are wonderful to sing, as they represent the highest art of secular polyphonic composition. The singing of madrigals can teach the student of epic verse much concerning the rhetorical expression of Italian Renaissance poetry.

## Solo Settings of Epic Verse

There is no lack of evidence that solos were sung. In his *Orlando innamorato*, Matteo Maria Boiardo references his singing narrator many times, though this might reflect a conventional rather than an actual practice. The Spanish courtier Luis Milán describes singing romances (ballads) of Charlemagne and his knights at the court of Valencia (123). The Italian philosopher Giordano Bruno relates how in 1584 he and his English friend John Florio (author of the first Italian-English dictionary) sang stanzas from *Orlando furioso* while traveling by boat on the Thames, even detailing which stanzas graced the boatman's ears (qtd. in Yates 309). And such practice was not reserved for the upper classes, as Montaigne's above quote demonstrates. Cervantes's Don Quixote hears a muleteer sing a version of the *Song of Roland* (part 2, ch. 9). Later in the 1700s Venetian gondoliers could be heard singing stanzas of *Gerusalemme liberata*. That Italian peasants were singing stanzas of Ariosto to the plucking of rustic lutes attests to the popularity of epic verse, but since the music was seldom written down, imitating their practice is not a straightforward enterprise.

## The Aria as a Melodic and Harmonic Vehicle for Epic Verse

It is possible to recover some of the melodies associated with epic verse in the Renaissance. The clearest example is the Spanish vihuelist Enríquez de

Ex. 1. Enríquez de Valderrábano (c. 1500–after 1557), "Ruggier, qual sempre fui," *Silva de Sirenas* (Valladolid, 1547)

Ruggier, qual sempre fui, tal esser voglio
fin alla morte, e più, se più si puote.
O siami Amor benigno o m'usi orgoglio,
o me Fortuna in alto o in basso ruote,
immobil son di vera fede scoglio
che d'ogn'intorno il vento e il mar percuote:
né già mai per bonaccia né per verno
luogo mutai, né muterò in eterno.
Ludovico Ariosto, *Orlando furioso*, Canto XLIV, 61

Ruggiero, what I have always been, so I wish to be
unto death, and more, if more is possible.
Whether Love be kind to me, or use me scornfully,
or whether Fortune wheel me high or low,
I am of true faith an unyielding rock
that winds and waves strike all roundabout:
nor ever, in fair seas or in foul,
have I yielded, nor shall I yield in eternity.
translation: Grant Herreid

Valderrábano's setting of a stanza from the *Orlando furioso*, the famous lines of steadfast faithfulness Bradamante swears to her lover Ruggiero (example 1).

Since the melody sets only the first two lines of the eight-line stanza, it would have to be sung four times, presumably with embellishments, to accommodate the remaining three couplets. Valderrábano's tune is accompanied by the same melody in the vihuela part, notated a third higher, creating a harmonious accompanying line. Curiously, this melody, identified by James Haar as the "Aria di Ruggiero," appears to be a traditional tune or aria associated with Ariosto's hero (97–98).[1] Haar found the tune woven into several of the polyphonic settings by Berchem. If this tune was popularly used for Ariosto's epic verse, sung in the streets and squares, it

Ex. 2. Jacquet de Berchem (c. 1510–c. 1565), "Tu m'hai, Ruggier, lasciata," *Primo, secondo et terzo libro del capriccio . . .* (Venice, 1561) Munich, Bayerische Staatsbibliothek

Tu m'hai, Ruggier, lasciata: io te non voglio,
né lasciarti volendo anco potrei;
ma per uscir d'affanno e di cordoglio,
posso e voglio, finire i giorni miei.
Di non morirti in gratia sol mi doglio;
che se concesso m'avessero i dei
ch'io fossi morta quando t'era grata,
morte non fu già mai tanto beata.
Ariosto, *Orlando furioso*, XXXII, 43

"You have left me, Ruggiero; I wish not to leave you,
nor would I be able to leave you if I wished;
but to escape from sorrow and grief
I can and wish to end my days.
'Tis only not to die in your grace that pains me,
for had the gods conceded to me
that I were dead while yet pleasing to you,
no death would ever have been so blessed."
translation: Grant Herreid

is likely that composers like Berchem strove to add a dimension of traditional practice into their own polyphonic settings of epic verse. Example 2 shows iterations of the tune as they appear in the tenor, altus, and cantus voices of a madrigal.

The word *aria* in this period describes more than simply a melody; it refers as much to the basic harmonic accompaniment over which a melody is (or, more properly, *melodic variations* are) composed or improvised. (A variant of the "Aria di Ruggerio's" harmonic progression would become a popular ground bass over which composers such as Antonio Cifra would set Ariosto, often for two voices in a virtuosic style.) The melody of the "Aria di Ruggiero," comprising two eleven-note phrases, will serve for any stanza of epic verse, or indeed any verse written in *ottave*, one couplet at a time, sung one syllable per note. The singer adjusted his or her delivery to accommodate the placement of the caesura, mark instances of enjambment, and add affective ornamentation, both to enhance the meaning of the words and to provide variety. The knowledge of when and how to employ these embellishments, and the technique to bring them off, must have been part of a professional singer's training.

## Composed Arias for Epic Verse

Some Renaissance composers provided generic arias, comprising both melody and bass, for singing stanzas of ottava rima and other forms of lyric verse. Labeled *aria di cantar ottave* or something similar, these settings were usually provided with a text, either set in a plain one-syllable-per-note style or with short melismas, rhythmic variation, and other musical effects proper to those specific words. Vincenzo Calestani gives us two such arias in his *Madrigali et arie* (1617). In "Modo di cantar ottave" ("A way to sing *ottave*"), like the "Aria di Ruggiero," each of the ottava's four couplets is composed of two eleven-note phrases, one syllable per note. Calestani sets only the first couplet (example 3).

The student singing verse to this straightforward setting, which easily accommodates the text of most any stanza, will discover that it requires adjustment and embellishment. Calestani helpfully demonstrates this practice in his second aria, "Altro modo di cantar ottave" ("Another way to sing *ottave*"), which entails both quatrains of an ottava by Ottavio Rinuccini. This aria is a *romanesca*, a popular melody and bass pattern often associated with the singing of *ottave*. The rhythms employed by Calestani in setting the first quatrain would not have suited the wording of the second

Ex. 3. Vincenzo Calestani, "Modo di cantar ottave," *Madrigali et arie* . . . (Venice, 1617) Reprinted in facsimile in *Italian Secular Song*, ed. Gary Tomlinson (Garland, 1986)

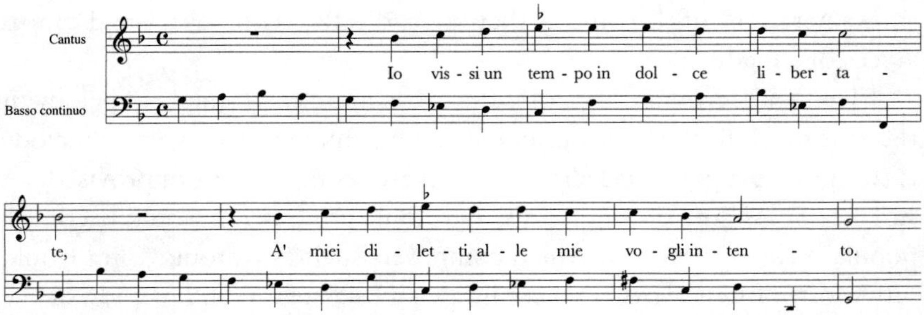


Io vissi un tempo in dolce libertate
 a' miei diletti, alle mie vogli intento;
tra riso, e canto consummai beate
 le notte ei giorni in me pago, e contento.
A' miei desir conforme era l'etate
 né sentivo d'Amor pena, o tormento.
E 'n così dolce, e si tranquilla vita
 era la gioia mia fatta infinita.
 Alessandro Ginori (fl. early 17th century)

Once I lived in sweet liberty,
 intent on my delights and my desires;
in laughter and in song I spent
 blessed nights and days, satisfied and content.
My age conformed to my desires,
 nor did I feel Love's pain or torment.
And in so sweet and tranquil a life
 my joy became never ending.
   translation: Grant Herreid

quatrain; the two settings provide students techniques for adjusting both rhythm and melody to reflect the scansion of each line, and the meaning of each word, as in the lamenting descending fourth that underpins the word "doglioso" (example 4).

## Ornamented Arias

Other examples elucidate the sort of embellishment proper, indeed necessary, for this art. Monteverdi gives us one in the "Notte che nel profondo oscuro seno" ("Night, in whose deep, dark bosom") passage of his *Combattimento di Tancredi e Clorinda* (1638). Monteverdi's narrator sings the

Ex. 4. Vincenzo Calestani, "Altro modo di cantar ottave," *Madrigali et arie* . . . (Venice, 1617) Reprinted in facsimile in *Italian Secular Song*, ed. Gary Tomlinson (Garland, 1986)

Piangono al pianger mio le fere e i sassi,  
  a' miei caldi sospir traggon sospiri,  
l'aer d'intorno nubiloso fassi  
  mosso anch' egli a pietà de' miei martiri.  
Ovunque io poso, ovunque io volgo i passi,  
  par che di me si pianga e si sospiri.  
Par che dica ciascun, mosso al mio duolo:  
  che fai tu qui, meschin, doglioso e solo?  
Ottavio Rinuccini (1562–1621)

Wild beasts and rocks weep at my weeping;  
  they draw forth sighs at my hot sighing;  
the air roundabout becomes cloudy,  
  moved also to pity at my torments.  
Where'er I stay, where'er I direct my footsteps,  
  it seems that all lament and sigh for me.  
It seems that each one says, moved by my grief,  
"What do you here, wretch, sorrowful and alone?"  
translation: Grant Herreid

first quatrain of this stanza from *Gerusalemme liberata* to an aria and then sings the second quatrain over the same bass harmonies—for example, the same aria but with extensive variation in both bass and melody. In comparing the two passages one can see the note values and inserted notes in the bass that support differences in the melody, embellishments that allow for Monteverdi's well-known affective elaboration and word-painting and that result in a heightened dramatic declamation. For example, inserting

Ex. 5. Claudio Monteverdi, "Combattimento di Tancredi e Clorinda," *Madrigali Guerrieri et Amorosi . . . Libro Ottavo* (Venice, 1638)

Notte, che nel profondo oscuro seno
chiudeste e nel oblio fatto sì grande,
degno d'un chiaro sol, degne d'un pieno
Theatro opre sarian sì memorande.
Piacciati ch'indi il tragga e 'n bel sereno
alle future età lo spieghi e mande.
Viva la fama lor e tra lor gloria
splenda dal fosco tuo l'alta memoria.
after Torquato Tasso, *Gerusalemme liberata*, XII, 54

Night, who in your deep dark bosom
enveloped in oblivion so great a deed;
worthy of bright sunlight, worthy of a full
theater would such memorable feats be.
May it please you that I bring it forth, and in clear light
reveal and transmit it to future ages.
Long live their fame, and amid their glory
may the noble memory of your darkness shine.
translation: Grant Herreid

an extra half note into the loosely structured bass pattern gives Monteverdi enough time to embellish the words "spieghi e mande" ("spread and send forth abroad") with a long scale-wise passage that runs down and up, illustrating the narrator's "spreading forth" the report of this duel. At the word "alta" ("high"), he inserts two half notes into the bass pattern while the melody dramatically rises an octave and a fourth. Monteverdi states that the singer may add his or her own ornamentation only in this section of the work (*Madrigals* [Dover] xvii), perhaps alluding to a tradition of highly embellished performance of epic stanzas (example 5).

Sigismondo d'India also gives examples of such variation in his *Le musiche* (1609), which includes arias for the performance of ottava rima. "Ottava in stile recitativo" ("Octave in recitation style") sets to an aria a stanza spoken by the enchantress Armida in *Gerusalemme liberata*. D'India's bass is repeated with quite a bit of rhythmic, and especially harmonic, variation, over which he employs striking chromatic coloration and dramatic melodic gesture: the bold upward leap of a fourth as she declares "per nom' Armida" ("by the name Armida"); the descending half steps at "Hor qui mancò lo spirto" ("Here she gave up her spirit") as she begins to faint; and the falling figure as she collapses at "E cadde tramortita" ("she fell in a swoon") all demonstrate the expressive possibilities of matching melodic gesture to textual action (example 6).

## A Singing Contest in Rome

Singers of the time, accustomed to the expressive challenges afforded by this compositional shorthand, must have been able to make such adjustments, whether spontaneously or in a more premeditated fashion. That this sophisticated style of singing epic verse was cultivated and prized in late-Renaissance society is illustrated by an account of a singing contest held in Rome in 1623 between two famous sopranos: Francesca Caccini (known as La Cecchina, daughter of Giulio Caccini, the most celebrated singing teacher of the day) and Adriana Basile (L'Adriana). As Timothy McGee describes it:

> [T]here was a difference of opinion among members of the Medici circle as to which of the two singers was the more talented. To resolve the dispute the poet Giovanni Battista Marini, a member of the circle, produced an *ottava rima* on the subject of Adonis, and the two sopranos were invited on successive evenings to demonstrate their talents

Ex. 6. Sigismondo d'India, "Ottava in stile recitativo," *Le Musiche* (Milan, 1609)

La tra 'l sangue e le morti egro giacente
    mi pagherai le pene, empio guerriero.
Per nome Armida chiamerai sovente
    ne gli ultimi singulti: udir ciò spero.
Or qui manco lo spirto alla dolente,
    né quest'ultimo suono espresse intero;
    e cadde tramortita e si diffuse
    di gelato sudore, e i lumi chiuse.
      Tasso, *Gerusalemme liberata*, XVI, 60

"There, lying feebly amid blood and death,
    you will repay my suffering, wicked warrior:
oft you will call Armida by name
    in your last gasps; this I hope to hear."
Here the grieving woman's spirit failed her,
    nor did she express this last utterance in full,
    but fell senseless, a frozen sweat
    spreading over her, and she closed her eyes.
        translation: Grant Herreid

> before a distinguished audience by improvising both melody and accompaniment without having seen the text beforehand. The judgement was that La Cecchina had the superior musical understanding (*di molto più sapere e padrona dell' arte*), whereas L'Adriana had a better voice and ability to express (*alquanto migliore voce et artifiziosa negli affetti*). The deciding factor, which caused the listeners to declare Francesca Caccini the winner, was her ability to match her performance to the text, the element that was usually singled out to praise her father's performances. (6)

Such a contest might have been an exceptional performance by two leading divas, but some familiarity with improvising musical settings of poetry was likely expected of every talented musician.

## Eighteenth-Century Arias from Gondoliers

Finally, a few melodies from the succeeding century survive in written form, arias that reflect a different practice of singing epic verse by a lower stratum of

Ex. 7. Giuseppe Tartini (1692–1770), "Aria di Tasso," published in Dr. Lev Ginsburg, *Tartini: His Life and Times* (Paganiniana Publications, 1981)

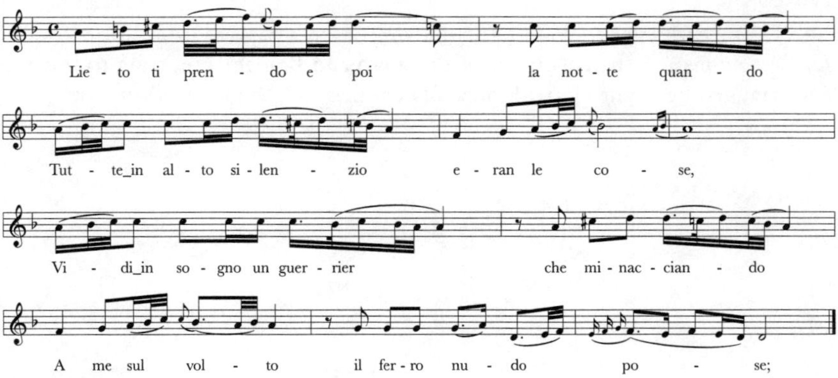


Lieto ti prendo; e poi la notte, quando
tutte in alto silenzio eran le cose,
vidi in sogno un guerrier che minacciando
a me su 'l volto il ferro ignudo pose.
Tasso, *Gerusalemme liberata*, XII, 36

"Happily I took you up; and then that night,
when everything was in total silence,
in a dream I saw a warrior threatening
me, with his naked sword poised above my head."
translation: Grant Herreid

society. In the 1700s the violinist-composer Giuseppe Tartini heard Venetian gondoliers singing stanzas of *Gerusalemme liberata*. Intrigued, he jotted down the melodies and texts, using the tunes as themes in some of his instrumental works (see Ginsburg 66–67). Another eyewitness noted that the gondoliers from neighboring canals would alternate in singing stanzas, one picking up the story where the other left off (Baretti 153–55). These two instances provide a few eighteenth-century melodies that the student may employ to sing stanzas of epic verse, melodies that can incorporate much melismatic ornamentation, as Tartini's "Aria di Tasso" demonstrates (example 7). Singing epic poetry, whether in front of an audience or simply to oneself, focuses attention on important elements of rhetorical delivery of Italian verse. But it also presents opportunities for passionate musical expression and embellishment that enhances meaning and comprehension. The power of music to amplify poetry's meaning was a commonplace of Renaissance thought, as expressed in a 1613 song by the English poet Thomas Campion performed in a masque at the court of James I: "Happy is he whose words can move, / Yet sweet notes help persuasion. / Mix your words with music then, / That they the more may enter" (257).

## Note

1. The early music group Ex Umbris recorded a passage from Boiardo's *Orlando innamorato* (the encounter of Ruggiero and Bradamante) sung to this aria and arranged by Grant Herreid, on a CD entitled *The Diamond of Ferrara*.

**Barbara Russano Hanning**

# Tasso and the Italian Madrigal

From the poem's first publication in 1581, Torquato Tasso's *Gerusalemme liberata* inspired at least three generations of madrigal composers, attracted by its emotional intensity and theatrical vividness. Certain stanzas, among them Armida's and Erminia's monologues (16.59 and 19.105), were repeatedly set to music because their emotional charge appealed to composers who were themselves forging a newly expressive musical language at the end of the sixteenth century. Moreover, in Tasso's epic, Armida's ravings no less than Erminia's laments were already couched in a language whose sounds were akin to music. In this respect, Tasso's poetry was a game changer, recognized as such by Claudio Monteverdi, one of the leading composers of the time (see Tomlinson). Whether Tasso imagined how his poetry would affect Monteverdi and others, he was in close touch with musicians at court. He fell in love with a singer more than once, and he likely envisioned Armida's enchanted garden as a realm of feminine artistry and passionate female lyricism, as well as of contemporary song.[1]

The Italian madrigal—small-scale vocal chamber music, usually set to preexisting love lyrics and performed by one or several singers with or without accompaniment—was, in its heyday, the most forward-looking, the most experimental, and, by the end of the century, the most dramatically expressive musical genre of the Renaissance. Dozens of madrigal settings of stanzas from the *Gerusalemme* were published, beginning with Tasso's contemporaries in Mantua and Ferrara—Giaches de Wert (1535–1596) and Claudio Monteverdi (1567–1643)—and then by early-seventeenth-century composers (among them Biagio Marini and Francesco Eredi) in other Italian cities (see Newcomb). Most of these works are now readily available in audio or digital formats.

This essay's goal is not so much to demonstrate how Tasso's poetry influenced the madrigal's development but rather to show how the inherent expressivity of Tasso's language lent itself to musical elaboration. By studying the musical settings discussed here, undergraduate and graduate students without knowledge of musical notation or technical vocabulary can understand why Tasso's language was so attractive to musicians and how composers responded to its powerful impact. Their responses varied from combining musical ideas in order to suggest the sounds of Armida's enchanted garden (as in Wert's setting of *Vezzosi augelli*, 16.12), to imitating Armida's cries of anger and indignation at Rinaldo's betrayal (as in Monteverdi's *Vattene pur, crudel*, 16.59). In each case the composer's musical choices match and highlight Tasso's ability to describe a lyrical scene or express the inarticulate elements of emotion. So, just as Tasso's language depicts a landscape or captures the inflections of a human voice gripped by powerful and uncontrollable emotions, the composer evokes nature or conveys despair, lament, anger, and so on with musical ideas and gestures that imitate Tasso's language. By perceiving those gestures and their motivating poetic content, students of literature gain new insight into Tasso's poetry and become more appreciative of its sonic and expressive values.

The first thing students should understand about the madrigal is that it was text-dependent, meaning that composers fashioned the music specifically to fit the words of each line of the poem. Now, the structure of the epic's ottava rima stanzas, rhyming *abababcc*, with each line having the same number of syllables, might lend itself to a formulaic musical style—one in which, say, the first two lines (*ab*) might serve for the rest of the stanza, with some variation or nuance provided by the singer. Indeed, earlier in the Renaissance, when epic poetry was declaimed or sung aloud, a series of stanzas was performed to the same musical formula, perhaps with improvised variations in the melody. (See Grant Herreid's essay in this volume.) This type of composition is called strophic and is common in hymn singing. But in the madrigal, which emerged in Italy in the 1530s, composers artfully fitted each line of the poem with new music in order to capture the words' changing meaning and expressive nuance. By definition, then, a madrigal is through-composed, meaning that it was composed throughout, with each line receiving an appropriate musical setting.

### ***Vezzosi augelli***
### (Wert, Madrigals, Book 8, 1586)

Something that differentiates the madrigal (and much other music) from poetry, recited or not, is that a poem's words have a necessary order, creating a succession of lines that unfold one at a time. In fact, often their meaning is not revealed until the series of words or lines form a complete phrase or sentence. But a madrigal composer who is in control of four or five voices simultaneously can combine, repeat, and rearrange words or phrases to create a composite soundscape, like a collage. This is what happens in Giaches de Wert's *Vezzosi augelli*,[2] a madrigal set to a stanza from the *Gerusalemme* most popular with composers: Tasso's description of Armida's enchanted garden (16.12). The words create images and evoke sounds:

> Vezzosi augelli infra le verdi fronde
> temprano a prova lascivette note;
> mormora l'aura, e fa le foglie e l'onde
> garrir che variamente ella percote.
> . . . . . . . . . . . . . . . . . . . . . . . . . . . . . .
> sia caso od arte, or accompagna ed ora
> alterna i versi lor la musica òra.
>
> Among the green fronds charming birds intone
> in tuneful counterpoint their wanton lays.
> The green leaves whisper and the soft waves moan,
> struck by the murmuring wind in varying ways.
> . . . . . . . . . . . . . . . . . . . . . . . . . . . . . . . . . . . . .
> the tuneful breeze, by chance or art, now sighs
> in concert, now in antiphon replies.

The composer assigns distinct musical ideas (motives) to different phrases and then combines them, so that while the higher singing voices imitate the birds in short, spritely notes ("Vezzosi augelli in fra le verde fronde"), the lower voices repeatedly intone the breeze's murmur in longer notes to the words "Mormora l'aura." Thus, rather than wait until line three to introduce the breeze's motive, Wert collapses the first and third lines of the stanza. A fruitful exercise might be to have groups of five students read aloud from the musical score (without singing) the words as the madrigal composer rearranged and superimposed them. The words would be aligned approximately thus:

| | | | | | | | |
|---|---|---|---|---|---|---|---|
| *Canto:* | Vezzosi augelli in fra le verde fron - | de | Temprano a prova | lascivette | no - | te | |
| *Quinto:* | Vezzosi augelli in fra le verde fron - | de | Temprano a prova | lascivette | no - | te | |
| *Alto:* | Vezzosi augelli in fra le verde fron - | de | Temprano a prova | lascivette lascivette | no - | | te |
| *Tenor:* | Mormora l'au - | | ra | | Mormora l'au- | | ra |
| *Bass:* | | | Mormora l'au-ra | | | | Mormora l'au-ra |

In this way, even before listening to a recording of the madrigal, students would experience the qualities of polyphony (the simultaneous sounding of different voice parts or lines of music), and they would understand that in this case polyphony transcended and enhanced the poetic text, in which only one thing at a time could be expressed. Wert fashioned a kaleidoscope of musical ideas—ideas suggested by the sound and shape of Tasso's words—to project a composite soundscape of the garden's enchantments, which could only be described cumulatively in the poem.

### *Forsennata gridava*
### (Wert, Madrigals, Book 8, 1586)

Several other stanzas in canto 16, in which things come to a head between Armida and Rinaldo, attracted many composers. When Rinaldo announces that he must leave her, Armida in her extreme distress runs after him to the shore and, Tasso comments, "makes her cries like heralds go before" (39). In Wert's setting, the next stanza (40) opens with those screams:

> Forsennata gridava: "O tu che porte
> parte teco di me, parte ne lassi,
> o prendi l'una o rendi l'altra, o morte
> dà insieme ad ambe. . . ."
>
> Distraught, she cried to him: "Oh you, who take
> Part of me with you, and leave part behind,
> take one or give the other back, or make
> both die. . . ."

The word "forsennata" implies a kind of madness: one could say Armida was "beside herself," driven "out of her mind" at the thought of being rejected and abandoned; so she cried out ("gridava"), emitting wails that could be heard at the shore even before she arrived. Wert translated the opening words' emotional charge directly into music, as one voice after the other (in his five-part setting) sings all the syllables of the first word, "forsennata," on one note, creating a tension from which explodes the word "gridava" in a huge upward leap (encompassing ten notes) to a pitch at the top of each singer's range, a pitch that is painfully prolonged like the scream that it imitates. That leap may be the largest in all madrigal literature, and the effect, as it echoes serially through the five voice parts, is hair-raising.

### *Qual musico gentil*
(Wert, Madrigals, Book 8, 1586)

In an effort to create larger-scale, semidramatic scenes, Wert was the first composer to set consecutive stanzas from the *Gerusalemme*. This one, beginning "Qual musico gentil" (16.43–47), follows soon after Armida arrives at the shore to remonstrate with her boy toy. Tasso introduces her four-stanza monologue with one in his own voice, or that of the narrator (43), in which he compares the pagan sorceress to a skillful musician who subtly prepares his listeners' minds with sweet harmony for the message he is about to deliver. Thus the manipulative Armida "does not, for all her soul's outcry, / wholly forget her craft and witchery, / but first prepares the ground by tuneful art / for what the voice imprints within the heart" (43). By comparing the sorceress to a musician, Tasso suggests that there is a self-conscious, staged quality about Armida's ensuing monologue. He thereby implicitly acknowledges that musical rhetoric was thought to play a very important persuasive role in late Renaissance Italy: witness the emergence of Orpheus on the operatic stage only a few decades later.

Wert sets Armida's monologue (44–47) in a fairly straightforward way, minimizing the composite, polyphonic style of *Vezzosi augelli*, and having all voices deliver Armida's words nearly simultaneously so that they are easily understood and can better persuade Rinaldo.

### *Vattene pur, crudel*
(Monteverdi, Madrigals, Book 3, 1592)

But Armida's pleas are to no avail, so she turns her wrath on her disloyal lover, ordering him to get out of her sight and virtually spitting out her words in short, staccato bursts (16.59):

> Vattene pur, crudel, con quella pace
> che lasci a me; vattene, iniquo, omai.
> Me tosto ignudo spirto, ombra seguace

indivisibilmente a tergo avrai.
Nova furia, co' serpi e con la face,
tanto t'agiterò quanto t'amai.

Well, go then, cruel man, in as much peace
as that you leave me here! Go, wretch! Go now!
Soon shall you find my naked spirit seize
upon your track, a vengeful ghost, I vow.
I'll haunt you as I loved, without surcease,
a blazing Fury crowned with serpent brow.

Monteverdi's madrigal owes much to Wert's *Forsennata gridava*; the opening syllables on a single repeated pitch ("Vattene pur") are followed by a large upward leap on the word "crudel," in imitation of Armida's shouted anger.[3] However, he uses only the three highest voices, silencing the two male voices at the beginning, perhaps in order to represent Armida's ravings more realistically in their high range. Especially worthy of attention is the stanza's sixth line: note the rhythmic agitation in the words of its first half, in which she threatens to destroy Rinaldo's peace of mind ("Tanto t'agiterò") and the long, open vowels in its second half, as she speaks of their past love ("quanto t'amai"). Monteverdi takes his cue from Tasso throughout this madrigal but especially by distinguishing the two halves of this line with musical contrast. Years later, the composer was explicit about Tasso's influence: it was, he says, "the divine Tasso" who taught him how to imitate the passions in music, "with all the propriety and naturalness" in his language (*Madrigali guerrieri et amorosi* [preface]; my trans.). By "propriety," of course, Monteverdi meant the poet's matching of emotion and meaning with appropriate-sounding words.

### *Vivrò fra i miei tormenti*
### (Monteverdi, Madrigals, Book 3, 1592)

Some stanzas that belong to Tancredi (12.77–79), the Christian knight in love with Clorinda, a warrior maiden who fights on the Muslim side, again show the attraction of Tasso's verse for a composer like Monteverdi. In a nighttime battle (a *combattimento* most famously set to music several decades later by the same composer) Tancredi unwittingly kills her and is himself wounded. Once he understands that it is Clorinda under the armor of the dead knight, he wonders that he can still be alive after committing such a horrific deed. But then he realizes that death would be too merciful because it would end his sorrows. Instead he is condemned to wander as a madman ("forsennato [that word again!] errante"), pursued by the ghosts of his past, fearful of the shadows, and shunning the sun because it was daylight that revealed Clorinda's identity (stanza 77).

The next stanza (78) demonstrates Tasso's affective language and reveals how, in Monteverdi's words, the poet guided him to imitate the passions in a natural way. Note the number of times some form of the exclamation "Alas!" appears ("oh lasso me"; or "ahi"). Also note the word repetition in line one: "Ma dove . . . dove restaro" and in line six: "Troppo e pur troppo prezioso pasto!" These repetitions lend an emotional force to Tancredi's sorrow, as though he were so distraught that he cannot speak fluently, emitting his words in short bursts. Monteverdi follows Tasso's lead by translating Tancredi's sobs ("ahi") into their musical equivalent—a long-held, sometimes dissonant note—and particularly by shaping the descending phrase "Ahi sfortunato!" ("Ah, hapless limbs"; line 7) into a wail. He then extracts it from the verse in which it is embedded and repeats it ten times during his setting of the last couplet.

### *Misera! non credea ch'agl' occhi miei* (Wert, Madrigals, Book 8, 1586)

We return to Giaches de Wert for one last example of how the inherent expressivity of Tasso's language lent itself to musical elaboration. When Erminia (the third person in the love triangle involving Tancredi and Clorinda) finds Tancredi lying unconscious and gravely wounded on the battlefield, she utters a doleful monologue, or lament, addressed to Tancredi (19.106–07). The lament, incidentally, was a type of poetry that would become very popular in early baroque vocal music precisely because it gave composers ample opportunity to imitate the passions.

> Misera! non credea ch'a gli occhi miei
> potessi in alcun tempo esser noioso.
> Or cieca farmi volentier torrei
> per non vederti, e riguardar non oso.
> Oimè, de' lumi già sì dolci e rei
> ov'è la fiamma? ov'è il bel raggio ascoso?
> de le fiorite guancie il bel vermiglio
> ov'è fuggito? ov'è il seren del ciglio?
>
> I never dreamed (ah, wretch!) that I could find
> a cause to look on you without delight.
> Gladly I'd gouge my eyes out and be blind

rather than see you thus. Ah, cursed sight!
Those lovely eyes, so cruel and so kind,
where has their fire, their proud gleam taken flight?
Those rosy cheeks, that calm and noble brow—
where have they gone? Where are they hidden now?

Again, Tasso's language is replete with exclamations, such as "Oimè!" (set to music as a descending sigh), and he strings together unanswerable questions, which the composer inflects with a rising melody, as they would be uttered in speech. As in other pieces by Wert examined here, the madrigal goes by quite quickly because the composer sets the octave in a compact and very speech-like way, using the rhythms that are inherent in the words and with very little word repetition in the music. Although the work is for five voices, Wert has the three top voices sing as one unit, the better to represent the sound of Erminia's words as though they were being declaimed on stage.

At the close of the monologue's second stanza (107), Erminia utters this quite shocking couplet: "Parte torrò di sue ragioni a morte, / baciando queste labbra essangui e smorte" (". . . so will I tear / from them some portion due to Death, / kissing these lips now drained of blood and breath").

Only here does the composer expand the peroration by repeating and combining the phrases "Parte torrò" (set to music the way it sounds: long, short, short, long) and "baciando queste labbra," emphasizing the jarring sentiments with audacious and harsh harmonies among the voices. Thus is Erminia's monologue brought to a satisfying conclusion, one that matches the audacity of Tasso's poetry.

In its dramatic vividness and affective language, Tasso's *Gerusalemme liberata* has all the trappings of opera, before opera existed. Indeed, while the sixteenth-century Italian madrigal was transformed and subsumed into other genres, parts of the *Gerusalemme* formed the basis for many operas in the seventeenth, eighteenth, and nineteenth centuries: Lully's *Armide* (1686), Handel's *Rinaldo* (1711), Gluck's *Armide* (1777), Rossini's *Armida* (1817), and Dvorák's *Armida* (1902–03), among others. Although Tasso's epic continued to be reprinted and became a literary classic, its formal, old-fashioned verse structure was too rigid for opera composers, who needed more flexible poetry—different types of verse for different styles of music: recitative, aria, and chorus. So various librettists through the centuries reworked Tasso's language but kept his exciting and illustrious characters, his thrilling tales of adventure and enchantment, and his heartrending scenes of lovers beguiled by magic and separated by war and death.

## Notes

1. For more on Tasso's influence on Monteverdi, see Mace; Tomlinson.

2. The music for this piece was composed by Giaches de Wert. It and Wert's other pieces discussed in this essay are available in his *Collected Works.* Performances of all four have been recorded by the early music ensemble ARTEK, directed by Gwendolyn Toth, and may be found at the group's *YouTube* channel (www.youtube.com/user/ARTEKearlymusic) in the "Gerusalemme Liberata" playlist, as well as individually on a variety of compact disc recordings by other ensembles.

3. The music for both pieces by Monteverdi discussed in this essay may be found in his *Madrigali a 5 voci, libro terzo.* Performances of both madrigals may also be found on the ARTEK *YouTube* channel cited in the previous note and individually on many other recordings.

**Roberto Puggioni**

# Teaching Tasso's *Gerusalemme liberata* through Italian Theater and Drama

Theatrical works inspired by Torquato Tasso's opus are significant in the multifaceted reception and interpretation of the Estense poet throughout history and factored largely in the rapid emergence of the *Gerusalemme liberata* as a modern classic, from the aftermath of the author's death throughout the seventeenth and eighteenth centuries and into early Romanticism. Similarly to what commonly occurs in other artistic fields (music, painting, dance, and cinema), the author's theatrical fortune was marked by borrowings, segmentations, hybridizations, and rewritings by playwrights according to the evolution in taste as well as formal dramatic and melodramatic innovations. Although both Tasso's biography (Pieri, "Dalla commedia dell'arte") and his dramatic works were subject to stage adaptations, it is mainly the *Gerusalemme liberata*'s most renowned figures and main narrative nuclei that became inexhaustible sources for dramatic reinterpretations. Sometimes the poem was the subject of ambitious integral transpositions, but most often it inspired adaptations or continuations of key episodes the poet left unresolved or ambiguous. Attention to this phenomenon in the classroom can shed light on the reception of the *Liberata* in modern culture.

The *Liberata*'s theatrical reception cuts across the centuries and involves hundreds of plays and performances inspired by the poem though they have yet to be systematically evaluated in their quantitative and qualitative heterogeneity. Nevertheless, several critical studies explore some examples of the poem's theatrical reception, especially in the seventeenth century, for which we have the most extensive scholarship (Stein, *Nel nome*; Gallinaro; Pieri, *Cavalieri*; Puggioni, *Torquato Tasso*).

We may consider three perspectives focusing on drama inspired by the poem: the chronological development, theatrical genres involved in the adaptations, and the characters and episodes of the *Liberata* privileged in dramatic texts. Such a framework can also be understood as a prerequisite for undertaking specific studies of some of these texts.

## Periodization

Concerning periodization, it should first be stated that there are no sufficiently comprehensive catalogs to obtain reliable cultural statistics. There is a conspicuous presence of these dramatic texts in the seventeenth century, a significant number of melodramas especially in the eighteenth century, and several musical works in the early nineteenth century, while original twentieth-century adaptations are harder to find. Moreover, the *Liberata* circulated among very different authors and performance contexts. It is worth remembering that there were plays designed not only for elite theaters but also for traditional folk theaters, such as the *maggi epici* of the Tuscan and Emilian Apennines (Cavallo, "L'Opera"; Palladini).

In a course focusing on a single century, the most logical choice would be the seventeenth century, for which—as mentioned above—there are comprehensive critical studies. In particular, the recent book by Thomas Stein as well as the pioneering study by Ilaria Gallinaro highlight the numerical strength of these theatrical rewritings: there are not fewer than eighty texts directly inspired by the poem in the course of the century. Traces of the *Liberata*'s influence are also found in many other cases, where Tasso's texts have been hybridized—for example, *I due anelli simili* (1637–64; "The Two Similar Rings"), a tragicomedy by the Genoese Anton Giulio Brignole Sale, which borrows significantly from both the poem and Tasso's tragedy *Torrismondo*. One could also include Angelo Ingegneri's tragedy *Tomiri* (1607), which in some parts, especially act 3, takes textual extracts and names from battle scenes between the crusaders and pagans in the *Liberata* 17–20 (Puggioni, "Conversione").

## Theatrical Genres

The variety of the poem's passions and events allows theatrical adaptations to feature different genres, especially in the seventeenth century, when Italian theater moves away from the constraints of classicism, mixing traditional forms and inventing new theatrical modes, also denominated in various ways by their authors (Capucci). In this context, the *Liberata* is perceived by playwrights as a real super-genre, as a hypotext comprising a complex repertoire of dramatic genres: Tasso is thus involved in the transformation of theatrical culture. Students can investigate a few examples: *Erminia* (1596–1606), by Eugenio Visdomini, written for the Academy of Innominati of Parma, is known as a "favola boschereccia" ("pastoral fable") (Denarosi); Tobia de Ferrari's *Sofronia* (1615) consists of "Tre intermedi" ("three intermezzos") (Stein, "Quando Olindo"); *Ermina* (1622) by Gabriello Chiabrera is a "tragedia" ("tragedy"); the *Goffredo* (1630) by Girolamo Manzone is presented as an "opera scenica" ("work on the stage"); *Gli incanti disciolti da Rinaldo* (1637) by Carlo Volpe is a "Ragionamento drammatico" ("dramatic conversation"); *L'Armida impazzita per amor di Rinaldo* (1677) by Giovanni Battista Toschi, dedicated to the Duke of Modena, is an "opera eroica" ("heroic opera"); *L'Erminia al Campo* (1688) by Giorgio Maria Rapparini is a "trattenimento musicale" ("musical entertainment"); *La vendetta invendicata di Armida* (1700) is an "Introduzione ad un ballo di Dame" ("introduction to a women's dance").

The above list also reveals the prevailing orientation in dramatic rewritings. Those playwrights who did not base their works on the poem's unabridged version, and who followed the rules of verisimilitude and convention to devise reasonably circumscribed plots, almost always used selective borrowings, creating dramatic texts using some core themes and characters. The widely shared esteem for Tasso's poem guaranteed that spectators would be familiar with the entire plot. Stage adaptations of the seventeenth century generally emphasized the poem's romance adventures, with particular attention to Erminia and Armida. Some theatrical developments offered a sequel to the love affairs that Tasso had left unresolved.

## Characters and Episodes

There is ample material for classroom discussion of the appropriation and theatrical rewriting of *Liberata*'s principal characters and episodes. Erminia's destiny in seventeenth-century drama is a significant example, closely tied to the enhancement of her pathetic qualities of simulator-dissembler and lover-enemy, and to the innocent fraud of which she is guilty in the poem (Zatti, *L'ombra del Tasso*). For the background to a large number of theatrical works inspired by this character (Stein, *Nel nome*), one may consider, for example, the above-mentioned tragedy *Erminia* by Gabriello Chiabrera, which ends with the heroine's suicide after the prince Tancredi refuses to marry her and bring her back with him to Italy.

Before Chiabrera's tragedy, two playwrights show Tasso's heroine in the stage form of the *intermedio* (Pontremoli): *La fuga d'Erminia* (1600; "The Escape of Erminia") by Giovanni Villifranchi (Pirruccio); and *De' successi di Erminia intermedi cinque* (1615; "Of the Successes of Erminia, Intermedio Five") by the Genoese Tobia de Ferrari. Although their works are fairly close to the poem, using large numbers of Tasso's verses, original heroic and seven-syllable verses of the two plays do not always lead to a harmonious outcome. Villifranchi focuses on the events from the sixth and seventh canto of the *Liberata*, Erminia's escape and pastoral interlude; de Ferrari aspires, instead, to a complete synopsis of the character's history. Villifranchi's reduction increases the elegiac character of the staging, which reverberates the tradition of pastoral poetry, while de Ferrari, without betraying his model, reshapes Tasso's heroine with some innovative features, such as her allusive sensuality in the epilogue.

*Erminia sul Giordano*, an opera by Giulio Rospigliosi, the future Pope Clement IX (D'Afflitto and Romei), staged for the first time in Rome in 1633, is instead a libretto that significantly diverges from canto 7 of the *Liberata*. The author intertwines Erminia's arrival by the Jordan River with the story of a pair of shepherds, Lidia and Selvaggio, who are protagonists of a real pastoral fable, almost an echo of *Aminta*; in this bucolic setting, he also introduces the characters of Tancredi and Armida. In a melodrama aimed at amplification of "meraviglia" (the marvelous), Tancredi will ensure the surprise happy ending, while the action of Armida will display the use of numerous scenic machines.

Very few authors dared to cover the entire poem. The first of these adaptations of the complete work—Cesare Abelli's *Gerusalemme liberata*—can be an interesting case study for the university classroom. Published in 1626 and conceived in the dramatic experiments of Bologna's Accademia dei Gelati (Calore), this eccentric tragedy, with its uncertain dramatic morphology and spectacular twists, expresses a taste already characteristic of baroque drama. Abelli's stated intention is to faithfully adhere to the storyline while transforming it from "epico" to "drammatico."

More specifically, as stated in the preface, the playwright wanted to represent the whole poem, while adapting it to the dramatic unities of time and place, "facendosi accadere tutti i Casi più tragici insieme nell'istessa notte del conquisto della Città" ("making all the most tragic events take place together in the same night as the conquest of the city"; my trans.).

In truth, the playwright significantly alters the poem's storyline. The plot is a generous rewriting of the best-known episodes, but it is based on a system of recovery and interference between episodes resting on a dramatic choice: most of the characters belong to the pagan front, except the choirs of women or Christians of Jerusalem, Vafrino, and Goffredo, to whom is entrusted exclusively the monologue of the final scene. The only character with a truly tragic stature is Aladino. This adaptation of Tasso's text produces a kaleidoscope of amazing theatrical sensations—"a curious farrago of absurdities," as one critic has put it (Corrigan 133–35)—in a plot characterized by misunderstandings and disguises, sometimes almost comical, inside the walls of Jerusalem, in the palace of Aladino, a place of visions, dreams, and intrigues. Thus Abelli's theatrical adaptation, while preserving the poem's ideological memory and principal action, nonetheless testifies to the aesthetic cultural changes and the loosening of the Aristotelian ties in the 1630s.

A university course on this subject can use different didactic options. If the priority is to relate the adaptations to the inherent theatricality of the *Gerusalemme liberata* itself, students must begin with a close reading oriented to this aspect. It will also be worth having as a background some passages from Tasso's *Discorsi dell'arte poetica* ("Discourses of Poetic Art") regarding the distinctive features of the epic as well as the similarities between epic narrative and dramatic texts, coupled with a brief excursus on sixteenth-century Italian theater culture. Subsequently, one can assign each student a canto or character, asking him or her to identify the theatricality of specific passages in relation to the author's descriptive art. Using Giovanni Careri's *La fabbrica degli affetti* ("The Factory of the Affections"), for example, students can focus on the verses in which Tasso elaborates a pictorial or theatrical view of the passions. Or, guided by the essay of Anna L. Lepschy and other related studies, the class can identify where the poem's dialogues are more markedly theatrical. Or still, based on the treatise of Andrea Perrucci, students can examine the octaves in which Tasso evokes a staged performance by highlighting the gestures and voice of his characters. The results of individual studies can then be compared and evaluated in the classroom.

Once students are familiar with the *Liberata*, they can study a range of plays inspired by the poem. The instructor can provide background on the dramaturgy of a particular time period, the peculiarities and developments of a specific theatrical genre, or the theatrical afterlife of certain key characters, asking students to reflect on the most meaningful differences between the poem and its theater interpretations. Although many plays are not available in modern editions, almost all can be downloaded from free online digital libraries—for example, that of the Biblioteca Braidense of Milan (www.braidense.it/cataloghi/catalogo_rd.php). The course can close with a discussion and evaluation of students' individual works, highlighting the difficulties that emerged in the course of the study as well as the aspects that students have most appreciated.

# Part IX

# The Italian Romance Epic in Modern Fiction and Video Games

**Stefano Nicosia**

# Rewriting Italian Romance in Twentieth-Century Italy

Writing about the history of Italian romance involves looking back at a history of rewritings: its prose and poems originate from and move toward narrations that combine and transform themselves, constantly recalling or concealing echoes of their genre. The twentieth century makes no exception, and Italian authors have a new vital interest in traditional romance that both inspires them and provides the key to their poetics. The creative use of romance literature traverses a vast range of forms and media, and the range itself can be considered a marker of the genre's resiliency.

In the following pages I refer to a broad idea of rewriting, one that demonstrates different kinds of reused traditional texts (anthologies, comic books, novels, short stories, prose versions of poems) with different aims: they can all be considered a way of writing on the palimpsest of Italian romance. In the twentieth century, in fact, there are such fascinating possibilities for working on and with romance, where new and original forms have been explored, that rewritings can constitute part of a course on the Italian romance epic for Italian majors.

## Calvino's Crossroads

The most famous example of the convergence between romance and contemporary writing is Italo Calvino, who builds his intellectual itinerary by constantly dialoguing with traditional romance as a way to ponder how far his work is from his canonical precedents, experiment with new narrative forms, and think about the contemporary world in relation to the past. Ariosto's *Orlando furioso* is for Calvino the classic par excellence, standing out as the most influential work for his form of writing. Furthermore, ten years after the most complex and fascinating tribute to romance, *Il cavaliere inesistente* ("The Nonexistent Knight"), we find another very clear example in *Il castello dei destini incrociati* (*The Castle of Crossed Destinies*). The latter is inspired by a deck of fifteenth-century tarot cards but is organized in the same style as *Orlando furioso*, a combination and intersection of narratives. Building a network of stories influenced by images, while using a structure and set of rules, Calvino recalls Ariosto's poem while also envisioning literature as a device made up of paths and plots. Connecting two tale-making machines—tarot cards and the *Furioso*—Calvino creates a combinatory game, an activity that fascinated him during the 1960s.[1] It is not by chance, then, that his last two stories are entitled "Storia dell'Orlando pazzo per amore" ("The Story of Orlando Mad Because of Love") and "Storia di Astolfo sulla luna" ("The Story of Astolfo on the Moon"), making the reference to Ariosto's poem even more explicit and even suggesting it as a key to the entire book. Moreover, understanding that "each story runs into another story . . . because the stories told from left to right or from bottom to top can also be read from right to left or from top to bottom" (Calvino, *Castle* 39), we can discern the process that presided over a centuries-long history of rewritings: the continual blending of stories and the reuse of characters, which is also one of the most important gifts western European romance has given us.

"Storia dell'Orlando pazzo per amore" shows the different stages of Orlando, Angelica, and Medoro's story (canto 23 of *Furioso*), reconstructed by using the tarots of one of the customers seated around the table, a silent warrior. The chapter's conclusion offers an interpretation of both the warrior's story and the poem itself: the world is meant to be read upside down, because its story is a story of balance, of harmony and disharmony. "Storia di Astolfo sulla luna," on the other hand, reflects on literature and on its (absence of) meaning, through the last tarot, which represents a poet: it recalls the scenes in canto 35 in which Saint John discloses to Astolfo the basics of poetry.

Calvino is interested in Ariosto because he creates a map of the world through narration. It is not about a sporadic application of plots and patterns; on the contrary, it is a way of raising Ariosto up to a narrative and ideological model (see Jossa, "Pazzia"). *Orlando furioso* seems to contain all the narrations, even those not written yet, a poem that stimulates questions about the world. This may be the meaning of the last part of Calvino's book, which demonstrates how it is possible to tell stories from other stories. The narrator in the *Castello*, after all, clearly knows Ariosto's poem, and (illegitimately?) overlaps his knowledge with other travelers' stories. Might this suggest that all readers utilize literature to interpret all other narrations, until they see no more than with the eyes of literature? Through a reading of Calvino's two stories in conjunction with the original episodes in the *Orlando furioso* (23.100–24.14 and 34.48–35.31), students can discuss not only the process of rewriting romance but more generally the nature and role of literature in human life.

## Gianni Celati: The Power of the Voice

Gianni Celati, on the other hand, is interested in the possibility of generating imaginary worlds and affirming values through words. In 1994 he published his prose version of Matteo Maria Boiardo's poem, *Orlando innamorato raccontato in prosa*. In this work, the remembrance of tradition—mainly meant to suggest a civilization based on narration—opposes the industrialization of literature and offers "una piccola patria per la mente" ("a small homeland for the mind"), "una piccola patria di sopravvivenza" ("a small homeland of survival"; x).[2] Celati here asserts a narrative approach based on the spoken word, an idea that truly belongs to his poetics. It is, therefore, a return to the origins, when the voice conveyed the stories and the ear embraced them.

Celati reminds us that knights' achievements have always been the subject of oral accounts. The desire to retell in prose a poem like Boiardo's *Innamorato* goes along with urging readers to embrace once again the oral dimension of these works. First of all, because this poem more than any other "accende la mia passione immaginativa" ("turns my imaginative passion on"), says Celati, and "stimola il mio desiderio di narrare" ("stimulates my desire to narrate"; ix)—that is to say, the poem succeeds in transforming the reader-listener into a new narrator—"il racconto che segue è stato scritto e pensato più come una recita che come un romanzo da leggere in silenzio" ("the following account was written and meant more as an oral performance rather than as a novel to be read in silence"; xi).

The book is made up of forty-three chapters, to be read "ad alta voce" with "gente simpatica" ("aloud" with "nice people"), trying to regain Boiardo's imagined gathering of eager listeners. Students may retell episodes from the poem aloud, to their classmates, or they may write down in prose Boiardo's *ottave*. They would then recognize Celati's work as a kind of rewriting, and they would better understand what switching from poetry to prose and from a written to an oral dimension means. Some episodes from Boiardo's *Innamorato* are particularly well rewritten by Celati: Angelica's arrival in the first canto (Celati 3–9 and *Orlando innamorato* 1.1.3–9); the battle in Albraca (Celati 73–87 and *Orlando innamorato* 1.10.1–11.46); Brandimarte and Fiordelisa's adventures (Celati 249–56 and *Orlando innamorato* 2.25.23–26.19).

## What If Orlando Had a Beak?

Since the earliest medieval versions, and then along the history of rewritings, romance has often been accompanied by (mostly silent) images. Comics, on the contrary, reverse the relation of text to image since illustrations take precedence over the written word. They can be more or less faithful to their models, more or less parodical, having diverse audiences and using different codes. In Italy, Disney comics have always held importance, being linked to the weekly issues of *Topolino*, printed in Italy since 1932 and still very popular. In fact, on several occasions Disney characters have become protagonists of stories inspired by Italian and world classics (for example, the series *I grandi classici Disney* and *Le grandi parodie Disney*).

A number of comics based on Italian Renaissance romance epics were published between the end of the 1950s and the end of the 1960s. *Paperin Meschino* (1958) is a comic inspired by Andrea da Barberino's *Guerrin Meschino*, followed by *Paperino il paladino* (1960), inspired by Boiardo's *Orlando innamorato*; *Paperin furioso* (1966); and *Paperopoli liberata* (1967). The latter title, with its allusion to Torquato Tasso's *Gerusalemme liberata*, is the Italian equivalent of *Duckburg Delivered*.[3] These comics can be used in the classroom to explore various issues, in particular the relation of the Renaissance work to a contemporary audience and a change of a narrative's medium.

First of all, in examining the settings of these parodies, one can choose comics with a particular focus, such as protagonists of the romance tradition who are reproduced or transformed; adventures that take place in the present age, as if the story were new rather than rewritten; or characters who are transported back into the past (by magic, for example) and who become protagonists of the chosen classic and encounter their chivalric ancestors. *Paperin Meschino*, *Paperino il paladino*, and *Paperin furioso*, for instance, are sorts of voyages into the past, while *Paperopoli liberata* is set in the present (although it clearly winks to the poem).

Something that immediately stands out in the third kind of story is the constant space-time paradox in which the characters live. They move in medieval-like settings, whose reenactment is, however, constantly denied by references to the contemporary age and by anachronisms, be they visual, linguistic, or cultural. In one of the *Paperino il paladino* cartoons, a painter—dressed like a sixteenth-century artist—paints a Kandisky-like picture (36); Gastolfo (Gladstone Gander-Astolfo) has a car horn on his sedan chair (47), and Gastolfo sings musical hits from 1959; in *Paperin Meschino*, Paperone (Scrooge McDuck) complains that bombs, guns, and steam power have not been invented yet, and so on. These infringements are very frequent, and the contamination between the two levels—the reconstruction of the classic's past and the winking to the contemporary age—is an inherent characteristic of these rewritings. All the adventures and magic objects are contaminated by the contemporary world: Atlante's castle can be destroyed by smashing his crystal-ball television; Saint John's cart is a rocket that takes Gastolfo to the moon, and so on.

Even though the Disney comic books are called parodies, they do not devalue the classic to which they are related. This modern genre does not diminish the classic but rather propels it toward a new life, with a new role. As Thierry Groensteen states, comics are a perfect means to rewrite in a desecrating fashion, for they combine two semiotic systems (text and images), are discontinuous, and provide an apt environment for collage and borrowed materials (145). Moreover, Disney comics offer a bridge made of images to works that are often already visually settled in the shared cultural memory. It is worth remembering, in fact, that these classic poems belong to the Italian cultural and educational canon. Students may find that the richness of references to the age of chivalry make the two worlds closer, removing a certain nuance of nostalgia.

In a discussion of these comic books students can also address the issue of nostalgia—that is, the conservative force that may emerge whenever we deal with a cultural heritage and thereby run the risk of erecting a stiff and arid museum rather than producing meaningful art. New forms of the chivalric tradition, by comparison, can be a way of allowing it to generate new meaning in the present. Students can discuss how some of the rewritings transform the classic into pop, thus bringing it closer to the contemporary age and debunking it without crushing it. How may irony (a postmodern one, as for some of our works) leave space between itself and the object, guaranteeing a healthy perspective from which to view the classic? In what other ways do comic books, while apparently reconstructing a world from the past, avoid a regressive nostalgia and offer a vital perspective on the classics?

Students can also examine how the characters' language comically imitates the poetry, increasing the effect of the story's setting. Dialogues, after all, are the best place to include explicit citations, for instance in *Paperin furioso*, when a herald announces the Moorish invasion with Ariosto's words (130). At the same time, students may also discuss the effect of the modernized language and colorful expressions not present in the original. How does the language convey values from centuries before? Does it need to be close to the original or mimetic of the present language? How can the images be a language themselves, with no need for further words? In discussing this topic, students can bring in their interdisciplinary experience, such as cinema and visual art studies as well as the study of or their experience with different registers in their own language.

The questions raised in the previous paragraphs can be applied to Pino Zac's *Orlando furioso* (1975), a masterful comic book that combines pure entertainment and rewriting at a high level.[4] Zac never forgets Ariosto's text, which often replaces dialogue or is used as captions. In fact, the book (thirty-six chapters, six pages each) reproduces quite accurately Ariosto's story (except for a few cuts). Furthermore, Ariosto's words always conclude each template, exactly where and how he had closed his own cantos. At the same time, Zac steps into the comic book and even directly involves the reader. He provides a reading guide, for example, explaining characters, places, and circumstances deemed unfamiliar to the modern reader (and this is a feature common to many rewritings, for example Celati's). Student can focus on moments in which the division between *diegesis* and reader is broken, such as the illustrated glossary at page 98, where the reader is actually represented on the page, joining the complex relationship among author, rewriter, and text. Here Zac himself steps into the comic to personally speak with Ariosto since the reader objects to the story. The authors (Zac and Ariosto) defend it, evoking the sixteenth-century *querelle* about the *Furioso*. Students may compare this same (but also different) need to speak to the readers, and these clear *mise en abymes*, across the centuries and across different media; they may reflect on how comics can use narrative devices associated with the romance epic.

Students can also consider how Pino Zac's book constantly converses with his contemporary readership by integrating the present into the chivalric plot. In some cases, the external world penetrates through anachronisms in the story: for example, the knights imprisoned by Atlante dream about cars, the herald becomes a mail carrier, Melissa the sorceress runs her own private practice as an occultist, and so on. In other cases, Zac deals even more directly with contemporary society and history by alluding to real events or people: Ruggiero's getting rid of Atlante's magic shield prompts a quick pacifist allusion to Richard Nixon and Leonid Brezhnev's meeting to discuss nuclear disarmament during the Vietnam war (123), and the desert hermit (canto 15) is transformed into an Al-Fatah militant (80), a nod to the Israeli-Palestinian conflict. Such references can be compared to Ariosto's allusions to the Italian wars in the early sixteenth century and in general to his historical references—for example, in the *proemi* to canto 14, 34 and 36, as well as in 26.31.7–8.

## A Chain of Rewritings

Students might also investigate how the style of the rewriting is in itself a way of interpreting the chivalric classics. Calvino and Zac, above all, choose an ironic and playful style, often caricature-like. Partially in harmony with the lightness of romance adventure, this style also offers an interpretative key to the source text. Rewritings can then be thought of as critical works, and they can also teach us about the rewriters' poetics and vision. Indeed, all the choices made by contemporary writers—from commentary on a selection of the poem (Manganelli) to a fictional Sicilian *cunto* (Bufalino)—tell us something about both themselves and the classic they've rewritten, and of course something about ourselves, the readers, who are challenged to extract meaning from their transformative process. The exploration of the above rewritings, and of others not mentioned here, can encourage students to think about the relation between literature and its readers and can stimulate them to continue this dialogue in a personal way, imagining methods of reinventing old chivalric stories for new audiences.

## Notes

1. In this decade he wrote the important essay *Cibernetica e fantasmi* (1967), joined the French OuLiPo, and took a deep interest in structuralism and semiotics.

2. Translations are my own.

3. They all can be easily found for classroom use.

4. Giuseppe Zaccaria (1930–85) was a well-known cartoonist and a film director, among whose works is a film, *Il cavaliere inesistente di Pino Zac*, inspired by Calvino's *Cavaliere inesistente* in 1971, currently available on *YouTube* (www.youtube.com/watch?v=-fBW5rk1dJ0&list=PLytkoX7KJ31JQmiVRJeCErhR4plxe7Mbu).

**Andrea Privitera**

# Teaching the Italian Renaissance Epic through Digital Role-Playing Games

In her contribution to the *Orlando furioso: Incantamenti, passioni e follie* exhibition catalog, Lina Bolzoni agrees with Johan Huizinga that Ludovico Ariosto embodies the *serio ludere* ("playing seriously") attitude of Leon Battista Alberti and Erasmus of Rotterdam ("L'*Orlando furioso*" 305; *Homo Ludens* 181). To support her claim, Bolzoni lists two baroque games inspired by *Orlando furioso*: the *Laberinto dell'Ariosto* ("Ariosto's Maze"), described by Emanuele Tesauro in *Il cannocchiale aristotelico* ("The Aristotelian Telescope"), and a chess table mentioned by Marco Aurelio Severino (310–12). In fact, the 2014–15 exhibition hosted at Palazzo Magnani in Reggio Emilia greeted its visitors with the display of a Game of the Goose-inspired tabletop panel made by comic book author Guido Crepax. Such a brilliant adaptation of *Furioso* let Crepax share the adventures of Orlando, Rinaldo, Ruggiero, and Angelica with his family (Parmiggiani 354–57).

Since games lend themselves to adapting a deeply metanarrative work such as Ariosto's, using them to teach *Orlando furioso* can be quite straightforward. Indeed, Crepax's work is only one among many intriguing educational games of this sort. Others include a pen-and-paper role-playing game created by Andrea Angiolino and Gianluca Meluzzi in 1993 (republished in 2002) and the collectable card game *Orlando's Wars*, designed by Enrico Maria Giglioli for the Palazzo Magnani exhibition. Even higher education successfully embraced this approach. In a recent course on the Italian Renaissance at the University of Kansas, Lawrence, Crystal Hall encouraged her students to design a tabletop game based on *Orlando furioso*, with positive results in terms of students' investment and learning outcome (55–62).

Expanding on Hall's ingenious example, I argue that video games may likewise stimulate participation in a Renaissance epic literature course. In addition to its appeal among undergraduates, gaming can also be a relevant learning tool. In the case of teaching Italian epic romances, digital role-playing games allow students to better familiarize themselves with such a daunting topic.

To begin, what are role-playing games? Following game designers Andrew Rollings and Ernest Adams's definition, role-playing games usually feature "strong storylines" and "configurable player-characters that improve with experience" (347). Players can customize several aspects of their in-game characters, including their feats and skills. For instance, one can play the same fantasy game as either a warrior, a thief, or a magician. In some games, players can even personalize their character's gender, race, and physical appearance. Once the game starts, the player-controlled character takes on a quest (which constitutes the main narrative of the game) and, potentially, a series of side quests.

While designing a survey course on the poems of Matteo Maria Boiardo, Ariosto, and Torquato Tasso for the Italian program at the University of Western Ontario, I realized that contemporary role-playing video games share several core traits with the epic romances of Renaissance Ferrara. For example, as Huizinga famously argues, European chivalric culture can be best explained in terms of aesthetics and play, in that the life of a knight resembles a game (*Waning* 65–74; *Homo Ludens* 179–80). Following Roger Callois's expansion of Huizinga's definition, we can refer to this game of chivalry as mimicry, a kind of play that consists "not only of deploying actions or submitting to one's fate in an imaginary milieu, but of becoming an illusory character oneself, and of so behaving" (135). From this perspective, mimicry is yet another word for role-playing (Burn 244).

Although Callois explains that games are either "ruled or make-believe" (127), role-playing video games are a mix of both, since player-controlled characters need to overcome a series of challenges in order to reach the end of the game. This logic, which in literature is the narrative plot, can be best defined in computer terms as the algorithm. The main difference between narrative and algorithm is that the latter is not as predominant as the former. The media theorist Lev Manovich maintains that the algorithm is a secondary form of representation in the information age, especially when compared to emergent structures such as the database or the navigable space. In other words, the algorithm exists only as yet another way to access the database or the space of a game. Although players are supposed to achieve a final goal, they may also spend hours exploring the game's world, learning about its lore and its customs. In sum, Manovich argues that video games are the result of narrative actions intertwined with exploration (212–86).

Indeed, both romance epics from the Italian Renaissance and contemporary role-playing video games share a heightened tension between narrative plot and spatial exploration. The movements of the characters in *Inamoramento de Orlando*, *Orlando furioso*, and *Gerusalemme liberata* closely resemble the balance between main quest and side quests in contemporary role-playing games. Players take detours from the main storyline, just as the knights of the chivalric narratives are constantly drawn away from their duties.

My survey course on epic romances, which I taught during the 2015 fall term at Western, welcomed a composite group of third- to fourth-year double majors in Italian and disciplines unrelated to the humanities. Because my students were unacquainted with literature, I actually included role-playing video games in my syllabus. By teaching the Italian epic romances through a cultural form that was more familiar to my students, I wanted to overcome the challenges they would face during the course. To further encourage participation, I had students read the texts both in Italian and in English, while I used Italian during lectures and for assignments. For the Italian editions of the poems, I provided my students with links to the free PDFs available on the *Biblioteca della letteratura italiana* Web site. For the Italian editions, I used the volumes edited by Aldo Scaglione (*Inamoramento*), Edoardo Sanguineti and Marcello Turchi (*Furioso*), and Lanfranco Caretti (*Liberata*). As for the translations, I adopted Charles S. Ross for Boiardo, Barbara Reynolds for Ariosto, and Max Wickert for Tasso.

At the very beginning of the course, I asked my students to play a role-playing game of their choice. There is a vast array of them available for the main platforms currently on the market, and their prices can suit all the students' pockets. A new game for PCs or consoles costs $40 to $60, but less recent and used games can be found for $5 to $20 through retailers or online distribution services. For the same price, students could also buy a role-playing game on their tablets or smartphones.

For my intent, I provided students with a list of games they could choose from in the syllabus. In doing so, I kept in mind a colleague's recommendation: asking students to play games published more than five to seven years ago might alienate them, whereas the main use of video games in a class on the Italian chivalric tradition is to help students grasp the course objectives through something more familiar. Therefore, unless specific old games have a particular nostalgic value to students, it would be better to use recent ones.

All the games in the syllabus emphasized character creation and free roaming through an open world and featured an unrealistic or ahistorical setting, such as Tolkienesque fantasy lands or space opera universes. These features helped students familiarize themselves with two aspects of the Renaissance chivalric tradition—which were also the two main objectives of the course. First, they clarified the historical distance between the medieval narratives of the Matter of France and Britain and the matters' literary reelaboration in fifteenth- and sixteenth-century Italy; second, they illustrated the wavering balance of epic and romance elements in *Inamoramento*, *Furioso*, and *Liberata*.

The first challenge I faced was to explain that a temporal distance exists between the reign of Charlemagne, its mythopoesis in European folk culture, and, finally, its literary reelaboration in early modern Italy. On our first meeting, I asked my students to write for the following class a brief description of the character they created in their chosen role-playing game. The purpose of this informal assignment was twofold. First, it allowed me to assess my students' writing skill in Italian. Above all, however, this task allowed me to introduce chivalric mimicry by discussing how the students enacted it on their own. In turn, the notion of mimicry keyed students into the gap between medieval narratives and the early modern historical context. After all, the distance between the Renaissance Este court and the stories of the paladins of France or the Crusaders is comparable to the distance between the story-world students experienced in their role-playing game and their everyday life.

As the course progressed, I addressed the narrative and game play aspects of the role-playing games. Some of them, like *Mass Effect* and *Star Wars: Knights of the Old Republic*, focus more on character development—skills, personality, and morality—and on the protagonist's goal. Other games, such as *Fallout 3* or *Skyrim* (*The Elder Scrolls V*), emphasize the vast world map the player can explore and pay less attention to the protagonist's identity. Likewise, users interact with the game in different fashions. Players of *Mass Effect* can spend hours on side quests, thus postponing the main narrative as much as possible. On the other hand, players of *Skyrim* can go through the main quest and finish the game by ignoring a large portion of the game map. I asked my students to discuss these dynamics in another written assignment. Students illustrated how they played the game, and I highlighted the differences between those who gave more importance to free roaming and those who aimed at the main storyline.

By pondering their experiences with character creation and game play, students could now recognize the uses of mimicry and narrative structures in Boiardo, Ariosto, and Tasso. As we read the first canto of *Inamoramento de Orlando*, students could understand the Este's self-legitimization through the arts in a neofeudal context. By addressing his audience of "signori e cavallier" ("lords and knights") (line 1), Boiardo effectively adapts Huizinga's game of chivalry in a different age, thus erasing the temporal and cultural distance between Charlemagne's court and Estense Ferrara.

Space, rather than time, seems to be the main concern of *Inamoramento*. In this unfinished poem, every journey has an objective: yet, as many of the plots remain unfulfilled, these journeys may become aimless romances. Boiardo's Orlando can be likened to a player who prefers to simply explore the game world. With this idea in mind, my students and I read the trials Orlando endures in order to find Angelica in Albraca (1.5–6). Students understood that, in this case, the journey itself is more important than its ending.

We could now read Ariosto's *Furioso* as a subversion of the romance tropes enacted in *Inamoramento*. Through David Quint's interpretation of the palace of Atlante narrative (*Furioso* 4 and 12), the class could consider these episodes as undermining Boiardo's mimicry and storytelling techniques ("Figure"). By comparing the Atlante cantos with Astolfo's journey to the moon (*Orlando furioso* 33–35), students acknowledged that Ariosto's exploration of space may not be a self-sufficient narrative mode; rather, it might be instrumental to a goal-oriented plot. This strategy, which was enacted by players who focused on the games' main quest, also allowed us to read Carlo and Ubaldo's adventure in the island of Fortune in *Gerusalemme liberata* 34–36.[1] When encouraged to consider these episodes in the poems' overarching structures, students could see how Ariosto and Tasso used digressions to delay the completion of the epic plot just as world exploration and side quests in a video game may delay the completion of the algorithm.

From a pedagogical point of view, I am glad to say that the course was a success. Students achieved the learning objectives I set for them, and they proved to be competent critical thinkers. In a midterm essay, a medical-science student drew a detailed and convincing comparison between the immersion of video games and the reprisal of chivalric mimicry in Renaissance Ferrara. My students also correctly identified narrative techniques from the chivalric poems in these games. For example, during an in-class presentation a biology student defined the player's ability to control the actions of different characters in *Knights of the Old Republic* as an example of *entrelacement* ("intertwining"), or the change of narrative focus between different characters in a chivalric poem. Also, this teaching method caught the attention of the media, as well as of teachers and scholars in the humanities. *Western News*, the University of Western Ontario's official weekly newspaper, ran a story about the use of video games in my course (Talbot).

In retrospect, I see my teaching experiment as a profoundly positive experience, one that I would love to further develop in future courses. I am convinced that, because of its flexibility, this approach can be tailored to suit the needs and learning aspirations of different groups of students. For example, one aspect of Renaissance literature that would be particularly appropriate for teaching through role-playing games is the *rifacimenti* ("rewritings") and *giunte* ("additions") of epic romances. These practices played a crucial role in the circulation of chivalric books in Renaissance Italy—for example Boiardo's poem was revised and continued by persons of letters and amateur writers alike. The rise of the printing press in the fifteenth century and the absence of copyright laws facilitated a bootleg and transformative culture similar to the one we have today.

In dealing with *rifacimenti* and *giunte*, students could be encouraged to modify their game with both official and unofficial add-ons. As not all games can be easily hacked by players, the instructor could comment on how the difference between open- and closed-source games is not unlike the difference in authorship between Boiardo, Ariosto, and Tasso. While *Inamoramento de Orlando*'s incompleteness invites other authors to continue or to rewrite the original, the closed-source poems of Ariosto and Tasso significantly limit their retellings and continuations.

In a more literature-oriented classroom, algorithms and navigable spaces could also introduce—and elaborate on—literary theory. Before dealing with Renaissance epic romances, the instructor could explain similar narrative differences in the narratives' sources, such as the *Chanson de Roland* and the romances by Chrétien de Troyes. While discussing Tasso, students could review the sixteenth-century debate on *epica* and *romanzo* by comparing its main issues to their game play experience. Is there a correct way to play a game or to read and write a poem? What might sixteenth-century literary theoreticians like Sperone Speroni or Giovambattista Giraldi Cinzio have thought of players not finishing a role-playing game? Would that be a failure or simply one way among many to experience a narrative work?

Finally, if I were to teach the same course to a media studies class, I would push students to engage not only the Renaissance texts but also video games in a more critical way. For instance, I would encourage them to focus on identity portrayal in media. Is there any difference in how race and gender are portrayed in contemporary role-playing games and in chivalric poems? Do these portrayals influence readers and players? Since the issue of identity and the desire to reshape it through media is as present today as it was five hundred years ago, discussing identity portrayal would be an excellent way to actualize Boiardo, Ariosto, and Tasso and to educate students to a more critical way of playing video games.

## Notes

This essay benefitted from dialogues with the participants of the "Teaching the Italian Renaissance Epic" panel at the 2015 American Association of Teachers of Italian Conference (AATI) in Siena, Italy, and the two meetings of the "Innovative Approaches of Teaching Italian" roundtable at the 2016 and 2017 American Association of Italian Studies (AAIS) and the Canadian Society of Italian Studies (CSIS) conferences. I would particularly like to thank Simone Bregni, Brandon Essary, Michael Maher, Chris Piccici, Alessio Tognetti, and Carolyn Zimmerman for the thought-provoking conversations. My attendance at the 2015 AATI conference, at which I read an early version of this essay, was supported by a travel grant generously awarded by the organizing committee. Cristina Caracchini, Maria Laura Mosco, and Luca Pocci also provided important suggestions for the design of the syllabus that inspired this work.

1. For this strategy at work in the above-mentioned stories, also see Quint, "The Boat of Romance."

# Part X

# Resources

Jo Ann Cavallo

## Primary Works in Translation

Although the vast majority of Italian romance epics are available only in their original language, there are an increasing number of translations that have made it possible to investigate the wider context of the genre even in comparative literature courses. Leslie Zarker Morgan has translated two early fourteenth-century Franco-Italian poems, "Berta and Milone" and "Orlandino," available online. Boccaccio's early epic poem in ottava rima, *Teseida delle nozze di Emilia*, is available in Vincenzo Traversa's translation as *Theseid of the Nuptials of Emilia. Cantari* by the fourteenth-century Florentine poet and storyteller Antonio Pucci are available in English with facing Italian text in editions by Thomas E. Vesce (*The Four Cantari*) and by Maria Bendinelli Predelli (*Gismirante*; *Madonna Leonessa*). For the Arthurian tradition in Italy, the *Tristano Panciatichiano*, *Tristano Corsiniano*, and *Tristano Riccardiano* have all been translated, the first two by Gloria Allaire and the third by Regina Psaki.

For the fifteenth century, substantial selections from Andrea da Barberino's prose *I reali di Francia* (*The Royal House of France*) and *L'Aspramonte* (*Aspramont*), as well as the anonymous Franco-Venetian *Fatti di Spagna* (*Exploits in Spain*), translated by Max Wickert (whose translations include Torquato Tasso's *Gerusalemme liberata* and *Rinaldo*), are currently online and will hopefully be available in print in the near future. Luigi Pulci's *Morgante Maggiore* has been translated by Joseph Tusiani as *Morgante: The Epic Adventures of Orlando and His Giant Friend Morgante.* The only complete translation of Matteo Maria Boiardo's *Orlando innamorato* is that by Charles S. Ross, discussed (along with partial translations) by Joshua Reid in this volume.

For the sixteenth century, Teofilo Folengo's *Baldus* is available in Ann Mullaney's translation with the original macaronic-Latin text on facing pages. For Ludovico Ariosto and Tasso, in addition to their major epic poems, translations of which are discussed by Reid in this volume, we can read excellent English-language versions of the former's *Cinque canti* and the latter's *Rinaldo*: *The Five Cantos* have appeared in prose translations by Morgan (1992) and by Alexander Sheers and David Quint with facing Italian text (1996); Wickert has recently rendered the *Rinaldo* in ottava rima verse (2017).

Translations of epics by three female poets were recently published thanks to the series The Other Voice in Early Modern Europe. Moderata Fonte's *Floridoro, A Chivalric Romance*, translated by Julia Kisacky, and

Margherita Sarrocchi's *Scanderbeide: The Heroic Deeds of George Scanderbeg, King of Epirus*, translated by Rinaldina Russell, were both published in 2006. These were followed in 2009 with the publication of Lucrezia Marinella's *Enrico; or, Byzantium Conquered: A Heroic Poem*, translated by Maria Galli Stampino. A fourth female-authored epic, Tullia d'Aragona's *The Wretch, Otherwise Known as Guerrino*, translated by John McLucas, is forthcoming in the same series.

Finally, two early seventeenth-century works written in ottava rima in dialogue with—or rather, in opposition to—the romance epic are also available in English translation. Alessandro Tassoni's mock-heroic epic *La secchia rapita* (1622) is available online in James Atkinson's verse translation *La secchia rapita; or, The Rape of the Bucket.* Selections from Giambattista Marino's mythological epic *Adone* (1623) were translated into blank verse by Harold Martin Priest as *Adonis.*

## Anthologies of Primary Works

Unicopli has a new Atlante series dedicated to anthologizing works by major Italian authors. A volume on Tasso, edited by Alessandro Bianchi and Rinaldo Rinaldi, was published in 2011, and a volume on Boiardo, edited by Cavallo and Corrado Confalonieri, appeared in 2018. Students with limited knowledge of Italian may find useful *Orlando furioso: A selection*, with its English-language introduction, notes, and vocabulary accompanying the Italian text. Giorgio Manganelli's commentary and selected readings of Pulci's *Morgante* (audio recording from 1972) are now available in print.

## Primary Works Online

Instructors and students can find primary Italian texts online at Biblioteca Italiana (www.bibliotecaitaliana.it), Biblioteca della Letteratura Italiana (www.letteraturaitaliana.net), and LiberLiber (www.liberliber.it/online). As always, these are not latest versions and generally lack critical apparatus.

## Audio Resources

An audio version of the entire *Orlando furioso* (2010) is available online through LiberLiber. Recorded selections from the *Orlando furioso* (proem, Orlando's folly, Astolfo on the moon), and *Gerusalemme liberata* (dedication, Erminia among the shepherds, the death of Clorinda), narrated by Moro Silo, are available on a fifty-minute CD entitled *I poemi epici del Rinascimento.*

## Prose Adaptations

In the mid-nineteenth century, the Palermitan Giusto Lo Dico combined several medieval and Renaissance epics into a three-thousand-page prose compilation entitled *La storia dei paladini di Francia cominciando da Milone conte d'Anglante fino alla morte di Rinaldo* ("The History of the Paladins of France from Count Milone of Anglante to the Death of Rinaldo"). Lo Dico's narrative follows the lives of Carolingian characters in chronological order, drawing from Tasso's *Rinaldo*, Cieco da Ferrara's *Mambriano*, Boiardo's *Orlando innamorato*, Ariosto's *Orlando furioso* and *Cinque canti*, Pulci's *Morgante*, and other chivalric texts lesser known today. Originally published in biweekly installments (1858–60), this massive compilation was frequently reprinted in the following decades and further expanded by Giuseppe Leggio (1870–1911), who added new episodes, beginning with the events surrounding Charlemagne's birth and youth as related in Andrea da Barberino's *Reali di Francia.*

Often referred to as the puppeteer's bible, *La storia dei paladini* provided an authoritative written version of stories already dramatized in puppet theaters and later became puppeteers' principal source, thus ensuring that medieval and Renaissance chivalric characters would remain familiar to the general population of Sicily, parts of southern Italy, and even the New World well into the twentieth century. The expanded version was most recently published in a thirteen-volume edition, *Storia dei paladini di Francia cominciando da Re Pipino fino alla morte di Rinaldo.*

If in the mid-nineteenth century one otherwise obscure individual refashioned the entire chivalric tradition in prose, in recent decades three prominent authors have undertaken prose renderings of three distinct chivalric epics: Italo Calvino's *Orlando furioso* (1970), Gesualdo Bufalino's *Guerrin meschino* (1993), and Gianni Celati's *Orlando innamorato raccontato in prosa* (1994).

For children, Sara Marconi has written four books recounting the adventures of Astolfo, Angelica, Bradamante, and Orlando (2014–15). Idalberto Fei's *Orlando furioso e innamorato* (2014) combines both poems along with some creative and practical readjustments. Cavallo's *Orlando innamorato di Matteo Maria Boiardo* (2001) is a bilingual prose version of Boiardo's poem abridged and translated for young readers.

## Comic Books

I Grandi Classici Disney and Le Grandi Parodie Disney included a number of comics based on Renaissance romance epics: *Paperin Meschino* (1958), based on Andrea da Barberino's *Guerrin Meschino*; *Paperino il paladino* (1960), loosely inspired by Boiardo's *Orlando innamorato*; *Paperin furioso* (1966), and *Paperopoli liberata* (1967), the latter two based on Ariosto's and Tasso's poems, respectively. See Stefano Nicosia's essay in this volume for a consideration of these books as well as Pino Zac's *Orlando furioso* (1975).

## Critical Readings for Instructors and Students

Scholarly works on the Italian romance epic are vast, and interest in the genre, if anything, is on the rise. The following section offers a brief overview of secondary literature, detailing the arc of the tradition, some individual authors, and reception in the arts. Additional readings are suggested throughout the volume by the contributors themselves.

### The Italian Romance Epic

Marco Villoresi usefully contextualizes Italy's chivalric literary tradition in two volumes: *La letteratura cavalleresca* and *La fabbrica dei cavallieri*. A bilingual journal devoted to Italian chivalric literature, *Letteratura cavalleresca italiana*, is scheduled to commence in 2018 under the direction of Christopher Kleinhenz and Davide Puccini.

### The Early Anonymous Tradition

For an overview in English, see Juliann M. Vitullo, *The Chivalric Epic in Medieval Italy*. For various permutations of the *Song of Roland* in Italy, see Giovanni Palumbo, *La* Chanson de Roland *in Italia nel Medioevo*. Bendinelli Predelli's essay in this volume includes bibliographical suggestions for the *cantari* tradition. For the *Entrée d'Espagne* and *La Spagna*, see Claudia Boscolo, *L'*Entrée d'Espagne, and Franca Strologo, La Spagna *nella letteratura cavalleresca italiana*, respectively. For the Arthurian tradition in Italy, see *The Arthur of the Italians*, edited by Allaire and Psaki.

### Individual Authors

#### LUIGI PULCI

Although Pulci's *Morgante* is recognized as a major literary work, it has received less scholarly attention than the three Ferrarese crowns. Recent critical works include Annalisa Perrotta's "Lo spazio della corte," Alessio Decaria's "Tra Marsilio e Pallante," and Alessandro Polcri's *Luigi Pulci e la Chimera*. In English, Edoardo Lèbano's introduction to Joseph Tusiani's translation is a good place to start for a concise introduction to the poem and relevant bibliography. In addition, Michael Murrin has a chapter on Pulci, "The Tactics of Roncesvalles," in *History and Warfare*. A volume of essays edited by James Coleman and Andrea Moudarres, *Luigi Pulci in Renaissance Florence and Beyond*, was published in 2017, and a special issue on the reception of the *Morgante* and *Orlando innamorato*, edited by Nicola Catelli and Giovanna Rizzarelli, is forthcoming in *Italian Studies*.

## MATTEO MARIA BOIARDO

Boiardo has received increased critical attention since the 1990s. Conferences for the five-hundred-year anniversary of the poem's definitive first edition led to two volumes of collected essays on Boiardo's literary opus: in Italian, *Il Boiardo e il mondo Estense*, edited by Giuseppe Anceschi and Tina Matarrese, which follows by almost three decades the volume by Anceschi, *Il Boiardo e la critica contemporanea*, and, in English, *Fortune and Romance: Boiardo in America*, edited by Cavallo and Ross, with essays by David Quint, Michael Murrin, James Nohrnberg, Werner Gundersheimer, and others.

Marco Praloran's *"Maraviglioso artificio"* focuses on the *Innamorato*'s innovative narrative strategies in negotiating between Carolingian and Arthurian structures, paying particular attention to the poem's use of *entrelacement*, transitions between episodes and the endings of *canti*, and virtuosic manipulation of narrative time. Raffaele Donnarumma's *Storia dell'*Orlando innamorato examines Boiardo's choices in creatively refashioning images, themes, and topoi from his classical and medieval sources. Cristina Zampese's *"Or si fa rosa or pallida la luna"* devotes attention to Boiardo's humanistic education, his translations of classical texts into the vernacular, and his reworking of classical sources in his lesser-known works as well as his major poem. Antonia Tissoni Benvenuti's introduction to the critical edition, *Inamoramento de Orlando*, proposes a revised dating, arguing that book 1 was not composed in the 1470s as previously believed, but rather during the latter years of Borso d'Este's reign (1466–71). Accordingly, book 2, with its greater interest in history and genealogy, would signal the shift to Ercole d'Este's patronage. Among earlier critical studies, Giovanni Ponte's *La personalità e l'opera del Boiardo* remains useful for its reach across Boiardo's opus.

In English, Ross's multipart introduction to his translation devotes sections to Boiardo's life and various aspects of the poem, including its plot, structure, and language. Murrin's chapter "Falerina's Garden" in *The*

*Allegorical Epic* offers a philosophical, political, historical, cosmological, and psychological reading of the *Innamorato*'s Garden of Orgagna, a death trap engineered by a malevolent fairy. Cavallo's *Boiardo's* Orlando innamorato explores the poem's creative imitation of biblical, classical, medieval, and early Renaissance intertexts in line with the ethical basis of fifteenth-century humanist poetical theory.

For the poem's publishing history, Neil Harris's *Bibliografia dell'* Orlando innamorato furnishes a rich description of all known editions from the late fifteenth century to 1900, with plot summaries of its various continuations (excluding Ariosto's *Orlando furioso*) and many illustrations. For Boiardo's biography, Tiziano Zanato's *Boiardo* (2015) is indispensable.

## LODOVICO ARIOSTO

For Ariosto, there are an unwieldy number of scholarly studies. Robert J. Rodini and Salvatore Di Maria's book-length annotated bibliography covering the years 1956 to 1980 is followed by Rodini's bibliographies, which provide guidance for the years 1980 to 1987 and 1986 to 1993. Two earlier books warrant special mention: Pio Rajna's *Le fonti dell'* Orlando furioso, a seminal work since its first appearance in 1876, posits Ariosto's extensive debt to previous sources, especially the classical epic and French-Italian medieval romance traditions; Michele Catalano's two-volume *Vita di Ludovico Ariosto* (1930) remains the most comprehensive source for Ariosto's life and works, with extensive documentation. Among recent Italian-language biographies, Giuseppe Sangirardi's *Ludovico Ariosto* views the author's life and works from the lens of psychoanalytic theory. In the absence of any comparable biographies of Ariosto in English, C. P. Brand's concise essay on Ariosto's life and times is still informative (in Brand, *Ludovico Ariosto*).

Essays by Marco Praloran on various aspects of the *Furioso*, including narrative temporality, the technique and thematics of duels, and the use of verbal tenses, are gathered in *Tempo e azione nell'* Orlando furioso. Alberto Casadei has also published substantial contributions on the *Furioso*, including *La strategia delle varianti*, *Il percorso del* Furioso, and, most recently, *Ariosto: I metodi e i mondi possibili*.

Turning to English-language studies dealing strictly with Ariosto, Albert Russell Ascoli's *Ariosto's Bitter Harmony*, following up on recent readings of the *Furioso* as reflective of a larger political and cultural crisis, maintains that the poem both evades and explores a series of crises, including the historical-political upheaval following the invasion of the Italian peninsula, the loss of faith in humanistic education, and the perceived limitations of language. Several scholars have examined Ariosto's representations of women and debated his position in the *querelle des femmes.* According to Pamela Joseph Benson, Ariosto defends women and attempts to counter his reader's potential misogynistic views, especially through his depiction of Bradamante (*The Invention of the Renaissance Woman*). Deanna Shemek argues that Ariosto's (often conflicting) arguments taken from the *querelle des femmes* disclose a reality more complex than the binary oppositions furnished by the *querelle* tradition ("Of Women, Knights, Arms, and Love"). Shemek's examination of Angelica and Bradamante as powerful female characters who act outside traditional gender roles focuses on their threat to both social hierarchy and societal order (*Ladies Errant*). Valeria Finucci's *The Lady Vanishes* contains five chapters on the *Furioso*'s female characters, arguing that in Renaissance Italy's masculinist ideology women must comply with the social order by accepting their feminine role (e.g., Bradamante) or else be expelled (e.g., Angelica).

Essays on single episodes of the *Furioso* may be particularly useful for courses that assign only excerpts. Robert W. Hanning examines how Polinesso's duplicity sets in motion a wave of deception that contaminates the other characters in the Ginevra and Ariodante episode ("Sources of Illusion"). Franco Masciandaro links the story of Gabrina to the episode of Orlando's madness, highlighting how the inability or categorical refusal to go beyond conventions and appearances leads to disaster in an ever-changing world subject to fortune, irrationality, and evil ("Folly in the *Orlando Furioso*"). David Marsh provides a positive assessment of the much-maligned story of Ruggiero and Leone, offering possible reasons for its inclusion in the 1532 edition ("Ruggiero and Leone"). David Quint discusses how Brandimarte's death at Lipadusa foreshadows both Ruggiero's foretold early death and Orlando's demise at Roncevaux ("The Death of Brandimarte").

Essays on a variety of topics can be found in *Ariosto Today*, edited by Donald Beecher et al., and in the 2018 Italian issue of *Modern Language Notes*. *Phaethon's Children*, edited by Dennis Looney and Shemek, goes beyond Ariosto to look at the Ferrarese court.

## TORQUATO TASSO

Angelo Solerti's three-volume *Vita di Torquato Tasso* remains the most comprehensive source of documentation for Tasso's life, while Claudio Gigante's *Tasso* is both authoritative and highly engaging. Focusing on Tasso's own private letters, Laura Benedetti traces the poet's persona across centuries and cultures ("L'amante di Orazio impazzì per Eleonora") and delves into his strategies dealing with the *Liberata*'s prepublication censorship ("Le ragioni della poesia: Torquato Tasso e Silvio Antoniano"). Tasso's poetic letters can be found in *Lettere poetiche*, edited by Carla Molinari, while his entire epistolary is available in the five-volume *Lettere*, edited by Cesare Guasti.

In English, Margaret W. Ferguson offers insights about the irreparable damage that befell Tasso's immediate family following Charles V's attempt to establish the Spanish Inquisition in Naples in 1547 ("Torquato Tasso: The Trial of Conscience" in *Trials of Desire*). Instructors and students can also consult C. P. Brand's *Torquato Tasso.*

There is vastly more scholarship on the *Gerusalemme liberata* than the earlier *Rinaldo*, an intriguing romance epic that warrants closer critical attention. Two recent essays that situate the *Rinaldo* in its literary context are Riccardo Bruscagli, "La materia del *Rinaldo*" and Matteo Navone, "Intersezioni di generi nel *Rinaldo*."

A major collection of essays dedicated to Tasso's opus is the three-volume *Torquato Tasso e la cultura estense*, edited Gianni Venturi. Guido Baldassari, who has himself written extensively on the *Gerusalemme liberata*, edits the journal *Studi tassiani*. Sergio Zatti examines the tensions between unity and diversity in the *Liberata*, linking Tasso's positive depiction of the heterogeneous Muslim underdogs to the genre of romance in *L'uniforme cristiano e il multiforme pagano*, and he finds an anti-imperialistic thrust in Satan's canto 4 speech condemning the Bible's (and, by implication, Christianity's) alleged propagandistic rewriting of history ("Dalla parte di Satana"). Bruscagli, while disputing Zatti's thesis that Tasso identified emotionally with the pagan enemy, nevertheless argues that the poem exposes the contradictions and ambiguities of crusading ideology (*Stagioni della civiltà estense*).

Several critical studies have focused on Tasso's three Muslim female protagonists, including Kristen Olsen Murtaugh, "Erminia Delivered"; Walter Stephens, "Saint Paul among the Amazons"; Marilyn Migiel, *Gender and Genealogy*; Benedetti, *Sconfitta di Diana*; and Melinda J. Gough, "Tasso's Enchantress."

## BOIARDO, ARIOSTO, AND TASSO

A number of scholars have focused on at least two of the three Ferrarese crowns, whether independently or in relation to one another. In *Boiardismo ariostesco*, Sangirardi uncovers the *Furioso*'s extensive narrative and linguistic borrowings from the *Innamorato*, arguing that Ariosto's frame of reference is not the chivalric romance per se but the chivalric romance as Boiardo had conceived it. Bruscagli's *Stagioni della civiltà estense* and *Studi cavallereschi* contain chapters on Boiardo, Ariosto, and Tasso, as well as lesser-known authors. Essays in *Boiardo, Ariosto e i libri di battaglia*, edited by Andrea Canova and Paola Vecchi Galli, also extend critical inquiry to lesser-known chivalric works.

Marco Dorigatti traces the meaningful use of genealogy in the *Innamorato* and *Furioso* in "Rugiero and the Dynastic Theme." Ross's *Custom of the Castle*, which explores legal and cultural conceptions of custom in France, Italy, and England through variations of a recurring romance episode, contains chapters on both Boiardo (Ranaldo at Castle Cruel) and Ariosto (Bradamante at the Rocca di Tristano). Jane Everson has argued for the importance of the Matter of Rome and, in particular, Boccaccio's *Teseida* for the development of the romance epic in Italy (*The Italian Romance Epic*). In *The World beyond Europe*, Cavallo examines the representation of eastern Asia, the Middle East, and northern Africa in the *Innamorato* and *Furioso*, discussing the poems' imaginary sites and geographic locations in the context of current events as well as ancient, medieval, and Renaissance texts influential at the time.

A number of studies extend the focus from Boiardo to Tasso and beyond. Murrin's *History and Warfare*, with its attention on technological developments in weaponry and the brutal reality of contemporary warfare in the early cinquecento, contains essays on Italian, English, and Iberian epics, including Agramante's war from the *Innamorato*, the siege of Paris from the *Furioso*, and the selective use of crusading history in the *Liberata*. Looney's *Compromising the Classics* investigates creative imitation in the chivalric poems of Boiardo, Ariosto, and Tasso, highlighting their reelaboration of classical and medieval sources, in particular Herodotus, Virgil, Ovid, and Dante. Cavallo's *The Romance Epics of Boiardo, Ariosto, and Tasso* traces the three Ferrarese crowns from a politically engaged Boiardo to an individualistic Tasso, with additional chapters devoted to Francesco Cieco da Ferrara's *Mambriano*, Gian Giorgio Trissino's *Italia liberata dai Goti*, and Bernardo Tasso's *Amadigi*.

Among studies concerned specifically with Ariosto and Tasso, *Renaissance Transactions*, edited by Finucci, offers ten essays by Italian and North American critics on a range of topics related to the *Furioso* and *Liberata*, including issues of national and religious identity, genre and gender, social and legal anthropology, and the politics of dissimulation. Tobias Gregory's *From Many Gods to One* contains chapters on Ariosto's and Tasso's uses of

God as a character in their poems. Ascoli's *A Local Habitation and a Name* includes essays on Ariosto and Tasso previously published in scholarly journals. In addition, some of Zatti's writings have been published in English in *The Quest for Epic*.

### Between Ariosto and Tasso

Other studies expand our knowledge of a very populated chivalric landscape in the wake of the *Furioso*'s success. Part 2 of Marina Beer's *Romanzi di cavalleria* devotes attention to the wealth of chivalric narratives published in the sixteenth century, followed by appendixes on works published between 1470 and 1600. Guido Sacchi's *Fra Ariosto e Tasso* offers a comprehensive examination and evaluation of new chivalric poems published between 1532 and 1581, identifying twenty-seven authors who composed a total of forty-three original works. Stefano Jossa's *La fondazione di un genere* investigates lesser-known works that help illuminate the playing field between the *Furioso* and the *Liberata*, highlighting the political ideology inherent in the works themselves.

### Women as Readers and Writers of Chivalric Poetry

Groundbreaking essays by Finucci ("La scrittura epico-cavalleresca al femminile") in 1995 and Virginia Cox ("Women as Readers and Writers of Chivalric Poetry") in 1997 first brought together Tullia d'Aragona, Moderata Fonte, Margherita Sarrocchi, and Lucrezia Marinella as female authors of chivalric narratives. For additional scholarly attention, the best starting place may be the introductions to these authors' respective works in the recent Italian editions and English translations. In addition, for D'Aragona, see Allaire, "Tullia d'Aragona's *Il Meschino*"; for Fonte, see Stephen Kolsky, "Moderata Fonte's *Tredici Canti del Floridoro*," and Paola Malpezzi Price, *Moderata Fonte*.

### Additional Chivalric Authors

Andrea da Barberino was immensely popular in the fifteenth century and beyond, but his works are only now appearing in English (thanks to Max Wickert, as noted above). Allaire has written a monograph (*Andrea da Barberino*) and several articles on his opus (see especially "Portrayals of Muslims").

Cieco da Ferrara is an early example of a chivalric poet following Boiardo's model, but his *Mambriano* (1490) has not been edited since 1926. Jane Everson, who is currently preparing a critical edition, has published several articles on this poem. See, for example, "Les personnages feminins dans le *Mambriano.*"

Pietro Aretino may be better known for some of his other works, but he is also the author of four chivalric poems at various stages of completion. Essays or book chapters on Aretino's chivalric opus include Bruscagli, "L'Aretino e la tradizione cavalleresca" (*Studi cavallereschi* 119–44), Luca Degl'Innocenti, "Testo e immagini nei continuatori dell'Ariosto," and Federica Capoferri, "De' gesti antiqui una chimera."

Teofilo Folengo has recently been the subject of a volume of essays in Italian and English by scholars working in North America, entitled *Folengo in America* and edited by Massimo Scalabrini. Scalabrini's earlier work, *L'incarnazione del macaronico*, also deals extensively with Folengo (19–82). See also Maria Cristina Cabani, "L'*Orlandino* di Folengo e il genere cavalleresco" and additional bibliographical suggestions in Stefano Gulizia's essay in this volume.

## The Literary Debate over the Epic in the Cinquecento

The publication of the *Orlando furioso* set in motion widespread discussion over the poem's canonicity and the characteristics of the genre. Daniel Javitch's *Proclaiming a Classic* explores the editorial strategies that promoted the poem's status as a classic. Bernard Weinberg surveys the critical debates in which literati defended the relative merits of Ariosto and Tasso in *A History of Literary Criticism in the Italian Renaissance* (see ch. 19, "The Quarrel over Ariosto and Tasso" [2: 954–990]; and ch. 20, "The Quarrel over Ariosto and Tasso (Concluded)" [2: 991–1073]). Francesco Sberlati's *Il genere e la disputa* shows how early literary interpretation and reception of the *Furioso* corresponded to changes in cultural ideology during the Counter-Reformation.

Two important participants in the debate over epic in the latter sixteenth century—whose works are also available in English translation—are Giovambattista Giraldi Cinzio and Torquato Tasso himself. Giraldi Cinzio's *Discorso dei romanzi* has been edited by Laura Benedetti, Giuseppe Monorchio, and Enrico Musacchio, with an in-depth introduction, appendixes, and extensive bibliography. It is translated by Henry L. Snuggs as *Giraldi Cinthio on romances.* In *The Genesis of Tasso's Narrative Theory*, Lawrence F. Rhu has published a translation of Tasso's early theoretical writings (Tasso's letter to his readers prefacing *Il Rinaldo* [1562], *Discourses on the Art of Poetry* [c. 1562–65; published in 1587], and the "Allegory" of the *Gerusalemme liberata* [1575–76]), along with an ample introduction that uses these texts to interpret the poems of Ariosto, Tasso, Spenser, and Milton. Tasso's later theoretical treatise, *Discorsi del poema eroico*, is also available in English: *Discourses on the Heroic Poem*, translated by Mariella Cavalchini and Irene Samuel.

## Background Studies

There are many studies of court culture in Renaissance Italy that can be useful in understanding the historical context of the romance epic. Cesare Vasoli's *La cultura delle corti* deals with court culture more generally, while Marco Folin's *Rinascimento estense* focuses directly on Ferrara. Giulio Bertoni's *La biblioteca Estense e la cultura ferrarese* contains inventories of books from the Estense library during the Renaissance.

In English, the volume of essays *Italy in Crisis: 1494*, edited by Everson and Diego Zancani, reflects on the consequences for Italian society and letters of the 1494 French invasion of the peninsula. Gundersheimer's *Ferrara: The Style of a Renaissance Despotism* is still the most comprehensive study in English on the historical context of the Estense court.

For insights into the geopolitical situation that can help ground the discussion of transcultural encounters in the romance epic, of particular interest are Giovanni Ricci's *Ossessione turca* and *I turchi alle porte*, as well as Maria Pia Pedani's *Venezia porta d'Oriente*. In English, see Margaret Meserve's *Empires of Islam* and Ayesha Ramachandran's *The Worldmakers*. Monique O'Connell's "The Italian Renaissance in the Mediterranean" provides an excellent frame of reference for a number of recent studies in the field.

## Critical Anthologies

*Poetry Criticism: Excerpts from Criticism of the Works of the Most Significant and Widely Studied Poets of World Literature* has the following entries: "Matteo Maria Boiardo," "Ludovico Ariosto," "Tasso," and "Italian Epic Poetry" (volumes 180, 175, 170, and 186, respectively). These entries include a biographical essay, a primary bibliography, and an ample selection of full-text or excerpted critical studies in English.

## Reference Works

Several print and online reference works contain entries on poets, works, and topics connected to the Italian Renaissance romance epic, such as the ongoing *Dizionario Biografico degli Italiani* (http://www.treccani.it/biografie)—although it is rather dated for many authors—and the *Enciclopedia italiana* (http://www.treccani.it/enciclopedia).

In English, the online *Literary Encyclopedia* (www.litencyc.com) has recent profiles by scholars currently working in the field, with updated bibliographies, on the following individuals and works: Andrea da Barberino, Luigi Pulci, Matteo Maria Boiardo, *Orlando innamorato*, Ludovico Ariosto, *Orlando furioso*, Teofilo Folengo, Laura Terracina, Torquato Tasso, *Gerusalemme liberata*, Lucrezia Marinella, *L'Enrico*, Sicilian puppet theater, Giusto Lo Dico, and the puppeteer Agrippino Manteo.

### Glossaries and Rhyme Dictionaries

For a glossary of the *Innamorato*, see Domizia Trolli's *Il lessico dell'*Inamoramento de Orlando. The *Rimario diacronico dell'* Orlando furioso, a two-volume set and DVD edited by Cesare Segre and others, provides a list of rhyme words for all three editions. The DVD also contains a digital copy of the 1532 *Furioso* edited by Debenedetti and Segre.

## World Maps

Students will be able to find many important world maps online. For an index of late medieval maps (1300–1500), visit www.henry-davis.com/MAPS/LMwebpages/LML.html. Maps particularly relevant for mapping the Italian Renaissance romance epic are the Catalan Atlas (1375) at the Bibliothèque nationale de France; the Estense-Catalan world map (1450–60) at the Biblioteca Estense, Modena; Fra Mauro's world map (1459) at the Correr Museum, Venice; and the Cantino planisphere (1502) at the Biblioteca Estense, Modena. Piero Falchetta has undertaken a monumental study of Fra Mauro's map (*Fra Mauro's World Map*), while Ernesto Milano examines the Cantino planisphere in the context of other world maps (*La carta del Cantino*). In addition, Martin Waldseemüller's world map (1507), at the Library of Congress in Washington, D.C., has been the focus of a vast interactive Web project by the Museo Galileo in Florence (exhibits.museogalileo.it/waldseemuller/index.html). For the relation of maps to the romance epic, as well as further bibliography, see Stephen McCormick's essay in this volume.

## Web Sites

A digital humanities project spearheaded by Daniel Leisawitz (Muhlenberg College) has led to the in-progress *Orlando Furioso Atlas* (www.furiosoatlas.com), featuring a digitized text of the poem linked to an interactive map (Waldseemüller's 1507 *Universalis Cosmographia*) on which are plotted the journeys of dozens of characters. According to Leisawitz, the site is designed to explore and analyze the modalities, patterns, and characteristics of travel in the *Orlando furioso* and will eventually include extensive bibliographies and content from users across the globe.

Various Web sites offer resources on artistic representations and performance traditions. The digital archive *L'*Orlando furioso *e la sua tradizione in immagini* (www.orlandofurioso.org) allows users to examine and compare illustrations and paratextual apparatus from the principal sixteenth-century editions of the *Furioso* and includes an extensive section on artwork inspired by the poem ("Opere d'arte"). A new archive showing the *Furioso*'s influence on the editorial format of other chivalric poems is in progress (see Rizzarelli's essay in this volume for both projects). The site *eBOIARDO* (Epics of Boiardo and Other Italian Authors: A Research Database Online) contains videos of theatrical adaptations, Sicilian puppet theater, and Maggio epico performances, as well as materials and links related to musical adaptations, artistic representations, and relevant world maps (edblogs.columbia.edu/eboiardo). The MLA Commons group linked to the Web site *Materials for Teaching the Italian Romance Epic* (commons.mla.org/groups/materials-for-teaching-the-italian-romance-epic) is open to all MLA members to discuss the topic and post materials.

*Performing Medieval Narrative Today* (mednar.org) contains several examples of performances of chivalric narratives by students and professionals, under the genres of romance and epic. It is continuously updated with clips from performances by students in Evelyn Birge Vitz's New York University course entitled Acting Medieval Literature.

## Reception in the Arts

For Pulci and Boiardo, see the forthcoming volume on the reception of the *Morgante* and *Orlando innamorato* edited by Catelli and Rizzarelli. For an overview of Tasso's reception in art and music, see Wickert's appendix to his translation, *The Liberation of Jerusalem* (400–03). Two volumes offer essays (in French) focusing on Tasso's reception in the various arts: *La* Jérusalem délivrée *du Tasse*, edited by Giovanni Careri, covers painting, music, and ballet, while *Les belles infidèles de la* Jérusalem deliverée, edited by Raymond Abbrugiati and José Guidi, explores the *Liberata*'s female characters in painting, opera, and cinema. Additional resources can be found under the "Web Sites" section above.

## Visual Arts

Giovanni Prampolini's *Le "Storie di Orlando"* offers descriptions and extensive color illustrations of artwork inspired by the poems of Boiardo and Ariosto from the Renaissance to the twentieth century. Prampolini also edited a volume with the 150 drawings of the *Furioso* that Jean-Honoré Fragonard prepared in the 1780s (*Le favole dell'Ariosto*). An English-language edition of these drawings, with essays by Elizabeth Mongan, Philip Hofer, and Jean Seznec, is also available (Fragonard). A selection of the *Furioso* illustrations that Gustave Doré published in 1879 can be found in *Doré's Illustrations for Ariosto's* Orlando furioso and, along with those of other French artists, in the volume *Imaginaire de l'Arioste*, edited by Michel Jeanneret and Monica Preti-Hamard.

A number of edited volumes focusing on visual art that was based on the *Orlando furioso* have been published in recent years. "*Tra mille carte vive ancora*," edited by Lina Bolzoni, Serena Pezzini, and Giovanna Rizzarelli, offers essays on the poem's iconographical history. *L'Arioste et les Arts*, edited by Michel Paoli and Monica Preti, includes essays on the visual arts in Ferrara, illustrations of the *Furioso*, and the poem's presence in European art. *Le sorti d'Orlando*, edited by Daniela Caracciolo and Massimiliano Rossi, was followed by the monumental *L'*Orlando furioso *nello specchio delle immagini*, edited by Lina Bolzoni, with twenty essays and 515 images of artwork (as well as performances) inspired by Ariosto's poems.

Ariosto's extensive artistic reception continues to be explored. Federica Caneparo's *"Di molte figure adornato"* features the numerous fresco cycles based on the poem, many hitherto receiving scant or no critical attention. Christian Rivoletti's *Ariosto e l'ironia della finzione* traces the *Furioso*'s reception in European letters and art from the sixteenth century to Calvino and contains an extensive bibliography (405–13). Among older studies, see Cesare Gnudi's "L'Ariosto e le arti figurative."

In English, Rensselaer W. Lee's *Names on Trees* focuses on visual representations of the Angelica-Medoro love story by sixteenth- to nineteenth-century illustrators and painters in Italy and beyond. See in particular chapter 3, "Angelica" (13–27).

There are also several studies devoted to Tasso and the visual arts. Along with those mentioned above (under Reception in the Arts), instructors and students can consult Giovanni Careri's *La fabbrica degli affetti*; Elena Fumagalli, Massimiliano Rossi, and Riccardo Spinelli's edited volume *L'arme e gli amori*; and the Centro di studi tassiani's conference proceedings, *Torquato Tasso e le arti*. In addition, Jonathan Unglaub looks specifically at the importance of Tasso's poetics for Poussin's artistic production.

There is also a vast and only partially documented tradition of chivalric narratives in popular art, in particular the panels of Sicilian carts, the *cartelli* announcing puppet plays, and the puppets themselves. Marcella Croce's *Pupi carretti contastorie* has recently come out in English as *The Chivalric Folk Tradition in Sicily*. For art related to Sicilian puppet theater, also see below.

## Music

For a detailed account of the musical culture in Renaissance Ferrara, see Lewis Lockwood. For a brief overview that draws in part on Lockwood's findings, see Leeman Perkins. For the use of music in the *Orlando innamorato*, see Cesare Ruini. The romance epic had an extensive reception in the field of music, from madrigals to melodrama to opera. In addition to the contributions of Grant Herreid, Barbara Russano Hanning, and Chris Picicci in this volume, see Elise B. Jorgens, Maria Antonella Balsano, and Edward Milton Anderson for Ariosto, and see Elizabeth Siberry for Tasso.

## Performance Arts

The most famous theatrical adaptation is Luca Ronconi's 1969 *Orlando furioso*, which stages various first-person narratives simultaneously so as to create an interactive experience. In 1998 Enrico Messina and Alberto Nicolino created the two-man play, *Hruodlandus: Libera rotolata medioevale*, which has since been superseded by two separate one-man performances: Messina's *Orlando: Furiosamente solo rotolando* (a revised version of the original play) and Nicolino's subsequent *Orlando furioso raccontato dal mago Atlante* (a new play incorporating some scenes from the earlier one). Paolo Panaro has peformed the opening canto of the *Orlando innamorato*, "La follia di Orlando" from the *Orlando furioso*, and the battle of Clorinda and Tancredi from the *Gerusalemme liberata*, as well as a monologue based on Folengo's *Baldus*.

Cavallo rendered episodes from Boiardo's *Orlando innamorato* into a trilogy of plays, which were performed by American university students and Italian actors in Italy under the direction of Vittorio Capotorto (*Orlando innamorato in commedia*, *Il giardino di Falerina*, *Le isole lontane*). The first play was translated into English by Cavallo and performed in New York in 2006 (*Orlando in Love*). The project is described in Cavallo's documentary, *Orlando innamorato: Un cammino epico-teatrale*.

For excerpts from most of the above-cited dramatic pieces and others, see "Theatrical Adaptations" on the *eBOIARDO* Web site. For a fuller account of recent performances inspired by Ariosto, see Francesca Bortoletti. For Tasso in theater through the centuries, see Roberto Puggioni, *Torquato Tasso nel teatro moderno*, as well as his essay in this volume.

### Cinema

The success of Ronconi's theatrical experiment with the *Orlando furioso* led to a 113-minute cinematic version as well as a television miniseries of five sixty-minute episodes. The film version is available on DVD. I have found student opinions to be mixed: while some found it heavy and pretentious without capturing the spirit of Ariosto's original text, others were fascinated by its avant-garde innovations and theoretical sophistication. On this production, see Bernardi. For a fuller account of films inspired by Ariosto and Tasso, see Edoardo Ripari (114–20). For incorporating film into courses on the epic, see Picicci's essay in this volume.

## Popular and Folk Performance Traditions

### Sicilian *Opera dei Pupi* (Puppet Theater)

In its heyday, from the mid-nineteenth to mid-twentieth centuries, puppet theater companies performed a cycle of plays in daily *puntate* that took well over a year to complete. Today's *pupari* (puppeteers) have drastically reduced their repertoire to a few select plays designed to hold the attention of a public unfamiliar with the larger context of chivalric narrative. The three most frequently staged episodes are 1) the battle between Orlando and Rinaldo for Angelica from the *Orlando innamorato*; 2) the madness of Orlando from the *Orlando furioso*; and 3) the battle of Roncevaux (mostly from Lo Dico's prose retelling of Pulci's *Morgante*, but sometimes from a return to earlier sources). Scenes from puppet plays, interviews with puppeteers, and documentaries are available on *eBOIARDO*.

Serious scholarly studies of this tradition initiate with the Sicilian ethnographer Giuseppe Pitrè (1841–1916). The scholar who put the tradition on the critical map, however, was Antonio Pasqualino, author of several foundational studies of puppet theater in Italian and English, including *L'Opera dei Pupi*, *Le vie del cavaliere*, "Humor and Puppets," and "Transformations of Chivalrous Literature." Alessandro Napoli, a member of a prominent puppeteer family, extended Pasqualino's work to the Catanese tradition. His *Il racconto e i colori* explores two aspects of Catanese puppet theater: the illustrated *cartelli* that regularly announced puppet performances and the *storie* that comprised the episodes dramatized on stage.

In English, John McCormick's *The Italian Puppet Theater* devotes attention to Sicilian *opera dei pupi* and includes a chapter by Alessandro Napoli on the Catanese tradition. For the distinctly Sicilian aspects of the art, see M. Croce (mentioned above) and Michael Buonanno. For an approach to teaching the Italian romance epic through Sicilian puppet theater, see Cavallo, "Encountering Saracens." For the analysis of an original play by the Napoli family, see Cavallo, "L'*Oro dei Napoli*." For a comparison of Sicilian puppet theater and the epic *maggio* (discussed below), see Cavallo, "Where Have All the Brave Knights Gone?" or the slightly updated Italian version, "L'Opera dei pupi e il maggio epico." For a sampling of non-Christian characters and non-European places in both performance traditions, see Cavallo, "Boiardo and Ariosto in Contemporary Sicilian Puppet Theater."

### *Burattini* (Glove Puppets)

Although chivalric stories are naturally linked to Sicilian *opera dei pupi* with its puppets constructed in wood, covered with metal, and supported by iron rods, there is also evidence of the same chivalric repertory in glove puppet theaters (*teatri di burattini*) of northern Italy. The best known of these today, thanks to Pietro Porta's extensive documentation of the theater's history, is that of the Sarina family, especially Peppino Sarina of Tortona, in the province of Alessandria. A summary of sixty-five plays from 1907 can be found in Giuseppe Bonavoglia and Giuseppe Decarlini.

### Tuscan-Emilian Epic *Maggio* (Folk Opera)

The *maggio epico*, also called *maggio drammatico* to distinguish it from *maggi lirici* (springtime festival songs), is a form of folk opera native to the Tuscan-Emilian Apennines. Ariosto is the most prevalent author in the *maggio* tradition, with numerous plays based on either the entire *Orlando furioso* or selected episodes. Among the earliest documented *maggi* are two from 1808 based on Ariosto and Tasso: the first, found in the Reggio Emilia Apennines and entitled simply *Maggio datto 1808*, dramatizes the Leone and Ruggiero episode, while the second, performed in the province of Pistoia, is one of numerous versions of the *Gerusalemme liberata* by the same name (see Giannini 142). Today the *maggio epico* is performed mostly on Sunday afternoons during the summer in mountain towns in the provinces of Reggio Emilia, Modena, and Lucca.

There are two documentaries on the *maggio* tradition available on DVD: Cavallo's *Il maggio emiliano: ricordi, riflessioni, brani*, also available on *eBOIARDO*, and Allieta Melchioni's *Cantare il Maggio*. Many *maggio* scripts have been published by the Centro tradizioni popolari and the Municipality of Villa Minozzo and can be found, along with additional information, on their Web sites, www.centrotradizionipopolari.it and www.comune.villa-minozzo.re.it, respectively. Scenes from epic *maggi* (including Luca Sillari's *Orlando innamorato* and the anonymous *Rodomonte*), interviews with *maggerini*, and several epic *maggio* scripts are available on *eBOIARDO*.

Scholarship on the *maggio epico* has been primarily in Italian and from the perspective of popular traditions. Two fundamental volumes for the genre are *"Vengo l'avviso a dare,"* edited by Romolo Fioroni and Giorgio Vezzani, and *Il Maggio Drammatico*, edited by Tullia Magrini. For a comparison of the epic *maggio* and Sicilian puppet theater, see Cavallo's above-mentioned article, "Where Have All the Brave Knights Gone?" For a comparison of the Ariostean *Rodomonte* and the Carolingian *Roncisvalle* in historical context, see Cavallo, "National Political Ideologies and Local *Maggio* Traditions."

### *Cuntisti-Contastorie* and *Cantastorie* (Storytellers and Singers of Tales)

Scattered evidence attests to improvised retellings and verse recitations of the epics of Boiardo, Ariosto, Tasso, and other chivalric authors from the Renaissance to the twentieth century. For the early period, see Marco Villoresi, "'Stati atenti e quïeti et ascoltati'" (for Boiardo) and Camilla Cavicchi (for Ariosto). Pitrè did the most to document this tradition during the 1800s. Rajna ("I 'Rinaldi'") and Benedetto Croce both penned essays on the storytellers in Naples, commonly referred to as "Rinaldi." When the American ethnomusicologist Alan Lomax traveled through the Italian peninsula with Diego Carpitella in the 1950s, he recorded "Battle between Orlando and Rinaldo" in Palermo by the *cuntista* Roberto Genovese, which is now available as part of the Alan Lomax Collection on Rounder Records.

### *Poeti contadini* (Peasant Poets)

There is a long independent tradition of *poeti contadini*—farmers, shepherds, and manual laborers—singing epic poetry. In 1581 Montaigne reports the extemporaneous poetry of an illiterate farm woman from Bagni di Lucca whose uncle used to read Ariosto and other poets in her presence when she was young (cited in Kezich, *Poeti contadini* 40–41). Giovanni

Kezich's *I poeti contadini*, revisited in English as *Some Peasant Poets*, documents the tradition of singing improvised epic poetry in competitions in central Italy. The latter work provides transcriptions of stanzas in both the original Italian and English translation, allowing students to enter the spirit of this tradition by comparing the competing ottava rima verses or devising their own.

## Notes on Contributors

**Karina F. Attar** is assistant professor of Italian and director of the Italian undergraduate program in the Department of European Languages and Literatures at Queens College, City University of New York. She has written articles on interfaith and cross-cultural encounters in the novellas of Giovanni Boccaccio, Giovambattista Giraldi Cinzio, Pietro Fortini, and Masuccio Salernitano, and coedited, with Lynn Shutters, *Teaching Medieval and Early Modern Cross-Cultural Encounters* (2014). Her current book project is tentatively titled *Scandalous Liaisons: Jews, Christians, and Muslims in the Italian Novella*.

**Maria Bendinelli Predelli** is professor emerita of Italian studies at McGill University. Her publications include *Alle origini del Bel Gherardino*; *Piccone e poesia: La cultura dell'ottava nel poema d'emigrazione di un contadino lucchese*; and *Cantari e dintorni*. She recently edited *La "Struzione della Tavola Ritonda" (I Cantari di Lancillotto)* and the English translations of Antonio Pucci's *Gismirante* and *Madonna Leonessa*. Her edition of the *Cantari della Guerra di Pisa*, by Antonio Pucci, appeared in 2017.

**Bryan Brazeau** is senior teaching fellow in liberal arts at the University of Warwick, where he previously worked on the Aristotle in the Italian Vernacular project as a research fellow. He is working on a monograph entitled "Hero of the Day: The Development of Christian Epic in Sixteenth-Century Italy," which examines depictions of interiority in early modern Italian Christian epic, and is the editor of a forthcoming collection, *Beyond Aristotle's* Poetics *in the Italian Renaissance: New Directions in Criticism and Reception*. His articles and book reviews have appeared in *MLN*, *History of European Ideas*, *Renaissance Quarterly*, *Quaderni d'Italianistica*, and *California Italian Studies*.

**Jo Ann Cavallo,** professor and chair of the Department of Italian, Columbia University, is author of *The World beyond Europe in the Romance Epics of Boiardo and Ariosto*; *The Romance Epics of Boiardo, Ariosto, and Tasso: From Public Duty to Private Pleasure*; and *Boiardo's Orlando innamorato: An Ethics of Desire*. She is coeditor of *Fortune and Romance: Boiardo in America* and *Speaking Truth to Power from Medieval to Modern Italy*. Her articles focus on Italian authors from the medieval to the modern period, folk traditions that dramatize epic narratives, and early Christian and gnostic literature.

**Allison DeWitt** is a PhD candidate at Columbia University in the Department of Italian and the Institute for Comparative Literature and Society. Her dissertation focuses on the use of geography in Dante's *Divine Comedy*, specifically representations of the Islamic world. It will be accompanied by a digital map on Columbia's *Digital Dante* site, for which she is an assistant editor. She has written and presented on the use of digital tools for research and the classroom and has worked extensively with the Center for Teaching and Learning on graduate student pedagogical development.

**Marco Dorigatti** is lecturer in Italian language and literature at Oxford University and has published numerous articles on Boiardo, Ariosto, and the chivalric literature of the Renaissance. He has also written studies on the modern period, including works on Grazia Deledda, Sibilla Aleramo, Giorgio Bassani, and Giuseppe Dessì, and on the cinema of Ingmar Bergman and Michelangelo Antonioni. He has published the first critical edition of Ariosto's *Orlando furioso secondo la princeps del 1516* (2006).

**Susan Gaylard** is associate professor of Italian studies and affiliate faculty in art history at the University of Washington, Seattle. She completed her PhD in Italian Studies at the University of California, Berkeley, and her research and teaching focus on intersections between textual and material culture—from printed portraits to the fashion industry. Her first book is titled *Hollow Men: Writing, Objects, and Public Image in Renaissance Italy*; her current project is *Beautiful Monsters: Erasing Women from Renaissance Histories.*

**Patricia E. Grieve** is the Nancy and Jeffrey Marcus Professor in the Humanities at Columbia University. Her work includes *The Eve of Spain: Myths of Origins in the History of Christian, Muslim, and Jewish Conflict* (2009), *"Floire and Blancheflor" and the European Romance* (1997), and *Desire and Death in the Sentimental Romance, 1440–1550* (1987). Her current book projects include *The Traveling Tale: Curiosity, Knowledge and Social Relevance in Ancient, Medieval and Early Modern Storytelling* and *Blood/Lust: Cultural Exchange and Conflict in the Early Modern Mediterranean.*

**Stefano Gulizia** is a fellow at New Europe College and holds a grant at the Herzog August Bibliothek in Wolfenbüttel. He specializes in intellectual history and philosophy, particularly with regard to early modern science, collecting, and sixteenth-century print culture. He is completing *Domesticating Aristotelian Learning in Seventeenth-Century Padua*, a book on the information technology of Galileo's entourage. In 2018 he began a research project on the Mediterranean republic of letters, partially funded by the Andrew W. Mellon Foundation and by a grant from the University of California.

**Julia L. Hairston** is academic director of the University of California, Rome, part of the University of California Education Abroad Program, where she teaches Italian literature. In addition to articles on Machiavelli, Ariosto, and Alberti, she has published a bilingual edition of the poems and letters of Tullia d'Aragona and coedited *The Body in Early Modern Italy* as well as an essay collection on gender in early modern Rome for *I Tatti Studies*. Her current projects include coediting a bilingual edition of d'Aragona's *Meschino* for the Other Voice in Early Modern Europe series and an intellectual biography of d'Aragona.

**Barbara Russano Hanning** is professor emeritus of music at the City College of New York and the Graduate Center of the City University of New York. She is the author of a book on the beginnings of opera and of various articles on sixteenth- and seventeenth-century Italian music, iconography of music, and eighteenth-century French subjects. She currently teaches a doctoral course in baroque music at the Juilliard School.

**Morten Steen Hansen** is full-time lecturer at the University of Washington, Seattle. His first book is entitled *In Michelangelo's Mirror: Perino del Vaga, Daniele da Volterra, Pellegrino Tibaldi*. He is working on a gender and Islam in the Tuscan Seicento, from Giovanni da San Giovanni to Carlo Dolci. His research interests include word-image relationships, social history, gender and sexuality, and image theology.

**Grant Herreid,** an early music specialist, performs frequently on early reeds, brass, strings, percussion, and voice with the groups Piffaro, Hesperus, My Lord Chamberlain's Consort, ARTEK, Elm City Consort, and others. On the faculty at Yale University, he directs the Yale Collegium Musicum and is artistic and music director of the Yale Baroque Opera Project. He also directs the New York Continuo Collective and devotes much of his time to exploring the unwritten traditions of early music, including recitation of Italian epic verse, with the ensembles Ex Umbris and Ensemble Viscera.

**Julia M. Kisacky** is senior lecturer in Italian at Baylor University. She is the author of *Magic in Boiardo and Ariosto* and various articles on Boiardo and Ariosto. She has translated Isabella Andreini's *Mirtolla: A Pastoral*, the first pastoral by an Italian woman; Valeria Miani's *Celinda: A Tragedy*, the only known Italian Renaissance tragedy written by a woman; and Moderata Fonte's *Floridoro: A Chivalric Romance*. Her cotranslation of selected correspondence of the Venetian artist Rosalba Carriera is forthcoming.

**Stephen P. McCormick** is associate professor of French and Italian at Washington and Lee University. His publications include articles on digital humanities and medieval studies in North America, the manuscript tradition of *Huon d'Auvergne*, as well as cartography and epic in Florentine humanism and Andrea da Barberino's *Ugone d'Alvernia*. His current project proposes an interdisciplinary analysis of Italian epic with geography, exploration, and map-making in fifteenth-century Florence and Venice. He is also participating in team-produced digital edition and translation of *Huon d'Auvergne*, a project funded by the National Endowment for the Humanities.

**John C. McLucas** is professor of Italian and Latin at Towson University. He has published articles on the *Orlando furioso*, the diachronic dialogue between Ariosto and Calvino, Tasso's Clorinda, Tullia d'Aragona's *Guerrino*, and women and war in sixteenth-century Italian literature. He is also the author of *Italian Reports on America, 1493–1522: Accounts by Contemporary Observers*, a book-length translation of sixteenth-century Latin documents, and the editor of the "Baltimore" volume of *Olifant*. His translation of Tullia d'Aragona's *Il Meschino, altramente detto il Guerrino*, edited by Julia L. Hairston, is forthcoming.

**Gael Montgomery** was visiting assistant professor of Italian at Miami University from 2012 to 2017. Her research interests, in addition to the Italian romance epic, include gender and sexuality in medieval and Renaissance Italian and French literature, *verismo*, and Italian Jewish studies.

**Leslie Zarker Morgan** is professor of Italian and French at Loyola University Maryland. She is the author of numerous articles about Franco-Italian literature and its context, editor of *La Geste Francor: Chansons de geste of Ms. Marc. Fr. XIII (=256)*, as well as coeditor of *Approaches to Teaching the* Song of Roland; *Epic Studies: Acts of the Seventeenth International Congress of the Société Rencesvals for the Study of Romance Epic, July 22–28, 2006*; *Franco-Italian and Italian Romance Epic*; and *Dante: Summa Medievalis*. She has translated Ariosto's *Five Cantos* and is currently completing an online team edition and translation of the Franco-Italian *Huon d'Auvergne*.

**Andrea Moudarres** is assistant professor of Italian at the University of California, Los Angeles. His forthcoming book, *The Enemy in Italian Renaissance Epic: Images of Hostility from Dante to Tasso*, examines the question of violence in internal and external forms of hostility. He is coeditor of two volumes: *New Worlds and the Italian Renaissance: Contribution to the History of European Intellectual Culture* (2012); and *Luigi Pulci in Florence and Beyond: New Perspectives on his Poetry and Influence* (2017). He has also published articles on Dante, Islam in quattrocento humanism, Machiavelli, Tasso, and Vico.

**Stefano Nicosia** completed his PhD in Italianistica in 2012 at Palermo University. He is the author of *La funzione Morgante: Persistenze e variazioni nel genere comico in ottave tra Cinque e Settecento* and *Ma tu che lavoro fai? Storie di editori* (2013), as well as articles on Italian literature. His interests include burlesque poetry, Italian romance, giants, and rewriting poetics. He is currently a high school teacher in Italy.

**Chris Picicci** is associate professor of Italian and director of Italian studies at Colorado State University, Pueblo, where he has taught since 2008. He received his PhD in romance languages and literatures at the University of Oregon, specializing in Italian and Spanish Renaissance epic poetry. His current research focuses on the intertextuality of the Italian epic tradition in Spanish epics of the New World. Other aspects of his scholarship include the impact of Petrarchan lyric, the distinction between author and narrator, and a broad range of topics on humanism and epos in Renaissance literature.

**Andrea Privitera** is a PhD candidate in comparative literature at the University of Western Ontario, in cotutelage with the University of Padua. He holds a *laurea triennale* and a *laurea specialistica* from the University of Padua and completed part of his master's studies at Charles University in Prague, Czech Republic. His research interests include Italian literature (especially Boccaccio, Boiardo, Ariosto, and Pasolini), literary theory, and media studies. His in-progress dissertation investigates romance from the perspective of Deleuze and Guattari's minor literature in *Inamoramento de Orlando*.

**Roberto Puggioni** is professor of Italian literature at the University of Cagliari. He is the editor of *Angelo Ingegneri, Danza di Venere* and author of *Ricerche tassiane*; *Lettere sul teatro: Percorsi nell'epistolografia scenica europea tra XVI e XIX secolo*; *D'annunziana: Un itinerario nella parola dell'Imaginifico*; *Drammaturgie: Generi teatrali e esperienze sceniche tra Cinquecento e Seicento*; and *Treni dannunziani*. He has edited the forthcoming volumes *Tasso nel teatro moderno* and *Filologia, Teatro, Spettacolo*. His current projects include allegory and theater, the Tuscan-Emilian epic *maggio*, landscape studies on modern Italian literature, and Grazia Deledda.

**Joshua Reid** is assistant professor of early modern studies in English in the Department of Literature and Language at East Tennessee State University. He has published on translation studies and the English Renaissance, Dantean portraiture, and English Renaissance translations of the *Orlando furioso* and *Gerusalemme liberata*. His current book project, *The Italian Romance Epic in English, 1590–1600*, will provide a comprehensive scholarly edition of the full and partial English Renaissance translations of Italian romance epics. He is a general editor for The Manchester Spenser, Manchester University Press's monograph series on the life and works of Edmund Spenser.

**Bernd Renner** is professor of modern languages and literatures at the City University of New York, Brooklyn College and the Graduate Center. He is the author of "*Difficile est saturam non scribere*"*: L'Herméneutique de la satire rabelaisienne*, editor of *"La Satire dans tous ses états": Le meslange satyricque à la Renaissance française*, and coeditor of *Illustrations inconscientes: Écritures de la Renaissance. Mélanges offerts à Tom Conley*. He is currently directing the *Brill Companion to Rabelais*, editing a critical edition of the "5e Livre apocryphe de Pantagruel (1549)," and working on a book on Renaissance satire from Pathelin to Du Bellay.

**Giovanna Rizzarelli** is assistant professor in Italian literature at the Scuola Normale Superiore in Pisa. She is the author of *"Se le parole si potessero scorgere": I* Mondi *di Doni tra Italia e Francia*, editor of *I* Marmi *di Anton Francesco*

*Doni*, and coeditor of *"Tra mille carte vive ancora": Ricezione del Furioso tra immagini e parole*; *L'ospite del libro: Sguardi sull'ospitalità*; and *C'è un lettore in questo testo? Rappresentazioni della lettura nella letteratura italiana*. She coedited, with Carlo Alberto Girotto, the critical edition of Doni's *Marmi* (2017). Her current projects include the literary representations of reading and readers in Italian literature, a monograph on the relation between words and images in illustrated editions of fifteenth- and sixteenth-century chivalric poems, and a coedited special issue of *Italian Studies* on the reception of Pulci's *Morgante* and Boiardo's *Inamoramento* from the end of the fifteenth century to the present.

**Charles S. Ross** is professor of English and director of the Comparative Literature Program at Purdue University. His books include the first-ever translation into English of Matteo Maria Boiardo's *Orlando innamorato*; *The Custom of the Castle from Malory to Macbeth*; *Elizabethan Literature and the Law of Fraudulent Conveyance*; a verse translation of Statius's *Thebaid*; *Fortune and Romance* (with Jo Ann Cavallo); *Lectura Dantis: Inferno* and *Purgatorio* (with Allen Mandelbaum and Anthony Oldcorn); *Shakespeare in Hollywood, Asia, and Cyberspace* (with Alexa Huang); and a restored and modernized edition of Sir Philip Sidney's *The Countess of Pembroke's Arcadia* (with Joel Davis, 2017).

**Janet Levarie Smarr** is professor of theater and Italian studies at the University of California, San Diego. She previously taught comparative literature at the University of Illinois, Urbana-Champaign, for twenty years. She is the author of *Italian Renaissance Tales*; *Boccaccio and Fiammetta*; *Boccaccio's Eclogues*; *Joining the Conversation: Dialogues by Renaissance Women*; and *Louise-Geneviève Gillot de Sainctonge: Dramatizing Dido, Circe, and Griselda*. She is also coeditor of *Boccaccio: A Critical Guide to the Complete Works*. Her recent projects include dramatizations of the Griselda story, women's versions of the Griselda story (not necessarily drama), and English theater and the *Decameron*.

**Maria Galli Stampino** is professor of Italian at the University of Miami, where she also serves as senior associate dean of academic affairs in the college of arts and sciences. She is the author of *Staging the Pastoral* and coeditor of the essay collections *Early Modern Habsburg* and *In Dialogue with the Other Voice in Sixteenth-Century Italy*. She edited both the critical edition of Lucrezia Marinella's *L'Enrico, ovvero Bisanzio acquistato* and her translation *Enrico; or, Byzantium Conquered: A Heroic Poem*. She is currently coediting and cotranslating Marinella's *Amore innamorato et impazzato*.

**Walter Stephens** is Charles S. Singleton Professor of Italian studies at Johns Hopkins University. His publications include *Giants in Those Days: Folklore, Ancient History, and Nationalism* and *Demon Lovers: Witchcraft, Sex, and* *the Crisis of Belief*, as well as the coedited essay collection *The Body in Early Modern Italy*. His current projects are an edition and translation of Gianfrancesco Pico's *Strix (The Witch)* and *De imaginatione*, a book on the love and lore of writing from Babylon to the electronic age, and a coedited volume, *Literary Forgery in Early Modern Europe, 1450–1800* (2019).

**Phillip John Usher** is associate professor of French and comparative literature at New York University. He is the author, translator, or editor of seven volumes. Regarding epic, he has published a translation of Ronsard's *Franciad* (2010), *Epic Arts in Renaissance France* (2014), and *L'aède et le géographe* (2018). His current research is featured on the blog *The Humanist Anthropocene* (thehumanistanthropocene.weebly.com/).

**Evelyn (Timmie) Birge Vitz** is professor of French at New York University. She has worked extensively on performance of medieval narrative, publishing widely on the issue. She codirects three performance Web sites, among them *Performing Medieval Narrative Today: A Video Showcase* (mednar.org/), on which hundreds of video clips from medieval narratives, many drawn from her course Acting Medieval Literature, are available. She is currently working on a book on testosterone in medieval literature. Her book *Invitations à la performance de récits français médiévaux: Virtuosité, spectacle, érotisme* will appear from Editions Paradigme in 2018.

# Works Cited


Abbrugiati, Raymond, and José Guidi, editors. *Les belles infidèles de la* Jérusalem deliverée*: La fortune du poème du Tasse, XVIe–XXe siècle.* Publications de l'université de Provence, 2004.

Abelli, Cesare. *La Gierusaleme liberata.* Tebaldini, 1626.

Acocella, Joan. "In the Blood: Why Do Vampires Still Thrill?" *The New Yorker*, 16 Mar. 2009, www.newyorker.com/magazine/2009/03/16/in-the-blood.

Agnelli, Giuseppe, and Giuseppe Ravegnani. *Annali delle edizioni ariostee con cxiv tavole fuori testo.* Zanichelli, 1933. 2 vols.

Akbari, Suzanne Conklin. *Idols in the East: European Representations of Islam and the Orient, 1100–1450.* Cornell UP, 2009.

Allaire, Gloria. *Andrea da Barberino and the Language of Chivalry.* U of Florida P, 1997.

———. "Cantare." *Medieval Italy: An Encyclopedia*, edited by Christopher Kleinhenz et al., Routledge, 2004, pp. 370–72.

———, editor. *The Italian Novella.* Routledge, 2003.

———. "Portrayals of Muslims in Andrea da Barberino's *Guerrino il Meschino.*" *Medieval Christian Perceptions of Islam: A Book of Essays*, edited by John Victor Tolan, Garland, 1996, pp. 243–69.

———. "Tullia d'Aragona's *Il Meschino* as Key to a Reappraisal of Her Work." *Quaderni d'Italianistica*, vol. 16, no. 1, 1995, pp. 33–50.

Allaire, Gloria, and F. Regina Psaki, editors. *The Arthur of the Italians: The Arthurian Legend in Medieval Italian Literature and Culture.* U of Wales P, 2014.

Anceschi, Giuseppe, editor. *Il Boiardo e la critica contemporanea: Atti del convegno di studi su Matteo Maria Boiardo.* Olschki, 1970.

Anceschi, Giuseppe, and Tina Matarrese, editors. *Il Boiardo e il mondo Estense nel Quattrocento.* Antenore, 1998. 2 vols.

Anconetani, Raffaella. "Il lessico della follia nell'*Orlando furioso.*" *Bollettino di italianistica*, new series, vol. 6, no. 1, 2009, pp. 15–58.

Anderson, Edward Milton. *Ariosto, Opera, and the Seventeenth Century: Evolution in the Poetics of Delight.* Olschki, forthcoming.

Andrea da Barberino. *Aspramont.* The Royal House of France (I Reali di Francia) *and Related Medieval Romances*, translated by Max Wickert, *Outriders Poetry Project*, www.outriderspoetryproject.com/uploads/4/6/1/4/4614234/_the_royal_house_of_france.pdf, pp. 231–436.

———. *L'Aspramonte.* Edited by Luigi Cavalli, Fulvio Rossi, 1972.

———. *L'Aspramonte, romanzo cavalleresco inedito.* Edited by Marco Boni, Palmaverde, 1951.

———. *Il Guerrin Meschino: Edizione critica secondo l'antica vulgata fiorentina.* Edited by Mauro Cursietti, Antenore, 2005.

———. *I Reali di Francia.* Edited by Giuseppe Vandelli and Giovanni Gamberin, Laterza, 1947.

———. *I Reali di Francia.* Introduced by Aurelio Roncaglia, notes by Fabrizio Beggiato, Gherardo Casini Editore, 1987.

———. *The Royal House of France.* The Royal House of France (I Reali di Francia) *and Related Medieval Romances*, translated by Max Wickert, *Outriders Poetry Project*, www.outriderspoetryproject.com/uploads/4/6/1/4/4614234/_the_royal_house_of_france.pdf, pp. 7–230.

Angiolino, Andrea, and Gianluca Meluzzi. Orlando furioso*: Gioco di ruolo dei paladini di Re Carlo.* Rose and Poison, 2002.

d'Aragona, Tullia. "Dialogo della Signora Tullia d'Aragona della infinità di amore." *Trattati d'amore del Cinquecento.* Edited by Giuseppe Zonta, Laterza, 1912, pp. 185–248.

———. *Dialogue on the Infinity of Love.* Edited and translated by Rinaldina Russell and Bruce Merry, U of Chicago P, 1997.

———. *Il Meschino, altramente detto il Guerrino. Fatto in ottava rima dalla signora Tullia d'Aragona. Opera nella quale si veggono e intendono le parti principali di tutto il mondo, e molte altre dilettevolissime cose, da essere sommamente care ad ogni sorte di persona di bello ingegno.* Gio. Battista et Melchior Sessa, Fratelli, 1560.

———. *Il Meschino detto il Guerrino.* Venice: Giuseppe Antonelli, 1839.

———. *The Poems and Letters of Tullia d'Aragona and Others.* Translated by Julia L. Hairston, Iter / Centre for Reformation and Renaissance Studies, 2014.

———. *Sweet Fire: Tullia d'Aragona's Poetry of Dialogue and Selected Prose.* Translated by Elizabeth A. Pallitto, George Braziller, 2005.

———. *The Wretch, Otherwise Known as Guerrino: A Bilingual Edition.* Edited by Julia L. Hairston, annotated by Julia L. Hairston and John C. McLucas, translated by John C. McLucas, Iter Press / Arizona Center for Medieval and Renaissance Studies, forthcoming.

Aretino, Pietro. *Poemi cavallereschi.* Edited by Danilo Romei, Salerno Editrice, 1995.

Ariosto, Ludovico. *Cinque canti.* Edited by Lanfranco Caretti, Einaudi, 1977.

———. *I cinque canti.* Ariosto, *Opere minori* [Segre], pp. 581–754.

———. *Cinque canti di un nuovo libro di M. Ludovico Ariosto.* Edited by Luigi Firpo, UTET, 1963.

———. *Cinque canti: Five Cantos.* Translated by Leslie Zarker Morgan, Garland, 1992.

———. *Cinque canti: Five Cantos.* Translated by Alexander Sheers and David Quint, U of California P, 1996.

———. *I frammenti autografi dell'* Orlando furioso. Edited by Santorre Debenedetti, Chiantore, 1937.

———. *I frammenti autografi dell'* Orlando furioso. Edited by Santorre Debenedetti, preface by Cesare Segre, Edizioni di Storia e Letteratura, 2010.

———. *Opere minori.* Edited by Cesare Segre, Ricciardi, 1954.

———. *Orlando furioso.* Edited by Emilio Bigi, Rusconi, 1982. 2 vols.

———. *Orlando furioso.* Edited by Lanfranco Caretti, Einaudi, 1966.

———. *Orlando furioso.* Edited by Edoardo Sanguineti and Marcello Turchi, *Biblioteca della letteratura italiana*, www.letteraturaitaliana.net/pdf/Volume_4/t325.pdf. Accessed 14 Dec. 2015.

———. *Orlando furioso*. Edited by Cesare Segre, Mondadori, 2004. Originally published in *Tutte le opere di Ludovico Ariosto*, vol. 1, Mondadori, 1964.
———. *Orlando furioso*. Translated by Guido Waldman, Oxford UP, 2008.
———. *Orlando furioso*. *LiberLiber*, 2010, www.liberliber.it/audiolibri/a/ariosto/index.php.
———. *Orlando furioso: A New Verse Translation*. Translated by David R. Slavitt, Belknap Press, 2009.
———. *Orlando furioso: A Selection*. Edited by Pamela Waley, Manchester UP, 1975.
———. *Orlando furioso di Ludovico Ariosto secondo le stampe del 1516, 1521, 1532 rivedute dall'Autore*. Edited by Filippo Ermini, Società Filologica Romana, 1909–13. 3 vols.
———. *Orlando furioso di messer Ludovico Ariosto*. Nicolo d'Aristotile detto Zoppino, 1536.
———. *Orlando furioso di m. Ludovico Ariosto*. Gabriele Giolito de Ferrari, 1542.
———. *Orlando furioso di m. Ludovico Ariosto*. Giovan Andrea Valvassori, 1553.
———. *Orlando furioso di m. Ludovico Ariosto*. Vincenzo Valgrisi, 1556.
———. *Orlando furioso di m. Ludovico Ariosto*. Francesco de Franceschi, 1584.
———. Orlando furioso *e* Cinque canti. Edited by Remo Ceserani and Sergio Zatti, UTET, 1997. 2 vols.
———. *Orlando furioso in English Heroical Verse*. Translated by John Harington, edited by Robert McNulty, Oxford UP, 1972.
———. *Orlando furioso secondo la princeps del 1516*. Edited by Marco Dorigatti, with Gerarda Stimato, Olschki, 2006.
———. *Orlando furioso secondo l'edizione del 1532 con le varianti delle edizioni del 1516 e del 1521*. Edited by Santorre Debenedetti and Cesare Segre, Commissione per i testi di lingua, 1960.
———. *Orlando furioso: The Frenzy of Orlando: A Romantic Epic*. Translated by Barbara Reynolds, Penguin, 1975–77. 2 vols.
———. *Orlando furioso traduzido en romance castellano*. Translated by Jerónimo de Urrea. University of Barcelona, stel.ub.edu/orlando/.
———. *The Satires of Ludovico Ariosto: A Renaissance Autobiography*. Translated by Peter DeSa Wiggins, Ohio UP, 1976.
———. *Tutte le opere di Ludovico Ariosto*. Edited by Cesare Segre, vol. 1, Mondadori, 1964.
———. "An Unknown English Translation from Ariosto: The Landlord's Tale, 1708." *Translation and Literature*, vol. 11, no. 2, Autumn, 2002, pp. 206–36.
Ascoli, Albert Russell. *Ariosto's Bitter Harmony: Crisis and Evasion in the Italian Renaissance*. Princeton UP, 1987.
———. *A Local Habitation and a Name: Imagining Histories in the Italian Renaissance*. Fordham UP, 2011.
*Aspramonte: Poema del Quattrocento*. Edited by Carmelina Sicari, Nuovo Umanesimo, 2003.
*Aspremont: Chanson de geste du XII*[e] *siècle*. Translated and edited by François Suard, Champion, 2008.
Attar, Karina F. "Genealogy of a Character: A Reading of Giraldi's Moor." *Visions of Venice in Shakespeare*, edited by Shaul Bassi and Laura Tosi, Ashgate, 2011, pp. 47–64.

———. "Muslim-Christian Encounters in Masuccio Salernitano's *Novellino*." *Medieval Encounters: Jewish, Christian and Muslim Culture in Confluence and Dialogue*, vol. 11, no. 1–2, Brill Academic Publishers, 2005, pp. 71–100.

Babb, Lawrence. *The Elizabethan Malady: A Study of Melancholia in English Literature from 1580 to 1642*. Michigan State UP, 1965.

Bacon, Roger. *The Opus Majus of Roger Bacon*. Edited by Robert Belle Burke, U of Pennsylvania P, 1928. 2 vols.

Bailey, Matthew. "Roland in Spain." Kibler and Morgan, pp. 109–14.

Bakhtin, Mikhail. "From the Prehistory of Novelistic Discourse." *The Dialogic Imagination*, translated by Caryl Emerson and Michael Holquist, U of Texas P, 1981, pp. 41–83.

———. *Rabelais and His World*. Translated by Hélène Iswolsky, Indiana UP, 1984.

Baldassarri, Guido, editor. *Quasi un picciolo mondo: Tentativi di codificazione del genere epico nel Cinquecento*. Edizioni Unicopli, 1982.

Balduino, Armando. "Letteratura canterina." *Boccaccio, Petrarca e altri poeti del Trecento*, Olschki, 1984, pp. 57–92.

———. "Le misteriose origini dell'ottava rima." Picone and Bendinelli Predelli, pp. 25–47.

Balsano, Maria Antonella, editor. *L'Ariosto, la musica, i musicisti*. Olschki, 1981.

Bandello, Matteo. *Le novelle del Bandello. Tutte le opere di Matteo Bandello*, edited by Francesco Flora, Mondadori, 1972.

———. *The Novels of Matteo Bandello*. Translated by John Payne, Villon Society, 1890.

Baretti, Giuseppe Marco Antonio. *An Account of the Manners and Customs of Italy*. London, 1769.

Barini, Giorgio, editor. *Cantari cavallereschi dei secoli XV e XVI*. Romagnoli dall'Acqua, 1905. *Internet Archive*, archive.org/details/cantaricavallere00bariuoft.

Bédier, Joseph. *Les légendes épiques: Recherches sur la formation des chansons de geste*. 3rd ed., Champion, 1926–29. 4 vols.

Beecher, Donald, et al., editors. *Ariosto Today: Contemporary Perspectives*. Toronto UP, 2003.

Beer, Marina. *Romanzi di cavalleria: Il "Furioso" e il romanzo italiano del primo Cinquecento*. Bulzoni, 1987.

Bendinelli Predelli, Maria. "Arthurian Material in Italian *cantari*." Allaire and Psaki, pp. 105–20.

———. *Cantari e dintorni*. Euroma–La Goliardica, 1999.

———. "Italian Cantari." *Oxford Bibliographies*, 2016, www.oxfordbibliographies.com/view/document/obo-9780195396584/obo-9780195396584-0199.xml.

———, editor. *La struzione della tavola ritonda (I cantari di Lancillotto)*. Società Editrice Fiorentina, 2015.

———. "The Textualization of Early Italian *Cantari*." *Textual Cultures of Medieval Italy*, edited by William Robins, U of Toronto P, 2011, pp. 145–64.

Benedetti, Laura. "L'amante di Orazio impazzì per Eleonora: Avventure e sventure del personaggio Tasso attraverso i secoli." *Italica*, vol. 75, no. 2, 1998, pp. 178–91.

———. "Le ragioni della poesia: Torquato Tasso e Silvio Antoniano." *Speaking Truth to Power from Medieval to Modern Italy*. Special issue of *Annali d'italianistica*, edited by Jo Ann Cavallo and Carlo Lottieri, vol. 34, 2016, pp. 243–59.

———. *Sconfitta di Diana: Un percorso per la* Gerusalemme liberata. Longo, 1996.

Bennett, Philip E. "Origins of the French Epic: The *Song of Roland* and Other French Epics." Kibler and Morgan, pp. 57–65.

Bensi, Mario, editor. *La canzone di Orlando*. Translated by Renzo LoCascio, introduced by Cesare Segre, BUR / Rizzoli, 1985.

Benson, Pamela Joseph. *The Invention of the Renaissance Woman: The Challenge of Female Independence in the Literature and Thought of Italy and England*. Pennsylvania State UP, 1992.

Berchem, Jacquet de. *Primo, secondo et terzo libro del capriccio*. Gardano, 1561.

Bernardi, Sandro. "From Poem to Theatre to Cinema: Luca Ronconi's *Orlando furioso*." Beecher, pp. 195–210.

Bertoni, Giulio. *La biblioteca Estense e la cultura ferrarese*. Ermanno Loescher, 1903.

Bianchi, Alessandro, and Rinaldo Rinaldi, editors. *Torquato Tasso*. UNICOPLI, 2011.

Bigazzi, Roberto. "Le novelle del *Furioso*." *Riscrittura Intertestualità Transcodificazione*: *Personaggi e scenari*, edited by Emanuella Scarano and Donatella Diamanti, Tipografia Editrice Pisana, 1994, pp. 47–57.

Bini, Mauro, editor. *Antichi planisferi e portolani: Modena, Biblioteca Estense Universitaria*. Y. Press, 2004.

Boccaccio, Giovanni. *Corbaccio*. Edited by Giorgio Padoan. *Tutte le opere di Giovanni Boccaccio*, edited by Vittore Branca, vol. 5.2, Mondadori, 1994, pp. 413–614.

———. *The* Corbaccio*; or, The Labyrinth of Love*. Translated and edited by Anthony Cassell, rev. ed., MRTS, 1993.

———. *Decameron*. Edited by Vittore Branca, Utet, 1956.

———. *Decameron*. Translated and edited by G. H. McWilliam, Penguin Books, 1972.

———. *Il Filocolo*. *Decameron, Filocolo, Ameto, Fiammetta*, edited by Enrico Bianchi et al., Ricciardi, 1952, pp. 767–899.

———. *Teseida, delle nozze d'Emilia*. Edited by Aurelio Roncaglia, G. Laterza and figli, 1941.

———. *Theseid of the Nuptials of Emilia*. Translated by Vincenzo Traversa, Peter Lang, 2002.

Bodel, Jean. *La chanson des Saisnes*. Droz, 1989.

Boiardo, Matteo Maria. *Boiardo*. Edited by Jo Ann Cavallo and Corrado Confalonieri, Unicopli, 2018.

———. *L'inamoramento de Orlando*. Edited by Antonia Tissoni Benvenuti and Cristina Montagnani, *Opere*, vol. 1, Riccardo Ricciardi, 1999. 2 vols.

———. *Orlando innamorato*. Edited by Riccardo Bruscagli, Einaudi, 1995. 2 vols.

———. *Orlando innamorato*. Translated by Charles S. Ross, U of California P, 1989.

———. *Orlando innamorato*. Edited by Aldo Scaglione, *Biblioteca della letteratura italiana*, www.letteraturaitaliana.net/pdf/Volume_3/t320.pdf. Accessed 14 Dec. 2015.

———. *Orlando innamorato; L'inamoramento de Orlando*. Edited by Andrea Canova, Rizzoli, 2011. 2 vols.

———. *Orlando innamorato: Orlando in Love*. Translated by Charles S. Ross, Parlor Press, 2004.

———. *Selections from Boiardo's* Orlando innamorato. Translated by Mark Staebler, Peter Lang, 1989. American University Studies, Series 2: Romance Languages and Literature 101.

Boiardo, Matteo Maria, and Francesco Berni. *Orlando innamorato di Matteo Maria Boiardo rifatto da Francesco Berni.* Edited by Severino Ferrari and Giovanni Nencioni, Sansoni, 1971. Originally published by Severino Ferrari and Giuseppe Albini, Sansoni, 1911.

Boitani, Piero. *The Shadow of Ulysses: Figures of a Myth.* Translated by Anita Weston, Clarendon Press, 1994.

Bolzoni, Lina, editor. *L'* Orlando furioso *e la sua tradizione in immagini.* www.orlandofurioso.org.

———, editor. *L'* Orlando furioso *nello specchio delle immagini.* Istituto della Enciclopedia Italiana fondata da Giovanni Treccani, 2014.

———. "L'*Orlando furioso* nello specchio delle immagini: Teatri della memoria e giochi fra Cinquecento e Novecento." Parmiggiani, pp. 305–13.

Bolzoni, Lina, et al., editors. *"Tra mille carte vive ancora": Ricezione del* Furioso *tra immagini e parole.* Maria Pacini Fazzi, 2010.

Bonavoglia, Giuseppe, and Giuseppe Decarlini. *Album Sarina.* Lions Club Tortona, 1990.

Bortoletti, Francesca. "La fortuna dell'*Orlando furioso* nelle arti performative: Scenario italiano." Bolzoni, *L'*Orlando furioso, pp. 689–724.

Boscolo, Claudia. *L'*Entrée d'Espagne: *Context and Authorship at the Origins of the Italian Chivalric Epic.* Oxford, 2017.

Braden, Gordon. "Edward Fairfax and the Translation of Vernacular Epic." *Tudor Translation*, edited by Fred Schurink, Palgrave Macmillan, 2011, pp. 161–74.

———. "Non-dramatic Verse: Epic Kinds." *The Oxford History of Literary Translation in English: Volume 2, 1550–1660*, edited by Gordon Braden et al., Oxford UP, 2010, pp. 167–93.

Bradley-Cromey, Nancy. *Authority and Autonomy in* L'Éntrée d'Espagne. Garland, 1993.

Bragaglia, Carlo, director. *La Gerusalemme liberata* [*The Mighty Crusaders*]. Italian screenplay by Sandro Continenza, English translation by Annalena Limentani and Frederica Nutter, MAX Film, 1958.

Branca, Vittore. "Nostalgie tardogotiche e gusto del fiabesco nella tradizione narrativa dei cantari." *Studi di varia umanità in onore di Francesco Flora*, Mondadori, 1963, pp. 88–108.

Brand, Charles P. "Ariosto's Continuation of the *Orlando innamorato.*" *Cultural Aspects of the Italian Renaissance: Essays in Honour of Paul Oskar Kristeller*, edited by Cecil H. Clough, Manchester UP, 1976, pp. 377–85.

———. *Ludovico Ariosto: A Preface to the* Orlando furioso. Edinburgh UP, 1974.

———. *Torquato Tasso: A Study of the Poet and His Contribution to English Literature.* Cambridge UP, 1965.

Brant, Sebastian. *The Ship of Fools.* Edited by Edwin H. Zeydel, Dover Publications, 2017.

Bredekamp, Horst. *Vicino Orsini und der heilige Wald von Bomarzo: Ein Fürst als Künstler und Anarchist.* Werner, 1985.

Bregoli Russo, Mauda. "L'astrologia, l'*Innamorato* del Boiardo e il *Milione* di Marco Polo." *Studi e problemi di critica testuale*, vol. 30, 1985, pp. 41–49.

Bright, Timothy. *A Treatise of Melancholie.* 1586. Columbia UP, 1940.

Brignole Sale, Anton Giulio. *I due anelli simili.* Edited by Romola Galli Tomasinelli, Sagep, 1980.

Brumbaugh, Barbara. "*Jerusalem Delivered* and the Allegory of Sidney's Revised *Arcadia.*" *Modern Philology*, vol. 101, no. 3, 2004, pp. 337–70.

Bruscagli, Riccardo. "La materia del *Rinaldo* di Torquato Tasso." *Boiardo, Ariosto e i libri di battaglia*, edited by Andrea Canova and Paola Vecchi Galli, Interlinea, 2007, pp. 511–28.

———. *Stagioni della civiltà estense*. Nistri-Lischi, 1983.

———. *Studi cavallereschi*. Società Editrice Fiorentina, 2003.

Bufalino, Gesualdo. *Il Guerrin Meschino: Frammento di un'opra dei pupi*. Bompiani, 1993.

Buonanno, Michael. *Sicilian Epic and the Marionette Theater*. McFarland and Company, 2014.

*Buovo d'Antona: Cantari in ottava rima*. 1480. Edited by Daniela Delcorno Branca, Carocci, 2008.

Burgess, Glyn, translator. *The Song of Roland*. Penguin, 1990.

Burn, Andrew. "Role-Playing." *The Routledge Companion to Video Game Studies*, edited by Mark J. P. Wolf and Bernard Perron, Routledge, 2014, pp. 241–50.

Burton, Robert. *The Anatomy of Melancholy*. New York Review Books, 2001.

Busby, Keith. *Codex and Context: Reading Old French Verse Narrative in Manuscript*. Rodopi, 2002. 2 vols.

Bynum, Carolyn Walker. "Medieval Wonder." *American Historical Review*, vol. 102, no.1, Feb. 1997, pp. 1–26.

Cabani, Maria Cristina. *Le forme del cantare epico-cavalleresco*. Pacini Fazzi, 1988.

———. "L'*Orlandino* di Folengo e il genere cavalleresco." *Rivista di letteratura italiana*, vol. 9, 1991, pp. 591–610.

Cachey, Theodore J., Jr. "Maps and Literature in Renaissance Italy." *The History of Cartography: Cartography in the European Renaissance*, vol. 3, edited by David Woodward, U of Chicago P, 2007, pp. 450–60.

Cairneross, Andrew S. "Shakespeare and Ariosto: *Much Ado About Nothing*, *King Lear*, and *Othello*." *Renaissance Quarterly*, vol. 29, no. 2, Summer 1976, pp. 178–82.

Calabritto, Monica. *The Subject of Madness: An Analysis of Ariosto's* Orlando furioso *and Garzoni's* L'Hospedale de' pazzi incurabili. University Microfilms International, 2001.

Calestani, Vincenzo. *Madrigali et arie. Italian Secular Song*, edited by Gary Tomlinson, vol. 2, Garland, 1986, pp. 39–40.

Callois, Roger. "The Definition of Play: The Classification of Games." *The Game Design Reader: A Rules of Play Anthology*, edited by Katie Salen and Eric Zimmerman, MIT P, 2006, pp. 123–55.

Calore, Marina. "La biblioteca drammatica degli accademici Gelati di Bologna: Saggio storico bibliografico." *Atti della Accademia delle Scienze dell'Istituto di Bologna, Cl. di Scienze morali, Rendiconti*, vol. 81, 1992–93, pp. 61–82.

Calvino, Italo. *Il castello dei destini incrociati*. Einaudi, 1973.

———. *The Castle of Crossed Destinies*. Translated by William Weaver, Secker and Warburg, 1977.

———. *Orlando furioso raccontato da Italo Calvino*. Einaudi, 1970.

———. Presentazione [Presentation]. *Orlando furioso*, edited by Lanfranco Caretti, Einaudi, 1992, pp. xxv–xlvi.

Cameron, Alice. *The Influence of Ariosto's Epic and Lyric Poetry on Ronsard and His Group*. Johns Hopkins UP, 1930.

———. *The Influence of Ariosto's Epic and Lyric Poetry on the Work of Amadis Jamyn*. Johns Hopkins UP, 1933.

Campbell, Kimberlee. "A Competitive Edge: Franco-Hispanic Rivalry and the Origins of the *Song of Roland*." Kibler and Morgan, pp. 115–23.

Campion, Thomas. *The Works of Thomas Campion*. Edited by Walter R. Davies, W. W. Norton, 1970.

Caneparo, Federica. *"Di molte figure adornato": L'*Orlando furioso *nei cicli pittorici tra Cinque e Seicento*. Officina libraria, 2015.

Canova, Andrea, and Paola Vecchi Galli. *Boiardo, Ariosto e i libri di battaglia*. Interlinea, 2007.

*Cantare di Madonna Elena*. Edited by Giovanni Fontana, Accademia della Crusca, 1992.

*Cantari d'Aspramonte inediti (Magl. 7. 682)*. Edited by Andrea Fassò, Commissione per i testi di lingua, 1981.

*I cantari del Danese*. Edited by Sara Furlati, Edizioni dell'Orso, 2003.

*Cantari di Fierabraccia e Ulivieri*. Edited by Elio Melli, Pàtron, 1984.

*Cantari di Griselda*. Edited by Raffaele Morabito. Japadre, 1988.

*I cantari di Rinaldo da Monte Albano*. Edited by Elio Melli, Commissione per i testi di lingua, 1973.

*Cantari di Tristano*. 1937. Edited by Giulio Bertoni, Mucchi, 1988.

*Cantari novellistici dal Tre al Cinquecento*. Edited by Elisabetta Benucci et al., introduced by Domenico De Robertis, Salerno, 2002. 2 vols. I novellieri italiani 17.

*Cantari religiosi senesi del Trecento*. Edited by Giorgio Varanini. Laterza, 1965. Scrittori d'Italia 230.

*Cantari tratti dal* Decameron. Edited by Paola Rada. Pacini, 2009.

Capata, Alessandro. *Semper truffare paratus: Genere e ideologia nel Baldus di Folengo*. Bulzoni, 2000.

Capodivacca, Angela Matilde. "The Witch as Muse: Macaronic Fantasy and Skepticism in Folengo's *Baldus*." Scalabrini, *Folengo*, pp. 122–52.

Capoferri, Federica. "De' gesti antiqui una chimera": I poemi cavallereschi di Pietro Aretino." *Rivista di studi italiani*, vol. 18, no. 2, 2000, pp. 44–67.

Capucci, Martino. Review of *Drammaturgia romana* by Saverio Franchi. *Rivista di letteratura italiana*, vol. 8, no. 1, 1990, pp. 205–13.

Caracciolo, Daniela, and Massimiliano Rossi, editors. *Le sorti d'Orlando: Illustrazioni e riscritture del* Furioso, Maria Pacini Fazzi editore, 2013.

Carbone, Lodovico. *Facezie*. Edited by Abd-el-Kader Salza, Giusti, 1900.

Careri, Giovanni. *La fabbrica degli affetti. La* Gerusalemme liberata *dai Carracci a Tiepolo*. Il saggiatore, 2010.

———, editor. *La* Jérusalem délivrée *du Tasse: Poésie, peinture, musique, ballet*. Klincksieck / Musée du Louvre / Istituto di Studi Rinascimentali, 1999.

Carne-Ross, D. S. "The One and the Many: A Reading of *Orlando furioso* Cantos 1 and 8." *Arion*, vol. 5, 1966, pp. 195–234.

Carrara, Enrico. *Da Orlando a Morgante*. L'Erma, 1932.

Casadei, Alberto. *Ariosto: I metodi e i mondi possibili*. Marsilio, 2016.

———. *Il percorso del* Furioso*: Ricerche intorno alle redazioni del 1516 e del 1521*. Il Mulino, 1993.

———. "Stanze 'Per la Storia d'Italia': Testo critico e commento." *La fine degli incanti: Vicende del poema epico-cavalleresco nel Rinascimento*, Franco Angeli, 1997, pp. 155–83.

———. *La strategia delle varianti: Le correzioni storiche del terzo* Furioso. Pacini Fazzi, 1988.

Castiglione, Baldassare. *The Book of the Courtier*. Translated by Charles S. Singleton, Doubleday, 1959.

———. *Il libro del cortegiano*. Edited by Walter Barberis, Einaudi, 1998.

Catalano, Michele. *Vita di Ludovico Ariosto: Ricostruita su nuovi documenti*. Olschki, 1930–31. 2 vols.

Catelli, Nicola, and Giovanna Rizzarelli, editors. *"Fortuna ogni ora più diversa": The Reception of the* Inamoramento de Orlando *and the* Morgante *(16th–20th centuries)*. Special issue of *Italian Studies* (forthcoming, 2019).

Cattaneo, Angelo. *Fra Mauro's Mappa mundi and Fifteenth-Century Venice*. Brepols, 2011. Terrarum Orbis 8.

Catullus, Gaius Valerius. *Poems 61–68*. Translated by John Godwin, Aris and Phillips, 1995.

Cavallo, Jo Ann. "Boiardo and Ariosto in Contemporary Sicilian Puppet Theater and the Tuscan-Emilian Epic *Maggio*." *Modern Language Notes*, vol. 133, 2018, pp. 48–63.

———. *Boiardo's* Orlando innamorato*: An Ethics of Desire*. Fairleigh Dickinson UP, 1993.

———. "Denying Closure: Ariosto's Rewriting of the *Orlando innamorato*." Cavallo and Ross, *Fortune*, pp. 97–134.

———. "Encountering Saracens in Italian Romance Epic and Its Folk Performance Traditions." *Teaching Medieval and Early Modern Cross-Cultural Encounters across Disciplines and Periods*, edited by Lynn Shutters and Karina L. Attar, Palgrave Macmillan, 2014, pp. 159–78.

———. *Il giardino di Falerina*. Scandiano and Vico del Gargano, Italy, 2001. *eBOIARDO*, edblogs.columbia.edu/eboiardo/theatrical-adaptations-2/giardino-falerina-play/. Theatrical adaptation.

———. *Le isole lontane*. Ugento, Italy, 2009. Theatrical adaptation.

———. *Il maggio emiliano: Ricordi, riflessioni, brani*. 2003. *eBOIARDO*, edblogs.columbia.edu/eboiardo/epic-maggio/il-maggio-emiliano/. Documentary.

———. "National Political Ideologies and Local *Maggio* Traditions of the Reggio Emilia Apennines: *Roncisvalle* vs. *Rodomonte*." *Conquistare la montagna: La storia di un'idea / Conquering Mountains: The History of an Idea*, edited by Carlo Baja Guarienti and Matteo Al Kalak, Mondadori, 2016, pp. 121–34.

———. "L'Opera dei pupi e il maggio epico: Due tradizioni a confronto." *Archivio antropologico mediterraneo*, vols. 5–7, 2002–04, pp. 157–70.

———. *Orlando in Love*. Naumburg Bandshell, Central Park, New York City, 2006. *eBOIARDO*, edblogs.columbia.edu/eboiardo/orlando-in-love-at-central-park/. Theatrical adaptation.

———. *Orlando innamorato di Matteo Maria Boiardo: Rielaborato e reso in versione abbreviata per ragazzi* [*Orlando in Love: Abridged and Translated for Young Readers*]. Edizioni Teatromania / Teatro Nuovo, 2001. *Columbia Academic Commons*, Columbia University Libraries, dx.doi.org/10.7916/D8WD3ZBF. Documentary.

———. *Orlando innamorato in commedia.* Scandiano, 2000. *eBOIARDO*, edblogs.columbia.edu/eboiardo/theatrical-adaptations-2/orlando-innamorato-in-commedia/. Theatrical adaptation.

———. *Orlando innamorato: Un cammino epico-teatrale dalla Rocca dei Boiardo . . . a Central Park ed ai castelli della Puglia.* Teatromania, 2006. *eBOIARDO*, edblogs.columbia.edu/eboiardo/theatrical-adaptations-2/documentary-orlando-innamorato-a-journey-in-epic-theater/. Documentary.

———. "L'*Oro dei Napoli*: Sicilian Puppet Theater Today." *Arba Sicula*, vol. 24, no. 1–2, 2003, pp. 92–107.

———. *The Romance Epics of Boiardo, Ariosto, and Tasso: From Public Duty to Private Pleasure.* U of Toronto P, 2004.

———. "Where Have All the Brave Knights Gone? Sicilian Puppet Theater and the Tuscan-Emilian Epic *Maggio*." *Italian Culture*, vol. 19, no. 2, 2001, pp. 31–55.

———. *The World beyond Europe in the Romance Epics of Boiardo and Ariosto.* U of Toronto P, 2013.

Cavallo, Jo Ann, and Charles S. Ross. "Teaching the *Innamorato*." Cavallo and Ross, *Fortune*, pp. 6–14.

———, editors. *Fortune and Romance: Boiardo in America.* Medieval and Renaissance Texts and Studies, 1998.

Cavicchi, Camilla. "Musici, cantori e 'cantimbanchi' a corte al tempo dell'*Orlando furioso*." *L'uno e l'altro Ariostro in corte e nelle delizie*, edited by Gianni Venturi, Olschki, 2011, pp. 263–89.

Céard, Jean. *La nature et les prodiges: L'insolite au seizième siècle.* Droz, 1977.

Celati, Gianni. *Orlando innamorato raccontato in prosa.* Einaudi, 1994.

Cerrai, Marzia. "Una lettura del *Furioso* attraverso le immagini: L'edizione giolitina del 1542." *Strumenti critici*, vol. 16, no. 1, 2001, pp. 99–133.

Cervantes Saavedra, Miguel de. *Don Quixote.* Translated by Edith Grossman, HarperCollins, 2003.

———. *El ingenioso hidalgo don Quijote de la Mancha.* Edited by Luis Andrés Murillo, Castalia, 1978.

Chamberlain, E. R. *The World of the Italian Renaissance.* Allen and Unwin, 1982.

*La Chanson de Roland.* Bodleian Library, Oxford, MS Digby 23.

*La Chanson de Roland.* Châteauroux, Bibliothèque municipale MS 1.

*La Chanson de Roland.* Venice, Biblioteca Nazionale Marciana, MS Fr. Z. 4 ($V^4$) = 225.

*La Chanson de Roland.* Venice, Biblioteca Nazionale Marciana, MS Fr. Z. 7 ($V^7$) = 251.

Chapman, Matthieu. "An Argument for Slavery in Robert Greene's Adaptation of Ariosto's *Orlando furioso*." *Medieval and Renaissance Drama in England*, vol. 29, 2016, pp. 175–90.

Chrétien de Troyes. *Le roman de Perceval; Ou, Le conte du graal.* Librairie Droz, 1959.

Cicero, Marcus Tullius. *Tusculan Disputations.* Translated by J. E. King, Harvard UP, 1966. Loeb Classical Library.

Cieco da Ferrara, Francesco Bello. *Libro d'arme e d'amore nomato Mambriano.* Edited by Giuseppe Rua, UTET, 1926. 3 vols.

Cioranescu, Alexandre. *L'Arioste en France des origins à la fin du XVIIIe siècle.* Éditions des Presses Modernes, 1939.

Cirot, Georges. "La maurophilie en Espagne au XVIe siècle." *Bulletin Hispanique*, vol. 40, no. 2, 1938, pp. 150–57.

Clements, Robert J., and Joseph Gibaldi. *Anatomy of the Novella: The European Tale Collection from Boccaccio and Chaucer to Cervantes.* New York UP, 1977.

Clubb, Louise George. *Italian Drama in Shakespeare's Time.* Yale UP, 1989.

Cohen, Jeffrey Jerome. *Of Giants: Sex, Monsters, and the Middle Ages.* U of Minnesota P, 1999.

Coleman, James, and Andrea Moudarres, editors. *Luigi Pulci in Renaissance Florence and Beyond: New Perspectives on His Poetry and Influence.* Brepols, 2017.

Colonna, Francesco. *Hypnerotomachia Polphili: The Strife of Love in a Dream.* Translated by Joscelyn Godwin, Thames and Hudson, 1999.

Columbus, Christopher. *The Four Voyages of Columbus: A History in Eight Documents, Including Five by Christopher Columbus, in the Original Spanish, with English Translations.* Translated by Lionel Cecil Jane, Dover Publications, 1988.

Contini, Gianfranco. "Come lavorava l'Ariosto." 1937. *Esercizî di lettura sopra autori contemporanei con un'appendice su testi non contemporanei*, Einaudi, 1974, pp. 232–41.

Corral, Pedro de. *Crónica del Rey don Rodrigo: Crónica sarracina.* Edited and introduced by James Fogelquist. Castalia, 2001. 2 vols.

Corrigan, Beatrice. "Tasso's Erminia in the Italian Theater of the Seicento." *Renaissance Drama*, vol. 7, 1964, pp. 127–50.

Cox, Virginia. "Epic and Romance: Ariosto." France, pp. 480–82.

———. "Moderata Fonte and *The Worth of Women.*" Fonte, *Worth*, pp. 1–23.

———. *The Prodigious Muse: Women's Writing in Counter-Reformation Italy.* Johns Hopkins UP, 2011.

———. *The Renaissance Dialogue.* Cambridge UP, 1992.

———. "Women as Readers and Writers of Chivalric Poetry in Early Modern Italy." *Sguardi sull'Italia: Miscellanea dedicata a Francesco Villari*, edited by Gino Bedani et al., Society for Italian Studies, 1997, pp. 134–45.

Cozzarelli, Julia M. "Genius, Madness, and Knowledge: Ficino, Landino, and Ariosto's Lovers." *Quaderni d'Italianistica*, vol. 26, no. 2, 2005, pp. 3–27.

Croce, Benedetto. "I 'Rinaldo' o i cantastorie di Napoli," *La critica*, vol. 34, 1936, pp. 70–74.

Croce, Marcella. *The Chivalric Folk Tradition in Sicily: A History of Storytelling, Puppetry, Painted Carts, and Other Arts.* McFarland, 2014.

———. *Pupi carretti contastorie: L'epica cavalleresca nelle tradizioni popolari siciliane.* Dario Flaccovio, 1999.

D'Afflitto, Chiara, and Danilo Romei, editors. *I teatri del Paradiso: La personalità, l'opera, il mecenatismo di Giulio Rospigliosi.* Maschietto and Musolino Protago, 2000.

Dalché, Patrick Gautier. *L'espace géographique au moyen âge.* Edizioni del Galluzzo, 2013.

———. "Le souvenir de la *Géographie* de Ptolémé dans le monde latin médiéval (V<sup>e</sup>–XIV<sup>e</sup> siècles)." *Euphrosyne*, vol. 27, 1999, pp. 79–106.

Daston, Lorraine. "Marvelous Facts and Miraculous Evidence in Early Modern Europe." *Critical Inquiry*, vol. 18, 1991, pp. 93–124.

Daston, Lorraine, and Katharine Park. *Wonders and the Order of Nature, 1150–1750.* Zone Books, 2001.

Davies, Owen. *Grimoires: A History of Magic Books.* Oxford UP, 2009.

Davies, Surekha. "The Wondrous East in the Renaissance Geographical Imagination: Marco Polo, Fra Mauro, and Giovanni Battista Ramusio." *History and Anthropology*, vol. 23, no. 2, 2012, pp. 215–34.

Dean, Trevor. "The Rise of the *Signori*." *Italy in the Central Middle Ages*, edited by David Abulafia, Oxford UP, 2004, pp. 104–24.

Debailly, Pascal. *La muse indignée: Tome 1: La satire en France au XVIe siècle.* Classiques Garnier, 2012.

Decaria, Alessio. Introduction. *Sonetti extravaganti.* Edited by Decaria, Società Editrice Fiorentina, 2013, pp. ix–ccxxii.

———. *Luigi Pulci e Francesco di Matteo Castellani.* Società Editrice Fiorentina, 2009.

———. "Tra Marsilio e Pallante: Una nuova ipotesi sugli ultimi cantari del *Morgante.*" *L'entusiasmo delle opere: Studi in memoria di Domenico de Robertis*, edited by Isabella Becherucci et al., Pensa Multimedia, 2012, pp. 299–340.

De Ferrari, Tobia. *De' successi di Erminia intermedi cinque cavati dalla* Gerusalemme *del Tasso.* Pinelli, 1615.

Degl'Innocenti, Luca. "Testo e immagini nei continuatori dell'Ariosto: Il caso uno e trino della *Marfisa* di Pietro Aretino illustrata coi legni del 'Furioso Zoppino.'" *Schifanoia: Notizie dell'Istituto di Studi Rinascimentali di Ferrara*, no. 34–35, 2008, pp. 193–204.

Dekker, Thomas. *The Honest Whore, Part I. The Dramatic Works of Thomas Dekker*, edited by Fredson Bowers, vol. 2, pp. 10–105.

Denarosi, Lucia. "L'*Erminia* di Eugenio Visdomini." *Schifanoia*, vol. 24–25, 2003, pp. 29–122.

D'India, Sigismondo. *Le musiche.* Simon Tim et Filippo Lomazzo, 1609. Civico Museo Bibliogafico Musicale, Bologna.

Di Tommaso, Andrea. "Insania and Furor: A Diagnostic Note on Orlando's Malady." *Romance Notes*, vol. 14, 1973, 583–88.

Doglioni, Giovanni Nicolò. "Life of Moderata Fonte." 1600. Fonte, *Worth*, pp. 31–40.

———. "Vita della Sig.ra Modesta Pozzo de' Zorzi, nominata Moderata Fonte, descritta da Gio. Nicolò Doglioni, l'anno MDXCIII." *Il merito delle donne ove chiaramente si scuopre quanto siano elle degne e più perfette de gli uomini*, edited by Adriana Chemello, pp. 3–10.

Dolce, Lodovico. *Apologia di Ludovico Dolcio contra ai detrattori dell'autore.* Orlando furioso *di messer Lodouico Ariosto con la giunta, nouissimamente stampato e corretto.* Mapheo Pasini, 1535.

Donato, Eugenio. " 'Per selve e boscherecci labirinti': Desire and Narrative Structure in Ariosto's *Orlando furioso.*" *Literary Theory / Renaissance Texts*, edited by Patricia Parker and David Quint, Johns Hopkins UP, 1986, pp. 33–62.

Donnarumma, Raffaele. *Storia dell'* Orlando inamorato*: Poetiche e modelli letterari in Boiardo.* Pacini Fazzi, 1996.

Doré, Gustave. *Doré's Illustrations for Ariosto's* Orlando furioso*: A Selection of 208 Illustrations.* Edited by Stanley Appelbaum, Dover, 1980.

Dorigatti, Marco. "Dalla parola al testo: Il cammino di Cesare Segre (1928–2014)." *Rassegna europea di letteratura italiana*, vol. 42, 2013, pp. 11–26.

———. "Rugiero and the Dynastic Theme from Boiardo to Ariosto." Everson and Zancani, pp. 92–128.

———. "Strutture filologiche: La tradizione testuale dell'*Orlando furioso*." *Lectura Ariosti*, edited by Franco Tomasi, SISMEL–Edizioni del Galluzzo, forthcoming.

Doroszlaï, Alexandre. *Ptolémée et l'hippogriffe: La géographie de l'Arioste soumise à l'épreuve des cartes*. Edizioni dell'Orso, 1998.

Dovizi, Bernardo, da Bibbiena. *La calandra / The Comedy of Calandro*. Giannetti and Ruggiero, pp. 1–70.

Duby, Georges. "Youth in Aristocratic Society." *The Chivalrous Society*, translated by Cynthia Postan, U of California P, 1977, pp. 112–22. Originally published as "'Les Jeunes' dans la société aristocratique dans la France du nord-ouest au XIIe siècle." *Annales*, vol. 19, no. 5, Sept.–Oct. 1964, pp. 835–46.

Duggan, Joseph J., general editor. *La Chanson de Roland: The Song of Roland: French Corpus*. Brepols, 2005. 3 vols.

———. "L'épisode d'Aude dans la tradition en rime de la *Chanson de Roland*." *Charlemagne in the North: Proceedings of the Twelfth International Conference of the Société Rencesvals, Edinburgh, 4 to 11 August 1991*, Société Rencesvals British Branch, 1993, pp. 273–79.

Duggan, Joseph J., and Annalee C. Rejhon, translators. *The Song of Roland: Translations of the Versions in Assonance and Rhyme of the Chanson de Roland*. Brepols, 2012.

Du Laurens, André (Andreas Laurentius). *A Discourse of the Preservation of the Sight: Of Melancholike Diseases, of Rhemes, and of Old Age*. Translated by Richard Surphlet, 1599. Oxford UP, 1938.

Durling, Robert M. "The Bower of Bliss and Armida's Palace." *Comparative Literature*, vol. 6, no. 4, 1954, pp. 335–47.

Edson, Evelyn. *The World Map, 1300–1492: The Persistence of Tradition and Transformation*. Johns Hopkins UP, 2007.

*The Elder Scrolls V: Skyrim*. Bethesda, 2011.

Ellero, Maria Pia. "Il lavoro delle api: La ricezione del *Furioso* nelle edizioni illustrate del secondo Cinquecento." Bolzoni et al., pp. 195–211.

Elliott, Alison Goddard, editor and translator. "Pamphilus." *Seven Medieval Latin Comedies*, Garland, 1984.

Elliott, Robert C. *The Power of Satire: Magic, Ritual, Arts*. Princeton UP, 1960.

*L'Éntrée d'Espagne*. Biblioteca Nazionale Marciana, Venice, MS Fr. Z. 21 ($V^{21}$) = 257.

L'Éntrée d'Espagne*: Chanson de geste franco-italienne*. Edited by Antoine Thomas, Firmin Didot, 1913. 2 vols.

L'Éntrée d'Espagne*: Rolando da Pamplona all'Oriente*. Edited by Marco Infurna, Carocci, 2011.

Erasmus, Desiderius. The Praise of Folly *and Other Writings*. Translated by R. M. Adams, Norton, 1989.

Espinosa, Nicolas. *La segunda parte de* Orlando, *con el verdadero sucesso de la famosa batalla de Roncesualles; fin y muerte de los doze Pares de Francia*. Martin Nucio, 1557.

Everson, Jane E. "The Epic Tradition of Charlemagne in Italy." *Cahiers de Recherches Médiévales et Humanistes / Journal of Medieval and Humanistic Studies*, vol. 12, 2005, pp. 45–81, crm.revues.org/2192.

———. "Every Picture Tells A Story: Illustrations for the *Orlando furioso* after 1542." *Sguardi sull'Italia: Miscellanea dedicate a Francesco Villari dalla Society for Italian Studies*, edited by Gino Bedani et al., W. S. Maney and Son, 1997, pp. 117–33. Vol. 3 of *Society for Italian Studies Occasional Papers.*

———. *The Italian Romance Epic in the Age of Humanism: The Matter of Italy and the World of Rome.* Oxford UP, 2001.

———. "Les personnages feminins dans le *Mambriano* de Francesco Cieco de Ferrara." *Charlemagne in the North*, edited by Philip E. Bennett et al., Société Rencesvals British Branch, 1993, pp. 281–90.

———. "Roland in the Italian Tradition." Kibler and Morgan, pp. 97–108.

Everson, Jane E., and Diego Zancani, editors. *Italy in Crisis: 1494.* Legenda, 2000.

Ex Umbris. "L'incontro fra Rugiero e Bradamante" ["The Meeting of Rugiero and Bradamante"]. *The Diamond of Ferrara: Music from the Court of Ercole I*, Dorian, 2001. CD.

Faini, Marco. *La cosmologia macaronica.* Vecchiarelli, 2010.

Falchetta, Piero. *Fra Mauro's World Map: With a Commentary and Translations of the Inscriptions.* Translated by Jeremy Scott, Brepols, 2006.

"Fall of Constantinople." *Wikipedia*, Wikimedia Foundation, 28 Oct. 2015, en.wikipedia.org/wiki/Fall_of_Constantinople. Accessed 30 Oct. 2015.

*Fallout 3.* Bethesda, 2008.

*Fatti di Spagna* [*Exploits in Spain*]. The Royal House of France (I Reali di Francia) *and Related Medieval Romances*, translated by Max Wickert, *Outriders Poetry Project*, www.outriderspoetryproject.com/uploads/4/6/1/4/4614234/_the_royal_house_of_france.pdf, pp. 437–534.

*Li fatti de Spagna: Testo settentrionale trecentesco già detto "Viaggio di Carlo Magno in Ispagna."* Edited by Ruggiero M. Ruggieri, Società tipografica modenese, 1951.

Fei, Idalberto. *Orlando furioso e innamorato.* Illustrations by Rita Petruccioli, La Nuova Frontiera Junior, 2014.

Feinstein, Wiley. "Dorinda as Ariostean Narrator in Handel's *Orlando.*" *Italica*, vol. 64, no. 4, 1987, pp. 561–71.

Ferguson, Margaret W. *Trials of Desire: Renaissance Defenses of Poetry.* Yale UP, 1983.

Fernando, Massimo, editor and translator. Berta e Milone*: Traduzione, commento, glossario. Academia*, uploaded by Massimo Del Bianco, www.academia.edu/9736338/Berta_e_Milone_-_Traduzione_commento_glossario.

Ferrero, Giuseppe Guido, editor. *Poemi cavallereschi del Trecento.* UTET, 1968.

Finucci, Valeria. *The Lady Vanishes: Subjectivity and Representation in Castiglione and Ariosto.* Stanford UP, 1992.

———. "Moderata Fonte and the Genre of Women's Chivalric Romances." Fonte, *Floridoro*, pp. 1–33.

———, editor. *Renaissance Transactions: Ariosto and Tasso.* Duke UP, 1999.

———. "La scrittura epico-cavalleresca al femminile: Moderata Fonte e *Tredici canti del Floridoro.*" *Annali d'italianistica*, vol. 12, 1994, pp. 203–31.

Fioroni, Romolo, and Giorgio Vezzani, editors. *"Vengo l'avviso a dare": Appunti per una bibliografia della drammatica popolare: Indagine sull'attività dei complessi del Maggio dell'Appennino reggiano e modenese, 1955–1982.* Centro Culturale "A. Benedetti" di Villa Minozzo, 1983.

Firenzuola, Agnolo. *Le novelle*. Edited by Eugenio Ragni, Salerno, 1971.

———. *Tales of Firenzuola*. 1889. Edited by Eileen Gardiner, Italica Press, 1987.

Folengo, Teofilo (Merlin Cocai). *Baldo*. Translated by Ann E. Mullaney, Harvard UP, 2007–08. 2 vols. I Tatti Renaissance Library 25.

———. *Il Baldo*. Translated by Giuseppe Tonna, edited by Carlo Tonna et al., Diabasis, 2004.

———. *Baldus*. Edited by Mario Chiesa, UTET, 1997. 2 vols.

———. *Orlandino*. Edited by Mario Chiesa, Antenore, 1991.

Foligno, Cesare. "Epistole inedite di Lovato de' Lovati e d'altri a lui." *Studi medievali*, vol. 2, 1906, pp. 37–58. *Internet Archive*, archive.org/details/studimedievali02cent.

Folin, Marco. *Rinascimento estense: Politica, cultura, istituzioni di un antico stato italiano*. Laterza, 2001.

Fonte, Moderata (Modesta Pozzo). *Floridoro, A Chivalric Romance*. Edited by Valeria Finucci, translated by Julia Kisacky, annotated by Finucci and Kisacky, U of Chicago P, 2006. The Other Voice in Early Modern Europe.

———. *Il merito delle donne ove chiaramente si scuopre quanto siano elle degne e più perfette de gli uomini*. Edited by Adriana Chemello, Eidos, 1988.

———. *Tredici canti del Floridoro*. Stamparia de' Rampazetti, 1581. *University of Chicago Library, Italian Women Writers*, artflsrv02.uchicago.edu/cgi-bin/philologic/navigate.pl?iww.40.

———. *Tredici canti del Floridoro*. Edited by Valeria Finucci, Mucchi Editore, 1995.

———. *The Worth of Women: Wherein Is Clearly Revealed Their Nobility and Their Superiority to Men*. Edited and translated by Virginia Cox, U of Chicago P, 1997.

Ford, John. *The Lover's Melancholy*. 'Tis Pity She's a Whore *and Other Plays*, edited by Marion Lomax, Oxford UP, 1995, pp. 1–80.

Fornari, Simone. *La spositione di m. Simon Fornari da Rheggio sopra l'Orlando furioso di m. Ludovico Ariosto*. Lorenzo Torrentino, 1549–50.

Foucault, Michel. "Of Other Spaces: Utopias and Heterotopias." Translated by Jay Miskowiec. *Diacritics*, vol. 16, no. 1, Spring 1986, pp. 22–27.

"Fourth Crusade." *Wikipedia*, Wikimedia Foundation. 19 Oct. 2015, en.wikipedia.org/wiki/Fourth_Crusade. Accessed 30 Oct. 2015.

Fragonard, Jean-Honoré. *Fragonard Drawings for Ariosto*. Pantheon Books, 1945.

France, Peter, editor. *The Oxford Guide to Literature in English Translation*. Oxford UP, 2000.

Franceschetti, Antonio. "La novella nei poemi del Boiardo e dell'Ariosto." *La novella italiana*, Salerno Editrice, 1989, pp. 805–40.

———. "Rassegna di studi sui cantari." *Lettere italiane*, vol. 25, 1973, pp. 556–74.

Freccero, Carla. "Politics and Aesthetics in Castiglione's *Il Cortegiano*: Book III and the Discourse on Women." *Creative Imitation: New Essays on Renaissance Literature in Honor of Thomas M. Greene*, edited by David Quint et al., Medieval and Renaissance Texts and Studies, 1992, pp. 259–79.

Freedman, Luba. "Titian's Ruggiero and Angelica: A Tribute to Ludovico Ariosto." *Renaissance Studies*, vol. 15, no. 3, 2001, pp. 287–300.

Freedman, Paul. *Out of the East: Spices and the Medieval Imagination*. Yale UP, 2008.

Friedman, John Block. *The Monstrous Races in Medieval Art and Thought.* Harvard UP, 1981.

Friedman, John Block, and Cristen Mossler Figg, editors. *Trade, Travel, and Exploration in the Middle Ages.* Garland, 2000.

Frye, Northrop. *The Anatomy of Criticism.* Princeton UP, 1957.

Fumagalli, Elena, et al. *L'arme e gli amori: La poesia di Ariosto, Tasso e Guarini nell'arte fiorentina del Seicento.* Sillabe, 2001.

Gadrat-Ouerfelli, Christine. *Lire Marco Polo au moyen âge: Traduction, diffusion et réception du* Devisement du monde. Brepols, 2015.

Gallinaro, Ilaria. *La non vera Clorinda: Tradizione teatrale e musicale della "Liberata" nei secoli XVII–XIX.* Franco Angeli, 1994.

Gaylard, Susan. "Castiglione vs. Cicero: Political Engagement or Effeminate Chatter?" *Italian Culture*, vol. 27, no. 2, 2009, pp. 81–98.

Gelli, Giambattista. *Circe: Consisting of Ten Dialogues between Ulysses and Several Men Transformed into Beasts.* Translated by Thomas Brown, edited by Robert Adams, Cornell UP, 1963.

Genovese, Roberto. "Battle between Orlando and Rinaldo." Edited by Alan Lomax and Diego Carpitella. *Italian Treasury: Sicily*, Rounder, 2000. CD.

*La Geste Francor: Chansons de geste of MS. Marc. Fr. XIII (=256).* Edited by Leslie Zarker Morgan, Arizona Center for Medieval and Renaissance Texts and Studies, 2009. 2 vols.

Giamatti, A. Bartlett. *The Earthly Paradise and the Renaissance Epic.* Princeton UP, 1966.

Giannetti, Laura, and Guido Ruggiero, translators. *Five Comedies from the Italian Renaissance*, Johns Hopkins UP, 2003.

Giannini, Giovanni. "Bibliografia dei Maggi stampati dalla tipografia Sborgi di Volterra." *Rassegna Volterrana*, vol. 2, no. 3, 1926, pp.141–68.

Gigante, Claudio. *Tasso.* Salerno, 2007.

Ginsburg, Lev. *Tartini: His Life and Times.* Translated by I. Levin, edited by Herbert Axelrod, Paganiniana, 1981.

Giraldi Cinzio, Giovambattista. "Cinthio's Tale of the Moor of Venice." Translated by John Edward Taylor, 1855. *An Anthology of Interracial Literature: Black-White Encounters in the Old World and the New*, edited by Werner Sollors, New York UP, 2004, pp. 85–95.

———. *Discorso dei romanzi.* Edited by Laura Benedetti et al., Millennium, 1999.

———. *Giraldi Cinthio on Romances; Being a Translation of the* Discorso intorno al comporre dei romanzi. Translated by Henry L. Snuggs, U of Kentucky P, 1968.

———. *Hecatommithi.* Edited by Susanna Villari, Salerno Editrice, 2012.

Gnudi, Cesare. "L'Ariosto e le arti figurative." *Signore cortese e umanissimo: Viaggio intorno a Ludovico Ariosto*, edited by Jadranka Bentini, Marsilio, 1994, pp. 13–47.

Góngora, Luis de. *Selected Poems of Luis de Góngora: A Bilingual Edition.* Edited and translated by John Dent-Young, U of Chicago P, 2007.

Gough, Melinda J. "Tasso's Enchantress, Tasso's Captive Woman." *Renaissance Quarterly*, vol. 54, 2001, pp. 523–52.

*Grande dizionario della lingua italiana.* Edited by Salvatore Battaglia and Giorgio Bàrberi Squarotti, Utet, 1961–2002.

Green, Richard Firth. *Elf Queens and Holy Friars: Fairy Beliefs and the Medieval Church*. U of Pennsylvania P, 2016.

Greene, Robert. *The Historie of* Orlando furioso, *One of the Twelue Pieres of France: As It was Plaid before the Queenes Maiestie*. London, 1594. *Early English Books Online*, University of Michigan, quod.lib.umich.edu/e/eebo/A02125.0001.001/1:2?rgn=div1;view=fulltext.

Gregory, Tobias. *From Many Gods to One: Divine Action in Renaissance Epic*. U of Chicago P, 2006.

Grendler, Paul F. *Schooling in Renaissance Italy: Literacy and Learning, 1300–1600*. Johns Hopkins UP, 1989.

Groensteen, Thierry. *La bande dessinée: Mode d'emploi*. Impressions Nouvelles, 2008.

Guazzoni, Enrico. *Gerusalemme liberata*. Guazzoni Film, 1918.

La guerra di Troia *in ottava rima*. Edited by Dario Mantovani, Ledizioni, 2013.

Gulizia, Stefano. Review of *Baldo* by Teofilo Folengo, translated by Ann E. Mullaney. *Renaissance Quarterly*, vol. 62, no. 4, 2009, pp. 1210–11.

———. "Scaffolding Folengo: Sites, Artifacts, and the Rise of Macaronic Design in Print Culture." Scalabrini, *Folengo*, pp. 153–95.

Gundersheimer, Werner. *Ferrara: The Style of a Renaissance Despotism*. Princeton UP, 1973.

Haar, James. *Essays on Italian Poetry and Music in the Renaissance*. U of California P, 1984.

Hairston, Julia L. "'Di sangue illustre and pellegrino': The Eclipse of the Body in the Lyric of Tullia d'Aragona." *The Body in Early Modern Italy*, edited by Julia L. Hairston and Walter Stephens, Johns Hopkins UP, 2010, pp. 158–75.

Hall, Crystal. "*Orlando furioso*: The Board Game." *SMART: Studies in Medieval and Renaissance Teaching*, vol. 20, 2013, pp. 51–66.

Hammond, Gerald. "English Translations of the Bible." *The Literary Guide to the Bible*, edited by Robert Alter and Frank Kermode, Belknap Press, 1987, pp. 647–66.

Hampton, Timothy. *Writing From History: The Rhetoric of Exemplarity in Renaissance Literature*. Cornell UP, 1990.

Hanning, Robert W. "Sources of Illusion: Plot Elements and Their Thematic Uses in Ariosto's Ginevra Episode." *Forum Italicum*, vol. 5, 1971, pp. 514–35.

Harley, J. B., and David Woodward, editors. *The History of Cartograhy*. U of Chicago P, 1987–2015. 6 vols.

Harris, Neil. *Bibliografia dell'* Orlando innamorato. Panini, 1988–91. 2 vols.

Hart, Thomas R. *Cervantes and Ariosto: Renewing Fiction*. Princeton UP, 1989.

Harvey, P. D. A. *Medieval Maps*. U of Toronto P, 1991.

Heddle, Donna. *John Stewart of Baldynneis'* Roland Furious*: A Scots Poem in Its European Context*. Brill, 2008. Brill's Studies in Intellectual History 158.

Heijkant, Marie-José. "'De re Artu parlar ciò che si scrisse': Orality in the Breton *cantari*." *"Der muoz mir süezer worte jehen": Liber amicorum für Norbert Voorwinden*, edited by Ludo Jongen, Rodopi, 1997, pp. 57–70.

Heikamp, Detlef. "Il Nano Morgante nel giardino del pensile degli Uffizi." *Giambologna, gli dei, gli eroi*, edited by Beatrice Paolozzo Strozzi and Dimitri Zikos, Giunti, 2006, pp. 294–301.

Hempfer, Klaus W. *Diskrepante Lekturen: Die* Orlando-Furioso-*Rezeption im Cinquecento. Historische Rezeptionsforschung als Heuristik der Interpretation.* F. Steiner Verlag, 1987.

Herodotus. *The Histories.* Translated by Tom Holland, Viking, 2013.

*Historia de los dos enamorados Flores y Blancaflor.* Edited by Adolfo Bonilla y San Martín, Ruiz Hermanos, 1916.

"Honors Colloquium." *Baylor University*, www.baylor.edu/honors_program/index.php?id=2148. Accessed 20 July 2015.

Horace. *Odes and Epodes.* Translated by Niall Rudd, Harvard UP, 2004.

Huet, Marie-Hélène. *Monstrous Imagination.* Harvard UP, 1993.

Huizinga, Johan. *Homo Ludens: A Study of the Play-Element in Culture.* Routledge, 1980.

———. *The Waning of the Middle Ages.* Penguin, 1987.

Huot, Silvia. *Outsiders: The Humanity and Inhumanity of Giants in Medieval French Prose Romance.* U of Notre Dame P, 2016.

Hurwood, Bernhardt J., translator. *The Facetiae of Giovanni Francesco Poggio Bracciolini*, edited by Marcello Ciccuto, Award Books, 1968.

Ingegneri, Angelo. *Tomiri, tragedia.* Carlino e Vitale, 1607.

Iser, Wolfang. *Der Akt des Lesens: Theorie asthetischer Wirkung.* Fink, 1976.

"Italian Epic Poetry." *Poetry Criticism*, edited by Lawrence J. Trudeau, vol. 186, Gale / Cengage Learning, 2017, pp. 1–161.

Izzo, Annalisa. "Entrelacement per immagini: Il racconto intercalato in alcune edizioni illustrate del *Furioso.*" *Narrazioni e strategie dell'illustrazione: Codici e romanzi cavallereschi nell'Italia del Nord (secc. XIV–XVI)*, edited by Annalisa Izzo and Ilaria Molteni, Viella, 2014, pp. 139–56.

Jackson, Guida M. *Encyclopedia of Traditional Epics.* ABC-CLIO, 1994.

Jacob, Christian. *L'empire des cartes.* Broché, 1992.

———. *The Sovereign Map.* Translated by Edward H. Dahl, U of Chicago P, 2005.

Jauss, Hans Robert. *Aesthetische Erfahrung und literarische Hermeneutik I.* Wilhelm Fink Verlag, 1977.

Javitch, Daniel. "Cantus Interruptus in the *Orlando furioso.*" *MLN*, vol. 95, no. 1, 1980, pp. 66–80.

———. "La nascita della teoria dei generi poetici nel Cinquecento." *Italianistica*, vol. 27, no. 2, 1998, pp. 177–97.

———. *Proclaiming a Classic: The Canonization of* Orlando furioso. Princeton UP, 1991.

———. *Saggi sull'Ariosto e la composizione dell'* Orlando furioso. Pacini Fazzi Editore, 2012.

Jeanneret, Michel, and Monica Preti-Hamard, editors. *Imaginaire de l'Arioste, l'Arioste imaginé.* Gourcuff Gradenigo, 2009.

Jones, Catherine M. *An Introduction to the Chansons de Geste.* UP of Florida, 2014.

———. "Roland versus Oliver." Kibler and Morgan, pp. 201–06.

Jorgens, Elise B. "Orlando Metamorphosed: Handel's Operas after Ariosto." *Parnassus: Poetry in Review*, vol. 10, no. 2, 1982, pp. 45–74.

Jossa, Stefano. *La fondazione di un genere: Il poema eroico tra Ariosto e Tasso.* Carocci, 2002.

———. "Pazzia e finzione: Appunti sul modello ariostesco nella letteratura del XX secolo." *Anticomoderno*, vol. 4, 1999, pp. 349–81.

Kennedy, William J. "Ariosto's Ironic Allegory." *MLN*, vol. 88, no. 1, 1973, pp. 44–67.

Kenseth, Joy, editor. *The Age of the Marvelous*. Hood Museum of Art, 1991.

Keyser, Sijbrand. *Contribution à l'étude de la fortune littéraire de l'Arioste en France*. M. Dubbeldeman, 1933.

Kezich, Giovanni. *I poeti contadini: Introduzione all'ottava rima popolare: Immaginario poetico e paesaggio sociale*. Bulzoni, 1986.

———. *Some Peasant Poets: An Odyssey in the Oral Poetry of Latium*. Peter Lang, 2013.

Kibler, William W. "Editions and Translations." Kibler and Morgan, pp. 9–19.

———. "Rencesvals: The Event." Kibler and Morgan, pp. 53–56.

Kibler, William W., and Leslie Zarker Morgan, editors. *Approaches to Teaching the* Song of Roland. Modern Language Association, 2006.

Kieckhefer, Richard. *Magic in the Middle Ages*. Cambridge UP, 1989.

Kitzes, Adam H. *The Politics of Melancholy from Spenser to Milton*. Routledge, 2006.

Kline, Naomi Reed. *Maps of Medieval Thought: The Hereford Paradigm*. Boydell Press, 2001.

Kolsky, Stephen. "Moderata Fonte's *Tredici Canti del Floridoro*: Women in a Man's Genre." *Rivista di studi Italiani*, vol. 17, 1999, pp. 165–84.

Kromm, Jane. *The Art of Frenzy: Public Madness in the Visual Culture of Europe, 1500–1850*. Continuum, 2002.

Lampe, E. L., and Philip Soergel. "Counter Reformation." *New Catholic Encyclopedia*, 2nd ed., vol. 4, Thomson Gale, 2003, pp. 308–14.

Laradje, Aline. *La Légende de Roland: De la genèse française à l'épuisement de la figure du héros en Italie*. L'Harmattan, 2008.

Latini, Brunetto. *Li livre dou trésor*. Edited by Paul Barrette and Spurgeon W. Baldwin, Garland, 1993. The Garland Library of Medieval Literature 90.

La Via, Stefano. "Dal Tasso a Monteverdi: Una lettura aristotelica del Combattimento di Tancredi e Clorinda." *L'arme e gli amori: Ariosto, Tasso and Guarini in Late Renaissance Florence*, edited by Massimiliano Rossi and Fiorella Gioffredi Superbi, Olschki, 2004.

Lèbano, Edoardo A. Introduction. Pulci, Morgante*: The Epic Adventures*, pp. xi–xxxiii.

———. "Luigi Pulci and Late Fifteenth-Century Humanism in Florence." *Renaissance Quarterly*, vol. 27, no. 4, Winter 1974, pp. 489–98.

Lecco, Margherita. "*Bruto di Bertagna* e Andrea Cappellano: Analisi delle fonti e considerazioni comparative su un *Cantare* del XIV secolo." *Forum Italicum*, vol. 38, no. 2, 2004, pp. 545–57.

Lee, Rensselaer W. *Names on Trees: Ariosto into Art*. Princeton UP, 1977.

———. "Poetry into Painting: Tasso and Art." Middlebury College, 1970.

Leisawitz, Daniel. "Why an Atlas?" *Orlando Furioso Atlas*, Sept. 2016, www.furiosoatlas.com/.

Lejeune, Rita, and Jacques Stiennon. *The Legend of Roland in the Middle Ages*. Translated by Christine Troloppe, Phaidon, 1971. 2 vols.

———. *La Légende de Roland dans l'art du moyen Age*. Arcade, 1967. 2 vols.

Lepschy, Anna L. "I discorsi della *Gerusalemme liberata*." *Lettere italiane*, vol. 37, no. 2, 1985, pp. 204–19.

Lescarbot, Marc. *De la défaite des Sauvages Armouchiquois par le Sagamos*. Jérémie Périer, 1607.

———. *Histoire de la Nouvelle-France*. Millot, 1609.

Levack, Brian P. *The Witch-Hunt in Early Modern Europe*. 3rd ed., Taylor and Francis, 2013.

Levtzion, Nehemia, and John F. P. Hopkins, editors. *Corpus of Early Arabic Sources for West Africa*. Cambridge UP, 1981.

Lewis, C. S. *The Allegory of Love*. 1936. Oxford UP, 1958.

———. *The Discarded Image*. 1964. Cambridge UP, 1970.

*Il libro di messer Tristano ("Tristano Veneto")*. Edited by Aulo Donadello, Marsilio, 1994.

Littlejohn, David. *The Ultimate Art: Essays around and about Opera*. U of California P, 1992.

Lockwood, Lewis. *Music in Renaissance Ferrara, 1400–1505: The Creation of a Musical Center in the Fifteenth Century*. Harvard UP, 1984.

Lo Dico, Giusto. *Storia dei paladini di Francia cominciando da Re Pipino fino alla morte di Rinaldo*. Edited by Felice Cammarata, Clio-Brancato, 1993 (vols. 1–9); and Brancato, 2000 (vols. 10–13).

Looney, Dennis. *Compromising the Classics: Romance Epic Narrative in the Italian Renaissance*. Wayne State UP, 1996.

Looney, Dennis, and Deanna Shemek, editors. *Phaethon's Children: The Este Court and Its Culture in Early Modern Ferrara*. Arizona Center for Medieval and Renaissance Studies, 2005.

Lord, Albert B. *Singer of Tales*. Harvard UP, 1960.

Lo Rito, Claudia. "Il perfetto cavaliere e l'uomo virtuoso nelle allegorie delle edizioni Giolito e Valvassori dell'*Orlando furioso*." Bolzoni et al., pp. 213–31.

Lot, Ferdinand. *Etude sur le Lancelot en prose*. 1918. Champion, 1954. Bibliothèque de l'Ecole des Hautes Etudes 226.

Lucian. *Works*. Translated by A. M. Harmon, vol. 1, Harvard UP, 1913.

"Ludovico Ariosto, 1474–1533." *Poetry Criticism*, edited by Lawrence J. Trudeau, vol. 175, Gale / Cengage Learning, 2016, pp. 1–157.

Luperini, Romano. *Insegnare la letteratura oggi*. Manni, 2013.

Lupton, Julia Reinhard. "Undressing Alcina: The *Orlando furioso* in Du Bellay's *Les Regrets*." *French Forum*, vol. 14, no. 3, Sept. 1989, pp. 291–301.

Lüttenberg, Thomas. "The Cod-Piece: A Renaissance Fashion Between Sign and Artefact." *Medieval History Journal*, vol. 8., no. 1, 2005, pp. 49–81.

Luzzati, Emanuele. *Dell'amore, dell'avventura. L'*Orlando innamorato. Interlinea, 2005.

Mac Carthy, Ita. *Women and the Making of Poetry in Ariosto's* Orlando furioso. Troubador, 2007.

Macdonald, Michael. *Mystical Bedlam: Madness, Anxiety, and Healing in Seventeenth-Century England*. Cambridge UP, 1981.

Mace, Dean. "Tasso, *La Gerusalemme liberata*, and Monteverdi." *Studies in the History of Music*, vol. 1, 1983, pp. 118–56.

Machiavelli, Niccolò. *The Chief Works and Others.* Translated by Allan Gilbert, Duke UP, 1965.

———. *La mandragola / The Mandrake Root.* Giannetti and Ruggiero, pp. 71–116.

*Maggio datto 1808.* Manuscript.

Magrini, Tullia. *Il Maggio Drammatico: Una tradizione di teatro in musica.* Analisi, 1992.

Maissen, Thomas. "Attila, Totila e Carlo Magno fra Dante, Villani, Boccaccio e Malispini: Per la genesi di due leggende erudite." *Archivio storico italiano*, vol. 152, 1994, pp. 561–639.

Malpezzi Price, Paola. *Moderata Fonte: Women and Life in Sixteenth-Century Venice.* Fairleigh Dickinson UP, 2003.

Manca, Joseph. "Boiardo and the Visual Arts in Ferrara: Comparisons and Convergences." Cavallo and Ross, *Fortune*, pp. 261–70.

Manetti, Antonio. *Fatso the Carpenter* [*La novella del Grasso Legnaiolo*]. *Italian Renaissance Tales*, translated by Janet Levarie Smarr, Solaris Press, 1983, pp. 105–33.

Manganelli, Giorgio. *Un'allucinazione fiamminga: Il* Morgante Maggiore *raccontato da Manganelli.* Edited by Graziella Pulce, Socrates, 2006.

Manovich, Lev. *The Language of New Media.* MIT P, 2001.

Marangoni, Marco. *In Forma di Teatro: Elementi teatrali nell'Orlando furioso.* Carocci, 2002.

Marconi, Sara. *Angelica, principessa combina-guai.* Lapis, 2014.

———. *Astolfo, cavaliere curioso.* Lapis, 2014.

———. *Bradamante, guerriera senza macchia.* Lapis, 2015.

———. *Orlando, paladino come nessun altro.* Lapis, 2015.

Mariani, Gaetano. Il Morgante *e i cantari trecenteschi: Saggi di letteratura italiana.* Le Monnier, 1953.

Marinella, Lucrezia. *Enrico; or, Byzantium Conquered: Heroic Poem.* Edited and translated by Maria Galli Stampino, U of Chicago P, 2009. The Other Voice in Early Modern Europe.

———. *L'Enrico, ovvero Bisanzio acquistato, poema eroico.* Edited by Maria Galli Stampino, Mucchi Editore, 2011.

Marinelli, Peter. *Ariosto and Boiardo: The Origins of* Orlando furioso. U of Missouri P, 1987.

Marino, Giambattista. *Adone.* Edited by Giuseppe Guido Ferrero, Einaudi, 1976.

———. *Adonis, Selections from l'*Adone. Translated by Harold Martin Priest, Cornell UP, 1967.

Marsh, David. "Ruggiero and Leone: Revision and Resolution in Ariosto's *Orlando furioso*." *MLN*, vol. 96, no. 1, 1981, pp. 144–51.

Martin, Craig. *Renaissance Meteorology: Pomponazzi to Descartes.* Johns Hopkins UP, 2011.

Masciandaro, Franco. "Folly in the *Orlando furioso*: A Reading of the Gabrina Episode." *Forum Italicum*, vol. 14, 1980, pp. 56–77.

*Mass Effect.* BioWare, 2007.

Massinger, Philip. *A Very Woman; or, The Prince of Tarent: A Tragi-comedy. The Plays and Poems of Philip Massinger*, edited by Philips Edwards and Colin Gibson, vol. 4, Clarendon Press, 1976, pp. 207–89.

"Matteo Maria Boiardo, 1441–1494." *Poetry Criticism*, edited by Lawrence J. Trudeau, vol. 180, Gale / Cengage Learning, 2016, pp. 1–148.

Maurer, Emil. *Manierismus: Figura serpentinata und andere Figurenideale: Studien, Essays, Berichte.* Wilhelm Fink Verlag, 2001.

Mayor, Adrienne. *The First Fossil Hunters: Dinosaurs, Mammoths, and Myth in in Greek and Roman Times.* 2000. Reprint, Princeton UP, 2011.

Mazzotta, Giuseppe. *The World at Play in Boccaccio's* Decameron. Princeton UP, 1986.

McCall, Timothy. "Brilliant Bodies: Material Culture and the Adornment of Men in North Italy's Quattrocento Courts." *I Tatti Studies in the Italian Renaissance*, vol. 16, no. 1–2, 2013, pp. 445–90.

McCormick, John, with Alfonso Cipolla and Alessandro Napoli. *The Italian Puppet Theater: A History.* McFarland, 2011.

McGee, Timothy J. "How One Learned to Ornament in Late Sixteenth-Century Italy." *Performance Practice Review*, vol. 13, no. 1, article 6, 2008, pp. 1–16, doi: 10.5642/perfpr.200813.01.06.

Melchioni, Allieta. *Cantare il Maggio.* 2016. DVD.

Meredith-Jones, Cyril, editor. *Historia Karoli et Rotholandi ou Chronique du Pseudo-Turpin.* 1936. Slatkine Reprints, 1972.

Meserve, Margaret. *Empires of Islam in Renaissance Historical Thought.* Harvard UP, 2008.

Messina, Enrico. *Orlando: Furiosamente solo rotolando.* 2006. *eBOIARDO*, 2015, edblogs.columbia.edu/eboiardo/theatrical-adaptations-2/enrico-messina/. Performance.

Messina, Enrico, and Alberto Nicolino. *Hruodlandus: Libera rotolata medioevale.* 1988. Performance.

Middleton, Thomas, and William Rowley. *The Changeling. Thomas Middleton: Five Plays*, edited by Bryan Loughrey and Neil Taylor, Penguin Books, 2006, pp. 345–421.

Migiel, Marilyn. *Gender and Genealogy in Tasso's* Gerusalemme Liberata. Edwin Mellen Press, 1993.

———. "Secrets of a Sorceress: Tasso's Armida." *Quaderni d'Italianistica*, vol. 8, no. 2, Winter 1987, pp. 149–66.

Milán, Luis. *Libro intitulado El Cortesano. Colleción de libros españoles raros ó curiosos, tomo séptimo*, Madrid, 1874, pp. 123–28.

Milano, Ernesto. *La carta del cantino e la rappresentazione della terra nei codici e nei libri a stampa della Biblioteca Estense e Universitaria.* Il Bulino, 1991.

Miller, Dwight. *Marcantonio Franceschini.* Artema / Compagnia di belle arti, 2001.

Milligan, Gerry. "The Politics of Effeminacy in *Il cortegiano.*" *Italica*, vol. 83, no. 3–4, 2006, pp. 345–66.

Milton, John. *John Milton: Complete Poems and Major Prose.* Edited by Merritt Y. Hughes, Bobbs-Company, 1957.

Moffitt, John. "An Exemplary Humanist Hybrid: Vasari's 'Fraude' with Reference to Bronzino's 'Sfinx.'" *Renaissance Quarterly*, vol. 49, no. 2, 1996, pp. 303–33.

Monfrin, Jacques. "Le *roman de Belris*, le *Bel Inconnu*, *Carduino.*" *Testi, co-testi e contesti del franco-italiano*, edited by Günter Holtus et al. Niemeyer, 1989, pp. 161–76.

Montaigne, Michel de. *Journal de Voyage de Michel de Montaigne, tome 2*. Rome, 1775.

Monteverdi, Claudio. *Madrigali a 5 voci, libro terzo*. Vol. 4, Fondazione Claudio Monteverdi, 1988.

———. *Madrigali guerrieri et amorosi*. Vincenti, 1638.

———. *Madrigals, book 8*. Dover, 1991.

Morabito, Raffaele. "The Italian *Cantare* between Orality and Writing." *Medieval Oral Literature*, edited by Karl Reichl, Walter de Gruyter, 2012, pp. 370–86.

Moretti, Franco. *Graphs, Maps, Trees: Abstract Models for a Literary History*. Verso, 2005.

Morgan, Leslie Zarker, editor and translator. "Berta and Milone." *The ORB: Online Reference Book of the Middle Ages*, 1996, the-orb.arlima.net/encyclop/culture/lit/italian/morgan4.html.

———. "Orlandino." *The ORB: Online Reference Book of the Middle Ages*, 1996, the-orb.arlima.net/encyclop/culture/lit/italian/morgan1.html.

Moses, Gavriel. "Tasso to Monteverdi: Intertextual Poetics." *Studies in the Italian Renaissance: Essays in Memory of Arnolfo B. Ferruolo*, Società Editrice Napoletana, 1985, pp. 245–59.

Murrin, Michael. *The Allegorical Epic: Essays in Its Rise and Decline*. U of Chicago P, 1980.

———. *History and Warfare in Renaissance Epic*. U of Chicago P, 1994.

———. *Trade and Romance*. U of Chicago P, 2013.

Murtaugh, Kristen Olsen. "Erminia Delivered: Notes on Tasso and Romance." *Quaderni d'Italianistica*, vol. 3, no. 1, 1982, pp. 12–25.

Napoli, Alessandro. *Il racconto e i colori: "Storie" e "cartelli" dell'Opera dei Pupi catanese*. Sellerio, 2002.

Nash, Ralph. Introduction. Tasso, Jerusalem Delivered*: An English Prose Version* [Nash], pp. ix–xxv.

Navone, Matteo. "Intersezioni di generi nel *Rinaldo* di Torquato Tasso." *Letteratura degli italiani: Rotte, confine, passaggi*, edited by Alberto Beniscelli et al., DIRAAS / Università degli Studi di Genova, 2012, www.italianisti.it/upload/userfiles/files/Navone%20Matteo_1.pdf.

Newcomb, Anthony. *The Madrigal at Ferrara, 1579–1597*. Princeton UP, 1980.

Nicholson, Eric. "Romance as Role Model: Early Female Performances of *Orlando furioso* and *Gerusalemme liberata*." *Renaissance Transactions*, edited by Valeria Finucci, Duke UP, 1999, pp. 246–69.

Nicolino, Alberto. *Orlando furioso raccontato dal mago Atlante*. 2011. *eBOIARDO*, 2012, edblogs.columbia.edu/eboiardo/theatrical-adaptations-2/alberto-nicolino/. Performance.

Nicolopulos, James. *The Poetics of Empire in the Indies: Prophecy and Imitation in* La Araucana *and* Os Lusíadas. Penn State UP, 2000.

Nohrnberg, James. *The Analogy of* The Faerie Queene. Princeton UP, 1976.

———. "Orlando's Opportunity: Chance, Luck, Fortune, Occasion, Boats, and Blows in Boiardo's *Orlando innamorato*." Cavallo and Ross, *Fortune*, pp. 31–75.

O'Connell, Monique. "The Italian Renaissance in the Mediterranean or between East and West: A Review Article." *California Italian Studies Journal*, vol. 1, 2010, pp. 1–30.

Olmi, Ermanno, director. *Il mestiere delle armi*. A-Film Distribution, 2001.

"Orlando's Wars. Gioco di carte." *Fondazione Palazzo Magnani*, www.palazzomag nani.it/2014/10/orlandos-wars-gioco-di-carte.

Orvieto, Paolo. "Sul rapporto Morgante-Orlando laurentiano." *Ritterepik der Renaissance: Akten des deutsch-italienischen Kolloquiums, Berlin 30.3–2.4.1987*, edited by Klaus W. Hempfer, Franz Steiner, 1989, pp. 145–53.

Ottonelli, Giovanni Domenico, and Pietro Berrettini. *Trattato della pittura et scoltura: Uso et abuso loro (1652)*. Edited by Vittorio Casale, Libreria editrice Canova, 1973.

Ovid. *Metamorfosi*. Edited by Alessandro Barchiesi, Fondazione Valla Mondadori, 2005.

Palladini, Irene. "I Maggi fra tradition orale et écriture." *La scena dell'oralità: Per una voce fuori luogo*, edited by A. Anastasi and V. Di Vita, Corisco edizioni, 2015, pp. 264–74.

Palumbo, Giovanni. *La* Chanson de Roland *in Italia nel Medioevo*. Preface by Cesare Segre, Salerno Editrice, 2013.

Panaro, Paolo. *La follia di Orlando dall'* Orlando furioso *di Ludovico Ariosto*. 2013. *YouTube*, www.youtube.com/watch?time_continue=1&v=4aA4UTm8_60. Performance.

———. Gerusalemme liberata *di Torquato Tasso*. 1992. *YouTube*, www.youtube.com/watch?time_continue=3&v=9qvMT4rSO7s. Performance.

———. Orlando innamorato, *canto 1*. 1993. *Performing Medieval Narrative Today*, 1996, mednar.org/2012/06/17/orlando-opening-canto/. Performance.

———. *Quel ch'avvelena Cipada a' tempi de Baldo*. 1995. *YouTube*, www.youtube .com/watch?v=vw12XwDomHY. Performance.

Paoli, Michel, and Monica Preti, editors. *L'Arioste et les Arts*. Musée du Louvre / Officina Libraria, 2012.

Paperino il paladino *e* Paperin Meschino. Edited by Gianni Bono, *I classici della letteratura*, vol. 25, RCS, 2013.

Paperopoli liberata *e* Paperin furioso. Edited by Gianni Bono, *I classici della letteratura*, vol. 14, RCS Libri, 2013.

Papio, Michael. *Keen and Violent Remedies: Social Satire and the Grotesque in Masuccio Salernitano's* Novellino. Peter Lang, 2000.

Paré, Ambroise. *Ambroise Paré on Monsters and Marvels*. Translated by Janis L. Pallister, U of Chicago P, 1983.

Paris, Gaston. *Histoire poétique de Charlemagne*. 1865. 2nd ed., Bouillon, 1905.

Parker, Patricia. *Inescapable Romance*. Princeton UP, 1979.

Parmiggiani, Sandro, editor. *L'*Orlando furioso*: Incantamenti, passioni e follie: L'arte contemporanea legge l'Ariosto*. Silvana, 2014.

Parry, Milman. "Studies in the Epic Technique of Oral Verse-Making: I. Homer and Homeric Style." *Harvard Studies in Classical Philology*, vol. 41, no. 80, 1930, pp. 1–50.

Pasolini, Pier Paolo. *Canzoniere italiano*. Vol. 1, Garzanti, 1972.

Pasqualino, Antonio. "Humor and Puppets: An Italian Perspective." *Humor and Comedy in Puppetry: Celebration in Popular Culture*, edited by Dina Sherzer and Joel Sherzer, Bowling Green State U Popular Press, 1987, pp. 8–29.

———. *L'Opera dei Pupi*. Sellerio, 1977.

———. "Transformations of Chivalrous Literature in the Subject Matter of the Sicilian Marionette Theater." *Varia Folklorica*, edited by Alan Dundes, Mouton, 1978, pp. 183–200.

———. *Le vie del cavaliere dall'epica medievale alla cultura popolare*. Bompiani, 1992.

Pasquini, Emilio. "Letteratura popolare e popolareggiante." *Storia della letteratura italiana: Il Trecento*, edited by Enrico Malato, vol. 2, Salerno, 1995.

Pedani, Maria Pia. *Venezia porta d'Oriente*. Il Mulino, 2010.

Perkins, Leeman. "Musical Culture in Late Quattrocento Ferrara: Local Traditions and Foreign Influences." Cavallo and Ross, *Fortune*, pp. 295–314.

Perrotta, Annalisa. "Lo spazio della corte: La rappresentazione del potere politico nel *Morgante* di Luigi Pulci." *Italianist*, vol. 24, 2004, pp. 141–68.

Perrucci, Andrea. *A Treatise on Acting, from Memory and by Improvisation (1699). Dell'Arte rappresentativa, premeditata ed all'improviso*, edited and translated by Francesco Cotticelli et al., Scarecrow Press, 2008.

Petrarch, Francesco. *Petrarch's Lyric Poems: The* Rime sparse *and Other Lyrics*. Translated and edited by Robert M. Durling, Harvard UP, 1976.

Pezzini, Serena. "The Digital Collections of Words and Images of the CTL - Scuola Normale Superiore: The Case of *Orlando furioso*." *Humanist Studies and the Digital Age*, vol. 3., no. 1, 2013, pp. 32–52.

———. "Il disegno dell'opera. Entrelacement e riprese nella illustrazioni dell'*Orlando furioso* edito da Valgrisi (1556)." *Le sorti d'Orlando. Il* Furioso *tra parole e immagini*, edited by Massimiliano Rossi and Daniela Caracciolo, Pacini Fazzi Editore, 2014, pp. 117–42.

Piatti, Barbara, and Lorenz Hurni. "Cartographies of Fictional Worlds." *The Cartographic Journal*, vol. 48, no. 4, 2011, pp. 218–23.

Pico della Mirandola, Gianfrancesco. *The Witch; or, On the Deception of Demons. The Renaissance in Europe: An Anthology*, edited by Peter Elmer et al., Yale UP, 2000, pp. 366–94.

Pico della Mirandola, Giovanni. *Oration on the Dignity of Man. The Renaissance Philosophy of Man*, edited by Ernst Cassirer et al., U of Chicago P, 1996, pp. 223–54.

Picone, Michelangelo, and Maria Bendinelli Predelli. *I Cantari: Struttura e tradizione: Atti del convegno internazionale di Montreal, 19–20 marzo 1981*. Olschki, 1984.

Picone, Michelangelo, and Luisa Rubini, editors. *Il cantare italiano fra folklore e letteratura*. Olschki, 2007. Biblioteca dell'Archivium Romanicum.

Pieri, Marzia. *Cavalieri armi amori: Una scorciatoia per il tragico. Eroi della poesia epica nel teatro del Cinque-Seicento*, edited by M. Chiabò and F. Doglio, Torre d'Orfeo, 2004, pp. 201–31.

———. "Dalla commedia dell'arte al sillabo: Varie sorti di Torquato mattatore." *Italianistica*, vol. 24, no. 2–3, 1995, pp. 593–614.

Piero da Siena. *La bella Camilla*. Edited by Vittorio Fiorini, introduced by Tommaso Casini, Commissione per i testi di lingua, 1969.

Pirruccio, Linda. *Giovanni Villifranchi: La "fabbrica" delle favole sceniche di Tasso e Ariosto*. Bulzoni, 2011.

Pitrè, Giuseppe. "La letteratura cavalleresca popolare in Sicilia." *Usi e costumi, credenze e pregiudizi del popolo siciliano*, vol. 1, pp. 119–336. Originally published in *Romania*, vol. 13, 1884, pp. 315–98.

Plato. The Republic *and Other Works.* Translated by B. Jowett, Doubleday, 1973.

Pliny the Elder. *Natural History: A Selection.* Translated by John F. Healey, Penguin Classics, 2001.

*I poemi epici del Rinascimento: Audio antologia della letteratura italiana*, vol. 5, Il Narratore, 2002.

Poggio Fiorentino. *Facezie.* Corbaccio, 1933.

Polcri, Alessandro. *Luigi Pulci e la Chimera: Studi sull'allegoria nel* Morgante. Società Editrice Fiorentina, 2010.

Poliziano, Angelo. *Stanze cominciate per la giostra di Giuliano de' Medici.* Edited by Vincenzo Pernicone, Loescher-Chiantore, 1954.

———. *Stanze, Fabula di Orfeo.* Edited by Stefano Carrai, Mursia, 1988.

———. *Stanze Orfeo Rime.* Edited by Davide Puccini, Garzanti, 1992.

Polo, Marco. *Le devisement du monde.* Edited by Philippe Ménard, vol. 1, Droz, 2001.

Ponte, Giovanni. *La personalità e l'opera del Boiardo.* Tilgher, 1972.

Pontremoli, Alessandro. *Intermedio spettacolare a Milano fra cinque e seicento.* Euresis, 1999.

*La ponzela gaia; Galvano e la donna serpente.* Edited by Beatrice Barbiellini Amidei, Luni, 2000.

Poole, Kevin R., editor and translator. *The Chronicle of Pseudo-Turpin: Book IV of the Liber Sancti Jacobi (Codex Calixtinus).* Italica, 2014.

Porta, Pietro. *Gente di Sarina: Il burattinaio Peppino Sarina e le comunità del Tortonese e dell'Oltrepò pavese nella prima metà del Novecento.* Diakronia, 1997.

Praloran, Marco. *"Maraviglioso artificio": Tecniche narrative e rappresentative nell'* Orlando innamorato. Pacini Fazzi, 1990.

———. *Tempo e azione nell'*Orlando furioso. Olschki, 1999.

Prampolini, Giovanni. *Le favole dell'Ariosto nei disegni di Jean-Honoré Fragonard.* Litostampa La Rapida, 2001.

———. *Le "Storie di Orlando": Rappresentazioni pittoriche e sceniche dell'* Innamorato *e del* Furioso. Litostampa La Rapida, 2000.

Pratt, Mary Louise. *Imperial Eyes: Travel Writing and Transculturation.* Routledge, 1992.

Presner, Todd, and David Shephard. "Mapping the Geospatial Turn." *A New Companion to Digital Humanities*, edited by Susan Schreibman et al., John Wiley and Sons, 2016, pp. 201–12.

Procaccioli, Paolo. "Girolamo Ruscelli (Viterbo ca. 1504–Venezia 1566)." *Autografi dei letterati italiani: Il Cinquecento*, edited by Matteo Motolese et al., vol. 1, Salerno, 2009, pp. 309–17.

Pucci, Antonio. *Apollonio di Tiro.* Edited by Renzo Rabboni, Commissione per i testi di lingua, 1996.

———. *Cantari della Reina d'Oriente.* Edited by Attilio Motta and William Robins, Commissione per i testi di lingua, 2007.

———. *The Four Cantari: English Verse Translation with Facing Italian Text and Literary Appraisal.* Edited and translated by Thomas E. Vesce, TEV Enterprises, 2003.

———. *Gismirante*; *Madonna Leonessa*. Edited and translated by Maria Bendinelli Predelli, University of Edinburgh Printing Services, 2013. British Rencesvals Publications 6.

Puggioni, Roberto. "La conversione a Melpomene: Tomiri di Angelo Ingegneri." *Drammaturgie Generi teatrali e esperienze sceniche tra Cinquecento e Seicento*, edited by Roberto Puggioni, Cuec, 2012, pp. 27–50.

———, editor. *Torquato Tasso nel teatro moderno*. Franco Angeli, forthcoming.

Pulci, Luca, and Luigi Pulci. *Il Cyriffo Calvanèo: La morte di Orlando*. Edited by Marzio Pieri, introduction by Marco Albertazzi and Luana Salvarani, La finestra Editrice, 2009.

Pulci, Luigi. *El famoso Morgante nella versione di Modena*. Edited by Marzio Pieri and Luana Salvarani, introduction by Marco Albertazzi, illustrated by Giovanni Tamburelli, La Finestra Editrice, 2008.

———. *Morgante*. 1955. Edited by Franca Ageno, Mondadori, 1994.

———. *Morgante*. Edited by Giuliano Dego, Rizzoli, 1992.

———. *Morgante*. Edited by Davide Puccini, Garzanti, 1989. 2 vols.

———. Morgante *e Lettere*. Edited by Domenico De Robertis, rev. ed., Sansoni, 1984.

———. Morgante *e opere minori*. Edited by Aulo Greco, UTET, 1997.

———. Morgante*: The Epic Adventures of Orlando and His Giant Friend Morgante*. Translated by J. Tusiani, introduction and notes by Edoardo A. Lèbano, Indiana UP, 1998.

Quint, David. "The Boat of Romance and Renaissance Epic." *Romance: Generic Transformations from Chrétien de Troyes to Cervantes*, edited by Kevin Brownlee and Marina Scordilis Brownlee, UP of New England, 1985, pp. 178–202.

———. "The Death of Brandimarte and the Ending of the *Orlando furioso*." *Annali d'Italianistica*, vol. 12, 1994, pp. 75–85.

———. *Epic and Empire: Politics and Generic Form from Virgil to Milton*. Princeton UP, 1993.

———. "The Figure of Atlante: Ariosto and Boiardo's Poem." *MLN*, vol. 94, no. 1, 1979, pp. 77–91.

———. "The Fortunes of Morgana: From Boiardo to Marino." Cavallo and Ross, *Fortune*, pp. 17–29.

Rabelais, François. Gargantua *and* Pantagruel. Translated by M. A. Screech, Penguin, 2006.

Raffaele da Verona. *Aquilon de Bavière, roman franco-italien en prose (1379–1407)*. Edited by Peter Wunderli, Niemeyer, 1982–2007. 3 vols.

———. *Giunta all'* Orlando innamorato. Edited by Gioachino Paparelli, Beta, 1971.

Rajna, Pio, editor. "Il Cantare dei cantari e il Serventese del Maestro di tutte l'Arti." *Zeitschrift für romanische Philologie*, vol. 2, 1878, pp. 220–54, 419–37; vol. 5, 1881, pp.1–40, www.classicitaliani.it/trecento/cantarecantari.htm.

———. "Contributi alla storia dell'epopea e del romanzo medievale. IX Altre orme antiche dell'epopea carolingia in Italia." *Romania*, vol. 26, 1897, pp. 34–73, gallica.bnf.fr/ark:/12148/bpt6k16034x/f40.image.

———. *Le fonti dell'* Orlando furioso. 1900. G. C. Sansoni Editore, 1975.

———. *La Geste Francor di Venezia (Codice Marciano XIII della serie francese).* Riproduzione fototipica. Bestetti e Tuminelli, [1925].

———. "I 'Rinaldi' o i cantastorie di Napoli." *Nuova Antologia*, Dec. 1878, pp. 557–79.

Ramachandran, Ayesha. *The Worldmakers: Global Imagining in Early Modern Europe.* U of Chicago P, 2015.

Reeves, Eileen. *Evening News: Optics, Astronomy, and Journalism in Early Modern Europe.* U of Pennsylvania P, 2014.

Reid, Joshua. *The Italian Romance Epic in English, 1590–1600.* Modern Humanities Research Association, forthcoming.

Renner, Bernd. "From *Satura* to *Satyre*: François Rabelais and the Renaissance Appropriation of a Genre." *Renaissance Quarterly*, vol. 67, no. 2, 2014, pp. 377–424.

Reuschel, Anne-Kathrin, and Lorenz Hurni. "Mapping Literature: Visualisation of Spatial Uncertainty in Fiction." *The Cartographic Journal*, vol. 48, no. 4, 2011, pp. 293–308.

Reynolds, Barbara. "Epic and Romance: Pulci and Boiardo." France, pp. 478–80.

———. "Epic and Romance: Tasso." France, pp. 482–83.

Rhu, Lawrence F. *The Genesis of Tasso's Narrative Theory: English Translations of the Early Poetics and a Comparative Study of Their Significance.* Wayne State UP, 1993.

Ricci, Giovanni. *Ossessione turca: In una retrovia cristiana dell'Europa moderna.* Il mulino, 2002.

———. *I turchi alle porte.* Il mulino, 2008.

Richman, Paula. "E. V. Ramasami's Reading of the *Ramayana*." *Many Ramayanas: The Diversity of a Narrative Tradition in South Asia*, edited by Paula Richman, U of California P, 1991, pp. 175–201.

Rigolot, François. "The Renaissance Crisis of Exemplarity." *Journal of the History of Ideas*, vol. 59, 1998, pp. 557–63.

Ripari, Edoardo. *Storia cinematografica della letteratura italiana.* Carocci, 2015.

Risi, Clemens. "Claudio Monteverdi's Combattimento di Tancredi e Clorinda (1624 or 1625): A Christian-Muslim Encounter in Music?" *Early Modern Encounters with the Islamic East: Performing Cultures*, edited by Sabine Schülting and Sabine Lucia Müller, Ashgate, 2012, pp. 153–66.

Rivoletti, Christian. *Ariosto e l'ironia della finzione: La ricezione letteraria e figurativa dell'* Orlando furioso *in Francia, Germania e Italia.* Marsilio, 2014.

Rizzarelli, Giovanna. "Tempo delle immagini e tempo del racconto nelle edizioni cinquecentesche illustrate dell'*Orlando furioso*." Bolzoni et al., pp. 161–93.

———. "Vedere il tempo. Strategie narrative nelle illustrazioni [dell'*Orlando furioso*]." Bolzoni, *L'* Orlando furioso *nello specchio delle immagini*, pp. 141–82.

Robey, David. *Sound and Metre in Italian Narrative Verse: An Analytical Database.* University of Reading, 3 Dec. 2007, www.italianverse.reading.ac.uk. Accessed 1 Oct. 2015.

Rodini, Robert J. "Selected Bibliography of Ariosto Criticism, 1980–87." *MLN*, vol. 103, 1988, pp. 187–203.

———. "Selected Bibliography of Ariosto Criticism: 1986–1993." *Annali d'Italianistica*, vol. 12, 1994, pp. 299–317.

Rodini, Robert J., and Salvatore Di Maria. *Ludovico Ariosto: An Annotated Bibliography of Criticism, 1956–1980.* U of Missouri P, 1984.

*Rodomonte.* Compagnia Maggistica Monte Cusna di Asta, 2005. *eBOIARDO*, ed blogs.columbia.edu/eboiardo/rodomonte/. Performance.

Rohmer, Éric. *Perceval le Gallois.* 1978. Fox Lorber Films, 2000.

Rollings, Andrew, and Ernest Adams. *Andrew Rollings and Ernest Adams on Game Design.* New Riders, 2003.

*Romanzo cavalleresco inedito.* Edited by Aurelia Forni Marmocchi, Pàtron, 1989.

Romizi, A. *Le fonti latine dell'Orlando furioso.* Paravia e comp., 1896.

Ronconi, Luca. *Orlando furioso.* 1974. Rai Trade, 2012. DVD.

Ronsard, Pierre de. *The Franciad.* 1572. Translated by Phillip John Usher, AMS Press, 2010.

———. *La Franciade. Œuvres complètes*, edited by Paul Lauonmier, vol. 16, Marcel Didier, 1950.

Rospigliosi, Giulio. *Erminia sul Giordano: Dramma musicale rappresentato nel palazzo dell'Ill. Ecc. Signore D. Taddeo Barberino posto in musica da Michelangelo Rossi.* Paolo Masotti, 1637.

Ross, Charles S. "Ariosto in Prose: Nuancing Shakespeare's *Taming of the Shrew.*" *Prose Studies*, vol. 29, no. 3, Dec. 2007, pp. 336–46.

———. *The Custom of the Castle from Malory to Macbeth.* U of California P, 1997.

———. Introduction. Ariosto, *Orlando furioso: A New Verse Translation*, pp. ix–xiv.

———. Introduction. Boiardo, *Orlando innamorato: Orlando in Love*, pp. xv–lxxxi.

Rouget, François. *Ronsard et le livre: Étude de critique génétique et d'histoire littéraire.* Vol. 2, Droz, 2012.

Ruini, Cesare. "La presenza della musica nell'*Orlando innamorato.*" *Il Boiardo e il mondo estense nel Quattrocento*, edited by Giuseppe Anceschi and Tina Matarrese, vol. 1, Antenore, 1998, pp. 323–36.

Sacchetti, Franco. *Tales from Sacchetti.* Translated by Mary G. Steegman, J. M. Dent, 1908.

———. *Trecentonovelle.* Edited by Valerio Marucci, Salerno Editrice, 1996.

Sacchi, Guido. *Fra Ariosto e Tasso: Vicende del poema narrativo.* Scuola Normale Superiore, 2006.

Saccone, Eduardo. *Il "soggetto" del* Furioso *e altri saggi tra Quattro e Cinquecento.* Liguori, 1974.

Saffioti, Tito. *I giullari in Italia. Lo spettacolo, il pubblico, i testi.* Xenia, 1990.

Said, Edward. *Orientalism.* Vintage Books, 1994.

Salernitano, Masuccio. *Novellino.* Edited by Salvatore Nigro, Rizzoli, 2000.

———. *Salernitano's Novellino.* Translated by W. G. Waters, Lawrence and Bullen, 1895.

Salwa, Piotr. "Appunti sulle novelle dell'*Orlando furioso.*" *Volteggiando sulle carte. Ludovico Ariosto e i suoi lettori*, edited by Enrico Garavelli, Université de Helsinki, 2011, pp. 29–44.

Sangirardi, Giuseppe. *Boiardismo ariostesco: Presenza e trattamento dell'* Orlando innamorato *nel* Furioso. Pacini Fazzi, 1993.

———. *Ludovico Ariosto.* Le Monnier, 2006.

———. "Les nouvelles du *Roland furieux.*" *Cahiers d'études italiennes*, vol. 10, 2009, pp. 115–28.

———. "Quanti sono i generi dell'*Orlando furioso*?" *Allegoria*, vol. 59, 2009, pp. 42–55.

Santoro, Mario. *L'anello di Angelica: Nuovi saggi ariosteschi*. Federico and Ardia, 1983.

Sarrocchi, Margherita. *Scanderbeide: The Heroic Deeds of George Scanderbeg, King of Epirus*. Translated by Rinaldina Russell, U of Chicago P, 2006.

———. *La Scanderbeide: Poema eroico*. Lepido Facij, 1606.

Sberlati, Francesco. *Il genere e la disputa: La poetica tra Ariosto e Tasso*. Bulzoni, 2001.

Scafi, Alessandro. *Maps of Paradise*. U of Chicago P, 2013.

Scalabrini, Massimo. "Contadini e mostri tra *Zanitonella* e *Baldus*." Scalabrini, *Folengo*, pp. 47–57.

———, editor. *Folengo in America*. Longo, 2012.

———. *L'incarnazione del macaronico*. Il Mulino, 2003.

Scarsi, Selene. *Translating Women in Early Modern England: Gender in the Elizabethan Versions of Boiardo, Ariosto, and Tasso*. Ashgate, 2010. Anglo-Italian Renaissance Studies.

Scott, Ridley, director and producer. *Kingdom of Heaven*. Written by William Monahan, Scott Free Productions, 2005.

Segre, Cesare. "Quattro tipi di follia medievale." *Fuori del mondo. I modelli nella follia e nelle immagini dell'aldilà*, Einaudi, 1990, pp. 89–102.

Segre, Cesare, et al. *Rimario diacronico dell'* Orlando furioso. IUSS Press, 2012. 2 vols.

Seneca. *Hercules furens*. *Tragedies, volume 8*, edited and translated by John G. Fitch, Harvard UP, 2002, pp. 35–159. Loeb Classical Library 62.

Sercambi, Giovanni. *Novelle*. Edited by Giovanni Sinicropi, Le Lettere, 1995.

Shakespeare, William. *King Lear*. Edited by Russell Fraser, New American Library, 1963. The Signet Classic Shakespeare.

———. *The Riverside Shakespeare*. Edited by G. Blakemore Evans, Houghton Mifflin, 1974.

Shakespeare, William, and John Fletcher. *The Two Noble Kinsmen*. Edited by Eugene M. Waith, Oxford UP, 1994.

Shemek, Deanna. *Ladies Errant: Wayward Women and Social Order in Early Modern Italy*. Duke UP, 1998.

———. "Of Women, Knights, Arms, and Love: The *Querelle des Femmes* in Ariosto's Poem." *MLN* vol. 104, 1989, pp. 68–97.

Short, Ian, editor and translator. *La Chanson de Roland*. 2nd ed., Le livre de poche, 1990.

Siberry, Elizabeth. "Tasso and the Crusades: History of a Legacy." *Journal of Medieval History*, vol. 19, 1993, pp. 163–69.

Sillari, Luca. *Orlando Innamorato*. Compagnia Maggistica Monte Cusna di Asta, Comune di Villa Minozzo, 2004.

Silverberg, Robert. *The Realm of Prester John*. Ohio UP, 1972.

Smarr, Janet Levarie. "Non-Christian People and Spaces in the *Decameron*." *Approaches to Teaching Boccaccio's* Decameron, edited by James H. McGregor, Modern Language Association, 2000, pp. 113–36.

Solerti, Angelo. *Vita di Torquato Tasso*. Loescher, 1895. 2 vols.

*Spagna ferrarese*. Edited by Valentina Gritti and Cristina Montagnani, Interlinea, 2009.

*La* Spagna *in prosa (Firenze, Biblioteca Laurenziana, Mediceo Palatino 101*[3]*)*. Edited by Frej Moretti, Edizioni ETS, 2011.

*La* Spagna *in rima del manoscritto comense*. Edited by Giovanna Barbara Rosiello, Edizioni dell'Orso, 2001.

"La *Spagna Magliabechiana* e la materia cavalleresca italiana: Edizione critica e studio del ms. BNCF, II, I, 57." Edited by Amélie Hanus. PhD dissertation, University of Namur, 2012.

La Spagna*: Poema cavalleresco del secolo XIV*. Edited by Michele Catalano, Commissione per i testi di lingua, 1939–40. 3 vols.

Spenser, Edmund. *The Faerie Qveene*. Edited by Albert Charles Hamilton, Hiroshi Yamashita, and Toshiyuki Suzuki, Pearson Longman, 2007. Longman Annotated English Poets.

Springer, Carolyn. *Armour and Masculinity in the Italian Renaissance*. U of Toronto P, 2010.

Staebler, Mark. Introduction. Boiardo, *Selections*, pp. 1–64.

Stampino, Maria Galli. "A Singular Venetian Epic Poem." Marinella, *Enrico*, pp. 1–66.

*Star Wars: Knights of the Old Republic*. BioWare, 2003.

Stein, Thomas. *Nel nome del gran Torquato:* Gerusalemme liberata *e drammaturgia secentesca*. Peter Lang, 2012.

———. "Quando Olindo diventa Aminta: Aspetti della fortuna teatrale di un episodio tassesco." *Studi Secenteschi*, vol. 42, 2001, pp. 59–84.

Stephens, Walter. *Demon Lovers: Witchcraft, Sex, and the Crisis of Belief*. U of Chicago P, 2002.

———. *Giants in Those Days: Folklore, Ancient History, and Nationalism*. U of Nebraska P, 1989.

———. "Saint Paul among the Amazons: Gender and Authority in *Gerusalemme liberata*." *Discourses of Authority in Medieval and Renaissance Literature*, edited by Kevin Brownlee and Walter Stephens, UP of New England, 1989, pp. 169–200.

———. "Skepticism, Empiricism, and Proof in Gianfrancesco Pico della Mirandola's *Strix*." *Magic, Ritual, and Witchcraft*, vol. 11, no. 1, Summer 2016, pp. 6–29.

———. "Writing." *The Classical Tradition: A Guide*, edited by Anthony Grafton et al., Harvard UP, 2010, pp. 990–95.

Stoppino, Eleonora. *Genealogies of Fiction: Women Warriors and the Medieval Imagination in the* Orlando furioso. Fordham UP, 2012.

*Storia di Stefano figliuolo d'un imperatore di Roma: Versione in ottava rima del* Libro dei Sette Savi. Edited by Pio Rajna, Commissione per i testi di lingua, 1968.

Strologo, Franca. La Spagna *nella letteratura cavalleresca italiana*. Antenore, 2014.

Struhal, Eva. "Reading with *Acutezza*: Lorenzo Lippi's Literary Culture." *The Artist as Reader: On Education and Non-education of Early Modern Artists*, edited by Heiko Damm, Michael Thimann, and Claus Zittel. Brill, 2013, pp. 105–27.

Sturm-Maddox, Sara. "'Non par orgoil, mais por senefiance': Roland Redefined in the *Entrée d'Espagne*." *Franco-Italian and Italian Romance Epic*, edited by Nancy Bradley-Cromey and Leslie Zarker Morgan. Special issue of *Olifant*, vol. 21, 1996–97, pp. 31–46, scholarworks.iu.edu/journals/index.php/olifant/article/view/19498/25618.

Suard, François. *Roland ou les avatars d'une folie héroïque*. Klincksieck, 2012. Les grandes figures du moyen âge.

Symonds, John Addington. *Renaissance in Italy: Italian Literature*. Vol. 1, Henry Holt, 1881.

Syson, Luke, and Dora Thornton. *Objects of Virtue: Art in Renaissance Italy*. J. Paul Getty Museum, 2001.

Talbot, Adela. "Making a Blockbuster out of the Renaissance." *Western News*, 11 Nov. 2015, news.westernu.ca/2015/11/making-a-blockbuster-out-of-the-renaissance/.

Tally, Robert T. *Spatiality*. Routledge, 2013.

———. "Translator's Preface." Westphal, pp. ix–xiii.

Taranto, Julius, and Kevin J. H. Dettmar. "The Secret of Good Humanities Teaching." *Chronicle of Higher Education*, 14 Sept. 2015, www.chronicle.com/article/The-Secret-of-Good-Humanities/233097. Accessed 28 Oct. 2015.

"Tasso." *Poetry Criticism*, edited by Lawrence J. Trudeau, vol. 170, Gale, 1991, pp. 213–322.

Tasso, Torquato. *Allegoria della Gerusalemme liberata*. Edited by Amedeo Quondam. *Tutte le opere*, edited by Amedeo Quondam, Lexis progetti editoriali, 1997. *Classici italiani*, www.classicitaliani.it/tasso/prosa/Tasso_allegoria_Gerusalemme.htm.

———. *Aminta*. Edited by Marco Corradini. Biblioteca Universale Rizzoli, 2015.

———. *Discorsi dell'arte poetica e del poema eroico*. Edited by Luigi Poma, Laterza, 1964.

———. *Discourses on the Art of Poetry. The Genesis of Tasso's Narrative Theory: English Translations of the Early Poetics and a Comparative Study of Their Significance*, translated and edited by Lawrence F. Rhu, Wayne State UP, 1993, pp. 99–153.

———. *Discourses on the Heroic Poem*. Translated by Mariella Cavalchini and Irene Samuel, Clarendon Press, 1973.

———. *Gerusalemme conquistata. Ms. Vind. Lat. 72 della Biblioteca nazionale di Napoli*. Edited by Claudio Gigante, Edizioni dell'Orso, 2010.

———. *Gerusalemme liberata*. Edited by Lanfranco Caretti, Einaudi, 2005. *Biblioteca della letteratura italiana*, www.letteraturaitaliana.net/pdf/Volume_5/t329.pdf. Accessed 14 Dec. 2015.

———. *Gerusalemme liberata*. Edited by Fredi Chiappelli, Rusconi, 1982.

———. *Gerusalemme liberata*. Edited by Franco Tomasi, Rizzoli, 2009. 2 vols.

———. *Il Gierusalemme*. Edited by Lanfranco Caretti, Zara, 1993.

———. *Godfrey of Bulloigne*. Translated by Edward Fairfax, edited by Kathleen Marguerite Lea and T. M. Gang, Oxford UP, 1981.

———. *Jerusalem Delivered*. Translated by Anthony M. Esolen, Johns Hopkins UP, 2000.

———. Jerusalem Delivered*: An English Prose Version*. Translated by Ralph Nash, Wayne State UP, 1987.

———. *Lettere*. Edited by Gesare Guasti, Le Monnier, 1852–55. 5 vols.

———. *Lettere poetiche*. Edited by Carla Molinari, Guanda, 1995.

———. *The Liberation of Jerusalem*. Translated by Max Wickert, introduced by Mark Davie, Oxford UP, 2009.

———. *Rinaldo*. Edited by Matteo Navone, Edizioni dell'Orso, 2012.

———. *Rinaldo*. Translated by Max Wickert, Italica Press, 2017.

———. *Torquato Tasso*. Edited by Alessandro Bianchi and Rinaldo Rinaldi, Unicopli, 2011.

———. *Tutte le poesie di Torquato Tasso*. Edited by Lanfranco Caretti, vol. 1, Mondadori, 1957.

Tassoni, Alessandro. *La secchia rapita*. Edited by Ottavio Besomi, Antenore, 1987.

———. *La secchia rapita; or, The Rape of the Bucket: An Heroi-comical Poem in Twelve Cantos*. Translated by James Atkinson, J. M. Richardson, 1825. 2 vols.

*Tavola Ritonda*. Edited by Emanuele Trevi, Rizzoli, 1999.

Ternaux, Jean-Claude. "La Franciade de Ronsard: Échec ou réussite?" *La Revue des amis de Ronsard*, vol. 13, 2000, pp. 117–35.

Thompson, Stith. *Motif-Index of Folk Literature: A Classification of Narrative Elements in Folktales, Ballads, Myths, Fables, Mediaeval Romances, Exempla, Fabliaux, Jest-books, and Local Legends*. Indiana UP, 1955–58.

Thorpe, Lewis, translator. *Einhard and Notker the Stammerer: Two Lives of Charlemagne*. Penguin, 1969.

Tissoni Benvenuti, Antonia. Introduction. *Inamoramento de Orlando*, edited by Tissoni Benvenuti and Cristina Montagnani. *Opere*, vol. 1, Ricciardi, 1999, pp. xi–xxxiii.

Tomlinson, Gary. "Madrigal, Monody, and Monteverdi's *Via naturale alla imitatione*." *Journal of the American Musicological Society*, vol. 34, 1981, pp. 60–108.

*Torquato Tasso e le arti: Convegno di studi promosso nel cinquantesimo di fondazione del Centro di studi tassiani*. Centro di studi tassiani, 2002.

*Il Tristano Corsiniano*. Edited and translated by Gloria Allaire, Brewer, 2015.

*Il Tristano Corsiniano*. Edited by Roberto Tagliani, critical ed., Accademia nazionale dei Lincei, 2011.

*Il Tristano Panciatichiano*. Edited and translated by Gloria Allaire, Brewer, 2002.

*Tristano Riccardiano*. Edited and translated by F. Regina Psaki, Brewer, 2006.

Tristano Riccardiano*: Testo critico di E. G. Parodi*. Marie-José Heijkant editor, Pratiche, 1991.

Trolli, Domizia. *Il lessico dell'* Inamoramento de Orlando *di Matteo Maria Boiardo: Studio e glossario*. Unicopli, 2003.

Turchi, Marcello. "Sui personaggi del *Furioso*." *Rassegna della letteratura italiana*, vol. 79, 1975, pp. 129–45.

Turner, Victor. *From Ritual to Theatre: The Human Seriousness of Play*. Performing Arts Journal Publications, 1982.

Tylus, Jane. "Reasoning Away Colonialism: Tasso and the Production of the *Gerusalemme liberata*." *South Central Review*, vol. 10, no. 2, 1993, pp. 100–14.

Ullendorff, Edward, and C. F. Beckingham, editors and translators. *The Hebrew Letters of Prester John*. Oxford UP, 1982.

Unglaub, Jonathan. *Poussin and the Poetics of Painting: Pictorial Narrative and the Legacy of Tasso*. Cambridge UP, 2006.

Urbaniak, Martyna. "Archivi digitali del CTL: Metodologie e strumenti per la ricerca letteraria tra parole e immagini." *Griselda online*, 2012, www.griselda online.it/dibattiti/fahreneit-151/archivi-digitali-ctl-urbaniak.html.html.

Usher, Phillip John. "Robert Garnier (1545–1590)." *The Literary Encyclopedia*, 13 Sept. 2012, www.litencyc.com/php/speople.php?rec=true&UID=1691.

Uther, Hans-Jörg. *The Types of International Folktales.* Suomalainen Tiedeakatemia, 2004.

Valderrábano, Enriquez de. *Libro de musica de vihuela, intitulado Silva de sirenas.* Minkoff Reprint, 1981.

Valesio, Paolo. "The Language of Madness in the Renaissance." *Yearbook of Italian Studies*, vol. 1, 1971, pp. 199–234.

Van Duzer, Chet. "*Hic sunt dracones*: The Geography and Cartography of Monsters." *The Ashgate Research Companion to Monsters and the Monstrous*, edited by Asa Simon Mittman and Peter J. Dendle, Ashgate, 2013, pp. 387–435.

———. *Sea Monsters on Medieval and Renaissance Maps.* The British Library, 2013.

Vasoli, Cesare. *La cultura delle corti.* Cappelli, 1980.

Venturi, Gianni, editor. *Torquato Tasso e la cultura estense.* Olschki, 1999. 3 vols.

Vergil, Polydore. *On Discovery.* Translated by Brian Copenhaver, Harvard UP, 2002.

Via, Claudia Cieri. "I trionfi, il mito e l'amore: La fascia superiore dei Mesi negli affreschi di Palazzo Schifanoia." *Atlante di Schifanoia*, Panini, 1989, pp. 41–44.

Vickers, Nancy J. "Re-membering Dante: Petrarch's 'Chiare, Fresche et Dolci Acque.'" *MLN*, vol. 96, no. 1, 1981, pp. 1–11.

Villegas, Antonio de. "Historia del abencerraje y la hermosa Jarifa." Cristóbal Pérez Pastor, *La imprenta en Medina del Campo*, Sucesores de Rivadeneyra, 1895, pp. 209–18. Originally published in *Inventario*, by Villegas, Francisco del Canto, 1577.

Villifranchi, Giovanni. *La fuga d'Erminia del sign: Torquato Tasso.* Ciotti, 1600.

Villoresi, Marco. *La fabbrica dei cavallieri: Cantari, poemi, romanzi in prosa fra Medioevo e Rinascimento.* Salerno, 2005.

———. *La letteratura cavalleresca: Dai cicli medievali all'Ariosto.* Carocci, 2000.

———. "'Stati atenti e quïeti et ascoltati': Le voci del Boiardo." *Rassegna Europea di letteratura italiana*, vol. 38, 2011, pp. 85–104.

Virgil. "Ecloga X." *Perseus Digital Library*, www.perseus.tufts.edu/hopper/text?doc=Verg.+Ecl.+10&fromdoc= Perseus%3Atext%3A1999.02.0056.

Vitullo, Juliann M. *The Chivalric Epic in Medieval Italy.* UP of Florida, 2000.

Waldman, Guido. Introduction. Ariosto, *Orlando furioso*, Waldman, pp. vii–xvii.

Weaver, Elissa B. "Lettura dell'intreccio dell'*Orlando furioso*: Il caso delle tre pazzie d'amore." *Strumenti critici*, vol. 11, 1977, pp. 384–406.

———. "A Reading of the Interlaced Plot of the *Orlando furioso*: The Three Cases of Love Madness." *Ariosto Today: Contemporary Perspectives*, edited by Donald Beecher et al., U of Toronto P, 2003, pp. 126–53.

Webster, John. "Duchess of Malfi." *The Tragedy of the Dutchesse of Malfy, As It Was Presented Privatly at the Black-friers, and Publiquely at the Globe by the Kings Maiesties Servants*, Chadwyck-Healey, 1994.

———. *The Duchess of Malfi.* Edited by Kathy Casey. Dover, 1999.

Weinberg, Bernard. *A History of Literary Criticism in the Italian Renaissance.* U of Chicago P, 1961. 2 vols.

Wert, Giaches de. *Collected Works.* Edited by Carol MacClintock and Melvin Bernstein, vol. 8, American Institute of Musicology, 1961–77.

Westphal, Bertrand. *Geocriticism: Real and Fictional Spaces.* Translated by Robert T. Tally, Palgrave Macmillan, 2011.

Wickert, Max. "Appendix: *Liberation of Jerusalem* in Literature, Art, and Music." Tasso, *Liberation*, pp. 400–03.

Wordsworth, John Craufurd. *Adventures in Literature.* Cranton, 1929.

Wright, Thomas. *The Passions of the Minde.* London, 1601.

Wrisley, David. "Spatial Humanities: An Agenda for Pre-modern Research." *Porphyra*, vol. 22, Fall 2014, pp. 96–107.

Yates, Francis. *The Art of Memory.* U of Chicago P, 1974.

Zac, Pino. *Orlando furioso.* Corno, 1975.

Zampese, Cristina. *"Or si fa rosa or pallida la luna": La cultura classica nell'* Orlando innamorato. Pacini Fazzi, 1994.

Zanato, Tiziano. *Boiardo.* Salerno Editrice, 2015.

Zatti, Sergio. "Dalla parte di Satana: sull'imperialismo cristiano nella *Gerusalemme liberata.*" *La rappresentazione dell'altro nei testi del Rinascimento*, edited by Sergio Zatti, Pacini Fazzi, 1998, pp. 146–82.

———. *Il* Furioso *tra epos e romanzo.* Pacini Fazzi Editore, 1990.

———. *Il modo epico.* Laterza, 2000.

———. *L'ombra del Tasso: Epica e romanzo nel Cinquecento.* Bruno Mondadori, 1996.

———. *The Quest for Epic: From Ariosto to Tasso.* Edited by Dennis Looney, translated by Sally Hill with Dennis Looney, U of Toronto P, 2006.

———. *L'uniforme cristiano e il multiforme pagano: Saggio sulla* Gerusalemme liberata. Il saggiatore, 1983.

# Index